Olive Schreiner

Olive Schreiner

Writing Networks and Global Contexts

Edited by
Jade Munslow Ong &
Andrew van der Vlies

EDINBURGH
University Press

Edinburgh University Press is one of the leading university presses in the UK. We publish academic books and journals in our selected subject areas across the humanities and social sciences, combining cutting-edge scholarship with high editorial and production values to produce academic works of lasting importance. For more information visit our website: edinburghuniversitypress.com

© editorial matter and organisation Jade Munslow Ong and Andrew van der Vlies 2024, 2025
© the chapters their several authors 2024, 2025

Edinburgh University Press Ltd
13 Infirmary Street,
Edinburgh EH1 ILT

First published in hardback by Edinburgh University Press 2024

Typeset in 10.5/13pt Sabon LT Pro
by Cheshire Typesetting Ltd, Cuddington, Cheshire

A CIP record for this book is available from the British Library

ISBN 978 1 3995 1253 4 (hardback)
ISBN 978 1 3995 1254 1 (paperback)
ISBN 978 1 3995 1255 8 (webready PDF)
ISBN 978 1 3995 1256 5 (epub)

The right of Jade Munslow Ong and Andrew van der Vlies to be identified as the editor of this work has been asserted in accordance with the Copyright, Designs and Patents Act 1988, and the Copyright and Related Rights Regulations 2003 (SI No. 2498).

Contents

Figures	vii
Acknowledgements	viii
Notes on Contributors	ix

    Olive Schreiner in the World: An Introduction   1
    Jade Munslow Ong and Andrew van der Vlies

PART I MODERNITY AND MODERNISM

1. Schreiner and the Machine   23
   Mark Sanders

2. The Bloomsbury Modernisms of Margaret Harkness and Olive Schreiner   39
   Jade Munslow Ong

3. Olive Schreiner and Virginia Woolf: Proto-Ecofeminists?   61
   Dan Wylie

PART II RACE AND ANTI-RACISM

4. Olive Schreiner and C. F. Andrews: Utopia and Paths to Anti-Racism and Decolonisation   85
   Barnita Bagchi

5. Turning Points: Olive Schreiner Changing Her Mind About Race Matters   99
   Liz Stanley

6. Olive Schreiner, Race and Black South Africa: #RhodesMustFall and a 'Prophetic Vision of the Future'   115
   Janet Remmington

7. The Influence of Olive Schreiner on Howard Thurman and, through Thurman, on Martin Luther King, Jr. 138
Heidi Barends

PART III PRINT, PUBLISHING AND TRANSLATION

8. Dreaming of Liberty: Olive Schreiner's Ambivalent Anarchism 157
Clare Gill

9. The Reception of Olive Schreiner's Work and Thought in the Dutch Press 177
Małgorzata Drwal

10. The Reception of Olive Schreiner in the Swedish Press, 1890–1920 199
Sanja Nivesjö

PART IV ANTIPODEAN SCHREINER

11. Olive Schreiner and the New Women of New Zealand: Feminist Solidarities Across the Southern Colonies 223
Emma Barnes

12. The Story of an Australian Farm: Olive Schreiner in Australia 244
Nicholas Jose, Alex Sutcliffe and Mandy Treagus

PART V SOUTH AFRICAN AFTERLIVES

13. Passing It On: Olive Schreiner and Bessie Head 269
Dorothy Driver

14. Coetzee's Schreiner, Schreiner's Coetzee: Provincialising Allegory 295
Andrew van der Vlies

15. Olive Schreiner In/Beyond the Museum 314
Paul Walters and Jeremy Fogg

Index 332

Figures

6.1 Performance artist Sethembile Msezane as the Zimbabwean Chapungu bird bearing witness to the dismantling of Rhodes's statue at the University of Cape Town. Her performance endured after the crowds dispersed. © David Harrison 119
6.2 Colour Bar Deputation to England 1909. Photograph with annotation included in Mweli Skota's *African Yearly Register, Who's Who*. Courtesy of Wits Historical Papers. 125
6.3 Olive Schreiner's message to the Universal Races Congress published in Sol Plaatje's *Tsala ea Becoana*, 28 October 1911. Courtesy of the National Library of South Africa, Cape Town. 128
10.1 Full-page illustration by Tyra Kleen from 'Nöjets Lustgård' (The Gardens of Pleasure). Schreiner, *Drömmar*, 22. Reproduction: National Library of Sweden. 204
10.2 Illustration by Tyra Kleen from 'Jag tyckte jag stod . . .' (I Thought I Stood). Schreiner, *Drömmar*, 49. Reproduction: National Library of Sweden. 205
10.3 Profile of Schreiner including a portrait drawn by Ivar Jonsson for the newspaper, *Södermanlands Dagblad*, 5 December 1899. Reproduction: Svenska Dagstidningar, National Library of Sweden. 209

Acknowledgements

We are grateful to all of our contributors for their generous efforts in bringing this volume together, and to our editorial assistants, Emma Barnes (also a contributor) and Hannah Helm, for the long hours and expert attention to detail that helped to see it over the line.

We would like to thank the Arts and Humanities Research Council (UK) for funding the South African Modernism 1880–2020 project [AH/T008733/1] of which this collection is part, the University of Salford for additional research funding, and Susannah Butler, Fiona Conn, Elizabeth Fraser and Jackie Jones at Edinburgh University Press for their guidance and help.

Thanks, too, to other friends and colleagues at the University of Salford, Adelaide University and Rhodes University for their support for this book project, and Mia Pike for the beautiful cover art.

Notes on Contributors

Barnita Bagchi is a feminist translator, literary and cultural critic, and cultural historian. She is Chair and Professor of World Literatures in English at the University of Amsterdam, Netherlands, and has published widely on utopia, histories of transnational and women's education, and women's writing in western Europe and south Asia. Her publications include a part-translation with introduction, *Sultana's Dream and Padmarag: Two Feminist Utopias*, by Rokeya Sakhawat Hossain (2005), an edited volume, *The Politics of the (Im)possible: Utopia and Dystopia Reconsidered* (2012), and an edited volume, *Urban Utopias: Memory, Rights, and Speculation* (2020). She is a Life Member of Clare Hall, University of Cambridge.

Heidi Barends attended the University of Stellenbosch from 2009 to 2011 where she completed a BA in Language and Culture. She then moved to the University of Cape Town where she completed her Honours, Masters and PhD degrees in English Studies, with her doctoral thesis (2018) focusing on the connections between the lives and works of white South African writer, Olive Schreiner, and African American writer, Pauline Elizabeth Hopkins. Heidi recently co-edited a written symposium on Dorothy Driver's edition of Olive Schreiner's *From Man to Man or Perhaps Only*—with Sanja Nivesjö in *The Journal of Commonwealth Literature*. She was involved in research and teaching at both the University of Cape Town (2014–2018) and Cape Peninsula University of Technology (2015–2018) while pursuing her studies, and currently serves as Academic Director at EDU Africa, an international education partner in Cape Town. Some of her research interests include transnational studies, feminist studies, critical race theory, social justice, and intercultural studies.

Emma Barnes is Lecturer in Nineteenth-Century and World Literatures and Knowledge Exchange Fellow at the University of Salford, and was Research Assistant on the AHRC-funded project, South African Modernism 1880–2020.

Dorothy Driver is Professor Emeritus at the University of Cape Town. From 2005 to 2016 she held a professorship in the Department of English and Creative Writing, Adelaide University, Australia, where she now has adjunct researcher status. Her most recent publications in Schreiner studies include a revised edition of *From Man to Man or Perhaps Only —* (2016; expanded and reformatted scholarly edition forthcoming Edinburgh University Press, and a readerly edition, both 2024); a booklet entitled *Olive Schreiner's Poetics of Plants* (2019) and a related essay, 'Invoking Indigeneity: Olive Schreiner and the Poetics of Plants', *Journal of Commonwealth Literature* (2021). Her publications on Bessie Head include early essays in CRNLE (2001) and WLT (1996), and a more recent essay on her life as a life-in-writing, forthcoming in the *Oxford Research Encyclopedia: African Women's History*.

Małgorzata Drwal is Assistant Professor at the Department of Dutch and South African Studies in the Faculty of English at Adam Mickiewicz University in Poznań, Poland, and research associate at the Department Afrikaans, University of Pretoria, South Africa. Her research interests include working-class literature, the sociology of literature, and cultural mobility. She is currently working on a project about the circulation of socialist and feminist thought between South Africa, the Netherlands, and Great Britain in the first half of the twentieth century. She has recently published in *Dutch Crossing, Tydskrif vir Letterkunde*, and contributed a chapter to *Working-Class Literature(s) Volume II: Historical and International Perspectives* (ed. by Lennon and Nilsson, 2020).

Jeremy Fogg was born in Johannesburg in 1951, and studied at the University of the Witwatersrand, Johannesburg College of Education and University of Cape Town. After thirteen years of teaching, Jeremy moved to Makhanda (then Grahamstown) to join AMAZWI South African Museum of Literature (then the National English Literary Museum). He worked here from 1986 to 2013 as Researcher, Archivist, Senior Curator, and Deputy Director, with particular oversight of Educational Outreach and the Schreiner House, Cradock. Jeremy has worked with Paul Walters on various Schreiner-related articles and publications.

Clare Gill is Lecturer in Victorian Literature at the University of St Andrews. Clare has research interests in the literature, culture and politics of the 1890s, nineteenth-century media history, the works of Olive Schreiner, and book history. She has published work on Schreiner, Marie Corelli, 1890s socialism, Victorian publishing and the Victorian press. She is the co-editor of *Women, Periodicals and Print Culture in Britain, 1830s–1900s: The Victorian Period* (Edinburgh University Press 2019), which was shortlisted for the 2020 Colby Prize. Clare's first monograph, *Olive Schreiner and the Politics of the Press*, will be published by Edinburgh University Press. She is also co-series editor (with Professor Andrew van der Vlies) of *The Edinburgh Edition of the Works of Olive Schreiner* and volume editor *of Olive Schreiner's Trooper Peter Halket of Mashonaland* (forthcoming, Edinburgh University Press).

Nicholas Jose is Emeritus Professor of English and Creative Writing at The University of Adelaide and Adjunct Professor in the Writing and Society Research Centre, Western Sydney University, where he is chief investigator in the research project 'Other Worlds: Forms of World Literature'. He has published seven novels, including *Paper Nautilus* (1987), *The Custodians* (1997), *The Red Thread* (2000) and *Original Face* (2005), and three collections of short stories. His non-fiction includes *Chinese Whispers, Cultural Essays* (1995) and an acclaimed memoir, *Black Sheep: Journey to Borroloola* (2002). As an essayist and scholar, he has written on Australian and world literature, including Chinese literature. He was general editor of the *Macquarie PEN Anthology of Australian Literature* (2009, also published as *The Literature of Australia*). His most recent publication, as co-editor, is *Antipodean China: Reflections on Literary Exchange* (2021).

Jade Munslow Ong is Associate Professor (Reader) in World Literatures in English at the University of Salford, UK, and Principal Investigator on the AHRC-funded research project, South African Modernism 1880–2020. She is author of *Olive Schreiner and African Modernism: Allegory, Empire and Postcolonial Writing* (2018), and articles and chapters on colonial and postcolonial African literatures, animals and the environment in Victorian and world literatures, and decolonising pedagogies in Further Education. Jade is also a BBC/AHRC New Generation Thinker who appears in programmes on BBC Radio 3.

Sanja Nivesjö is a Swedish Research Council postdoctoral researcher at Uppsala University, Sweden and University of Salford, UK. Her research interests focus on Southern African literatures and questions of sexuality, gender, race, space, and temporality. In her current project she examines the portrayal of interracial love in Southern African literature,

1900–1950. Together with Heidi Barends she has edited a symposium on Dorothy Driver's edition of Schreiner's novel *From Man to Man* (1926) with the *Journal of Commonwealth Literature* (2021). She has also published 'Making Space for Women's Sexual Selves in Olive Schreiner's *From Man to Man*' in the special issue 'Commemorating the Olive Schreiner Centenary', *English in Africa* (2021).

Janet Remmington is a research associate at the Humanities Research Centre, University of York, and African Literature Department, University of the Witwatersrand. She was co-editor of *Sol Plaatje's Native Life in South Africa: Past and Present* (2016), which won the 2018 Best Edited Collection Prize from South Africa's National Institute for Humanities and Social Sciences. Other publications include articles in *Journal of Southern African Studies*, *Studies in Travel Writing*, and *Research in African Literatures*, as well as chapters in *Sea Narratives: Cultural Responses to the Sea, 1600–Present* (2016), *Fighting Words: Fifteen Books that Shaped the Postcolonial World* (2017), and *The Edinburgh Companion to British Colonial Periodicals* (forthcoming in 2023). She has a PhD in English and Related Literature from the University of York, and Masters degrees in English, Creative Writing, and African Studies from the Universities of Cape Town, Royal Holloway (London), and Oxford respectively, as well as a Postgraduate Diploma in Advanced Studies in Publishing from Oxford Brookes University. Janet combines her research and writing interests with a professional career in publishing.

Mark Sanders is Professor of Comparative Literature and English at New York University and Extraordinary Professor of Afrikaans and Dutch at Stellenbosch University. Mark specialises in African literatures, literary theory, and interdisciplinary approaches to literature, law, and philosophy. He is author of several books, including *Learning Zulu: A Secret History of Language in South Africa* (2016), *Ambiguities of Witnessing: Law and Literature in the Time of a Truth Commission* (2007), *Gayatri Chakravorty Spivak: Live Theory* (2006), and *Complicities: The Intellectual and Apartheid* (2002). Sanders was recently awarded a fellowship by the Stellenbosch Institute for Advanced Study (STIAS) for his new book project, *A Will for the Machine: Automation, Computerization, and the Arts in South Africa*.

Liz Stanley is Professor of Sociology at the University of Edinburgh and a Fellow of the Academy of Social Sciences. She is Principal Investigator for the Olive Schreiner Letters Online and remains actively engaged in

Schreiner research as well as its successor project on Whites Writing Whiteness. She has published seventeen books, including three on Olive Schreiner and her work, most recently *Reintroducing Olive Schreiner: Intersectionality, Decoloniality and the Schreiner Theoria* (2022). For further information including extensive publications list see https://www.sps.ed.ac.uk/staff/liz-stanley and for the Olive Schreiner Letters Online see https://www.oliveschreiner.org.

Alex Sutcliffe is an MPhil student in the Department of English, Creative Writing, and Film at the University of Adelaide. Alex's research interests include the Bildungsroman, Australian modernism, and promises in literature.

Mandy Treagus is Associate Professor of English at the University of Adelaide. Mandy's research interests span literature, film, photography and visual art forms, in the context of archival sources. Her publications include the monograph *Empire Girls: The Colonial Heroine Comes of Age* (2014), and the co-edited collections: (with M Tonkin, M Seys and S.C. De Rosa), *Changing the Victorian Subject* (2014), and (with M Keown and A Taylor), *Anglo-American Imperialism and the Pacific Discourse of Encounter* (2018).

Andrew van der Vlies is Professor in the Department of English, Creative Writing, and Film at the University of Adelaide in Australia, and Extraordinary Professor at the University of the Western Cape, South Africa. A graduate of Rhodes and Oxford Universities, he is the author of essays and chapters on South African literatures, art history, gender studies, and print cultures, and of the books *Present Imperfect: Contemporary South African Writing* (2017) and *South African Textual Cultures* (2007). He is co-editor of *The Bloomsbury Handbook to J. M. Coetzee* (with Lucy Graham, 2023) and *South African Writing in Transition* (with Rita Barnard, 2019), and editor of Zoë Wicomb's *Race, Nation, Translation: South African Essays* (2018) and *Print, Text, and Book Cultures in South Africa* (2012).

Paul Walters is Emeritus Professor of English at Rhodes University, Makhanda (Grahamstown), South Africa. He has worked as lecturer in the USA and South Africa, and from 1979 was based at Rhodes University, where he was appointed as the first incumbent of the HA Molteno Chair in 1982, and made Emeritus Professor in 2009. Paul's childhood included trips to the Schreiner burial site and extended winter stays on a Karoo farm, which awoke a lifelong love of the region, its peoples and literatures. Paul has been a sometime Rhodes representative on the AMAZWI South African Museum of Literature Council, and is one of the lead organisers of the annual Schreiner Karoo Writers Festival. With joint author Jeremy Fogg, Paul has published regularly on Schreiner.

Dan Wylie is Professor Emeritus at Rhodes University, Makhanda (Grahamstown), South Africa. He founded the Literature and Ecology Colloquium in 2004, and has published widely in the field of ecocriticism, as well as in literary animal studies, early Zulu history, Zimbabwean literature and poetry. His books include *Myth of Iron: Shaka in History* (2006), *Intimate Lightning: Sydney Clouts, Poet* (2017), and *Death & Compassion: The Elephant in Southern African Literature* (2018).

Olive Schreiner in the World: An Introduction

Jade Munslow Ong and Andrew van der Vlies

The essays collected in this volume consider the significance and influence of South African-born writer, activist and thinker Olive Schreiner (1855–1920) in international and multidisciplinary contexts – literary, intellectual, political, cultural – in her own time and in ours. The scholarly engagements collected here account in new ways for under-examined aspects of her linked aesthetics and politics as they relate – amongst other of Schreiner's very many interests – to feminism, modernism, socialism and anti-racism in the colonial and metropolitan contexts in and between which she moved during her own life. They also explore revealing and sometimes unexpected connections and affinities that link Schreiner's work with its widespread influence and afterlife. Here contributors consider the nature of transmissions, translations, adaptations and memorialisation of Schreiner and her work since her death in 1920, across the globe and into the twenty-first century.

Schreiner has long been regarded as the first significant Anglophone novelist to emerge from what is now South Africa, her first and most famous book, *The Story of an African Farm* (1883), heralded both as the region's first serious novel and as an important contribution to the fiction of the 'New Woman' in the broader Anglosphere and beyond, a significant forerunner to such *fin-de-siècle* writers as Sarah Grand, Mona Caird and George Egerton.[1] *African Farm* immediately elicited many letters from readers who recognised their own plights in those of Schreiner's protagonists; the author recounted in a letter that she had 'got scores, almost hundreds of letters about it from all classes of people, from an Earl's son to a dressmaker in Bond Street, and from a coal-heaver to a poet'.[2] The novel circulated widely in what Ann Ardis calls a 'semi-underground economy' amongst freethinkers, anti-imperial and anti-racist activists and suffragists during the late nineteenth and early twentieth centuries.[3] Later, Schreiner's 1890 collection of allegories, *Dreams*, and her 1911 proto-feminist polemic, *Woman and Labour*, served as important touchstones for figures such as Charlotte Perkins Gilman, Constance Lytton and Vera Brittain.[4] The young Rebecca West, not yet a published novelist, commented in *The Freewoman* in 1912 that Schreiner was 'less a woman than a geographical fact' so enormous was her reputation in proto-feminist circles – and so synonymous was she with the land of her birth that inspired her most memorable fiction.[5]

Born on 24 March 1855, the ninth of twelve children, to Gottlob, a German-born missionary, and his English-born wife, Rebecca Lyndall, at the Wittebergen mission on the mountainous north-eastern border of the Cape Colony, Schreiner would spend her childhood and early adulthood in the arid interior of the Colony before journeying to London in early 1881. The constraints of gender and barriers of race and class that she sought to overcome in the deeply divided colonial and metropolitan situations she inhabited are everywhere evident in her behaviours, beliefs and politics, and in the friendships that they were enabled by – and enabled in turn. Once in London, Schreiner became a familiar of such anti-establishment intellectuals as Henry Havelock Ellis, Karl Pearson, Eleanor Marx and Edward Carpenter, and while she returned to southern Africa for long stretches on several occasions, she would spend the rest of her life navigating intellectual allegiances to overlapping circles in both northern and southern hemispheres.[6]

In her work on the 'affective communities' that emerged at the *fin de siècle* around connected British-Indian radicalisms (that included Carpenter), Leela Gandhi discusses how the 'politics of friendship' enabled 'unlikely conjunction[s]' of seemingly unconnected strands of radical thought, such that varied positions including '(proto-)posthumanist spiritualism and religious heterodoxy, pro-suffrage activism and socialism' might all 'be regarded as varieties of anti-imperialism'.[7] Instances of 'critical conjuncture' were created, Gandhi explains,

> when some of the selves who make up a culture loosen themselves from the security and comfort of old affiliations and identifications to make an unexpected 'gesture' of friendship toward all those on the other side of the fence. [. . .] A breach, that is, in the fabric of imperial inhospitability.[8]

Though Schreiner falls outside the national parameters of Gandhi's study, she can also be described in these terms; her 'gestures of friendship' – expressed both personally and through her writing – extended well beyond her South African and British contexts. As Simon Lewis has pointed out, work that focuses only on the British-South African axis tends to obscure wider, entangled, sometimes occluded networks of influence or affiliation that trouble assumptions about centre-periphery paradigms for understanding colonial-era cultural and intellectual contexts.[9]

By contrast, 'Schreiner's experience provides evidence for the ways in which [...] transnational inter-discursivity worked', Lewis contends, illustrating the point by considering how the many and varied books Schreiner encountered at family homes and in circulating libraries in the rural Cape Colony brought multiple transnational influences to bear on the development of her 'theological unorthodoxy' in particular.[10] 'The vectors of knowledge-as-power are complicated and multi-directional', Lewis demonstrates (echoing, for example, though differently framed, Laura Chrisman's call for scholars of culture under late imperial conditions to 'disaggregate' the metropolis).[11] It is the direction and scale of these vectors, in Schreiner's time and into our own, that this book contributes to charting.

The fifteen chapters that follow draw on evidence from Schreiner's political and literary writings, as well as letters that attest to her friendships and networks, to demonstrate distinct, situated understandings of the significance of her politics and aesthetics for a range of individual writers, thinkers, coteries, communities and audiences globally and across a variety of fields and in multiple forms. The collection is organised into five sections: 'Modernity and Modernism'; 'Race and Anti-Racism'; 'Print, Publishing and Translation'; 'Antipodean Schreiner'; 'South African Afterlives'. Broadly speaking, the essays move from analysis of Schreiner and her 'writing networks' to the 'global contexts' of her influence and afterlives, though there are a number of shared and overlapping concerns across the volume as a whole. The collection thus represents the first attempt to collate works that address the international impacts of, and global responses to, Schreiner and her writings from the late-nineteenth to the twenty-first centuries. The geopolitical diversity of the chapters is matched by its theoretical and methodological diversity, spanning (amongst others) Marxism, eco-feminism, translation, print cultures, postcolonialism, epistolary studies and museum studies. Contributors combine macro-level analysis of Schreiner and her work in the context of global networks and world systems, with micro-level formal analysis of texts produced by Schreiner and other key figures with whose work hers has been compared.

Whilst the collection as a whole adopts a diachronic approach, individual chapters offer synchronic focus on specific letters, published writings, spaces (homes and museums), personal and textual connections, publishers and readers, and translations, in order to consider particular textual and intellectual moments, and to trace the movement of Schreiner's ideas and forms across regions and centuries. In this way, the collection maps transhistorical, transnational and multidirectional lines of influence, collaboration, confluence and cultural impact that originate with Schreiner.

Modernity and Modernism, Affect and Affiliation

Schreiner's coming to consciousness as a keen observer of social relations in the Cape Colony during the 1860s and 1870s, witness to the forces of industrialisation and a nascent global resource capitalism that would drive Britain's conflict with the Dutch republics (with which Schreiner came to sympathise) as much as it would fuel the First World War, made her a prescient commentator on what later theorists would cast as the discontents of western modernity in the later nineteenth century. A number of scholars have traced these lines of argument in Schreiner's corpus of fiction and polemic alike, perhaps none as insightfully as Carolyn Burdett, who wrote more than two decades ago that 'Schreiner saw South Africa placed to make a unique historical wager with modernity and progress': 'modernization in South Africa was experienced as an act or an event, belligerently visible, freed of the mystifications of history, and quite unlike the seemingly inevitable, unfolding process of European modernity'.[12]

We have come, in the years since, to see Schreiner's analysis at the heart of her experiments with form; Jed Esty and others have given us the language to recast what some metropolitan critics had hitherto regarded as inconsistencies or unevenness in some of her work (not least *African Farm*'s sometime pastiche-like quotation of genres and styles) as an implicit critique of western narratives of progress – exemplified in the novel of *Bildung* – and as evidence of a sophisticated and 'systematic assimilation of an uneven and markedly colonial temporality into [. . .] plot structure, characterization, and figurative language'.[13] Jade Munslow Ong has more recently made the bold but justified claim that 'Schreiner provides the primary example of a South African modernist pioneer', one whose modernism emerged out of what Fredric Jameson considers a necessary 'situation of incomplete modernization [. . .] that reproduces the appearance of First World social reality [. . .] but whose underlying structure is in fact much closer that of the Third World'.[14] That is, Schreiner 'lived the inequalities of, and defamiliarisation processes generated by, the imposition of European economic, political and culture structures detached from African ways of life'; as a result, she was able to 'enter the philosophical terrain of modernism earlier than' her Euro-modernist counterparts because she 'did not require the same levels of conscious abstraction in order to understand and respond to the uneven dynamics of capitalist modernity'.[15]

The first three chapters – by Mark Sanders, Munslow Ong and Dan Wylie – variously take up the challenge of reading, or rereading, Schreiner in relation to her engagements with 'Modernity and Modernism' (the section's title). They demonstrate how, in her fictional and polemical writing and letters, Schreiner responded to the technological advances, urbanisation and industrialisation of the later stages of the Industrial Revolution, and the gendered, ecological, political and social effects of the spread of global capitalism through empire. They show too how Schreiner devised and mobilised resistant feminist and socialist politics and nature-based ethics to counter the damaging effects of these distinctly modern experiences. Sanders's analysis of Schreiner and the machine focalises key aspects of Schreiner's artistic and political thinking on *woman and labour* (also the title of Schreiner's 1911 polemic), industrialism and new technologies, and the overlapping position of the artist and/as engineer. Picking up on ideas of working women in her chapter on the converging modernisms of Schreiner and Margaret Harkness, Munslow Ong then argues that the Bloomsbury friendships and networks of which Schreiner and Harkness were part created the context for both to develop shared socialist and feminist ideas that they conveyed through linked literary techniques. Wylie's chapter on Schreiner and Virginia Woolf is similarly concerned with ideas held in common between women writers, albeit with a specific focus on their engagements with nature, so that Wylie reads both as proponents of burgeoning eco-feminist ideas in modern literature.

What emerges across the collection, including in chapters by Dorothy Driver, Barnita Bagchi, Emma Barnes, and collaborating authors Nicholas Jose, Alex Sutcliffe and Mandy Treagus, are a number of South-South connections established through Schreiner's own personal and political networks, as well as the creation, production, circulation and consumption of Schreiner's writings, from South Africa and Britain to Botswana, India, Australia and New Zealand. These periphery-to-periphery contact zones generate new centres of thought, as scholars such as Elleke Boehmer, Isabel Hofmeyr, Michelle Williams, Porscha Fermanis, Sarah Comyn and others have demonstrated in nuanced studies of particular cross-cultural or contact-zone exchange in recent decades.[16] This book builds on their work, evidencing the value of a methodology that focuses the insights of a number of critical orientations – literary critical, print-cultures, sociological – on a single author's life and work (and, crucially, cross- and inter-textual legacies). The connections charted in these chapters stand alongside the more familiar connections made between Southern Africans over time (see chapters by Driver and by Andrew van der Vlies), between South Africa and the UK, as well as in the USA, Sweden and the Netherlands (contexts that are the subject of chapters by Heidi Barends, Clare Gill, Sanja Nivesjö and Małgorzata Drwal).

In all cases, the work in this volume is driven by a shared impetus to uncover and analyse the anticipatory and galvanising roles of political and artistic forces that emerge from Southern Africa through case studies on Schreiner. In investigating the spread and circulation of South African literary forms and ideas around the globe, the collection challenges the dictum 'first the West and then the rest' by revealing Schreiner as a wellspring for key aspects of anti-racist, modernist, utopian, feminist and eco-feminist thought that travelled to other parts of Africa, India, the USA, Western Europe, Australasia and beyond. In a broader context, the collection contributes to ongoing discussions about the role of the Global South, and particularly Southern Africa, in shaping global political and literary futures.[17] The collection thus aims to generate new currents in Schreiner Studies by speaking to recent debates around global and world literature. As it is, the 'global turn' in Postcolonial Studies that took place in the early 2000s and sought to offer new accounts of, and ways of reading, a world emerging after twentieth-century decolonisation, has not yet had a significant impact on Schreiner scholarship. Existing criticism that addresses the international reach of Schreiner's personal networks and writings remains scattered and piecemeal, though recently John Hilton has published on Schreiner's friendship with Mohandas Gandhi, and Drwal analysed Schreiner's influence on Dutch feminist Aletta Jacobs.[18]

Schreiner's writing networks and global contexts were expansive even within her lifetime, in part due to her distinctively peripatetic lifestyle. She straddled nations and national definitions, both in her self-description as an 'English-South African' and in her relentless travel within and across national borders.[19] Though she spent most of her life in South Africa, she also lived in various places across England, as well as Switzerland, Italy and France.[20] Schreiner's itinerancy was driven by various factors: economic need and career opportunities, changing friendships and relationships, the search for environments that were better for her health, and her own restless energies. From her earliest years, Schreiner devised stories and allegories as she marched up and down on stoeps outside her childhood homes – a habit and strategy that she continued to rely on in adulthood as a way of activating thought. For example, in an 1898 letter to her brother William Schreiner, she describes how, '[a]fter I had finished [*Trooper*] Peter Halket [*of Mashonaland*]' (her blistering literary attack on Cecil Rhodes), 'I spent three days & nights almost entirely without sleep pacing up & down my verandah, trying to decide whether I should publish it or not'.[21]

The protagonists in Schreiner's novels and allegories are similarly mobile, often travelling across lands and seas in search of places and communities that might accommodate their 'queerness'.[22] Though Schreiner never seemed to settle, her fondness for Matjiesfontein is telling, as the small Central Karoo village grew up around a station on the railway connecting Cape Town to Kimberley and so provided opportunities for swift returns and departures. Schreiner's view of Matjiesfontein as sanctuary and haven, as well as its importance to her political vision and changing ideas about race, are highlighted in both Munslow Ong and Liz Stanley's chapters.

Nation, Race, Sex, Class

Schreiner's movements across South Africa and Western Europe went hand in hand with her efforts to seek out new forms of cultural and linguistic exchange. As a child, she was permitted to speak only English at home, and was once beaten by her mother for exclaiming in Cape Dutch: 'Ach!'.[23] Schreiner remained conversant in this proto-Afrikaans however, and showed great interest in learning other languages, including French and Italian.[24] In 1890, she wrote to her friend Karl Pearson, statistician and eugenicist (probably in an attempt to impress him), that she planned 'to spend some years in the interior of Africa'; she was learning an indigenous language, she told him (probably isiXhosa), 'so that I shall be able to study the people'.[25] Instantiations of Schreiner's learning and changing thinking about race appear throughout the collection, including in chapters by Stanley, Bagchi, Janet Remmington, and Driver. Schreiner's interactions with San, Khoikhoi and mixed-race labourers, a coloured woman whose baby she helped to deliver, her reading of W. E. B. DuBois and support for Black South African leaders such as Solomon T. Plaatje (amongst other examples), illustrate her developing understanding of sundering racial divides and gross inequalities and are identified as key to inspiring her efforts in later adulthood to counter racism in its many forms.[26]

Schreiner's political connections to, and interest in, India and its struggles for independence were in part formed through her friendship with Gandhi. In his book about Indians in South Africa, Gandhi claims that he 'had the privilege of being familiar with' Schreiner, and was particularly admiring of the fact that she 'was as simple in habits and humble in spirit as she was learned' and appeared to make no distinction 'between her Negro servants and herself'.[27] Gandhi was particularly grateful that '[t]his gifted lady lent to the Indian cause the whole weight of her influence over the Europeans of South Africa'.[28] Bagchi's chapter in this collection enriches our understanding of Schreiner's Indian connections and shared anti-colonialism through comparative analysis of Schreiner's writings and those of missionary and social reformer Charles Freer Andrews (also a friend of Gandhi's). Key agents involved in South African and Indian anti-colonial resistance, campaigns and writing are thus revealed as connected through the parallel development of key themes and ideas in their work, as well as through mutual associates.

Bagchi's essay provides an important bridge to the second section of the book, 'Race and Anti-Racism'. By placing Schreiner's later writings in conversation with work by Andrews (by way of their mutual friendship with Gandhi), Bagchi reveals novel correlations and connections between key aspects of South African and Indian anti-colonial, anti-racist, utopian and spiritual/religious thought. Stanley, in her analysis of three key 'turning points' evidenced in Schreiner's letters and inspired by her reading, charts Schreiner's changing opinions on race and the development of her anti-racist thinking. The final two chapters in this section, by Remmington and Barends, segue from Schreiner's *writing networks* to the *global contexts* of her life and works up until the present day. Remmington begins by discussing the evolution of Schreiner's ideas about race through her relationship and break with Rhodes, then turns outwards to examine Schreiner's responses to political events and the developing framework of discriminatory legislation, her social and political networks that included key Black intellectuals and politicians such as Sol Plaatje, all while positioning Schreiner as 'agent and icon' of race advocacy even in the present day.[29] Finally, Barends examines the influence of Schreiner on a leading figure of the American Civil Rights movement, Howard Thurman, and how, through Thurman, Schreiner's work reached Martin Luther King Jr.

The anti-racist and anti-colonial dimensions of Schreiner's work form an important thrust of other work presented in this collection, too, and offer a corrective to the fact that it was Schreiner's feminism that long provided the primary focus of critical, cultural and fictional engagements with the author and her writing. This is captured well in the 2015 blockbuster film *Suffragette*, in which a copy of *Dreams* is passed among members of the Women's Social and Political Union. In the climactic scene at the 1913 Epsom Derby, the character based on the historical figure Emily Davison hands *Dreams* to the (fictional) Maud Watts before being trampled to death under the hooves of the King's horse. The film closes with lines from 'Three Dreams in a Desert', a short allegory from the collection. As this recent filmic representation indicates, Schreiner was an important figure in the context of emerging white middle-class feminism in Britain, but as Barnes argues in her chapter, the intertextual presence of Schreiner's work in New Woman writing from Aotearoa New Zealand, clear in novels by Louisa Alice Baker and Jane Mander, reveals Schreiner's extraordinary geographical reach within her lifetime. Barnes's work also provides a newly gendered and feminist understanding of what Comyn and Fermanis have dubbed 'the southern archive', which 'provide[s] a counterbalance to northern biases and [...] new purchase on nation-centred literary paradigms' to reveal 'south-south transnational exchanges and structural homologies between southern genres, themes and forms'.[30] This is confirmed by the Australian analysis offered by Jose, Sutcliffe and Treagus. Schreiner's Australian contemporaries, feminist novelists Catherine Helen Spence and Catherine Martin, were keenly aware of, and impressed by, Schreiner's work, and a range of resonances and reminiscences connect the three writers' politics as well as the plots of their novels.

Schreiner also found a ready readership amongst working-class women. As her close friend, Mary Brown, recalled:

> I asked a Lancashire working woman what she thought of *Story of an African Farm* and a strange expression came over her face as she said 'I read parts of it over and over.' 'What parts?' I asked, and her reply was 'About yon poor lass' (Lyndall), and with a far-off look in her eyes added 'I think there is hundreds of women what feels like that but can't speak it, but *she* could speak what we feel'.[31]

The affective and politicised responses of working women to Schreiner's writings crossed class boundaries, just as Schreiner herself sought to befriend prostitutes, studying and writing about prostitution, and investigating and condemning the lived impacts of the punitive Contagious Diseases Acts. Schreiner often lived alone, and as a result fell afoul of English landladies and police who made assumptions about her unmarried status, regular male visitors and habit of walking alone in the streets.[32] These discriminatory interactions were subsequently narrativised in Schreiner's strident public and literary attacks on the sexual exploitation of women within and outside of marriage, informing her forceful criticisms of gender-based oppression in feminist tracts and shorter allegories as well as the book she regarded as her magnum opus, the posthumously published *From Man to Man, Or Perhaps Only*.[33]

Transnational Print Cultures and Literary Afterlives

As the example of the Lancashire woman illustrates, the reach of Schreiner's writing extended far beyond her personal and political networks to multiple contexts of reception. Stanley points out that 'many individual people who came across [Schreiner's] work [. . .] felt their ideas and lives changed by it'.[34] Such readers found a support in Schreiner's writing to assuage their own sense of being at an angle to majority society; for other such readers who found one another, being linked by a common love of Schreiner's work generated new communities, often out of view of the mainstream. Indeed, Schreiner herself was particularly keen that her writing reach diverse readers across social strata and the world. In 1892, she wrote to publisher T. Fisher Unwin to remind him that she had

> insisted on an African Farm being published at 1/- (one shilling) because the book was published by me for working men. I wanted to feel sure poor boys like Waldo could buy a copy, & feel they were not alone.[35]

This contrasts with her claim that her 1890 collection, *Dreams*,

> is not published by me with the special intention of reaching the poor. I would prefer the rich to have it. If I dedicated it to the public for whom I intended it, I should dedicate it ('To all Capitalists Millionaires & Middle-men – in England & America, & all high & mighty persons').[36]

Short stories and vignettes collected in *Dreams*, as well as later publications such as *Trooper Peter Halket of Mashonaland*, often seem to speak directly to and challenge 'capitalists', 'millionaires' and 'middle-men', who are condemned for their exploitation and harming of others; at the same time, however, Schreiner's allegories enact a kind of double address, including the dissident, marginal or marginalised individuals and subcultures that comprised so much of her readership. The nameless, genderless or gender-crossing, synecdochal, prosopopoeiac and child characters – including, for example, the worker, prostitute, Life, Joy and unnamed I – that populate Schreiner's various dream allegories combine a sense of the familiar generated by religious imagery, language and settings, with an openness of form that enables individual interpretation and readerly self-recognition.

Despite these universalising strategies, Schreiner's writings neither dissolve into abstraction nor erase cultural and social difference. She often incorporates specific references to European cities or rural and wilderness settings in the Cape, and depicts recognisable power dynamics, for example between master and servant. In consequence, the local and global, individual and collective continually collapse and merge in Schreiner's work, and the great variety of contexts in which it circulated compounded its interest for new audiences. Stanley notes that Schreiner was a 'major intellectual presence for other circles and collectivities of people' across a range of regional contexts, from Southern Africa to Europe and North America, and further afield to Japan, Russia, and elsewhere.[37] Apollon Davidson and Irina Filatova produced an early account of the publication history of Schreiner's literature and non-fiction in Russia, and in her introduction to a collection of short essays on Schreiner, Itala Vivan discussed the Italian reception of the first translation of *African Farm*.[38] More recently, there have been analyses of Japanese translations of Schreiner's work in the New Woman magazine *Seitō* (Bluestocking), and critical commentary on the role played by Schreiner's writings in Japanese feminist debates on motherhood, including by critics Jan Bardsley, Hiroko Tomida and Vera Mackie.[39]

As this brief account of some of the contexts canvassed in extant scholarship suggests, the transnational and historical span of Schreiner's work meant that it appeared in a range of cultural and political locations, across various print media, and in translation, accruing new readers with their own presumptions and preoccupations along the way. Each mediated encounter with a differently contextualised version of a 'Schreiner' text activated new latent meanings. As Van der Vlies wrote in an account of the reception history of *African Farm*:

> the mediation of Schreiner's text by its changing material manifestations, and the manner in which multiple interest groups interpreted Schreiner's own perceived national and geographic origins and affiliations, provides evidence to challenge and extend work on colonial writing in general, and so-called 'South African' writing in particular, providing a salutary lesson in the conditional, ideological, and provisional nature of any attempt to claim a work of literature for any strictly circumscribed category or tradition – including that of a national literature.[40]

Schreiner's transatlantic influence is the focus of both Barend's chapter and the first chapter in the third section in this volume, 'Print, Publishing and Translation'. Here Gill analyses the publication and reception of Schreiner's work in the anarchist press, both in the UK and USA. Turning to the periodical press in the Netherlands, Drwal takes in a broad range of examples to examine how a 'pillarised' Dutch society – to use the term that describes the separation of public life into confessional and ideological pillars – mobilised Schreiner and her writings to support a variety of political, cultural and social positions. The Swedish press is the focus of Nivesjö's chapter, in which she looks at translations of, and engagements with, Schreiner's *The Story of an African Farm*, *Dreams* and *Woman and Labour*.

These chapters greatly expand our understanding of the geographical, temporal and political parameters of Schreiner's work, but other essays have their eye on question of publishing cultures, too, whether in English or in translation. Jose, Sutcliffe and Treagus briefly reference Chinese translations of Schreiner's writings, for example; Remmington's study of Schreiner's relations with Black intellectuals in South Africa engages perforce with African-language newspaper contexts; while the difficulty of publication for some later writers deeply influenced by Schreiner is a running theme in Driver's chapter, too. Reception, translation and adaption become metaphors – and in some cases synonyms – as work like Schreiner's accrues cultural resonances in particular times and places that are sometimes difficult to recognise or reconstruct in the present. The influence of Schreiner on Bessie Head and on J. M. Coetzee, posited by Driver and Van der Vlies respectively, is of this order: Schreiner's work has become symbolic capital for investment or disavowal in complex ways that suggest that the history of writerly authority (and the authority of received reputation) has much to tell us about regional and national literary genealogies.

Southern Hemisphere Afterlives

The final two sections in the collection each trace some of these genealogies in striking ways, and in both 'cases' in the Southern Hemisphere. The two chapters gathered under the sign 'Antipodean Schreiner' uncover the influence of Schreiner's feminist and modernist aesthetics and politics on New Zealand and Australian writers. Barnes investigates the influence of Schreiner's politics and fiction on contemporaneous New Women writers from Aotearoa New Zealand in the context of an intercolonial white feminist network spanning Southern-hemisphere nations. The co-authored chapter by Australian writers and scholars Jose, Sutcliffe and Treagus begins by analysing the influence of Schreiner's work on Australian writers Spence, Martin, Miles Franklin and Henry Handel Richardson, before arguing for the importance of Schreiner in the development of Australian modernism by uncovering the intertextual importance of Schreiner's *African Farm* for Australian Nobel Laureate in Literature, Patrick White.

In the final section of the collection, 'South African Afterlives', the Southern-hemisphere focus returns us to South Africa and the intergenerational dynamics of three major writers: Schreiner, Head and Coetzee. Driver's essay traces the probable influence of Schreiner on Head; the younger writer once even referred to herself as a 'reincarnated' Schreiner. Driver's opening gambit is to ask the reader to imagine the 'poor coloured woman' who Schreiner describes as having given birth 'in the road' in a diary entry from January 1881,[41] as forerunner not only of the mixed-race infant that unsettles a bourgeois family in Schreiner's *From Man to Man* (1926), but also of a mixed-race character in Head's 1971 novel, *Maru*. Driver asks us to consider how a literary 'tradition' comes to be constructed, and how 'writing (and its meaning) is transmitted from one generation to the next'.[42] A similar interrogation structures Van der Vlies's chapter, in which the transmission is from Schreiner to Coetzee. Starting with a series of mixed messages from the Nobel laureate that both claim and disavow her influence, Van der Vlies considers the possibility of Schreiner's work serving as 'maternal' influence rather than in a line of direct indebtedness or patronage: Coetzee himself claimed such a form of descent, and this essay considers what this could mean in relation to the lines one might trace between *Trooper Peter Halket of Mashonaland* (1897), the last sustained work of allegorical fiction Schreiner would publish in her lifetime, and Coetzee's first published book, *Dusklands* (1974).

In the final chapter in the section, Paul Walters and Jeremy Fogg offer a historicised account of the Olive Schreiner House as heritage and tourist site of vital educational, cultural and commemorative importance. Here is influence and afterlife of a different, and very tangible, order. Schreiner tourism is a small but nonetheless fascinating phenomenon, facilitated by the work of the curators of the Schreiner House in Cradock as well as organisers of the annual Cradock-based Karoo Writers Festival, which has run since 2010 and continues to draw new audiences to Schreiner and her circles.[43] It is possible too to visit Schreiner's sarcophagus atop Buffelskop, a mountain on the outskirts of town, and book overnight stays in the tiny Olive Schreiner Cottage in Matjiesfontein, where she lived for a number of years and where she reportedly entertained both Rhodes and Rudyard Kipling.

Perhaps in part due to her comparatively small *oeuvre*, Schreiner sometimes seems to fall between the cracks and crevasses that exist within and amongst disciplines: her nationality is weighted against her in conventional selections of Victorian literature; she fails to register as even a minor modernist by comparison to writers such as Virginia Woolf and Katherine Mansfield; and her contexts of writing mean that, at best, she figures as a kind of pre-postcolonial pioneer – one who stands outside the period typically associated with the literature of decolonisation. Yet Schreiner does have a place in repertoires of postcolonial and world literatures and cultures, not least because her work continues to appear in transformed and transmedial adaptations across languages, forms, cultures and locations. By way of only a few examples: Schreiner is the subject of a poem, play and creative essay by Leontia Flynn, Stephen Gray and Doris Lessing, respectively; Schreiner's final resting place appears in poems and stories by Roy Campbell, Etienne van Heerden and Caitlin Stobie; and *African Farm* has been adapted for stage, radio and film by Marion Baraitser, Lindiwe Dovey and David Lister.[44] We ourselves chose a quote from *African Farm* as the epigraph to the short film *All That Is Buried*, which was made in association with our AHRC-funded project, *South African Modernism 1880–2020* (from which this collection also arises). In addition, growing critical and public interest in Schreiner's life and writings has been fuelled by initiatives such as the Olive Schreiner Letters Online project (led by Stanley), recent republications of Schreiner's works, including Driver's edition of *From Man to Man*, Stanley's *The Dawn of Civilisation*, and Barbara Black, Carly Nations and Anna Spydell's *Dreams*, a forthcoming Edinburgh edition of selected writing by Van der Vlies, Driver, Burdett and Gill, as well as the film *Suffragette* (2015), mentioned above.

Schreiner's legacy does not 'belong' to or in any single national or language context; to claim as much would be to ignore the findings of nearly every essay in this collection. The legacy is, however, perhaps most contested in the country of the author's birth in the wake of some of the reckonings with the aftermath of racial segregation three decades after the end of formal apartheid. Schreiner's own (and confessed) childhood racism, often uncritical use of racist language in her earliest writings, and the point made by Stanley that 'Schreiner wrote in the context of imperialism, racism and the origins of the apartheid state in South Africa, so that she is sometimes seen as an emblematic "white South African" and tainted by everything this has come to mean', have perhaps prevented any close association between Schreiner's life and writings with the liberation struggles of South Africa.[45] Her vociferous public and literary attacks on Rhodes notwithstanding, Schreiner rarely figures as a major historical antecedent of mid- and late-twentieth- and twenty first century resistance movements, anti-colonial and anti-apartheid activism or decolonising campaigns.

This point is also noted in Remmington's chapter, which points out that the 2015 #RhodesMustFall student movement 'did not at the time specifically link its twenty-first century protest action to the vocal, multi-sited anti-Rhodes activism of the past, including that of Schreiner'.[46] Certainly the post-apartheid Rainbow Nation had its own iconic freedom fighters and had little need to look back to a long-departed daughter of white European missionaries to find additional heroes. Likely this is also the case for decolonial activists today. And yet telling glimpses of Schreiner's voice and art appear in various accounts of South Africa's long struggle for self-determination and freedom from minority rule: in exhibitions in the Schreiner House in Cradock and the Amazwi South African Museum of Literature in Makhanda (Grahamstown); in a small glass case housing a copy of *The Story of an African Farm* with explanatory caption in the Apartheid Museum in Johannesburg; and in Schreiner's posthumous 2003 award of South Africa's national Order of Ikhamanga in Gold for 'her exceptional contribution to literature and commitment to the struggle for human rights and democracy'.[47]

The essays in this collection are our collective contribution to further confirming Schreiner's ongoing presence and importance in colonial and post-colonial South Africa and beyond. Taken together, they make the argument for a 'new' Schreiner studies, one that draws on recent developments in scholarship on global and peripheral modernisms, activist networks and intersectional alliances, posthumanism, memory studies and intermediality, to position the study of Schreiner and her legacies as significant for understanding literary and social archives, race and gender performance, and the circulation of ideas, from the nineteenth century to the present day.

Works Cited

Ardis, Ann. *New Women, New Novels: Feminism and Early Modernism.* New Brunswick: Rutgers University Press, 1990.

—. 'Organizing Women: New Woman Writers, New Woman Readers, and Suffrage Feminism.' In *Victorian Women Writers and the Woman Question*, edited by Nicola Diane Thompson, 189–203. Cambridge: Cambridge University Press, 1999.

Bardsley, Jan. 'The New Woman of Japan and the Intimate Bonds of Translation.' In *Translation in Modern Japan*, edited by Indra Levy, 213–33. London: Routledge, 2017.

Baraitser, Marion. The Story of an African Farm: *A Dramatisation of Olive Schreiner's Novel.* London: Oberon Books, 2000.

Bjørhovde, *Rebellious Structures: Women Writers and the Crisis of the Novel 1880–1900.* Oslo: Norwegian University Press, 1987.

Boehmer, Elleke. *Empire, the National, and the Postcolonial 1890–1920: Resistance in Interaction.* Oxford: Oxford University Press, 2002.

Bristow, Joseph. 'Introduction'. In *The Story of an African Farm*, by Olive Schreiner, vii–xxix. Oxford: Oxford University Press, 1992.

Burdett, Carolyn. *Olive Schreiner and the Progress of Feminism: Evolution, Gender, Empire*. Houndmills, Basingstoke: Palgrave, 2001.

Campbell, Roy. 'Buffel's Kop'. In *Adamastor*, 27. London: Faber & Faber, 1930.

Chrisman, Laura. *Rereading the Imperial Romance: British Imperialism and South African Resistance in Haggard, Schreiner, and Plaatje*. Oxford: Clarendon, 2000.

Comaroff, Jean, and John L. Comaroff. *Theory from the South or, How Euro-America is Evolving toward Africa*. New York: Routledge, 2016.

Comyn, Sarah, and Porscha Fermanis, 'Rethinking Nineteenth-Century Literary Culture: British Worlds, Southern Latitudes and Hemispheric Methods'. *Journal of Commonwealth Literature*, online ahead of print (2021): 1–18.

—, eds. *Worlding the South: Nineteenth-Century Literary Culture and the Southern Settler Colonies*. Manchester: Manchester University Press, 2021.

Davidson, Apollon, and Irina Filatova. 'Olive Schreiner: A Century in Russia'. *English in Africa* 20, no. 1 (May 1993): 39–48.

Dovey, Lindiwe, dir. *Perfect Darkness*. 2008.

Drwal, Małgorzata. 'The Feminism of Olive Schreiner and the Feminism of Aletta Jacobs: The Reception of Schreiner's *Woman and Labour* in the Netherlands.' *Dutch Crossing: Journal of Low Countries Studies* 45, no. 1 (2021): 77–92.

Esty, Jed. 'The Colonial Bildungsroman: *The Story of an African Farm* and the Ghost of Goethe'. *Victorian Studies* 49, no. 3 (2007): 407–30.

First, Ruth, and Ann Scott. *Olive Schreiner*. New Brunswick: Rutgers University Press, 1980.

Flint, Kate. *The Woman Reader: 1837–1914*. Oxford: Clarendon, 1993.

Flynn, Leontia. 'Olive Schreiner'. *Drives*, 12. London: Jonathan Cape, 2008.

Gandhi, Leela. *Affective Communities: Anticolonial Thought, Fin-de-Siècle Radicalism, and the Politics of Friendship*. Durham: Duke University Press, 2006.

Gandhi, Mohandas K. *Satyagraha in South Africa*. Madras: Triplicane, 1928.

Gavron, Sarah, dir. *Suffragette*. 2015.

Government of South Africa. 'Recipients of the National Order Awards, 2003'. https://www.gov.za/sites/default/files/schreiner.pdf.

Gray, Stephen. *Schreiner: A One-Woman Play*. Claremont: David Philip, 1983.

Heilmann, Ann. *New Woman Strategies: Sarah Grand, Olive Schreiner, Mona Caird*. Manchester: Manchester University Press, 2004.

Hilton, John. 'Gandhi, Carpenter, Schreiner and the Crisis of Modern Civilisation at the Turn of the 20th Century'. *African Studies* 74, no. 2 (2015): 157–74.

Hofmeyr, Isabel, and Michelle Williams, eds. *South Africa and India: Shaping the Global South*. Johannesburg: Wits University Press, 2011.

Jameson, Fredric. 'Modernism and Imperialism.' In *Nationalism, Colonialism and Literature*, by Terry Eagleton, Fredric Jameson and Edward Said, 42–66. Minneapolis: University of Minnesota Press, 1990.

Lessing, Doris. 'Olive Schreiner'. In *Time Bites*, 195–200. London: Harper Perennial, 2004.

Lewis, Simon. 'The Transnational Circulation of Dissent: Olive Schreiner and the Colonial Counter-Flows of Unitarian Freethinking.' *Safundi* 14, no. 1 (2013): 1–15.
Lister, David, dir. *Bustin' Bonaparte: The Story of an African Farm*. 2004.
Mackie, Vera. *Feminism in Modern Japan: Citizenship, Embodiment and Sexuality*. Cambridge: Cambridge University Press, 2003.
Munslow Ong, Jade. *Olive Schreiner and African Modernism: Allegory, Empire and Postcolonial Writing*. London: Routledge, 2018.
Satpathy, Sumanyu, ed. *Southern Postcolonialisms*. New Delhi: Routledge, 2009.
Schreiner, Olive. 'An English-South African's View of the Situation: Words in Season'. In *Words in Season: The Public Writings with Her Own Remembrances Collected for the First Time*, 59–101. Johannesburg: Penguin Books, 2005.
—. *Dreams*, edited by Barbara Black, Carly Nations and Anna Spydell. Ontario: Broadview, 2020.
—. *From Man to Man, or Perhaps Only*, edited by Dorothy Driver. Claremont: University of Cape Town Press, 2015.
—. [as Ralph Iron.] *The Story of an African Farm*. 2 vols. London: Chapman and Hall, 1883.
—. *Trooper Peter Halket of Mashonaland*. London: T. Fisher Unwin, 1897.
—. *Woman and Labour*. London: T. Fisher Unwin, 1911.
Stanley, Liz. *Imperialism, Labour and the New Woman: Olive Schreiner's Social Theory*. Durham: Sociologypress, 2002.
—. *Olive Schreiner's The Dawn of Civilisation & Other Unpublished Wartime Writings*, edited by Liz Stanley. Edinburgh: X Press, 2018.
Stanton-Sharma, Simon, and Maire Tracey, dirs. *All That is Buried*. 2022.
Stobie, Caitlin. 'Striking Rocks'. In *Thin Slices*, 41. Birmingham: Verve Poetry Press, 2022.
Tomida, Hiroko. 'The Controversy over the Protection of Motherhood and its Impacts upon the Japanese Women's Movement'. *European Journal of East Asian Studies* 3, no. 2 (2004): 243–71.
Van der Vlies, Andrew. *South African Textual Cultures*. Manchester: Manchester University Press, 2007.
Van Heerden, Etienne. 'The Resurrection of Olive'. *Iowa Review* 21, no. 2 (1991): 15–29.
Vivan, Itala. 'Introduzione'. In *Storia di una fattoria Africana* by Olive Schreiner, translated by Riccardo Duranti, v–xix. Florence: Giunti Astrea, 1986.
—. 'Introduction.' In *The Flawed Diamond: Essays on Olive Schreiner*, edited by Itala Vivan. 9–25. Sydney: Dangaroo Press, 1991.
West, Rebecca. *The Young Rebecca: Writings of Rebecca West 1911–1917*, edited by Jane Marcus. London: Macmillan, 1982.
West-Pavlov, Russell, ed. *The Global South and Literature*. Cambridge: Cambridge University Press, 2018.

Letters

Olive Schreiner to Samuel Cron Cronwright-Schreiner, 23 April 1915. *Olive Schreiner Letters Online*.

Olive Schreiner to The Editor of *The Standard*, 4 January 1887. *Olive Schreiner Letters Online*.
Olive Schreiner to Henry Havelock Ellis, 21 October 1884. *Olive Schreiner Letters Online*.
Olive Schreiner to Henry Havelock Ellis, 29 October 1885. *Olive Schreiner Letters Online*.
Olive Schreiner to Henry Havelock Ellis, 7 February 1888. *Olive Schreiner Letters Online*.
Olive Schreiner to Karl Pearson, 25 October 1886. *Olive Schreiner Letters Online*.
Olive Schreiner to Karl Pearson, 11 November 1890. *Olive Schreiner Letters Online*.
Olive Schreiner to William Philip Schreiner, 29 June 1898. *Olive Schreiner Letters Online*.
Olive Schreiner to T. Fisher Unwin, 26 September 1892. *Olive Schreiner Letters Online*.

Notes

1. See Bjørhovde, *Rebellious Structures*, 21–233; Heilmann, *New Woman Strategies*, 4–6; Ardis, *New Women, New Novels*, 31.
2. Schreiner to Pearson, 25 October 1886, *Olive Schreiner Letters Online (OSLO)*.
3. Ardis, 'Organizing Women', 192.
4. Flint, *The Woman Reader, 1837–1914*, 242–43.
5. Bristow, 'Introduction', xxvi, quoting West ('So Simple', *The Freewoman*, 12 October 1912), *The Young Rebecca*, 73.
6. Schreiner lived in South Africa again between October 1889 and May 1893, October 1893 and January 1897, August 1897 and December 1913, and from August 1920 until her death in December.
7. Gandhi, *Affective Communities*, 9, 8.
8. Gandhi, *Affective Communities*, 189.
9. Lewis, 'The Transnational Circulation of Dissent', 6.
10. Lewis, 'The Transnational Circulation of Dissent', 1–2.
11. Lewis, 'The Transnational Circulation of Dissent', 2. Chrisman, *Rereading the Imperial Romance*, 7–8.
12. Burdett, *Olive Schreiner and the Progress of Feminism*, 149, 149–50.
13. Esty, 'The Colonial Bildungsroman,' 408.
14. Munslow Ong, *Olive Schreiner and African Modernism*, 10; Jameson, 'Modernism and Imperialism,' 60.
15. Munslow Ong, *Olive Schreiner and African Modernism*, 8, 9–10.
16. See Boehmer, *Empire, the National, and the Postcolonial*; Hofmeyr and Williams, *South Africa and India*; Comyn and Fermanis, *Worlding the South*.
17. See Satpathy, *Southern Postcolonialisms*; Comaroff and Comaroff, *Theory from the South, Or, How Euro-America is Evolving Towards Africa*; and West-Pavlov, ed., *The Global South and Literature*, for example.

18. See Hilton, 'Gandhi, Carpenter, Schreiner'; Drwal, 'The Feminism of Olive Schreiner'.
19. Schreiner, 'An English-South African's View of the Situation,' 59. This was originally published as a three-part essay titled 'An English-South African's View of the Situation: Words in Season' in *South African News* 1, 2 and 3 in June 1899.
20. Schreiner was in Europe between 1881 and 1889, and again in 1893, 1897, and between 1913 and 1920.
21. Olive Schreiner to William Schreiner, 29 June 1898, OSLO.
22. The subtitle of Schreiner's first (unfinished) novel, *Undine*, is 'A Queer Little Child'.
23. See First and Scott, *Olive Schreiner*, 48.
24. See Schreiner to Cronwright-Schreiner, 23 April 1915; Schreiner to Havelock Ellis, 21 October 1884; and Schreiner to Havelock Ellis, 7 February 1888, all at OSLO.
25. Schreiner to Pearson, 11 November 1890, OSLO.
26. 'Coloured' is still widely used in South Africa to refer to people of mixed-race descent who predominantly live in the Cape, though the term is increasingly contested.
27. Gandhi, *Satyagraha in South Africa*, 281.
28. Gandhi, *Satyagraha in South Africa*, 281.
29. Remmington, 'Olive Schreiner, Race and Black South Africa', 130.
30. Comyn and Fermanis, 'Rethinking Nineteenth-Century Literary Culture', 1.
31. Quoted in First and Scott, *Olive Schreiner*, 121.
32. See Schreiner to Havelock Ellis, 29 October 1885, OSLO.
33. Schreiner wrote a public letter to the editor of *The Standard* complaining about the behaviour of a policeman who accosted her when she was with her friend, Bryan Donkin, outside her lodgings at night. See Schreiner to The Editor of *The Standard*, 4 January 1887, OSLO.
34. Stanley, *Imperialism, Labour and the New Woman*, 18.
35. Schreiner to Unwin, 26 September 1892, OSLO. Waldo is the poor farm labourer in Schreiner's first novel, *The Story of an African Farm* (1883).
36. Schreiner to Unwin, 26 September 1892, OSLO.
37. Stanley, *Imperialism, Labour and the New Woman*, 18.
38. Davidson and Filatova, 'Olive Schreiner: A Century in Russia'; Vivan, 'Introduction', in *The Flawed Diamond*, 9. See also Vivan's 'Introduzione' to the first Italian translation of *African Farm*, *Storia di una fattoria Africana*, v–xix.
39. See Bardsley, 'The New Woman of Japan'; Tomida, 'The Controversy over the Protection of Motherhood'; and Vera Mackie, *Feminism in Modern Japan*, 55.
40. Van der Vlies, *South African Textual Cultures*, 12.
41. Schreiner, '3 January 1881', quoted in Cronwright-Schreiner, *The Life of Olive Schreiner*, 142; reprinted in Schreiner, *From Man to Man or Perhaps Only*, 433.
42. Driver, 'Passing It On: Olive Schreiner and Bessie Head', 272.
43. Lead organisers of the festival include Paul Walters and Jeremy Fogg.
44. See Flynn, 'Olive Schreiner'; Gray, *Schreiner: A One-Woman Play*; Lessing, 'Olive Schreiner'; Campbell, 'Buffel's Kop'; Van Heerden, 'The Resurrection

of Olive'; Stobie, 'Striking Rocks'; Baraitser, *The Story of an African Farm*; Dovey, *Perfect Darkness*; and Lister, *Bustin' Bonaparte*.
45. Stanley, *Imperialism*, 108.
46. Remmington, 'Olive Schreiner, Race and Black South Africa', 117.
47. See Government of South Africa, 'Recipients of the National Order Awards, 2003'.

Part I

Modernity and Modernism

Chapter 1

Schreiner and the Machine
Mark Sanders

Olive Schreiner's *The Story of an African Farm* (1883) is a novel replete with acts of wanton cruelty inflicted by the stronger on the weak. Of these acts, the one that has always stood out for me, because it is the crushing of the soul of a youth, is when Bonaparte Blenkins grinds into the ground the miniature that Waldo Farber has constructed of a sheep-shearing machine that he has designed. The sadistic act of an ignorant charlatan who has ingratiated himself with the farm's proprietress leaves Waldo speechless, its effect left to be figured only by the narrator's description of Waldo's dog's mutilation of a dung beetle, the Sisyphus of the African insect world: 'And it was all play, and no one could tell what it lived and worked for. A striving, and a striving, and an ending in nothing'.[1] Waldo, the son of the farm's German overseer, never reconstructs his model. His eventual fate is to leave the farm and seek work in town, where he will labour for this master and that.[2] The destruction of his machine is thus also the destruction of an ideal for the good life – of living and working for something, not somebody – that Waldo shares with Lyndall, beloved friend of his childhood and Schreiner's immortal heroine. Before his father's death, and before Blenkins's ascension as 'master of th[e] farm', work on the farm is different to work in town.[3] In Schreiner's version of the pastoral, farm labour leaves time for contemplation, for the life of the mind, whereas, with wage labour, such time is negated or restricted.[4] Blenkins, who tells Waldo 'no more minding of sheep and reading books at the same time', is the malign agent of personal, social and symbolic catastrophe, precipitating Waldo Farber's fall into soul-destroying wage labour.[5]

This framework determines the meaning of Waldo's machine. It is a child of his imagination. Schreiner's novel tends to figure the work of the creative mind as gestation and parturition.[6] The model of the shearing machine, which is his 'secret,' has taken Waldo 'nine months' to construct.[7] When he trustingly shows it to Blenkins, we read:

> There was never a parent who heard deception in the voice that praised his child – his first-born. Here was one who liked the thing that had been created in him. He forgot everything. He showed how the shears would work with a little guidance, how the sheep would be held, and the wool fall into the trough. A flush burst over his face as he spoke.[8]

Although perhaps surprising, is the machine an intrusion into the pastoral idyll, a symbolic contradiction between the industrial and the agrarian? This is the pattern identified in *The Machine in the Garden*, Leo Marx's classic study of nineteenth-century American pastoral. In Schreiner's rendition of the pastoral, which predates widespread industrialisation in South Africa (even as an incipient mechanisation is evident in agriculture, and registered in Schreiner's novel),[9] Waldo's machine is not out of place in *The Story of an African Farm*'s rustic setting, as the locomotive or steamship was disruptive to the pastoral idyll for most American writers of the mid-nineteenth century.[10] A different figuring applies in this particular South African case.

The crux is that Waldo's design for this intricate mechanism is work that is not alienated; this is possible, for him, historically, given his status within the pastoral space of the farm.[11] But his machine is also a work of art – or *better* than what might come to mind as a work of art when compared, as the book compares it, to the wood-carving done by Waldo to mark his father's grave after the destruction of his machine: '[t]his was but a thing he had made, laboured over, loved and liked—nothing more—not his machine'.[12] The notion of a machine as a work of art burns bright in the constellation of ideas that inform *The Story of an African Farm*. Engineer and artist could still have been thought together in the mid-Victorian era. Take Ralph Waldo Emerson, for example, who, as Leo Marx explains, constitutes something of an exception among the American writers of his time, with regard to the machine.[13] As Emerson wrote in his essay, 'Art' (1841), '[b]eauty must come back to the useful arts, and the distinction between the fine and the useful arts be forgotten'.[14] The American transcendentalist was one of Schreiner's great early influences, as the names of Waldo and Em, as well as her own pseudonym (Ralph Iron) bear witness.[15] We need not attribute Waldo's machine to Emerson, however, in order to discern the basic pattern. Having discerned it, one could perhaps even say that, in Waldo's early life, *techne* has not quite fully undergone the epochal bifurcation of art (*Kunst, die Künste*) and technology (*Technik*) of which Heidegger speaks in 'The Question Concerning Technology'.[16] For a time before his eventual fate is sealed,[17] Waldo Farber is not a proletarian but *homo faber*, maker of a machine for shearing sheep.[18] In a word, an artist for the industrial age.

Aside from being an example of labour that is not alienated, a creation of the mind of a labourer who has not fallen, and, perhaps for that very reason, a work of art, Waldo's design is for a machine that will alleviate human labour. That much ought to be plain – yet in *The Story of an African Farm* it is not made explicit. For that, we must turn to subsequent works by Schreiner, in which the ambiguities of mechanical alleviation are made apparent. Although the figure of the inventor is not absent from those texts, he is no longer portrayed as an artist, but rather as a worker among workers.[19]

Having left a largely agrarian South Africa in 1881 and spent the next eight years in England, Schreiner had experienced life in an industrialised society and participated in the feminist and socialist debates of the Men and Women's Club that responded to the profound social changes of the time. The emphasis of the works about labour that she wrote after her return to South Africa in 1889 is almost completely on the consequences of mechanisation for workers. In the series of texts from 1890 to 1911 that Carolyn Burdett expertly interprets as being in critical dialogue with Karl Pearson's social Darwinism, especially its eugenics, Schreiner explores the consequences of the fact that machines relieve certain tasks done by workers.[20] Because machines then commonly substitute for the workers who performed those tasks, this is not necessarily the boon for women that it might appear. The boon of mechanisation, Schreiner argues, accrues disproportionately to men, who are better placed to find alternative employment. As a consequence, women, who are less well placed to do so than men, revert to a sexual parasitism of wife, mistress or prostitute – none of whom, according to Schreiner, performs productive labour.

This is the argument in its fullest elaboration, as set out in *Woman and Labour*, published in 1911. But Schreiner does not reach her conclusions about the machine immediately. In 'Three Dreams in a Desert', an allegory first published in 1890, the dreamer hears proclaimed an epochal change in which the labour of women will be relieved by 'Mechanical Invention':

> The Age-of-muscular-force is dead. The Age-of-nervous-force has killed him with the knife he holds in his hand; and silently and invisibly he has crept up to the woman, and with that knife of Mechanical Invention he has cut the band that bound the burden to her back. The Inevitable Necessity is broken. She must rise now.[21]

Although its effects are not inevitable, because they depend on women helping themselves, there is no suspicion that 'Mechanical Invention', having relieved her of her burden, is anything but a catalyst to her rising.[22] Like many thinkers of her era, Schreiner thought in terms of broadly defined historical epochs; as Burdett points out, this applied not just to the social Darwinists, but also to Mill, who, employing conventional terms for social progress, had also distinguished an 'age of muscular force' from an 'age of mental force'.[23]

In the sequence of evolutionary epochs distributed between 'primitive' and 'civilised' that she delineated in her notes for a never published introduction to a centenary edition of Mary Wollstonecraft's *A Vindication of the Rights of Woman*, Schreiner maintains that

> [t]he 'worst' point in relations between the sexes (that is, when sexual differentiation is greatest) . . . is found in advanced agricultural and slave-owning cultures where 'a great degree of civilization has been attained, but where machinery plays a small part, and human muscular force is everywhere the energy used in production'. In this state, women are excluded from socially useful labour and their lives are predominantly defined by sexual roles.[24]

As Burdett points out, 'Schreiner will later develop this idea in her concept of "sex-parasitism"'.[25] Contrasted with both the slave-owning or agrarian 'civilised' societies of the past, as well as with 'primitive' society, is modern industrial society, which is also termed 'civilised'. In those '"civilised" societies' (Burdett summarises):

> technological innovation means that women need no longer be barred from work denied them because of their inferior muscular power, nor yet enslaved in 'primitive' toil. Technology produces the need for a new type of labour which will liberate women into a fulfilling, socially useful existence which, at the same time, is freed from the hand-to-mouth struggle for immediate physical survival.[26]

It was in two articles on 'The Woman Question' published in 1899 (and later incorporated in *Woman and Labour*) that Schreiner developed her concept of sex parasitism.[27] As Burdett shows, these articles reverse the valence that Schreiner had given to modern technology; far from freeing women, it renders them redundant as workers. Men are also replaced by machines, but 'unlike the man, the modern woman has an alternative to working – she can live through "the passive performance of sexual functions alone". She is seduced into a dependency which will eventually result in degeneracy and decay'.[28]

My goal is not to attempt to improve on Burdett's highly convincing account of how Schreiner's argument in *Woman and Labour* may be seen as an acceptance of the social Darwinist premise that women's labour ought to be socially useful, but a rejection of the corollary that such labour be defined, whether entirely or partially (the logical outcome of Pearson's eugenics), as reproductive or maternal.²⁹ My goal is more modest: to specify, with greater clarity, how Schreiner refigures the machine and its use in order to arrive at the conclusions that Schreiner does. Like Burdett, although I attach to them a different significance, I find a clue in what Schreiner says in her introduction to *Woman and Labour* about 'Three Dreams in a Desert'. As Schreiner notes, this was taken from her book, 'Musings on Woman and Labour', the manuscript of which was destroyed by fire during the Anglo-Boer War.³⁰ 'In addition to the prose argument,' she writes, referring to that book,

> I had in each chapter one or more allegories; because while it is easy clearly to express abstract thoughts in argumentative prose, whatever emotion those thoughts awaken I have not felt myself able adequately to express except in the other form.³¹

As Schreiner adds in a footnote, referring to 'Three Dreams', 'I have felt that perhaps being taken from its context it was not quite clear to everyone'.³² Although what that context was will never be known with certainty, when, nineteen years later, if the allegory is placed in the context of the 'fragment' that was published as *Woman and Labour*, the emotion associated with 'Mechanical Invention' – at least as it can be gauged from the argumentative prose of the book – is of a different valence.³³ Phrased in Proppian narratological terms, as far as woman is concerned, 'helper' has turned into 'antagonist'. With this role reversal, the affective values have also been reversed: the affect associated with the machine has turned into its opposite. In Freudian terms, the one once beloved has become a persecutor, with a resultant paranoid shading attaching to the machine.

In *Woman and Labour*, the assurance of '[s]he must rise now' is gone.³⁴ Schreiner shows how the invention of machines and their use in farming, industry and warfare, has been a pivotal historical turning point in relations between men and women, because of how, as in earlier epochal turning points in human history, it has changed the division of labour. 'But now, again a change has come', Schreiner writes, '[s]omething that is entirely new has entered into the field of human labour, and left nothing as it was'.³⁵ Schreiner continues, specifying what change has come for men:

> In man's fields of toil, change has accomplished, and is yet more quickly accomplishing, itself.
> On lands where once fifty men and youths toiled with their cattle, today one steam-plough, guided by but two pair of hands, passes swiftly; and an automatic reaper in one day reaps and binds and prepares for the garner the produce of fields it would have taken a hundred strong male arms to harvest

in the past. The iron tools and weapons, only one of which it took an ancient father of our race long months of stern exertion to extract from ore and bring to shape and temper, are now poured forth by steam-driven machinery as a millpond pours forth its water; and even in war, the male's ancient and especial field of labour, a complete reversal of the ancient order has taken place. Time was when the size and strength of the muscles in a man's legs and arms, and the strength and size of his body, largely determined his fighting powers, and an Achilles or a Richard Coeur de Lion, armed only with his spear or battle-axe, made a host fly before him; today the puniest mannikin behind a modern Maxim gun may mow down in perfect safety a phalanx of heroes whose legs and arms and physical powers a Greek god might have envied, but who, having not the modern machinery of war, fall powerless. The day of the primary import to humanity of the strength in man's extensor and flexor muscles, whether in labours of war or of peace, is gone by for ever; and the day of the all-importance of the culture and activity of man's brain and nerve has already come.[36]

Although Schreiner does not ignore the resulting unemployment among men of the labouring classes,[37] her main point is that, by sparing men of the need to perform muscular labour, just as they free beasts of burden, machines have made it possible for men to enter fields of intellectual work.[38] This liberation is unequal. Referring to the causes represented by the labour movement and the women's movement, Schreiner writes: 'the two problems are not identical'.[39] Women, whose traditional work is now also being done by machines, are not freed by mechanisation because 'artificial constrictions and conventions' prevent women from entering other occupations, or lead to their exploitation for low wages, and they are barred from training in the trades and professions.[40] Their reproductive labour, including childrearing, which has been replaced by organised schooling, has also become less valuable.[41] From the earliest pages of *Woman and Labour*, the cry thus wells up: '[g]ive us labour and the training which fits for labour! We demand this, not for ourselves alone, but for the race'.[42] The cry of 'modern European women' is, in the light of these changes, for 'new forms of labour and new fields for the exercise of their powers'.[43]

Let us examine more closely how Schreiner figures the machine. Mechanisation plays a direct role in systematically making women into unproductive sex parasites dependent on men:

At the present day, so enormous has been the advance made in the substitution of mechanical force for crude, physical, human exertion (mechanical force being employed today even in the shaping of feeding-bottles and the creation of artificial foods as substitutes for mother's milk!), that it is now possible not only for a small and wealthy section of women in each civilised community to be maintained without performing any of the ancient, crude, physical labours of their sex, and without depending on the slavery of, or any vast increase in the labour of, other classes of females; but this condition has already been reached, or is tending to be reached, by that large mass of women in civilised societies, who form the intermediate class between poor and rich. During the next fifty years, so rapid will undoubtedly be the spread of the material conditions of civilisation, both in the societies at present civilised and in the societies at present unpermeated by our material civilisation, that the ancient forms of female, domestic, physical labour of even the women of the poorest classes will be little required, their place being taken, not by other females, but by always increasingly perfected labour-saving machinery.

Thus, female parasitism, which in the past threatened only a minute section of earth's women, under existing conditions threatens vast masses, and may, under future conditions, threaten the entire body.

If woman is content to leave to the male all labour in the new and all-important fields which are rapidly opening before the human race; if, as the old forms of domestic labour slip from her for ever and evitably, she does not grasp the new, it is inevitable, that, ultimately, not merely a class, but the whole bodies of females in civilised societies, must sink into a state of more or less absolute dependence on their sexual functions alone.

As new forms of natural force are mastered and mechanical appliances perfected, it will be quite possible for the male half of all civilised races (and therefore ultimately of all) to absorb the entire fields of intellectual and highly trained manual labour; and it would be entirely possible for the female half of the race, whether as prostitutes, as kept mistresses, or as kept wives, to cease from all forms of active toil, and, as the passive tools of sexual reproduction, or, more decadently still, as the mere instruments of sexual indulgence, to sink into a condition of complete and helpless sex-parasitism.[44]

Several aspects of this passage stand out. First, as in her introduction to Wollstonecraft, Schreiner distinguishes 'civilisation' and 'material civilisation'. The first term assimilates England, ancient Greece and Rome; upper-class and bourgeois domestic life has evolved in the former to make it comparable to the latter. The second term refers to the newer evolution under industrial capitalism, in which mechanisation has played a key role and threatens to bring about a new division of labour that, although not the same as in slave-owning societies, will have the same effect for upper-class women, and unprecedented effects for women of the other classes Schreiner identifies. This final implication means that the same fate awaits women in countries that are not yet industrialised, ultimately all of the planet's women. Second, although the fate of women of different social classes is differentiated, the eventual fate of all women will be practically the same. Atop Schreiner's threefold class division (rich, poor, and intermediate) a threefold taxonomy of sex parasitism is mapped. The kept wife among the rich finds her mirror image in the poor prostitute; one surmises that the kept mistress emerges from the intermediate stratum. Third, Schreiner is making a prediction.

What she describes has not yet happened but will take place '[d]uring the next fifty years'. Fourth, what she describes is 'evitable,' should 'woman grasp the new'. This, one assumes, is not the same as the appeal for new forms of labour associated with the Women's Movement, but rather its necessary volitional precondition.

There is something curious about the scenario presented by Schreiner. Historically, machines certainly did substitute for muscular force and, for that reason, transformed industry in late-eighteenth- and nineteenth-century England and the United States. Machines also certainly displaced workers because of this substitution. However, the reorganisation of production in factories also led to an increase in the number of workers employed, and in the hours that they worked. Notably, factories, especially those manufacturing textiles and clothing, employed women and children in great numbers. 'In so far as machinery dispenses with muscular power', wrote Karl Marx in *Capital* (1867), with an appreciation of the irony of a substitute for labour creating more labourers,

> it becomes a means for employing workers of slight muscular strength, or whose bodily development is incomplete, but whose limbs are all the more supple. The labour of women and children was therefore the first result of the capitalist application of machinery! That mighty substitute for labour and for workers, the machine, was immediately transformed into a means for increasing the number of wage-labourers by enrolling, under the direct sway of capital, every member of the worker's family, without distinction of age and sex.[45]

And Frederick Engels is often quoted for confidently asserting in *The Origin of the Family, Private Property, and the State* (1884) that 'the first premise for the emancipation of women is the re-introduction of the entire female sex into public industry'.[46] A friend of Eleanor Marx, Schreiner would no doubt have been familiar with the historical developments as Marx described them, and with Engels's subsequent inferences. And she was probably also familiar with August Bebel's observation in *Woman in the Past, Present and Future* (1879) that the growing diversity of women's occupations was, in part, due to mechanisation.[47] As is well known, by the end of the nineteenth century, the development of capitalism in England and the United States had given rise to a vast apparatus of clerical work – in accounting, record-keeping and communications. It was into this increasingly mechanised sphere that women would be drawn in growing numbers, as they had been into factories a century before.

But when Schreiner sees parasitism and prostitution as a direct outcome of mechanisation, she is not making a historical argument – at least not one limited to historical actuality. There is, to be sure, a transhistorical argument in *Woman and Labour* that surveys the past. Although the longer epochal evolutionary framework of the lost manuscript is compressed, the book gives a sweeping account of how, if women and men once laboured side by side, the work traditionally done by women was by turns usurped by men. Having been deprived of work, woman turns into a sex parasite – whether as wife, mistress or prostitute. Whereas in early 'civilised' times, such as in ancient Greece, this is linked to slave labour, in more recent times this is linked to mechanisation.

This is where Schreiner's account takes a surprising turn. 'Woman', Schreiner writes, has been 'rob[bed] ... not merely in part but almost wholly, of the more valuable of her ancient domain of productive and social labour'.[48] In the textile and clothing industries, in food production and provision, and in domestic work, it is men with machines who have robbed her by gaining employment in those fields. A powerful moral point is made when Schreiner refers to the first of these fields. Our spinning wheels are broken', Schreiner writes:

> in a thousand huge buildings steam-driven looms, guided by a few hundred thousand hands (often those of men), produce the clothings of half the world; we dare no longer say, proudly, as of old, that we and we alone clothe our people.[49]

In the second field of labour, a 'man-driven motor-car' delivers fresh bread, and accompanying it is the 'male-and-machinery manipulated butter pat'.[50] Having been robbed by men with machines of her labour in these three spheres of 'the entire field of woman's ancient and traditional labours, fully three-fourths of it have shrunk away for ever, and th[e] remaining fourth still tends to shrink'.[51] Schreiner thus appeals for machine-operating jobs for women, and for ownership of the means of production: 'we demand in the factory, the warehouse, and the field, wherever machinery has usurped our ancient labour-ground, that we also should have our place, as guiders, controllers, and possessors'.[52] Historically, however, even if female proprietorship is not the rule in England, women being employed to guide and control machines, especially in factories, is by 1911 well established.[53]

Direct references in *Woman and Labour* to actual employment patterns due to mechanisation are relatively few and, when we find them, can be of questionable historical accuracy. When Schreiner writes in parentheses that the hands guiding machines in the textile and clothing mills are 'often those of men', it is instructive to turn to the empirical – to what the allegorical 'hunter' in *The Story of an African Farm* encounters as the 'almighty mountains of Dry-facts and Realities'.[54] Although it may be historically accurate that proportionately more men were working in cotton and woollen manufacture by 1911, women continued to predominate in these industries.[55] Schreiner's appeal for machine-minding jobs is thus odd, when considered in historical context, since women occupy most of these jobs in the industries to which she attaches the highest importance. One could go on in this vein, were one to consider her relative neglect of office work.[56]

How to make sense of this discrepancy between Schreiner's description of epochal change, and what is known about her epoch? When she refers to earlier eras, Schreiner makes broad transhistorical arguments based on what she knew about the actuality of those eras and is indebted to ones made by social Darwinists. When she refers to her own era, her argument is speculative. Should she have expressed it in the form of an allegory, that modality might have been clearer; what is certain is that the emotional tone with which she makes it is different from 'Three Dreams' – not triumphant but tragic. Mechanisation as catastrophe. What is important to note, however, is that she writes: '[i]t is possible . . .'.[57] Although she does state, polemically, that three-fourths of women's ancient and traditional labours have shrunk away, she is not in fact saying, in the key paragraphs on mechanisation and parasitism, that what she describes is actual. It will take place over 'the next fifty years'. The speculative scenario there depends on all work except childbearing and female sex work being done by men with machines.[58] Although Schreiner confidently makes a transhistorical argument – men usurp women's labour with the aid of machines – that extends into her own era, she is not quite saying that what she declares to be 'possible' is actual in that era.

Schreiner is thus committed to a view that, in both its speculative and polemical form, makes female parasitism in its three forms inevitable due to the mechanisation of work. The only quarter of her labour left is that which confines her to her sexual being – bearing children; being used sexually by men, either as a prostitute or as kept mistress. Is it fair to interpret this tragic view as projecting the fate of married upper-class and bourgeois women onto women in general? The former remain barred from the professions but might be in a position to depend wholly on the labour of their husbands; unmarried or working-class women cannot necessarily depend on the labour done by males. As Schreiner acknowledges, although it works for the future benefit of all women, 'the Woman Labour Movement has taken its rise . . . among the wealthy, cultured, and brain-labouring classes'.[59] Perhaps more than she acknowledges, however, the vector of parasitism imaginable for the wives of wealthy men is here transposed into a vector of prostitution for poor and unmarried women, and of kept-mistresshood for women of the intermediate class. For those women, mechanical invention means not '[s]he must rise', but *she must fall*.[60]

Schreiner is perhaps not the only one, among writers of the middle class of her era, to have imagined such a fall. Even the authors of 'typewriter-girl novels', who acknowledged the role played by that machine in dramatically increasing the number of women office workers by the *fin de siècle*, and hence assisting her emancipation, could plot her fall.[61] Think of Monica Madden in George Gissing's *The Odd Women* (1893), who, educated but poor, is offered a career at Rhoda Nunn's typing bureau, but opts instead for an unhappy union with a man of means. But isn't explaining this fable in terms of the class-bound character of the author's vision all too pat, as predictable as the fable itself? In Schreiner's case, a mission-educated colonial governess turned author, there is surely a grain of truth to an explanation in this mode.[62] There may, in *Woman and Labour*, be a tripartite occupational division being tacitly mapped onto the two threefold differentiations of class and sex parasitism – professional/factory worker/office worker – that is not purely descriptive but also evaluative.

If we set such explanations aside, what remains in Schreiner's case is the singularity of her commitment to an idea of women, as labouring human beings, as reducible to a kind of 'bare life' of sexual use – whether as wives, mistresses or prostitutes. This commitment's deeper motivations, should they lie in a sexual fear or wish and whether they relate consequently to the break with Pearson, the beloved having in phantasy become persecutor, will have to be explored on another occasion. For the present, suffice it to say that it is the machine, in its historical actuality (given an opening in some of Schreiner's less credible empirical claims), that asserts itself. And, more than anything perhaps, it places in relief the speculative nature, and gives relevance to the emotional tone, so utterly changed in relation to the machine, of Schreiner's final tragic view of mechanisation for women. Her vision in *Woman and Labour* is, in many respects, as far as can be from that of *The Story of an African Farm*. Perhaps the major difference is that the capacity for reproductive labour that functions as a metaphor for Waldo's creativity and inventiveness has become a master signifier for personal and social degeneration; flying in the face of the fact of greater opportunities to work because of mechanisation, this functions as a vector for a tragic inevitability. Although crushed in the early novel, and become woman's antagonist in the late treatise, the machine returns. Even if the full significance of mechanisation for women is obscured by the tendency of Schreiner's late text, the machine can be heard as insisting, with a whir and a click (sounds that one might fancy Waldo's sheep-shearing machine having made), that it, too, alongside women and men, and beasts of burden, has a say in making what human beings helplessly call history.

Works Cited

Bebel, August. *Woman in the Past, Present and Future*. Translated by H. B. Adams Walther. London: Zwan Publications, 1988.
Burdett, Carolyn. *Olive Schreiner and the Progress of Feminism: Evolution, Gender and Empire*. Basingstoke and New York: Palgrave, 2001.
Emerson, Ralph Waldo. 'Art'. In *Essays and Representative Men*. London: Collins Clear-Type Press, n.d., 206–18.
Engels, Frederick. *The Origin of the Family, Private Property, and the State: In the Light of the Researches of Lewis H. Morgan*. Moscow: Progress Publishers, 1948.
Heidegger, Martin. 'The Question Concerning Technology'. In *The Question Concerning Technology and Other Essays*, translated by William Lovitt, 3–35. New York: Harper, 1977.
Hobson, J. A. *The Evolution of Modern Capitalism: A Study of Machine Production*. 4th ed. Abingdon: Routledge, 2013.
Marx, Karl. *Capital: A Critique of Political Economy*, translated by Ben Fowkes. New York: Vintage, 1977.
Marx, Leo. *The Machine in the Garden: Technology and the Pastoral Ideal in America*. New York: Oxford University Press, 1964.
Mill, John Stuart. *Principles of Political Economy With Some of Their Applications to Social Philosophy*. 7th ed. London: Longmans, 1871.
Sanders, Mark. *Complicities: The Intellectual and Apartheid*. Durham: Duke University Press, 2002.
Schreiner, Olive. *Dreams*. Boston: Little, Brown, 1929.
—. 'Introduction to the Life of Mary Wollstonecraft and the Rights of Woman'. *History Workshop* 37 (1994): 188–93.
—. *The Story of an African Farm*. Harmondsworth: Penguin, 1993.
—. *Woman and Labour*. London: Virago, 1978.
Wånggren, Lena. *Gender, Technology and the New Woman*. Edinburgh: Edinburgh University Press, 2017.

Acknowledgement

I would like to thank Jade Munslow Ong and Dan Wylie for their suggestions during the early evolution of my chapter, and Christina Chalmers for her excellent research assistance, which helped me to bring it to completion.

Notes

1. Schreiner, *The Story of an African Farm*, 107. The same words appear as the epigraph to the second part of the book, see page 135.
2. Waldo, to be sure, returns to the farm, but, although still deeply pensive and sensitive to the world around him, there is no sense that he regains the ability to invent or to create art: 'He was an uncouth creature with small learning, and no prospect in the future but that of making endless tables and stone walls, yet it seemed to him as he sat there that life was a rare and very rich thing.' Schreiner, *The Story of an African Farm*, 299. Still only a young man, Waldo dies before he can get up.
3. Schreiner, *The Story of an African Farm*, 103.
4. After leaving the farm, Waldo finds work as a shop clerk, and then as a transport-rider, before returning to town to work as a packer at a wholesale store. In a letter describing his work as a transport rider, he reflects on the soul-destroying effects of manual work: 'My body was strong and well to work, but my brain was dead. ... You may work, and work, and work, till you are only a body, not a soul. Now, when I see one of those evil-looking men that come from Europe – navies, with the beast-like, sunken face, different from any Kaffir's – I know what brought that look to their eyes; and if I have only one inch of tobacco I give them half. It is work, grinding, mechanical work, that they or their ancestors have done, that has made them into beasts. You may work a man's body so that his soul dies. Work is good. I have worked at the old farm from the sun's rising till its setting, but I have had time to think, and time to feel.' Schreiner, *The Story of an African Farm*, 256. The last job that he finds gives him the means to subscribe to a library, and time to read his books. But he lacks intellectual companionship. See Schreiner, *The Story of an African Farm*, 259.
5. Schreiner, *The Story of an African Farm*, 104. On the farm, the changes in Waldo's work and status are racially coded. There are signs, subtle and not, that, when Blenkins becomes 'master', he treats Waldo as if he were his Black servant or slave. The most obvious is the whipping that he gives the youth. Less so is that, after his father's death, Waldo is assigned tasks that, when his father was alive, would be performed by the 'Kaffir boys'. He even calls himself a 'servant'. Schreiner, *The Story of an African Farm*, 124–26, 108, 38–39, 157.
6. Schreiner, *Story of an African Farm*, 106. For a more detailed account of the complex relationship between sexual and intellectual life in Schreiner's novel, see Sanders, *Complicities*, 24–38.
7. Schreiner, *The Story of an African Farm*, 77, 107.
8. Schreiner, *The Story of an African Farm*, 106.
9. One of Blenkins's tall tales is that, 'I bought eight thousand pounds worth of machinery – winnowing, ploughing, reaping machines; I loaded a ship with them. ... Where is the ship with the things? Lost – gone to the bottom!' Schreiner, *The Story of an African Farm*, 61.
10. See Marx, *Machine in the Garden*, 15–16, 28–29.
11. The question of whether anything comparable might be possible for the Black farmworkers is never broached. The closest that the book comes to

opening the question is when, as a boy, Waldo imagines 'one of the . . . old wild Bushmen' who must have painted the rock paintings found beneath a shelving rock in a koppie on the farm. The painter, with his race, is assumed, however, to have been slaughtered into extinction by 'the Boers'. Schreiner, *The Story of an African Farm*, 49–50.
12. Schreiner, *The Story of an African Farm*, 156. Like the machine, the carving has taken him 'nine months'. Schreiner, *The Story of an African Farm*, 158.
13. Marx, *The Machine in the Garden*, 229–42.
14. Emerson, 'Art', 217. Emerson continues: 'It is in vain that we look for genius to reiterate its miracles in the old arts; it is its instinct to find beauty and holiness in new and necessary facts, in the field and road-side, in the shop and mill. Proceeding from a religious heart it will raise to a divine use the railroad, the insurance office, the joint-stock company, our law, our primary assemblies, our commerce, the galvanic battery, the electric jar, the prism, and the chemist's retort, in which we seek now only an economical use. Is not the selfish and even cruel aspect which belongs to our great mechanical works – to mills, railways, and machinery – the effect of the mercenary impulses which these works obey? When its errands are noble and adequate a steamboat bridging the Atlantic between Old and New England, and arriving at its ports with the punctuality of a planet, is a step of man into harmony with nature.' Emerson, 'Art', 217–18. Although, in *The Story of an African Farm*, Waldo's invention 'forgets' the distinction between the fine and useful arts, and the novel frequently depicts its inventor in harmony with nature, it should also be noted that Waldo, muttering to himself, envisions his machine as a source of fame and profit: '"Over the whole world – the whole world – mine, that I have made!" . . . "And fifty pounds – a black hat for my dadda – for Lyndall a blue silk, very light; and one purple like the earth-bells, and white shoes." He muttered on – "A box full of books. They shall tell me all, all, all," he added.' Schreiner, *The Story of an African Farm*, 97.
15. See Sanders, *Complicities*, 34.
16. Heidegger, 'The Question Concerning Technology', 34.
17. In a corresponding episode of colonial anti-intellectualism, Blenkins, egged on by Tant' Sannie, throws a volume of J. S. Mill's *Principles of Political Economy* in the fire. That Waldo has been reading a 'chapter on property . . . Communism, Fourierism, St Simonism', thereby entering into the question of how the surplus created by the worker is distributed, may perhaps be read as foreshadowing his destiny as a proletarian. Schreiner, *The Story of an African Farm*, 108–14. The two episodes are joined in Waldo's mind. Schreiner, *The Story of an African Farm*, 119–20. For the relevant chapters in the book that is burned, see Mill, *Principles of Political Economy*, vol. 1, Book 2, 254–69. The first English translation of volume 1 of Marx's *Capital*, by Samuel Moore and Edward Aveling, appeared in 1887, a few years after the publication of Schreiner's novel.
18. In German, a *Färber* is a dyer.
19. 'The brain of one consumptive German chemist, who in his laboratory compounds a new explosive, has more effect upon the wars of the modern peoples than ten thousand soldierly legs and arms; and the man who invents one new labour-saving machine may, through the cerebration of a

few days, have performed the labour it would otherwise have taken hundreds of thousands of his lusty fellows decades to accomplish.' Schreiner, *Woman and Labour*, 41.
20. Burdett, *Olive Schreiner*, 46–85.
21. Schreiner, *Dreams*, 57. As Lena Wånggren, quoting this passage in an epigraph to her book, observes, by the *fin de siècle*, '[r]eading the New Woman in terms of the figure's connection to technologies and social practices of the time provides a way of understanding how certain technologies come to work as "freedom machines", as visual emblems connected to the New Woman and signifying female emancipation.' Wånggren, *Gender, Technology and the New Woman*, 2.
22. Schreiner, *Dreams*, 59.
23. Burdett, *Olive Schreiner*, 195, n102.
24. Burdett, *Olive Schreiner*, 55–56, quoting Schreiner, 'Introduction to the Life of Mary Wollstonecraft', 192.
25. Burdett, *Olive Schreiner*, 56.
26. Burdett, *Olive Schreiner*, 56.
27. Burdett, *Olive Schreiner*, 59–60.
28. Burdett, *Olive Schreiner*, 59.
29. Schreiner, *Woman and Labour*, 60–61.
30. In the same introduction, Schreiner details the genesis of the book from her 'early youth' up until 1899, its destruction, and her subsequent efforts, under wartime internment, to rewrite it. As she explains, *Woman and Labour* is a fragment of the whole, mainly from the chapter on parasitism, which was one of twelve chapters. Schreiner, *Woman and Labour*, 11–25.
31. Schreiner, *Woman and Labour*, 16.
32. Schreiner, *Dreams*, 16 n1.
33. 'The allegory "Three Dreams in a Desert" which I published about nineteen years ago', dates the introduction to 1909. Schreiner, *Woman and Labour*, 16 n1.
34. Schreiner, *Dreams*, 57.
35. Schreiner, *Woman and Labour*, 40.
36. Schreiner, *Woman and Labour*, 40–41.
37. See Schreiner, *Woman and Labour*, 42–44.
38. 'Yet it is only upon one, and a comparatively small, section of the males of the modern civilised world that these changes in the material conditions of life have told in such fashion as to take all useful occupation from them and render them wholly or partly worthless to society. If the modern man's field of labour has contracted at one end (the physical), at the other (the intellectual) it has immeasurably expanded! If machinery and the command of inanimate motor-forces have rendered of comparatively little value the male's mere physical motor-power, the demand upon his intellectual faculties, the call for the expenditure of nervous energy, and the exercise of delicate manipulative skill in the labour of human life, have immeasurably increased.' Schreiner, *Woman and Labour*, 44–45.
39. Schreiner, *Woman and Labour*, 120.
40. Schreiner, *Woman and Labour*, 24, 120–24, 153–61, 195–96. For an account of how what he terms the 'liberal callings' remained largely closed

to women in the late nineteenth century, see Bebel, *Woman in the Past, Present and Future*, 112, 117–18, 130–36.
41. Schreiner, *Woman and Labour*, 54–67.
42. Schreiner, *Woman and Labour*, 33.
43. Schreiner, *Woman and Labour*, 67.
44. Schreiner, *Woman and Labour*, 114–16.
45. Marx, *Capital*, 517.
46. Engels, *The Origin of the Family*, 74.
47. Bebel, *Woman in the Past, Present and Future*, 105–108.
48. Schreiner, *Woman and Labour*, 50.
49. Schreiner, *Woman and Labour*, 50.
50. Schreiner, *Woman and Labour*, 50–51.
51. Schreiner, *Woman and Labour*, 66–67.
52. Schreiner, *Woman and Labour*, 71.
53. J. A. Hobson, for example, noted that '[t]he tendency of machine industry to displace male by female labour is placed beyond all question by the statistics of occupations in England, which show since 1861 a regular and considerable rise in the proportion of women to men workers in most branches of manufacture where machinery is most fully applied.' Hobson, *Evolution of Modern Capitalism*, 350.
54. Schreiner, *The Story of an African Farm*, 166. The allegory was reprinted in Schreiner, *Dreams*, 11–37.
55. See Hobson, *Evolution of Modern Capitalism*, 452–53.
56. In England by 1911, 25 per cent of clerical workers were women, an increase from only 15 per cent in 1901. In 1911, more than 50 per cent of telephone and telegraph workers were women. Hobson, *Evolution of Modern Capitalism*, 453.
57. Schreiner, *Woman and Labour*, 116.
58. See Schreiner, *Woman and Labour*, 116.
59. Schreiner, *Woman and Labour*, 123.
60. Schreiner, *Dreams*, 57.
61. For a nuanced account of women typists in English popular literature of the period, see Wånggren, *Gender, Technology and the New Woman*, 34–61.
62. Schreiner is clear, however, that when political life and certain professions remain restricted, to be an author reveals a limit as much as an opportunity. This is, incidentally, a condition that the writer shares with the typist: '[e]ven in the little third-rate novelist whose works cumber the ground, we see often a pathetic figure, when we recognise that beneath that failure in a complex and difficult art, may lie buried a sound legislator, an able architect, an original scientific investigator, or a good judge. . . . Both the creative writer and the typist, in their respective spheres, are merely finding outlets for their powers in the direction of least resistance. The tendency of women at the present day to undertake certain forms of labour, proves only that in the crabbed, walled-in, and bound conditions surrounding woman at the present day, these are the lines along which action is most possible to her.' Schreiner, *Woman and Labour*, 158–59.

Chapter 2

The Bloomsbury Modernisms of Margaret Harkness and Olive Schreiner
Jade Munslow Ong

Bloomsbury's status as a uniquely privileged site of modernist innovation is largely based on the art, writing, relationships and philosophies of the 1920s writers and thinkers known as the 'Bloomsbury Group'. Yet forty years earlier, the area hosted other writers and intellectuals who contributed to the development of literary modernisms. Olive Schreiner and Margaret Harkness were two such antecedents, and members of various and overlapping women's clubs, friendship circles, debating societies and progressive organisations that comprised earlier Bloomsbury groups of the late-1880s.

During this period, Harkness produced her first two novels and a number of short stories, while Schreiner wrote a series of allegories collected as *Dreams* (1890). Harkness's second novel, *Out of Work* (1888), and Schreiner's allegory 'The Sunlight Lay Across My Bed' (1890) are considered here in the context of the writers' friendship, and as formally distinct, yet politically and aesthetically related, works of proto-/modernist socialist literature. Connections between Harkness's Naturalism, Schreiner's use of allegory, and literary modernism are established through reference to Georg Lukács's work on the ideology of modernism, which is expanded to address what Jed Esty describes as the 'lacunae' of Lukács's 'relative lack of interest in women's writing', and 'two other, perhaps interconnected, blind spots in that thinker's oeuvre: modernism and imperialism'.[1] Following Esty in globalising Lukács in order to read the overlapping and co-determined modernisms of Harkness and Schreiner, it becomes possible to see how their writings 'transferred the unfolding dynamic of modern history from the national frame of reference to a global one, retaining a reality principle adequate to objective social conditions but jettisoning the Lukácsian norm of universal (if uneven) progress'.[2] As such, both Harkness and Schreiner's writings represent classed experiences typically occluded or denied by dominant cultures; use distinctive narratorial voices and proto-/modernist perspectival shifts to dialectically explore diverse subject, cultural and political positions; and present street-level views and sounds of the imperial metropole as a place for contemplation, connection, action and (potential) liberation.

Bloomsbury Connections

Despite the presence of co-existing and allied narrative devices, images and arguments across the work of both Harkness and Schreiner, their outputs did not emerge from a clearly defined modernist coterie, neither do they cohere as a unified artistic movement, nor represent a single school of political or philosophical thought. Where Emile Zola's controversial and path-breaking Naturalism provided the formal inspiration for Harkness's fiction, Schreiner took her stylistic cues from a different literary genealogy, namely the religious texts of her missionary upbringing in colonial South Africa. Schreiner's allegorical South African modernism can therefore be distinguished from the French Naturalist inheritances of Harkness's proto-/modernism, even as the writers mobilised similar strategies and shared tropes to some common political ends. The causes uppermost in their 1880s writing differed too: Harkness prioritised socialist argument, while Schreiner combined and shuttled between socialist, anti-imperialist and feminist interests. Even their friendship with one another formed a similarly fluctuating pattern alternating between periods of closeness and tension.

Schreiner first arrived in Bloomsbury in March 1882, joining her brother William in Guildford Street.[3] As Anna Snaith explains, the area was often 'the first port of call for colonial travellers given the area's bohemian associations', and Schreiner was one of a number of colonial writers whose 'encounters with metropolitan writers and the cultural spaces of the city are an important, yet often overlooked, part of the history of modernist London and its literary networks'.[4] Schreiner was initially unhappy in London, but by December 1884 was writing to her friend, sexologist Henry Havelock Ellis, that she intended to find 'rooms in the heart of Bloomsbury & that might do me good'.[5] Despite ultimately finding accommodation elsewhere, Schreiner still spent much time in the area, attending meetings at the Men and Women's Club at UCL, as well as the Fellowship of the New Life at 29 Doughty Street, alongside intellectuals and progressives such as Havelock Ellis, Edward Carpenter and Karl Pearson. At the same time, Schreiner made a number of new literary friends and acquaintances who were themselves pioneering new literary forms at the *fin de siècle*. These included Symbolist poets Amy Levy, Arthur Symons and Philip Bourke-Marston; Aesthetes Oscar Wilde and Vernon Lee (Violet Paget); Imperial Romance novelist Henry Rider Haggard; and New Woman writer Mona Caird. Schreiner also attended talks and plays by leading playwright, George Bernard Shaw, and even fended off the romantic advances of the Naturalist novelist George Moore.[6]

Another of Schreiner's new London friends was Bloomsbury resident Harkness.[7] The first mention of Harkness in Schreiner's extant correspondence appears in a letter to her brother, William, in June 1884: 'I went to Camden Church this morning with a Miss Harkness, a girl I like much & who is making a path for herself in the world'.[8] The two women likely bonded over shared political and creative interests, but they also had other experiences in common, as both had felt intellectually stifled in their youth, had initially pursued careers in nursing, published their fiction under male pseudonyms, and were then unmarried professional writers at a time when marriage was still considered the chief objective for middle-class women.[9]

Schreiner's early warmth towards Harkness did not last, however, and her letters from 1886 and 1887 reveal an increasing sense of Harkness as a drain on her energy and resources. In a March 1887 letter to Havelock Ellis for example, Schreiner complains that:

> The time with Maggie – has been so terrible. I have been nearly mad. She has no money and she came thinking I would support her and I can't. [. . .] God knows I am so weak, and not a human soul puts out its hand to help me, only to demand love from me, and I am bankrupt, I am dying, I have nothing more to give. I'm not physically dying, but dying in a more terrible way. . . . . Now these women, Mrs. – and Mrs. – and Maggie – have just crushed me.[10]

Despite the ill-feelings evident here (that would resurface), there appears to have been a period of personal and professional reconciliation in 1888, the year in which Harkness published her second novel, *Out of Work* (which Schreiner duly read), as well as the allegory 'The Gospel of Getting On', which bore a dedication '(To Olive Schreiner.)'.[11]

The Reading Room at the British Museum in Bloomsbury provided a particularly important centre of intellectual life for Schreiner and Harkness in the late-1880s. Here they met with other female radicals and thinkers to discuss socialist and feminist texts, and social and political questions of the day. According to Deborah Epstein Nord, these 'outsider' women, which included Harkness's cousin Beatrice Potter (later Webb), Dollie Radford, Eleanor Marx, Constance and Clementina

Black, as well as Levy, comprised 'a loosely organized community or network' of 'unmarried women' who 'understood their own marginality not only – perhaps not even primarily – as a condition of their sex but also as a product of their socialist politics, of their aspirations to enter male-dominated areas of work, or of their religion or class'.[12] The Bloomsbury setting made these meetings possible because, as Nord explains, London 'represented the antithesis of those private and protected spaces that middle-class women traditionally had occupied'.[13] A similar view is expressed by Levy in her 1888 essay, 'Women and Club Life', in which she writes that

> in class-room and lecture-theatre, office and art-school, college and clubhouse alike, woman is waking up to a sense of the hundred and one possibilities of social intercourse; possibilities which, save in exceptional instances, have hitherto for her been restricted to the narrowest of grooves.[14]

Levy draws here on her own experiences, as it was in the Bloomsbury-based reading group with Harkness and Schreiner that she found a community in which women were able to cultivate new ideas, friendships, conflicts and intimacies.

As a result of this access to new networks and spaces in which to develop their politics and craft, female authors were able to contribute in larger numbers and more significant ways to new literary cultures of the late-nineteenth and early-twentieth centuries. Sandra Gilbert and Susan Gubar were early to recognise this, stating 'that in their problematic relationship to the tradition of authority, as well as to the authority of tradition, women writers are the major precursors of all twentieth-century modernists, the *avant garde* of the *avant garde*, so to speak'.[15] In the years since, Bonnie Kime Scott, Lisa Rado, Rita Felski, Marianne De Koven and others have done much to expand our understanding of the role of women writers in pioneering and participating in developments in literary modernisms. This chapter on Harkness and Schreiner is a contribution to this ongoing work.

Harkness's Proto-/modernism: Voice, Perspective, Dialectic

In 1888, Friedrich Engels received a copy of Margaret Harkness's first novel, *A City Girl* (1887), from its publisher, Vizetelly.[16] In response, Engels wrote to Harkness a now oft-cited and frequently anthologised letter, in which he described the novel as '*ein kleines Kunstwerk*' [a little work of art], albeit with some reservations:

If I have anything to criticise, it would be that perhaps after all, the tale is not quite realistic enough. Realism, to my mind, implies, besides truth of detail, the truthful reproduction of typical characters under typical circumstances. [...] In the *City Girl* the working class figures are a passive mass, unable to help itself and not even making any attempt at striving to help itself. [...] The rebellious reaction of the working class against the oppressive medium which surrounds them, their attempts – convulsive, half-conscious or conscious – at recovering their status as human beings, belong to history and must therefore lay claim to a place in the domain of realism.[17]

Engels's interpretation of Realism as simply 'truthful' representation is allied to his argument that it serves as the most effective literary vehicle for handling 'the fights of the militant proletariat'.[18] He evidences his claim by comparing Honoré de Balzac's Realism with Zola's Naturalism, identifying Balzac as 'a far greater master of realism than all the Zolas *passés, présents et a venir* [past, present and future]' due to his ability to capture 'the necessity of the downfall of his favourite nobles [...] and that he saw the real men of the future'.[19] Engels draws this distinction in order to critique Harkness's use of Naturalist forms indirectly, negatively judging Zola against Balzac as a way of encouraging Harkness to turn towards the latter's more 'realistic' methods, which he felt provided better means for conveying and supporting the socialist cause.[20] Engels closes the letter with the leading question: 'how do I know whether you have not had very good reasons for contenting yourself, for once, with a picture of the passive side of working-class life, reserving the active side for another work?'.[21]

It is likely that Engels's letter had some impact, as Harkness's second novel, *Out of Work*, does portray the 'active side' of the working classes by taking as its subject a real historical event: the unemployed riots that took place in London in 1887. Harkness does not, however, retreat to older forms of Realist representation, pushing instead in the direction of modernism by experimenting with new forms, manipulating or discarding the elements of Naturalist writing that she finds unequal to the challenge of confronting the dire social conditions of urban-industrial capitalism. The 'continuity from Naturalism to the Modernism of our day' – as theorised by Lukács – is therefore relevant here, as he outlines a developmental narrative that usefully connects the two movements. Lukács explains, however, that the 'continuity' he maps is 'restricted [...] to underlying ideological principles', their shared 'psychopathology', 'neurosis', 'static approach to reality' and acceptance of the status quo. For these reasons, he considers Naturalism overly-deterministic, modernism narcissistic and eccentric, and both severely limited in their political utility.[22]

Given the uncompromising nature of these claims, it may seem counter-intuitive to engage Lukács in my reading of Harkness, because although *Out of Work* retains the elements of Naturalist writing that reveal the workings of power, and while characters are committed to unavoidable downwards trajectories as they attempt to survive the modern world, Harkness's particular proto-/modernism in no way evades the 'Real'. Her novel explicitly addresses social conditions to argue for major reform. Esty offers a solution to this conundrum, arguing that it is possible to 'turn Lukács against Lukács and rethink the modernist novel not as a testament to late bourgeois inwardness and decadence but as an art form partially determined by objective social conditions in the Age of Empire'.[23] By globalising Lukács (as Esty does) in order to read Harkness's (and later Schreiner's) writings, it becomes possible to trace what 'Lukács misses about modernism: the representation of layered, even apparently autotelic, subjectivity in the metropole can refer to determinate or objective social conditions, and those social conditions include the colonial dimensions of European experience'.[24]

In Naturalist novels, the inborn qualities of non-agentive characters typically combine with external events to drive them towards inevitable misery, ruin and death. Harkness, by contrast, divorces issues of heredity from environmental conditions in deciding individual fates. In *Out of Work*, her characters Jos and Squirrel are placed (as Naturalist characters often are) in increasingly appalling situations in order to represent the dirt, poverty, prejudice and disease experienced by impoverished inhabitants of the city, or what Lukács describes as 'the torments which the transition to the capitalist system of production inflicted on every section of the people, the profound moral and spiritual degradation which necessarily accompanied this transformation on every level of society'.[25] Crucially, however, Jos and Squirrel's decline is propelled only by their place in a historically-specific and grossly unfair society, so that inherited characteristics play no role in determining their journeys or destinations. By jettisoning the biological determinism of Naturalist writing whilst retaining an emphasis on the role of the environment in shaping individual destinies, Harkness argues that it is *structural* rather than *innate* conditions that cause and perpetuate the plight of London's unemployed. As she indicates in the novel, the conditions of industrial capitalism, made possible by the wealth of empire, need not be permanent or inevitable, but must be wholly transformed by radical political change.

One of the ways that Harkness reaches out from Realism and Naturalism towards modernist expression is in her experiments with narrative voice. As in other Naturalist novels, *Out of Work* frames the progression of events using evolutionary principles relating to the struggle for life in hostile situations, and pessimistic and deterministic strategies are used to represent the realities of Victorian working-class experiences. Harkness does not, however, replicate the detached narrative style that accompanies the Naturalist method of scientific enquiry in literature. She instead devises a continually present narrator to provide political commentary on the action in the novel, as exemplified by this description of the unemployed working-class character, Jos:

> [an] intelligent observer, seeing him that Sunday afternoon, would have noticed something about his appearance that had nothing to do with his character, further than as an environment that might modify it in some directions and transform it in others. The flesh of his face was falling away, and by so doing was leaving the skin loose [. . .] His face showed the first signs of starvation – signs easily interpreted by one who has studied the painful science of keeping alive on next-to-nothing, but never understood by those who receive their daily bread without effort or consideration.[26]

Narrators in mid-century social problem novels, including those written by Charles Dickens, Elizabeth Gaskell and Benjamin Disraeli, typically protect and shelter middle-class readers by working to establish their complicity and trust. They guide readers through the city slums, echoing and reinforcing middle-class notions of charity, morality and Christianity as the means to address issues of poverty and unemployment. Working-class and impoverished characters such as Dickens's Oliver Twist or Gaskell's Jem are then permitted to rise above the horrors of life for the poor because they possess inherent (and unrealistic) middle-class values, sensibilities and spiritualities. Harkness's narrator does not reassure. Instead, middle-class readers are exhorted to be 'intelligent observers' rather than 'those who receive their daily bread' and do nothing to share it.[27] The ironic use of devotional language exposes the prejudices, hypocrisies and complacencies of the middle-classes, undermining both moralistic cultural forms, and the idea that Christian charity poses a solution to socio-economic problems. The narrator thus establishes a view – maintained throughout the novel – of religion as ideology that masks and sustains the sundering inequalities of late-nineteenth century British capitalism.

Harkness's use of ventriloquism and repetition also anticipate later modernist experiments in free indirect discourse. These techniques are adopted to express mobile and shared feelings and perspectives, creating a sense of the persistence and pervasiveness of the poverty and undernourishment experienced by so many Londoners in 1887. The pivotal word, ''ungry', is introduced in the opening chapter, in which a

Wesleyan Minister delivers a sermon in honour of the Jubilee celebrations, only to be interrupted by one of the congregation. As the Minister gives thanks to the imperial monarch, '[o]ur Queen [who] rules over a kingdom upon which the sun never sets', decrying 'sceptics' and 'unbelievers', a man interjects: '"Sir," asked a voice, "'ave you ever been 'ungry?"'.[28] He poses the question a number of times: '"'Ave you ever been 'ungry?", he repeated, determined to have an answer, "'ungry?"'.[29] The man is ushered out, but the word continues to reverberate across the novel: 'pageants are waning, and loyalty is dying, and kings and queens are fading away. And all this because the people are tired of being 'ungry'.[30] Later, when Jos is forced to move to a doss-house, he sees '[c]rouching on the floor, gnawing a bone, was a man closely resembling the "'ungry" man' and the child Squirrel asks: '"Aren't you 'ungry?"'.[31] The ventriloquised and repeated ''ungry' inherits additional meanings with each usage, as the narrator and characters become aware of, empathise with, or experience, extreme poverty and starvation.

The word also often appears as part of a question, as in another example when Jos joins a crowd of unemployed men at the docks looking for a work, and the narrator asks: 'Has no artist sympathy enough with suffering humanity to visit the dock gates some early morning, and afterwards show Christian England what it is to be "'ungry"?'.[32] In response, the narrator then adopts a different perspective to argue against artistic representation of the men gathering at the docks in search of work: 'But why should any artist waste his time there? The upper ten would only turn away from the sorrows of that lowest ten if painted, and say, "How vulgar! How disgusting!"'.[33] Here again, the narrator assumes the role of ironic commentator in order to illustrate the combined unevenness of capitalist development, pushing middle-class readers to reconsider their own roles and values in the context of a major social crisis, whilst the resonating ''ungry' and haunting presence of the ragged man provides another reminder that real lives are at stake. The recurring loops back to the opening chapter through the echoing ventriloquism and lingering figure also serve to create a modernist sense of entrapment, capturing both the persistence of gnawing hunger, and a sense of the huge and increasing numbers of starving people in London as more and more voices declare that they too are ''ungry'.

Harkness's ability to narrativise complex and changing feelings and experiences is not only confined to instances of ventriloquism and repetition. In the following chapter, 'The Class-Leader Comes to Tea', she demonstrates great perspectival dexterity in presenting a scene through the shifting inner emotions and opinions of three female characters: Mrs Elwin, Mary Anne and Polly. As the servant Mary Anne moves between rooms, she struggles to muster interest in the conversations amongst William Ford, Polly and Mrs Elwin because '[p]eople without titles she thought commonplace, unless they belonged to that wonderful order of being who hover betwixt earth and heaven, namely, actors and actresses', and her thoughts quickly run to her own 'love-scenes [. . .] [that] she herself played with the butcher boy'.[34] The roaming narrative voice then enters Mrs Elwin's thoughts as she 'watched the young man's face, and while watching she made up her mind about something, – something that took away her appetite, and led her to tilt the bottle of rum into her tea-cup'; and the chapter ends with Polly, who 'vacillate[s] from pillar to post' between her suitors Jos and William, eventually saying aloud 'I wish Jos would go away'.[35] These intersecting streams of consciousness provide differing views on the action and interior worlds of characters in the novel, presaging a method that would become a hallmark of modernist writing. Where Balzac's omniscient narrators and Zola's documentary-style narration endeavour to create the sense of objective reality through detached reporting of phenomena and events as they unfold, Harkness instead utilises shifting narrative focalisations to demonstrate the existence of multiple realities or truths. The result is not, however, the lack of agency, psychopathology, inaction or paralysis that Lukács considers the inevitable result of Naturalist and modernist forms. Rather Harkness strives to represent complex subjectivities without retreating into solipsism and apathy, as her proto-/modernist techniques retain the political impetus of the novel by presenting high-level critiques of capitalist exploitation, located in historical reality, brought close by the thoughts and experiences of working-class characters.

Schreiner's Socialist Allegory: Representing the Real

Schreiner's experiments in accessing the 'Real', Harkness's relationship with Schreiner, and Zola's permeating presence in the literary cultures of the *fin de siècle*, can be traced across a number of Schreiner's letters from 1888. Sometime between April and October of that year, Schreiner wrote to Harkness's cousin, Potter: 'I think Maggie's book [*Out of Work*] first rate. Great improvement on the last; though that was good. It is the little touches that are so true to life'.[36] Had *Out of Work* adhered precisely to the conventions of Zolaesque Naturalism it is unlikely that it would have garnered Schreiner's praise, as in a January letter to Havelock Ellis in which she describes Zola as 'a man of power almost of genius', though goes on to claim: 'I hate Zola & that school more

& more send me any of their novels you get in English, I will return them faithfully!!!!!'.³⁷ In November she writes to Havelock Ellis again, this time turning from mention of Zola to her own work on an Introduction to a new reprint edition of Mary Wollstonecraft's *A Vindication of the Rights of Woman* (1792):

> If you have one of Zola's novels in French you might send it me. [. . .] My Mary Wollstonecraft is going on. It is all poetry from the first to the last, except a few sentences. There are six or seven allegories in it; I've tried to keep them out, but I can't. I have come to the conclusion that only poetry is truth. That other forms are <u>parts</u> of truth, but as soon as a representation has all parts, then it is poetry. As soon as there is the form and the spirit, the passion and the thought, then there is poetry, or the <u>living</u> reality. I don't mean that I attain to true poetry – all I mean is that what makes a man strive after and seek to see the thing in that way is that it is the reality. It's the other that's fancy and fiction, and this that is real.³⁸

As Schreiner's epistolary record shows, she was reading novels by both Harkness and Zola in 1888, working on both the Wollstonecraft Introduction and 'The Sunlight Lay Across My Bed', and at the same time shaping her own ideas about how to represent 'truth' in fiction.³⁹ It is clear from the letters that she felt little affinity for Zola's writings, expressing instead a preference for 'poetry'. As she explains, her use of the term 'poetry' does not refer to metrical composition or verse, rather serves as a way to describe allegory, a form that for Schreiner encapsulated 'spirit', 'passion' and 'thought'. It was through allegory, rather than Realism or Naturalism, that Schreiner established her own unique modernism as a way of representing the 'Real' and expressing radical arguments in fiction.

Though Harkness and Schreiner's writings of the late-1880s emerged from discrete literary influences and traditions, Schreiner's allegory 'The Sunlight Lay Across My Bed' bears comparison with Harkness's *Out of Work* due to its underpinning ethical socialism, experiments with narrative voice, and presentation of competing views as dialectical process. This in turn provides evidence of their shared proto-/modernist praxis – a reading partially enabled by turning once more to Lukács, who writes:

> Modern allegory, and modernist ideology, [. . .] deny the *typical*. By destroying the coherence of the world, they reduce detail to the level of mere particularity (once again, the connection between modernism and naturalism is plain). Detail, in its allegorical transferability, though brought into a direct, if paradoxical, connection with transcendence, becomes an abstract function of the transcendence to which it points. Modernist literature thus replaces concrete typicality with abstract particularity.⁴⁰

As well as continuing to define modernism as a kind of second-generation Naturalism, Lukács also describes modernism as allegorical in character. His explanation that allegory, Naturalism and modernism all emerge as 'a moral protest against capitalism' also does much to illuminate the political intent of Harkness and Schreiner's writing.[41] Yet the next stage of Lukács's argument, that modernism inevitably becomes ideological, forming a new typology that is the 'immutable *condition humaine*', has limited applicability to *Out of Work* and 'The Sunlight Lay Across My Bed', which remain grounded in specific historical responses to specific historical situations.[42] In Lukács's view, Naturalism and modernist allegory consistently fail to critique the capitalist system of production that gave rise to them in the first place, resulting in spiritual degradation, superficiality and fragmentation, and ending as 'gesture [. . .] destined to lead nowhere; it is an escape into nothingness'.[43] His complaint here is that modernism, or more properly, ideological modernism, presents human experience in universalising ways detached from the 'concrete typicality' of historical referents.[44] Thus 'modernism's allegorical approach' – which for Lukács is exemplified by Franz Kafka's writings – fails 'to achieve that fusion of the particular and the general which is the essence of realistic art'.[45] In other words, modernism remains an aesthetic endeavour that never confronts the 'Real'.

Though 'The Sunlight Lay Across My Bed' does indeed depict transcendent allegorical visions, the story does not, in my view, '[become] an abstract function of the transcendence to which it points' because the visions are shaped and bookended by direct engagement with the condition of the working classes, who are also racialised and gendered.[46] The allegory thus remains tied to specific localities, histories and socially determined situations associated with London, without divorcing these experiences from the global circuits of capital that made them possible. As such, Schreiner's allegory explicitly expresses hope and resistance rather than apathy and neurosis, providing exactly a 'fusion of the particular and general' that Lukács laments the loss of in modernist literature.

In her important account of Schreiner's influence on Harkness, Angharad Eyre explains that they had 'a shared philosophy of religion re-visioning' that shaped their 'positions on Christianity and socialism, and prompted [Harkness] to undertake experiments with form and genre'.[47] Though Schreiner's 'The Sunlight Lay Across My Bed' was published two years after Harkness's 1888 'The Gospel of Getting On', they were written at around the same time, and have in common the reformulation of Christianity for socialist purposes. 'The Sunlight Lay Across My Bed' is told from the perspective of a narrator who drifts in and out of sleep, dreaming of Heaven and Hell. In a key scene, God takes the narrator to a banquet house, where men and women pray to God and then gorge themselves on wine. The wine is then revealed as the blood of people crushed in a wine-press concealed behind a curtain, and the narrator watches as:

> Mothers whispered to their children, 'Do not drink all, save a little drop when you have drunk.' And when they had collected all the dregs, they slipped the cups out under the bottom of the curtain without lifting it. After a while the curtain left off moving.
> I said to God, 'How is it so quiet'
> He said, 'They have gone away to drink it.'
> I said, 'They drink it – their own!'
> God said, 'It comes from this side of the curtain, and they are very thirsty'.[48]

The dregs represent the necessary product; the wine consumed by the feasting crowd the surplus product. In this way, Schreiner allegorises the deathly industrial processes of imperial capitalism as the violently exploited, expendable workers are given no alternative to auto-vampirism as a means for survival. As Carly Nations points out, there are gendered and racialised dynamics at work here too, because 'the bodies of those in the wine press' are 'marginalized bodies – both female and colonized. In Schreiner's Hell, women suffer for the sake of men and, more specifically, Black men and women suffer for the sake of white indulgence and white willful ignorance'.[49] When a 'bloodless', 'wine-pressed hand' appears from behind a curtain, the crowd become afraid, men rush to beat it back, and leave only 'a small stain upon the floor'.[50] They then resume their revelries and gluttony: '[m]en and women sat at the tables quaffing great bowls', 'pledged each other in the wine, and kissed each other's blood-red lips', and 'women dyed their children's garments in the wine, and fed them on it till their tiny mouths were red'.[51] In 'The Sunlight Lay Across My Bed', religion is practised by a self-serving, fearful, hedonistic and sadistic leisure class, whilst the horror-reworking of the Eucharist allegorically defamiliarises Christianity as an ideology that obscures and sustains capitalist modes of production. Importantly, this view of the relationship between religion and capitalism was also shared by Harkness, and is traceable in her allegory dedicated to Schreiner, in which only '[a] few Socialists' remain who 'follow Jesus of Nazareth'.[52] As Eyre explains, the allegory expresses Harkness's view 'that socialists were the only true nineteenth-century Christians', and as such, provides evidence that 'Harkness not only admired Schreiner, but believed that they were workers in a shared mission'.[53]

The dialectical purpose of Harkness and Schreiner's writings emerges in their presentation of competing views to establish new historical understanding, albeit expressed through divergent methods derived from Naturalism (in the case of Harkness) and allegory (in the case of Schreiner). In Harkness's novel, narratorial impositions, ventriloquism and perspectival shifts make possible contrasts between the glory of empire celebrated in the Queen's Jubilee and the horrors of poverty and starvation in the metropolitan imperial centre; the pitting of Christianity against socialism; and the battle between love and economic security as a primary reason for marriage. In Schreiner's allegory, dialogue and setting are used to dialectical effect so that visions of Hell are contrasted with visions of Heaven, and the narrator and God engage in interpretations and reinterpretations of scenes of the afterlife in order to generate evolving insights. Like Harkness, Schreiner uses shifting viewpoints, questions and repetition to reflect changing perceptions. When, for example, the narrator and God come to some ruins, the narrator asks:

'It was a banquet-house?'
God said, 'Ay, a banquet-house.'
I said, 'There was a wine-press here?'
God said, 'There was a wine-press.'[54]

The narrator's dawning realisation about the extent of the damage wreaked by the industrial production of blood-wine prompts 'further, yet further' visions of a world that initially appeared beautiful and joyful, but which is 'pitfall', poison, death and suffering.[55] Now 'the plains, the mounds are burial heaps', 'the stones I hear them crying aloud', men dance to 'time beaten in with sobs; and their wine is living!'.[56]

Schreiner's allegory thus provides striking and memorable scenes of societal hypocrisy and capitalist exploitation, but as Laura Chrisman points out: '[t]he most glaring problem of such an approach is its totalitarianism. The transformation by, or resistance from within, any of its social elements is impossible'.[57] Lukács's arguments about the universalising tendencies of modernism are once again recalled, as the limits of Schreiner's critical socialism are indeed evident in the presentation of dialectical synthesis as utopian vision rather than the outcome of class struggle: in the 'highest' Heaven, writes Schreiner, 'it grew so bright I could not see things separately; and which were God, or the man, or I, I could not tell; we were all blended'.[58] Yet, as Esty explains, 'globalizing Lukács allows us to read modernist bohemian tales of colonial alienation not just as negative allegories of the agonized soul under reification, but as positive (in the epistemological sense) allegories of a world system in which colonial difference runs athwart universal progress'.[59] The return to the city at the end of 'The Sunlight Lay Across My Bed' is therefore also a return to the 'concrete typicality' that Lukács requires of the 'Real', providing a reminder of the combined and uneven development of the capitalist world-system that cuts across, without undermining, the imperative and yet impossible aims of Schreiner's utopian, socialist and post-colonial vision.

The Sights and Sounds of the City

Both Harkness's *Out of Work* and Schreiner's 'The Sunlight Lay Across My Bed' depict London as place of gross inequality and deprivation that at the same time gives rise to new communities and forms of resistance. In *Out of Work*, dioramas and soundscapes of the city are mediated by the narrator and characters to convey differing ideas about class, politics and social conditions. When, for example, the lower middle-class character Polly walks the streets of Whitechapel, she sees men 'stood about public houses. Children crowding the pavements. Here and there a hurdy-gurdy kept the people dancing, boys with boys, girls with girls, even mothers nursing babies'.[60] Middle-class prejudices are implicated in Polly's perception as she feels she 'had nothing in common with the young women, whose untidy clothes and hair made her shudder'.[61] Even when, as Nadia Valman observes, 'she notices the appreciative glances that denote their shared interest in female clothing and appearance', Polly rejects any possibility for 'sympathy across class', which in turn 'signals the harsh individualism that will make Polly a key agent in the fall of Jos Coney and the novel's tragic conclusion'.[62] Polly's disgust, and by extension, the assumed disgust of Harkness's reading audience, is unmistakeable in the description of her 'pass[ing] through some of the worst streets our metropolis can boast of, full of degraded human beings, filthy overcrowded houses, and shops that sell adulterated grocery, putrid meat, watered milk, and second-hand clothing'.[63]

A negative perception of the inhabitants of the city remains in place at the outset of a later chapter, 'Work at the Docks', which opens with a description of the area outside Fenchurch Street Station:

> Half-past six is an unpleasant hour in that part of the city. The streets look greasy. There are not enough people about to enliven the houses. Shops have shutters up; untidy girls are scrubbing doorsteps; no one is there, except men on their way to work, old women going to market, and that scum of the populace who sleep in any hole they can, and live in any way they may;

bleating sheep and lowing cattle are being driven along by butchers; yawning policemen are talking over a suicide here, a murder there; lean dogs are acting as scavengers; ragged children are seeking breakfast in dust heaps and gutters. The damp morning air is adding to the unpleasant smells in the atmosphere.[64]

The passage homes in on sensory experience, loading negative adjectives to depict the dirt, noise and smells of the slums, viewed with disgust from a narrative perspective allied to a middle-class reading audience. This conventionally social realist content and tone is brought a little nearer to modernist forms of representation by the lengthy parataxic sentence, comprised predominantly of monosyllabic words designed to capture the isolating, fragmenting effects of capitalism, and often overwhelming immediacy of experience on the city streets. Making a similar point in her work on soundscapes in Harkness's first novel, *A City Girl*, Ruth Livesey states that '[i]n the decades that follow Harkness's novel this disintegrative auditory principle became a keynote of modernist experiment in the forms of vorticism and futurism'.[65]

Later in 'Work at the Docks', the city dioramas and soundscapes shift in their mediation so that the differing cognitions of narrator and characters are either contrasted or merged. This is evident in the line immediately following the passage quoted above, as the description is sharply undercut by a narratorial interjection, the exclamation: 'Little wonder that public-houses entice customers!'.[66] This expression of sympathy by the ever-present narrator contrasts with the earlier description of East End streets, articulating an alternative viewpoint that encourages a move towards new historical understanding of social problems. Then again in the subsequent line, there is another perspectival and aural transferral, so that the eyes and ears through which the reader experiences the city now belong to the unemployed working-class character, Jos. Through his narrative focalisation, London's poor are no longer kept at bay, as Jos is invited to 'Tumble in!' a train carriage of 'forty men, all untidy, unshaven, hungry people [. . .] All had unbrushed hair, muddy boots, filthy hands and dirty faces; some were sleeping, some were smoking, three or four were trying to laugh at the others'.[67] Now Jos jostles alongside others en route to Tidal Basin in search of work. He hears individual voices, snatches of conversation and greetings; he witnesses small acts of generosity, and gestures of friendship: '[i]t was "Ulloa, Tom!" and "Well Bill!" at every platform, a desire to share tobacco, to show kindness, and receive favours'.[68] Importantly too, the fragmented cacophonies of the city that Livesey identifies, and which Harkness sees as consequence of urban-industrial capitalism, do not, in *Out of Work*, preclude possibilities for connection, reciprocities and compassion. This is exemplified by moments of aural harmony, as in the example where 'the men began to sing: – "Starving on the Queen's highway."'.[69] In this way, Jos's street-level view of the city establishes London as a place in which communities are made, collective resistance becomes possible, and, to quote Engels once more, 'the active side' of 'working-class life' becomes visible.[70]

Schreiner's 'The Sunlight Lay Across My Bed' also begins and ends in London's East End, and auditory principles are similarly central to Schreiner's representation.[71] The allegory opens 'In the dark one night' as the narrator lies on a bed listening to the sounds of the city outside the window:

> I heard the policeman's feet beat on the pavement; I heard the wheels of carriages roll home from houses of entertainment; I heard a woman's laugh below my window – and then I fell asleep. And in the dark I dreamt a dream. I dreamt God took my soul to Hell.[72]

When the narrator awakes after a second dream about Heaven, the sounds of the city are heard once again through the bedroom window:

> In the streets below, men and women streamed past by hundreds; I heard the beat of their feet on the pavement. Men on their way to business; servants on errands; boys hurrying to school; weary professors pacing slowly the old street; prostitutes, men and women, dragging their feet wearily after last night's debauch; artists with quick, impatient footsteps; tradesmen for orders; children to seek for bread.[73]

As in the example from *Out of Work*, Schreiner here captures the fragmented, unequal experiences of life in the metropole through parataxis and contrast, with each phrase describing distinct groups of people divided by class, gender, age and profession. The rhythmic soundscape of the London streets emerges in the anaphora, repetition and metrical monosyllables sounding out the footsteps of the walkers.[74] The poetic techniques create an upswell until 'the broken barrel-organ on the street corner sobbed' and the narrator's heartbeats fall in time with the feet on the pavement, '[crying] out with every throb, "Love! – Truth! – the Beautiful! – the Beautiful!" It was the music I had heard in Heaven that I could not sing there'.[75] Like the voices rising together in song in Harkness's *Out of Work*, the synthesis between the narrator's dream visions and experience of London express hope for new human connections as the route to a better world.

Forms and Farewells

Though Schreiner and Harkness took their leading aesthetic pointers from distinct literary genealogies, their writings of the late-1880s arrived at corresponding ideas, images and methods that enabled them to express shared socialist arguments. The women and their work were shaped by their interactions with one another and associated literary and radical circles, as well as their experiences of London, and adoptions and adaptions of Naturalist and allegorical forms. Though highly divergent texts in many ways, both *Out of Work* and 'The Sunlight Lay Across My Bed' experiment with narrative voice, shifting perspectives, dialectical processes, and city dioramas and soundscapes, demonstrating techniques that critics would later identify as modernist. Harkness and Schreiner's importance as proto-/modernist writers and thinkers emerges in these innovations, which yet manage to avoid the psychopathology and inaction laid out by Lukács's concept of modernist ideology, because they retain a focus on the 'concrete typicality' of the social conditions caused by urban-industrial capitalism.[76]

For a brief period in the late-1880s, then, Bloomsbury provided intellectual and imaginary spaces for Schreiner and Harkness to nurture and develop shared politics and aesthetics. Their friendship did not last, however, as Schreiner found Harkness increasingly predatory and draining. On 11 October 1889, Schreiner returned to South Africa, keen by then to sever all ties. She was alarmed, therefore, to hear from publisher W. T. Stead in late 1890 or early 1891 that Harkness intended to visit her in Matjiesfontein. Schreiner wrote to Stead to tell him that 'I have come out to Africa entirely that I might be alone' and asked him: 'Will you show this letter to Miss Harkness because she might not understand if you did not'.[77] In another letter, sent to her sister-in-law, Frances (Fan), Schreiner wrote:

> Do you remember my telling you and Will about a ~~M~~ woman who had caused me no end of trouble & would come out after me & stay with me. Well Mr Fort has just sent me a cutting from a paper in which it is said that she is coming out to ~~stay~~ pay a visit to her friend Olive Schreiner in South Africa!!!
>
> I really came out to this country greatly to get ride [sic] of her. If you ever see me bolt suddenly into your house in Hoff street you will know I am escaping from her [...] You can't have any idea what a nightmare that woman is to me. <u>Please don't</u> say anything to your friends or anyone, but if a tall thin woman comes to ask you or Will what my address is you wire up to me, & I shall not be in Matjiesfontein when she comes here![78]

In the end, Schreiner took the matter into her own hands, writing what remains the only (and incomplete) extant letter between the two women. It is clearly intended as a final missive, as Schreiner warns Harkness not to visit her, and delivers the brutal directive: 'There is no need for us simply to write to say we are alive & well. I should always see in the papers if you were ill, you would always see from the papers if I were ill or dead'.[79] Despite this, an old or lingering affection is discernible towards the end of the letter, as the final lines above her signature read: 'I believe you will yet do greater & greater good work in our world. I wish that all good & success always be with you'.[80]

Works Cited

Chrisman, Laura. 'Allegory, Feminist Thought and the *Dreams* of Olive Schreiner'. *Prose Studies: History, Theory, Criticism* 13, no. 1 (May 1990): 126–50.

Esty, Jed. 'Global Lukács'. *Novel* 42, no. 3 (Fall 2009): 366–72.

Eyre, Angharad. 'Socialism, Suffering, and Religious Mystery: Margaret Harkness and Olive Schreiner'. In *Margaret Harkness: Writing Social Engagement 1880–1921*, edited by Flore Janssen and Lisa C. Robertson, 167–81. Manchester: Manchester University Press, 2019.

Frierson, William C. 'The English Controversy Over Realism in Fiction 1885–1895.' *PMLA* 43, no. 2 (June 1928): 533–50.

Gilbert, Sandra, and Susan Gubar. 'Introduction: The Female Imagination and the Modernist Aesthetic. *Women's Studies* 13, no. 1 (1986): 1–10.

Law, John [Margaret Harkness]. *Out of Work*. London: Merlin Press, 1990.

—. 'The Gospel of Getting On (To Olive Schreiner.)' *To-day: Monthly Magazine of Scientific Socialism* 52 (March 1888): 83–4.

Levy, Amy. 'Women and Club Life'. In *The Complete Novels and Selected Writings of Amy Levy 1861–1889*, edited by Melvyn New, 532–38. Gainesville: University Press of Florida, 1993.

Livesey, Ruth. 'Soundscapes of the City in Margaret Harkness, *A City Girl* (1887), Henry James, *The Princess Casamassima* (1885–86), and Katharine Buildings, Whitechapel'. In *Margaret Harkness: Writing Social Engagement 1880–1921*, edited by Flore Janssen and Lisa C. Robertson, 111–29. Manchester: Manchester University Press, 2019.

Lukács, Georg. *Studies in European Realism: A Sociological Survey of the Writings of Balzac, Stendhal, Zola, Tolstoy, Gorki and Others*, translated by Edith Bone. London: Hillway, 1950.

—. *The Meaning of Contemporary Realism*. Translated by John and Necke Mander. London: Merlin Press, 1969.

Nations, Carly. '"Made Alive": Olive Schreiner's *Dreams* and the Embodied Vision of Equality'. *Nineteenth-Century Gender Studies* 17, no. 2 (Summer 2021): https://ncgsjournal.com/issue172/nations.html.

Nord, Deborah Epstein. *Walking the Victorian Streets: Women, Representation and the City*. Ithaca and London: Cornell University Press, 1995.
Schreiner, Olive. 'The Sunlight Lay Across My Bed'. In *Dreams*, 131–82. London: T. Fisher Unwin, 1890.
—. 'Introduction to Mary Wollstonecraft's *A Vindication of the Rights of Woman*'. In *Words in Season: The Public Writings with Her Own Remembrances Collected for the First Time*, 19–28. Johannesburg: Penguin Books, 2005.
Snaith, Anna. *Modernist Voyages: Colonial Women Writers in London*. Cambridge: Cambridge University Press, 2014.
Valman, Nadia. 'Walking Margaret Harkness's London'. In *Margaret Harkness: Writing Social Engagement 1880–1921*, edited by Flore Janssen and Lisa C. Robertson, 57–73. Manchester: Manchester University Press, 2019.

Letters

Friedrich Engels to Margaret Harkness, April 1888. In *European Literature from Romanticism to Postmodernism: A Reader in Aesthetic Practice*, edited by Martin Travers, 122–4. London and New York: Continuum, 2001.
Olive Schreiner to Henry Havelock Ellis, 24 January 1884. *Olive Schreiner Letters Online*.
Olive Schreiner to Henry Havelock Ellis, 17 December 1884. *Olive Schreiner Letters Online*.
Olive Schreiner to Henry Havelock Ellis, 13 July 1885. *Olive Schreiner Letters Online*.
Olive Schreiner to Henry Havelock Ellis, 26 July 1885. *Olive Schreiner Letters Online*.
Olive Schreiner to Henry Havelock Ellis, 22 March 1887. In *The Letters of Olive Schreiner 1876–1920*, edited by S. C. Cronwright-Schreiner, 112. London: T. Fisher Unwin, 1924.
Olive Schreiner to Henry Havelock Ellis, 2 November 1887. *Olive Schreiner Letters Online*.
Olive Schreiner to Henry Havelock Ellis, 2 November 1888. In *The Letters of Olive Schreiner 1876–1920*, edited by S. C. Cronwright-Schreiner, 145. London: T. Fisher Unwin, 1924.
Olive Schreiner to Henry Havelock Ellis, 17 March 1889. *Olive Schreiner Letters Online*.
Olive Schreiner to Margaret Harkness, January–February 1891. *Olive Schreiner Letters Online*.
Olive Schreiner to Beatrice Potter, April–October 1888. *Olive Schreiner Letters Online*.
Olive Schreiner to Frances (Fan) Schreiner, Jan 1891–Dec 1892. *Olive Schreiner Letters Online*.
Olive Schreiner to Will Schreiner, 3 June 1884. *Olive Schreiner Letters Online*.
Olive Schreiner to William Thomas Stead, March–December 1890. *Olive Schreiner Letters Online*.

Notes

1. Esty, 'Global Lukács', 367.
2. Esty, 'Global Lukács', 369.
3. Olive Schreiner arrived in England in March 1881 and visited friends and family in Eastbourne, Burnley and Ventnor before moving to London.
4. Snaith, *Modernist Voyages*, 9, 2.
5. Schreiner to Havelock Ellis, 17 December 1884, *Olive Schreiner Letters Online* (hereafter *OSLO*).
6. Schreiner to Havelock Ellis, 13 July 1885, *OSLO*.
7. Harkness lived in Bloomsbury in the early 1880s but moved to the East End in 1886.
8. Olive Schreiner to Will Schreiner, 3 June 1884, *OSLO*.
9. Schreiner came to Britain to train as a nurse but had to abandon this plan due to ill health, while Harkness trained at Westminster and Guy's hospitals and worked as a nurse. Schreiner published under the pseudonym 'Ralph Iron', and Harkness as 'John Law'.
10. Schreiner to Havelock Ellis, 22 March 1887 in Cronwright-Schreiner, *The Letters of Olive Schreiner*, 111–12. The editorial team of the definitive *Olive Schreiner Letters Online* note that the original version of this letter no longer exists, and so the accuracy of the version published in the Cronwright-Schreiner collection cannot be gauged.
11. Law [Margaret Harkness], 'The Gospel of Getting On', 83.
12. Nord, *Walking the Victorian Streets*, 197, 181, 183–84.
13. Nord, *Walking the Victorian Streets*, 182.
14. Levy, 'Women and Club Life', 532–3. This essay was originally published in the first edition of Oscar Wilde's magazine *The Woman's World*. Schreiner also published allegories in *The Woman's World*.
15. Gilbert and Gubar, 'Introduction', 1.
16. Publisher Henry Vizetelly was convicted of obscenity in 1888 and again in 1889 for publishing English translations of Emile Zola's novels. He was sentenced to three months imprisonment, and Schreiner was amongst the many writers who signed a petition for his release. See Frierson, 'The English Controversy over Realism', 542.
17. Friedrich Engels to Margaret Harkness, April 1888, in Travers, 122, 123.
18. Engels in Travers, 123.
19. Engels in Travers, 123, 124. Though Engels does not make this clear, Naturalism and Realism are in fact closely related literary forms, and Zola once even named Balzac as the true father of Naturalism.
20. Interestingly, Schreiner wrote to Havelock Ellis on 26 July 1885 to tell him that 'M Harkeness [sic] brought me yesterday Balzacs "Physiologie du Mariage."' *Olive Schreiner Letters Online*.
21. Engels in Travers, 124.
22. Lukács, *The Meaning of Contemporary Realism*, 29, 31, 34.
23. Esty, 'Global Lukács', 366.
24. Esty, 'Global Lukács', 370.
25. Georg Lukács, *Studies in European Realism*, 12.
26. Law, *Out of Work*, 40.

27. Law, *Out of Work*, 40.
28. Law, *Out of Work*, 11, 13.
29. Law, *Out of Work*, 13.
30. Law, *Out of Work*, 51.
31. Law, *Out of Work*, 111, 112.
32. Law, *Out of Work*, 131.
33. Law, *Out of Work*, 131.
34. Law, *Out of Work*, 145, 146.
35. Law, *Out of Work*, 146, 151.
36. Schreiner to Beatrice Potter, April–October 1888, OSLO.
37. Schreiner to Havelock Ellis, 24 January 1884, OSLO.
38. Schreiner to Havelock Ellis, 2 November 1888 in Cronwright-Schreiner, *The Letters of Olive Schreiner*, 145. The original version of this letter was destroyed, and so its accuracy can now not be gauged. Schreiner never actually completed her Introduction, which was only published in full for the first time in 2005. See Schreiner, 'Introduction to Mary Wollstonecraft's *A Vindication of the Rights of Woman*', 19–28.
39. References to writing 'The Sunlight Lay Across My Bed' appear in various of Schreiner's letters from late 1887–1889. See for example Schreiner to Havelock Ellis, 2 November 1887; Schreiner to Havelock Ellis, 17 March 1889, OSLO.
40. Lukács, *Contemporary Realism*, 43.
41. Lukács, *Contemporary Realism*, 29.
42. Lukács, *Contemporary Realism*, 31.
43. Lukács, *Contemporary Realism*, 29.
44. Lukács, *Contemporary Realism*, 43.
45. Lukács, *Contemporary Realism*, 45.
46. Lukács, *Contemporary Realism*, 43.
47. Eyre, 'Socialism, Suffering, and Religious Mystery, 167.
48. Schreiner, *Dreams*, 144.
49. Nations, 'Made Alive', 11.
50. Schreiner, *Dreams*, 145–46.
51. Schreiner, 'Sunlight', 148–49.
52. Law, 'The Gospel of Getting On', 84.
53. Eyre, 'Socialism, Suffering, and Religious Mystery', 167, 170.
54. Schreiner, *Dreams*, 155.
55. Schreiner, *Dreams*, 157.
56. Schreiner, *Dreams*, 157.
57. Chrisman, 'Allegory, Feminist Thought and the *Dreams* of Olive Schreiner', 146.
58. Schreiner, *Dreams*, 178.
59. Esty, 'Global Lukács,' 371.
60. Law, *Out of Work*, 70.
61. Law, *Out of Work*, 71.
62. Valman, 'Walking Margaret Harkness's London', 66.
63. Law, *Out of Work*, 71.
64. Law, *Out of Work*, 126.
65. Livesey, 'Soundscapes of the City,' 124.
66. Law, *Out of Work*, 127.

67. Law, *Out of Work*, 127, 128.
68. Law, *Out of Work*, 129.
69. Livesey, 'Soundscapes of the City', 112; Law, *Out of Work*, 128.
70. Engels in Travers, 124.
71. See Schreiner to Havelock Ellis, 17 March 1889, *Olive Schreiner Letters Online*.
72. Schreiner, *Dreams*, 133.
73. Schreiner, *Dreams*, 180–81.
74. Schreiner, *Dreams*, 133.
75. Schreiner, *Dreams*, 182.
76. Lukács, *Contemporary Realism*, 43.
77. Schreiner to Stead. Letter recorded as 'after start March 1890; before end December 1890' but may possibly have been sent in 1891, *OSLO*.
78. Olive Schreiner to Frances (Fan) Schreiner. Letter recorded as 'after start 1891; before end 1892', *OSLO*.
79. Schreiner to Harkness. Letter recorded as 'after start January 1891; before end February 1891', *OSLO*.
80. Schreiner to Harkness. Letter recorded as 'after start: January 1891; before end February 1891', *OSLO*. Schreiner does include a lengthy postscript, which is incomplete due to missing pages.

Chapter 3

Olive Schreiner and Virginia Woolf: Proto-Ecofeminists?
Dan Wylie

Both Olive Schreiner and Virginia Woolf draw on a well-worn trope of birth and development: the insect chrysalis. In an 1886 letter, Schreiner compared the 'receptive state' of a creative mind to that of the voracious caterpillar, which then turns into a chrysalis, apparently dead, immobile and impervious, '& then at last out comes the butterfly'.[1] Some forty years later, sitting in a favourite countryside 'hollow', Woolf's reaction to observing a 'caterpillar, now becoming a Chrysalis', was rather different: 'A horrid sight: head turning from side to side, tail paralyzed; brown colour, purple spots just visible; like a snake in movement'.[2] This is an initial hint of echoes and congruities in the two writers' treatment of the natural world, as well as of certain divergences of attitude.

Karel Schoeman remarked that Schreiner at times exemplified Woolf's ambition for the woman writer to find a 'room of [her] own',[3] a comparative angle that has not been much exploited. In fact, the parallels are numerous and close, surprisingly so given that Schreiner's topographical milieux – largely the remote, scrubby villages and hills of South Africa's Karoo semi-desert – could scarcely be further removed from the urban and bookish socialising of Woolf's Bloomsbury. These two women lived almost at opposite poles of the imperial axis: Schreiner was a rare voice of dissent in a colony still sparsely populated by white settlers and their descendants, surrounded by wildness and Indigenous peoples, while Woolf flourished at the heart of the great imperial metropolis itself and its intensively domesticated countryside. Nonetheless, their lives overlapped in time and space. Schreiner, thirty years Woolf's senior, was despite her isolation well-apprised of Europe's intellectual currents, helped by substantial sojourns in England and the Continent. Both writers even resided in London simultaneously, though there is no evidence they ever met. We have no record of Woolf's feelings about Schreiner's *The Story of an African Farm* (1883), though she did comment publicly on Samuel Cronwright-Schreiner's publication of a selection of his late, estranged wife's letters in 1925. Woolf was characteristically waspish but illuminating, finding Schreiner too 'egotistical' and only 'half of a great writer'.[4] That Schreiner influenced Woolf directly, despite the latter's dismissal, has been suggested by Elaine Showalter (in 1993) and explored as a possibility by Jade Munslow Ong (more recently).[5] Whether this was the case, or they converged independently on ambient, modernist cultural concerns and techniques, the profile of their works is substantially parallel: each produced a clutch of ground-breaking novels, a considerable body of short fiction, overtly feminist tracts, numerous essays and thousands of letters and pages of diaries.

Their respective feminist credentials are now exhaustively established – largely independently, though Maria Saracino delineates selected feminist connections between them. Their works devoted to exposing the oppression of women and objecting to masculinist warfare – Schreiner's *Women and Labour* (1911), Woolf's *A Room of One's Own* (1929) and *Three Guineas* (1938) – are remarkably congruent. Both wrote prefaces to Mary Wollstonecraft's *A Vindication of the Rights of Women* (1792). Though she referred to 'the woman question' rather than 'feminism', as Woolf did later, there seems no reason to quibble with characterising Schreiner as 'protofeminist', as do encyclopaedists Gareth Cornwell, Dirk Klopper and Craig Mackenzie.[6] '*Eco*feminist' is a different proposition. Both oeuvres are certainly replete with references to the natural world, material and imaginative. These are largely unfocused, but generate rich ruminations on human-natural relations, plant and animal presences, the effects of evolutionary science and possibilities for an ethical but non-religious sense of underlying unity. In parallel but separate strands, those representations have lately been subjected to closer scrutiny.

In Schreiner's case, scholarship has been overwhelmingly dedicated to her engagement with the 'Woman Question' and with politics, war and race, excepting Jane Wilkinson's 1991 foray into relations between 'Nature and art' in *The Story of an African Farm*. Joyce Avrech Berkman's otherwise penetrating study, *The Healing Imagination of Olive Schreiner* (1989), ignores how the natural world manifestly provides both author and characters with solace, a source of 'interknitted sympathy' to challenge binarist thinking.[7] Excepting recent essays by Dorothy Driver (on plants) and Valerie Stevens (on pets), Schreiner's attachments to the Karoo landscape, her invocations of the animal and the vegetal, and extrapolations of Darwinian theory, have been universally recognised but acknowledged largely in comments as scattered as are Schreiner's own. To my knowledge, only Andrew McMurray (1994) has made a start: in an essay focused only on *African Farm*, he argues that the absorption of characters into the very ground, and Schreiner's melding of genders, broach an explicitly ecofeminist perspective.

In Woolf's case, plant- and animal-studies threads within ecocriticism have taken discussion considerably further than in Schreiner's. In several books, contributors offer discussions on Woolf's engagement with trees, flowers, landscapes and gardens, sundry animals and biological science.[8] Though much pre-empts or echoes my sketches below, relatively little is explicitly ecofeminist, and definitions and approaches vary widely. For example, Bonnie Kime Scott, a prime mover of 'eco-Woolfian' activity, acknowledges that her earlier location of ecofeminism in Woolf's evocation of earth-goddess figures is not agreeable to all feminists.[9] Nonetheless, Justyna Kostkowska argues, Woolf may be called both 'ecofeminist' *and* 'environmentalist'.[10] What, then, are the connections between each writer's feminism and their representations of 'nature'? And can Schreiner also be invoked as at least a 'proto-ecofeminist'?

Who's afraid of an ecofeminist?

In proposing to apply the term 'ecofeminist' to Schreiner and Woolf, certain difficulties arise. Firstly, having been coined only in 1974 by Françoise D'Eaubonne, the term may be too anachronistic a measure of either. Secondly, taking an ecocritical or ecofeminist literary *reading* differs from deciding whether or not the *writer* 'was' an ecofeminist in action or philosophy. The relationship between these approaches can be slippery, as between author and fictional character. It is often assumed that Lyndall and Rebekah are effectively mouthpieces for Schreiner's own ideas; and Woolf herself remarked of the characters in *The Waves* that 'we are the same person, and not separate people'.[11] However, some caution is appropriate here. Analogously, the self-portrayals discernible in letters and diaries, whilst not formally fictions, are nevertheless verbal constructions, subject to heterotopic compilation and construal.

A third difficulty is the diversified terrain of ecofeminist thought itself. Proponents disagree over whether or not to closely tie 'women' to 'nature'; there are 'spiritual' and 'social-constructionist', 'socialist' and 'transformative' iterations,[12] more recently also postcolonial, queer, animal-, plant-, and multispecies-orientated modes of ecocriticism. Scholars wrestle with apparently ineluctable tensions between a narrow ecofeminism that threatens to essentialise 'nature' or 'woman', and a broader anti-dualistic conceptualisation that threatens to blur or erase the 'feminist' element altogether, and thus lose its 'critical force'. Greta Gaard adds:

Rather than perpetuate the gendered and essentialist culture-nature dualism, [some] argue for the agency of nature and for a material feminism that reconceptualizes nature in ways that accounts for 'intra-actions' [...] between phenomena that are material, discursive, human, more-than-human, corporeal, and technological.[13]

Still useful is Gaard's 1993 definition:

[E]cofeminism's basic premise is that the ideology which authorizes oppressions such as those based on race, class, gender, sexuality, physical abilities, and species is the same ideology which sanctions the oppression of nature. [...] Its theoretical base is a sense of self most commonly expressed by women and various other non-dominant groups – a self that is interconnected with all life [and that] makes moral decisions on the basis of an ethic of responsibilities or care.[14]

Much of this echoes, for example, Woolf's gestures towards 'pattern', or Schreiner's iterations of 'unity', in their critiques of patriarchy and reason, and their calls for an ethic of nurturing. The question remains, nevertheless, about just how coherently and explicitly either writer linked the oppressions of women and of nature in practice.

Observations and intimations

'We begin with noticing', write Anna Tsing and Heather Swanson, with a curiosity about 'both lively and destructive connections' that have been obscured by the 'seductive simplifications' and 'singular notions of modernity'.[15] Both Schreiner and Woolf were keen observers of their respective natural worlds, from tiny insects to whole landscapes. The young Woolf was drafted by her father into not uncommon 'amateur naturalist' mode, retaining a good taxonomic knowledge of butterflies into adulthood. Both were tomboyish and outdoorsy as youngsters, both developing a lifelong 'joy of walking', through which 'the current of sensations & ideas' might become 'a fine thin sheet of perfect calm happiness'.[16] From observation can flow love. In the 'Times and Seasons' interlude in *African Farm*, Schreiner captures the process:

The rocks have been to us a blur of brown; we bend over them, and the disorganized masses dissolve into a many-coloured, many-shaped, carefully arranged form of existence [...] rainbow-tinted crystals, half-fused together [...] The flat plain has been to us a reach of monotonous red. We *look at* it, and every handful of sand starts into life. That wonderful people, the ants, we *learn to know*; see them make war and peace, play and work, and build their huge palaces. [...] The bitto flower has been for us a mere blur of yellow; we *find* its heart composed of a hundred perfect flowers, the homes of the tiny black people with red stripes.¹⁷

Looking, learning, discovering, finally humanising and identifying with even the inanimate. Schreiner wrote to Carpenter in 1887: '[s]ometimes you know I cannot believe that these chairs & tables & the walls & all the things about me are not alive. I love them so, inanimate things'.¹⁸ In 'The mark on the wall', Woolf also begins with furniture. The narrating consciousness wakes from dreams of horror, gratefully

> worshipping the chest of drawers, worshipping solidity, worshipping reality, worshipping the impersonal world which is a proof of some existence other than ours. [. . .] Wood is a pleasant thing to think about. It comes from a tree; and trees grow, and we don't know how they grow. For years and years they grow, without paying any attention to us, in meadows, in forests [. . .] I like to think of the tree itself: first the close dry sensation of being wood; then the grinding of the storm; then the slow, delicious ooze of sap.¹⁹

She goes on to imagine the tree feeling the feet of insects upon it, and, even after being felled, enjoying 'a million patient watchful lives still [. . .], all over the world, in bedrooms, in ships, on the pavement, lining rooms'. She rather winsomely imagines the tree as 'full of peaceful thoughts, happy thoughts'.²⁰ Despite the ironic touches, Woolf's word 'worshipping' intimates that natural processes circulate both in and beyond human agency and vision. Although expressed in anthropomorphic, even near-numinous terms, she is not so far from extensive recent research suggesting that plants and their networked symbionts are in some fashion sentient, even agentive. Such intimations typically arose in solitude, in favourite contemplative places. One of Schreiner's was a sheltered ravine, a scene reiterated in *Undine* and *African Farm*; Woolf's was a particular 'hollow' where she felt she

> entered into a sanctuary; a nunnery; had a religious retreat; of great agony once; & always some terror: [. . .] & got then to a consciousness of what I call 'reality': [. . .] something abstract; but residing in the downs or sky; beside which nothing matters; in which I shall rest & continue to exist.²¹

For both, streams also served to release thought. Woolf, finding in a sense 'a room of one's own' in nature, begins the work of that title with her 'sitting on the banks of a river a week or two ago in fine October weather, lost in thought [which] – to call it by a prouder name than it deserved – had let its line down into the stream'.²² This reappears ecstatically with Rhoda in *The Waves*, who, sitting 'by the stream's trembling edge [. . .] thaws', becomes 'unsealed' and 'incandescent', immersed 'in a deep tide fertilising'.²³ A parallel stream-bank contemplation appears in the second section of Schreiner's essay 'The Dawn of Civilisation'. After meditating on war and objections to it, reminiscent of *Three Guineas*, Schreiner inserts a 'homely personal confession of a believer in human unity':

> When a child, not yet nine years old, I walked out one morning [. . .] till I came to a place where a little stream ran [. . .] between soft, earthy banks; at one place a large slice of earth had fallen away from the bank on the other side, and it had made a little island a few feet wide with water flowing all around it. It was covered with wild mint and a weed with yellow flowers and long waving grasses. [. . .]
> My heart was heavy [. . .] the whole Universe seemed to be weighing on me. [. . .] And then, as I sat looking at that little, damp, dark island, the sun began to rise. It shot its light across the long, grassy slopes of the mountains and struck the little mound of earth in the water. [. . .] And, as I looked at that almost intolerable beauty [. . .] I seemed to see a world in which creatures [were] no more hated and crushed, in which the strong helped the weak, and men understood each other, and forgave each other [. . .] and I was in it, and a part of it. And there came to me, as I sat there, a joy such as never besides have I experienced.²⁴

Repeatedly, she revelled in non-human, more-than-human presences, from 'red sand' to sky, stars and mountains, perhaps most readily to the tactile beauty of plants as 'living things'.²⁵

In a very different milieu, the family retreat at St Ives, Woolf wrote similarly:

> I was looking at the flower bed by the front door; 'That is the whole', I said. I was looking at a plant with a spread of leaves; and it seemed suddenly plain that the flower itself was part of the earth; that a ring enclosed what was the flower; and that was the real flower; part earth; part flower.²⁶

Woolf experiences this fusion as a 'shock', a 'revelation'. 'Nature' does not remain objectively 'out there': it becomes 'real' and 'whole' for Woolf 'by putting it into words', and through that fusion of 'severed parts' she finds 'a great delight':

> From this I reach what I might call a philosophy; at any rate it is a consistent idea of mine; that behind the cotton wool is hidden a pattern; that we – I mean all human beings – are connected with this; that the whole world is a work of art; that we are parts of the work of art. [. . .] We are the thing itself.²⁷

The point here is – as numerous recent critics argue – there can be no concept of 'nature' distinct from human perception; it acquires significance only through the imagination. Donna Haraway argues that there is only 'natureculture' and 'symbiogenesis'.[28] Artistry itself offers a portal into integration, into a kind of phenomenological ecosystem that includes the human imagination. Thus in *The Waves*, while others merely 'brush the surface of the world', Woolf depicts Louis as similarly 'alone' and integrating,

> standing by the wall among the flowers. [. . .] I hold a stalk in my hand. I am the stalk. My roots go down to the depths of the world, through earth dry with brick, and damp earth, through veins of lead and silver. I am all fibre.[29]

This is not far from Schreiner's delving beneath the surface of things to recognise common organic patternings. In dissecting a dead goose, 'we' discover that

> [e]ach branch of the blood vessels is comprised of a trunk, bifurcating and rebifurcating into the most delicate, hair-like threads, symmetrically arranged. We are struck with its singular beauty [. . .] Of that same exact shape and outline is our thorn-tree seen against the sky in mid-winter; of that shape also is delicate metallic tracery between our rocks; [. . .] so shaped are the antlers of the horned beetle.[30]

This is not the diagrammatic Darwinian tree of evolutionary genealogies, more an intimation of belonging through analogy, or what Haraway calls 'involutionary' interrelations.[31] The two metaphors are not mutually exclusive: both imaginaries imply that one 'sap flows through us all' within a complex immensity that 'we among the branches cannot see'. Schreiner resists, moreover, the caricature of the Darwinian sense of Nature as a 'chance jumble', a 'weltering chaos', and postulates rather a 'deep union', a unified 'living thing, a *One*'.[32]

Still, being diminished to a single twiglet in that vast tree, or contemplating such dissolutions of self, can also be existentially terrifying. At points Schreiner felt reduced to meaninglessness, a 'miserable worm, a speck within a speck, an imperceptible atom'.[33] It can even become paranoiac, as for Septimus Warren Smith in *Mrs Dalloway*. Even at their strongest, intimate observations and concomitant responses of love, belonging and interfusion are necessary but not sufficient conditions for ecofeminism. Contradictory implications evident in even these few examples also haunt ecofeminism as a project, pre-eminently the juxtapositions of violence and love, and the shift from materiality to language and representation. There is no simple move from aesthetics to ethics, from the material to the imaginary, from solitude to social responsibility, from diversity to unity.

How unified is 'unity'?

In *From Man to Man*, Rebekah, who professes to have advanced from a Christian view of the universe as 'a thing of shreds and patches', a 'heap of toys', to one of 'a whole [that] lives in all its parts',[34] thinks:

> Between the furthest star and the planet earth we live on, [. . .] between man, plant, bird, beast and clod of earth, everywhere the close internetted lines of interaction stretch; nowhere are we able to draw a sharp dividing line, nowhere find an isolated existence.[35]

Schreiner herself wrote:

> When I was a little child of five & sat alone among the tall weeds at the back of our house, this ?perpee perception of the unity of all things, & that they were alive, & that I was part of them, was as clear & overpowering to me as it is today.[36]

Woolf is more tentative, but Eleanor in *The Years* asks the crucial questions:

> [I]s there a pattern, a theme, recurring, like music, half-remembered, half foreseen? [. . .] a gigantic pattern, momentarily perceptible? The thought gave her extreme pleasure: that there was a pattern. But who makes it? Who thinks it?[37]

Intimations of 'unity' (with the material cosmos, with other animals, occasionally even with other humans), induces impulses or hopes of recharged love and generosity. How sustainable, and how ecofeminist, are Schreiner and Woolf's respective intimations?

Schreiner in particular seems torn between expressing her sense of underlying unity in religious or in scientific-materialist terms. Effectively, like her era more generally, she was in transition between the two – between, as it were, the Book of Genesis and Herbert Spencer's *First Principles*, working through a wider 'secularisation of the moral imagination'.[38] She wrote to Karl Pearson in 1886:

> I wish you could go once to my old African world & know what it is to stand quite alone on a mountain in the still blazing sunshine, & the clear, clear blue above you, & the great unbroken plains stretching away as far as you can see, with out a trace of the human creature [. . .] then you would know how the one God was invented. [. . . W]hen one is in contact with that vast, dry, bright nature, one is conscious of oneself, of inanimate nature – & of something else. It is this something else that has framed those religions in which there is one, sole, almighty God.[39]

She wrote similarly to Rev. Lloyd in 1892: '[t]he stars are wonderful, the light, in a human eye is wonderful, the growing of a seed is wonderful; but is there anything more wonderful than the power which keeps together the particles, which in fact <u>constitutes</u> them?'.[40] This is integrative thinking of an intense order, but is it necessarily feminist?

Such observations have prompted Ruth Knechtel, for one, to recruit Schreiner to a modernised brand of 'pagan animism', or 'pantheism' (the two are not quite the same thing). In practice, Knechtel spends most of her article exploring Schreiner's abiding recourse to the nurturing and the maternal, and is rather thin on animism itself. She quotes Graham Harvey's loose definition of the 'new animists', who 'celebrate plurality, multiplicity, the many, and their entwined passionate entanglements'.[41] Closer to Schreiner's tenor is Bron Taylor's definition:

> *Animism* is a term that most fundamentally reflects a perception that spiritual intelligences, or life-forces, animate natural entities and living things. [. . .] Animism may also involve communication or even communion with such intelligences or life-forces. Such a worldview usually enjoins respect if not reverence for and veneration of such intelligences and forces.[42]

Schreiner's depiction of Rebekah, sitting on a hilltop and experiencing the 'strange impersonal [. . .] Nirvana like quiet' of contemplating nature,[43] is one of many possible supportive examples.

Despite animism's turn towards earthy, organic, and ethically loaded continuities, Knechtel does not connect it with ecofeminism as such. She might well have done so, since Schreiner's apprehensions of beauty in nature repeatedly spill into caring reverence of an explicitly maternal kind. Moreover, these apprehensions are frequently refracted through natural comparisons; or, more accurately, human nurturing is seen as continuous with, and/or inspired by, nurturing amongst non-human creatures. She wrote, for instance, of

> mornings in the bush at Ganna Hoek, where I used to go & lie under the rock & the birds used to come quite close to me & make love [. . .] & one saw in one's mind all the love & wonder to the end the little eggs coming, & the nest & the new little lives.[44]

The crucial phrase there is 'in one's mind': the continuity is in a sense an imaginary, a construction. This welding of the natural and maternal is, nevertheless, one with which at least some ecofeminists would agree.

Assertions of 'unity' can drift into vacuous statements or endless deferrals, precisely because it can only manifest experientially, at the very edge of the inexpressible (as indeed Spencer had argued). As Schreiner stated, '[w]ords are very poor things'.[45] Similarly, Woolf professed to entertain some sort of 'transcendental' philosophy, but shied from expressing it further. How would one tell whether the perception of pattern (or unity, or Spencer's 'Unknown Reality',[46] or divine writ) is pre-existent or purely imagined? How to reconcile such notions with observable conflicting, fragmenting, decaying realities? It might be more analytically fruitful for now to approach the issue in more circumscribed ways (as in practice do many ecofeminists). We can provisionally parse three interconnected spheres within which both writers tried to transcend established dichotomies: male/female, human/animal and spiritual/Darwinian.

Sex manifestation

Crucial to the explicitly feminist project of countering patriarchal dominance is questioning, realigning or reconceptualising the dualism of female and male. Both Schreiner and Woolf resoundingly critiqued masculinist dominance, from war-mongering to constraining women within marriage, in the labour market and above all in creative opportunity. How to address, escape or transform this systemic problem is the trickier question. Both writers, interestingly, have been aligned with an idealised projection of *androgyny*, offered as a means to transcend prevailing, heteronormative rigidities of sex and gender. In both cases the avowed androgyny has further been posited as symbolic of wider boundary-blurring or -erasure. Woolf scholars point to the ambiguous protagonist of *Orlando* (1928) and the brief discussion of androgyny in 'A Room of One's Own', which has been both praised and roundly critiqued.[47] In any event, Woolf makes no connection of androgyny to the natural world, or to anything recognisably ecofeminist. Nor does Schreiner's parallel formulation of the 'new man' and 'new woman', by which the former potentially evinces qualities of 'tenderness', the latter of 'virile' strength. Inner personal re-socialising, she hoped, might thereby effect societal transformation. Berkman entitles one chapter of *The Healing Imagination* 'The Androgynous Vision',[48] although this was a notion about which Schreiner could be 'vague and inconsistent'.[49] Even Schreiner's most fluid and rebellious characters – Lyndall, Gregory Rose, Rebekah – reflecting their creator's own ambivalences, *fail* to attain a successful or matured androgyny.

Still, Berkman highlights Schreiner's insistence on 'the circumstantial, heterogeneous, and versatile nature of gender traits and roles'.[50] She refers tangentially to a remarkable passage in Schreiner's uncompleted preface to Wollstonecraft's *Vindication*,[51] in which Schreiner knowledgeably outlines the 'exceedingly protean shapes' and 'wonderful transformations' in sexual identities in other realms of nature.[52] In some sea-creatures, she elaborates, the male form is dominant; in some insects the female. In the snail, 'both male and female are contained perfectly in each individual'.[53] Some birds are monogamous, some polygamous; some fish swap gender roles; sea-horse males carry the young. The full history of this variability is 'yet to be written', she notes, but even a 'cursory glance' reveals that 'nothing has been more fluid [. . .] than the sex manifestations', including within the 'narrower limits' of human relations.[54] To Pearson she insisted that, in exploring the origins of sex, 'we must study not only the human embryo, but the first forms of life', and that in experimenting with sexuality her argument was 'drawn mainly from the laws of growth in the animal world (say, the growth of a shell-fish!)'.[55] Sexuality was variable but fundamental, and ecosystemic: 'Every material and external social surrounding affecting sex manifestation and sex conditions reacts on all else'.[56] Though Schreiner's feelings about sexuality, motherhood and matrimony in her own life proved periodically conflicted, here she certainly approaches certain ecofeminist views. (Woolf, in contrast, decried what she called 'the religion & superstition [. . .] the hush & mystery of motherhood').[57] This all overlaps with our other spheres of interest – continuity with the animals, and Darwinian perspectives.

One with animals

Both Woolf and Schreiner evinced a range of responses to animal life, many if not most sympathetic, even familial. Both wielded continuities and contrasts between 'human' and 'animal' to critique human limitations and pretensions. But to what extent can their empathetic relationship with animals be deemed either 'ecological' or 'feminist'? An allied problematic here is the conventional distinction between domestic and wild. Most treatments of 'ecology' deal with relations between humans and 'nature-as-wilderness'. 'Wild' by definition is that which is distinct from the acculturated human, so it requires some redefinition of terms to extend an 'ecosystem' to the domestic sphere of pets, who are at once liminal to and enabling of both wildness and human nurturing.[58] Schreiner and Woolf owned pets, primarily dogs, adoring and identifying with them to varying degrees. From Woolf's diaries and letters one gains the impression that dogs were ever-present but not exactly central to her attentions. *Flush* is famously her spaniel's-view fictional account of the Brownings' life-world; she termed Flush, like at least one of her series of family pets, 'a human dog'.[59] *Flush* is anthropomorphically empathetic and insightful about an imagined dog experience of the world, especially via scent, and even dreams. There are limits, however, both technically and personally, and ultimately it was the human life she was interested in illuminating.[60] (The same can be said of the snail's-eye view of people deployed in her short piece 'Kew Gardens').

For her part, Schreiner loved her own little dog Neta so much she insisted he be buried alongside her and her infant daughter on the heights of Buffelskop. Her fiction also offers examples of domesticated animals serving as vectors for compassion and caring. Her closest parallel to Flush is Doss, the dog in *African Farm* who acts materially and metonymically on many levels to breach the membranes between established categories, the human/animal dualism being only one.[61] Doss is, as Lyndall herself says, 'profoundly suggestive'.[62] At two points, foreshadowing similar scenes in *Flush*, Schreiner 'reveals' the very content of Doss's dreams, thereby enacting some coalescing of 'inner' worlds – but still 'only' imagined.

Doss is also the recipient of a mildly abusive kick from the departing villain, Bonaparte Blenkins.[63] Cruelty, the obverse of animal-human communality, is almost entirely perpetrated by men in these parallel depictions by each author. Woolf's *Diary* for 31 July 1918 recounts that she 'saw a dead horse [...] rather pathetic to me – to die in Oxford Street one hot afternoon, & to have been only a van horse'.[64] In the essay 'Dawn of Civilisation' (penned just down the road the year before), Schreiner writes:

> Three times I had seen an ox striving to pull a heavily loaded waggon up a hill, the blood and foam streaming from its mouth and nostrils as it struggled, and I had seen it fall dead, under the lash.[65]

She connects this viscerally with broader, systemic behaviours. She had also seen, for example, 'bands of convicts going past to work on the roads' with 'the terrible look in their eyes of a wild creature', and separately 'a pack of dogs set on by men to attack a strange dog, which had come among them and done no harm to anyone': 'Why did everyone press on everyone and try to make them do what they wanted? Why did the strong always crush the weak? Why did we hate and kill and torture?'.[66] Schreiner's sense that cruelties against racially different humans and against animals are allied in motivation and means, brings her close to another core assertion of modern ecofeminism: that the different vectors of violence are at their root patriarchal. As she encapsulated it: 'the man with the gun was always there'.[67] The syndrome extends from the domestic to the wild. Schreiner's essay continues: 'In the bush in the kloof below I had seen bush-bucks and little long-tailed monkeys that I loved so shot dead, not from any necessity but for the pleasure of killing'.[68] Rebekah in *From Man to Man* would save the wild creatures that her hunter husband Frank would sooner kill and indifferently kick aside. She summarises: 'what I wanted from living things was what they could give me, not what I could take from them'.[69]

Woolf's references to animal cruelty, though present, are sporadic and inconsistent. A visit to the zoo, for instance, seems torn between joyful excitement and sympathy for 'an Indian buffaloe [sic], with ingrowing toenails, poor beast, in a grotto of grey stone'.[70] On one issue she did engage more forcefully: the public debate over the Plumage Bill. She pronounced herself 'wholly against the plumage trade', while admitting that she still wore ostrich feathers, and ultimately her concern was over women's dignity, not the welfare of egrets, let alone their native environments:

> To torture birds is one thing, and to be unjust to women is another [. . .] I am not writing as a bird, not even as a champion of birds; but as a woman [. . .] it seems to me more necessary to resent such an insult to women [. . .] than to protect egrets from extinction.[71]

This hardly seems committed ecofeminism. It should not occlude, however, Woolf's gestures towards commonality with animals: she recalls once 'lying on the side of a hollow [. . .] & seeing a red hare loping up the side & thinking suddenly "This is Earth life". I seemed to see how earthy it all was, & I myself an evolved kind of hare'.[72] However, she did not take this very far in an ecofeminist direction.

Schreiner's assertions of human-animal commonalities are more systematically embedded within wider nature to create what might be termed an ecology of binding emotion. Schreiner (or Rebekah) postulates human caring as a seamless continuation of natural cooperation. While acknowledging struggle and predation, Rebekah argues that 'to regard this destructive element in existence as the keynote to life on earth is a strange inversion'.[73] Citing, among other examples, meerkats' 'passionate devotion and self-sacrifice' for the good of the group, she discerns a 'binding moving creative force [that] moves at the very heart of things':

> From the mysterious drawing together of amoeba to amoeba, their union and increase, on through all the forms of sentient life [. . .] always this stretching-out, uniting, creative force [. . .] drawing together creatures of like and unlike kinds, bringing into all the forms of friendship and union and love, it lies at the root of existence.[74]

Schreiner's formulation foreshadows both various ecofeminists and the biology of symbiosis post-Lynn Margulis. Surely she would be fascinated and encouraged by the so-called 'Postmodern Synthesis' of recent studies into microbial and bacterial roles in horizontal gene transfer, multispecies existence and symbiogenesis (a term in circulation as early as 1910). According to Haraway, feminist thought has been instrumental in the field.[75] Such challenges to patriarchal reason's exclusionary parsing of physical from psychical, material from spiritual, constitute another central plank of ecofeminism's project.

Darwin's entangled bank

As we have seen, Woolf's and Schreiner's respective intuitions of, or desires for, underlying patterns or 'creative forces' governed by cooperation or even love seem at least quasi-spiritual, allied to a sort of moralistic animism. This runs counter to their awareness of a prevailing notion of Nature being no more than a meaningless broil of uncaring predation – in crude shorthand, 'Darwinian'. Both writers were acquainted with the epoch-making works of Charles Darwin (the Woolf and Darwin families were friends). Though it is often asserted that Woolf 'read Darwin', and she and her characters refer at times to evolutionary notions (primordial swamps, descent from the apes), she scarcely incorporated evolutionary ideas in more depth than those omnipresent in common discourse. The echoes of Darwin are perhaps strongest in *The Voyage Out*, the solitary novel of hers venturing into a non-English wilderness. Woolf had not visited the Amazon herself and, Gillian Beer suggests, drew in part on Darwin's earlier *Voyage of the Beagle*.[76] Nevertheless, the descriptions of the jungle were designed primarily, Woolf wrote in 1916, 'to give the feeling of a vast tumult of life, as various and disorderly as possible'.[77] That sense of unpredictable changes unfolding with neither discernible teleology nor a favoured position for humans, of processes characterised primarily by unforgiving predation, was what frightened most people about Darwinism. Yet such tumult was present, Woolf discerned with the greater precision of first-hand observation, even in 'soft & sappy'[78] English environs. In a particularly arresting passage, she described how birds, though beautiful, stab 'savagely' into an 'unlit world' of rotting leaf and mould and

> spiked the soft, monstrous body of the defenceless worm, pecked again and yet again, and left it to fester. Down there among the roots where the flowers

decayed, gusts of dead smells were wafted; drops formed on the bloated sides of swollen things. [...] Yellow excretions were exuded by slugs, and now and again an amorphous body with a head at either end swayed slowly from side to side.[79]

Though conveyed with disgust rather than scientific detachment, this ecosystemic description strongly resembles Darwin's own image in *Origin of Species* of the 'entangled bank', whose 'web of complex relations' exemplified the perpetual 'war between insect and insect – between insects, snails, and other animals with birds and beasts of prey – all striving to increase, and all feeding on each other and on the trees or their seeds'.[80] That the process involved 'great destruction'[81] was undeniable, but Darwin also stressed that he used the phrase 'Struggle for Existence' in 'a large and metaphorical sense'[82] that included the mutualisms and symbiotic dependencies that would be amplified by later ecofeminists. Moreover, he was far from insensitive to 'beautiful diversity',[83] even a kind of 'grandeur'[84] in the process. His theory was also premised on evolutionary and genealogical kinship with other life-forms, as much as on the separation of species over time.

Schreiner responded to evolutionary ideas as presented first by Spencer, who in certain respects differed from Darwin, and later by Darwin himself (she read *Descent of Man* rather than *Origin of Species*). An admixture of these ideas was incorporated into Rebekah's extended rumination on the evolutionary emergence of the human in *From Man to Man*. Rebekah (and presumably Schreiner herself) recorded reading Darwin's more technical work, *Variation of Plants and Animals under Domestication*.[85] The quasi-Socratic argument pursued through the crucial 'Raindrops in the Avenue' chapter comes close to broaching ecofeminist ideas. It deserves more thorough analysis than critics have accorded it. Neither Carolyn Burdett's nor Hilary Bedder's analyses pick up an ecofeminist thread, though both touch on Spencer's influence – notably Rebekah's use of his (not Darwin's) coinage 'survival of the fittest', and the idea that observable physical laws course through both non-human nature and human society in a progression towards complexity and perfection. To material processes, Bedder argues, Schreiner wished to 'add the noumenal', though 'add' feels wrong: Schreiner/Rebekah seek something more integral if ultimately inexplicable.[86]

That the idealism of *From Man to Man* remains unfulfilled (and is perhaps unfulfillable) manifests in Rebekah's gloomy fate. Schreiner's hopeful vision that 'what you strive for something strives for; *and nothing in the Universe is quite alone*' (Schreiner's italics), tended periodically to wilt in a world

> where creature preys on creature, and man, the strongest of all, preys more than all [. . .] In a world where the little ant-lion digs his hole in the sand and lies hidden at the bottom for the small ant to fall in and be eaten, and the leopard's eyes gleam yellow through bushes as it watches the little bush-buck coming down to the fountain to drink, and millions and millions of human beings use all they know, and their wonderful hands, to kill and press down on others, what hope could there ever be?[87]

This perennial, irresolvable issue could at times reduce Schreiner to existential despair, moments at which she lost sight of the ideal of systemic change and reform of the patriarchy, ecofeminism's overarching goal. Ultimately she felt she had control only of the personal: '[i]n your own heart strive to kill out all hate'.[88] There is something of the New Testament in that formulation.

Conclusion

Much might be added to this sketch. It seems pointless, if not impossible, to try securely to align either Woolf or Schreiner with any of the sub-strands of ecofeminism: one can cherry-pick gestures presaging several of them. Broadly, however, the two writers, in challenging 'unfeeling human systems of oppression and domination', surely probe several of the questions with which Rosemarie Tong concludes – pre-eminently, what it will take to 'stop thinking dichotomously [and] to stop destroying what we are in fact: an interdependent whole, a unity that exists in and through, and not despite, its diversity'.[89] Though both writers attacked patriarchy in multiple ways, neither absolved women entirely either, thus moving already towards some ecofeminists' attempts to transcend sex/gender identifications. Both noted human assaults on the natural world, at times with misanthropic bite: humans, in their 'congested' cities, were a 'stain', lamented Schreiner.[90] Rebekah scoffs on her behalf at man's self-flattery in 'destroying all he can destroy, and using and consuming all he can use or consume'.[91] A century later, in the midst of anthropogenic mass extinctions, we are reaping the desiccated fruits of that implacable destructiveness. Though we must probably agree with Bonnie Kime Scott that Woolf – likewise Schreiner – cannot be judged as more than 'proto-ecofeminist';[92] the perspectives they foreshadow are more necessary than ever before in human history.

Works Cited

Bedder, Hilary. 'Olive Schreiner's *From Man to Man*: Alternative Models of Reality and the Problematics of Human Reasoning'. *English in Africa* 47, no. 2 (2020): 99–118.
Beer, Gillian. *Virginia Woolf: The Common Ground*. Edinburgh: Edinburgh University Press, 1996.
Berkman, Joyce Avrech. *The Healing Imagination of Olive Schreiner: Beyond South African Colonialism*. Amherst: University of Massachusetts Press, 1989.
Briggs, Julia. *Virginia Woolf: An Inner Life*. London: Penguin, 2005.
Burdett, Carolyn. *Olive Schreiner and the Progress of Feminism: Evolution, Gender, Empire*. Basingstoke: Palgrave, 2001.
Clayton, Cherry, ed. *Olive Schreiner*. Johannesburg: McGraw-Hill, 1983.
Cornwell, Gareth, Dirk Klopper and Craig Mackenzie, eds. *The Columbia Guide to South African Literature in English since 1945*. New York: Columbia University Press, 2011.
Darwin, Charles. *The Origin of Species by Means of Natural Selection*, edited by J. W Burrow. Harmondsworth: Penguin, 1968.
Driver, Dorothy. 'Olive Schreiner's Poetics of Plants'. Amazwi Museum: Makhanda, 2019.
Gaard, Greta, ed. *Ecofeminism: Women, Animals, Nature*. Philadelphia: Temple University Press, 1993.
—. 'Ecofeminism Revisited: Rejecting Essentialism and Re-placing Species in a Material Feminist Environmentalism'. *Feminist Formations* 23, no. 2 (2011): 26–53.
Haraway, Donna. 'Symbiogenesis, Sympoiesis and Art Science Activisms for Staying with the Trouble'. In *Arts of Living on a Damaged Planet: Ghosts and Monsters of the Anthropocene*, edited by Anna Tsing, Heather Swanson, Elaine Gan and Nils Bubandt. Minneapolis: University of Minnesota Press, 2017.
Kissack, Mike and Michael Titlestad. 'Olive Schreiner and the Secularization of the Moral Imagination'. *English in Africa* 33, no. 1 (2006): 23–46.
Klopper, Dirk. 'Between Man, Woman and Dog: Olive Schreiner's *The Story of an African Farm*.' *Safundi* 19, no. 4 (2018): 419–37.
Knechtel, Ruth. 'Olive Schreiner's Pagan Animism: An Underlying Unity'. *English Literature in Transition*. 53, no. 3 (2010): 259–78.
Kostkowska, Justyna. *Ecocriticism and Women Writers*. London: Palgrave Macmillan, 2013.
McMurray, Andrew. 'Figures in a Ground: An ecofeminist study of Olive Schreiner's *The Story of an African Farm*'. *Canadian Studies in English* 20, no. 4 (1994): 431–48.
Munslow Ong, Jade. '"Too uncompromising a figure to be so disposed of": Virginia Woolf and/on Olive Schreiner'. *English Studies in Africa* 65, no. 1 (2022): 31–45.
Saracino, Maria. 'The Diamond and the Flaw'. In *The Flawed Diamond: Essays on Olive Schreiner*, edited by Itala Vivan, 146–59. Sydney: Dangaroo Press, 1991.

Schoeman, Karel. *Olive Schreiner: A Woman in South Africa 1855–1881*. Jonathan Ball: Parklands, 1991.

Schreiner, Olive. 'The Dawn of Civilisation'. In *Words in Season*, edited by Stephen Gray, 205–14. Johannesburg: Penguin, 2005.

—. *From Man to Man or Perhaps Only –*, edited by Dorothy Driver. Claremont: University of Cape Town Press, 2015.

—. 'Introduction to *A Vindication*'. In *Words in Season*, edited by Stephen Gray, 19–28. Johannesburg: Penguin, 2005.

—. *The Story of an African Farm*. Oxford: Oxford University Press, 1998.

Scott, Bonnie Kime. 'Virginia Woolf and Critical Uses of Ecofeminism'. *Virginia Woolf Miscellany*, 81 (2012): 8–10.

Showalter, Elaine. 'Introduction'. In *The Story of an African Farm*, vii–xxi. New York: Bantam, 1995.

Spencer, Herbert. *First Principles*. 5th ed. London: Williams & Norgate, 1890.

Stevens, Valerie. 'Human-Animal "Mother-love" in Novels by Olive Schreiner'. *English Literature in Transition* 61, no. 2 (2018): 147–73.

Swanson, Heather, Anna Tsing, Nils Bubandt and Elaine Gan. 'Introduction: Bodies Tumbled into Bodies'. In *Arts of Living on a Damaged Planet: Ghosts and Monsters of the Anthropocene*, edited by Anna Tsing, Heather Swanson, Elaine Gan and Nils Bubandt. Minneapolis: University of Minnesota Press, 2017.

Taylor, Bron. 'From the Ground Up: Dark Green Religion and the Environmental Future'. In *Ecology and the Environment: Perspectives from the Humanities*, edited by Donald Swearer, 89–107. Cambridge: Harvard University Press, 2008.

Tong, Rosemarie Putnam. *Feminist Thought*. 2nd ed. St Leonards NSW: Allen & Unwin, 1998.

Wilkinson, Jane. 'Nature and Art in Olive Schreiner's *The Story of an African Far*'. In *The Flawed Diamond: Essays on Olive Schreiner*, edited by Itala Vivan, 107–20. Sydney: Dangaroo Press, 1991.

Woolf, Virginia. *A Room of One's Own*. San Diego: Harcourt Brace, 1957.

—. *Congenial Spirits: The Selected Letters of Virginia Woolf*, edited by Joanne Trautmann Banks. New York: Harcourt Brace Jovanovich, 1989.

—. *Flush*, edited by Kate Flint. Oxford: Oxford University Press, 1998.

—. *Moments of Being: Autobiographical Writings*, edited by Jeanne Schulkind. London: Pimlico, 2002.

—. 'Mark on the Wall'. In *Street Haunting*. London: Penguin, 2005.

—. *The Diary of Virginia Woolf*, edited by Anne Olivier Bell. 4 vols. New York: Harcourt Brace Jovanovich, 1977.

—. *The Waves*. London: Penguin, 1991.

—. *The Years*. London: Vintage, 2000.

—. *Three Guineas*. New York: Harcourt Brace & Co, 2001.

Wylie, Dan. 'The Anthropomorphic Ethic: Fiction and the Animal Mind in Virginia Woolf's *Flush* and Barbara Gowdy's *The White Bone*'. *Interdisciplinary Studies in Literature and Environment* 9, no. 2 (2002): 115–32.

—. 'Review: Kostkowska, *Ecocriticism and Women Writers*'. *Partial Answers* 12, no. 2 (2014): 396–400.

Letters

Olive Schreiner to Edward Carpenter, 28 December 1887. *Olive Schreiner Letters Online.*
Olive Schreiner to Henry Havelock Ellis, 25 December 1884. *Olive Schreiner Letters Online.*
Olive Schreiner to Henry Havelock Ellis, 13 May 1890. *Olive Schreiner Letters Online.*
Olive Schreiner to J. T. Lloyd, 29 October 1892. *Olive Schreiner Letters Online.*
Olive Schreiner to Karl Pearson, 16 June 1886. *Olive Schreiner Letters Online.*
Olive Schreiner to Karl Pearson, July 1886. *Olive Schreiner Letters Online.*
Olive Schreiner to Karl Pearson, 10 July 1886. *Olive Schreiner Letters Online.*
Olive Schreiner to Karl Pearson, 10 September 1886. *Olive Schreiner Letters Online.*
Olive Schreiner to Karl Pearson, 25 January 1887. *Olive Schreiner Letters Online.*

Notes

1. Schreiner to Pearson, July 1886, *Olive Schreiner Letters Online*, (OSLO).
2. Woolf, *Diary*, 1:43.
3. Schoeman, *Schreiner*, 338.
4. Quoted in Clayton, *Schreiner*, 93–4.
5. Showalter, 'Introduction'; Munslow Ong, 'Too uncompromising'.
6. Cornwell, *South African Literature*, 150.
7. Berkman, *Healing Imagination*, 159.
8. See Alt, *Virginia Woolf and the Study of Nature* (2010); Czarnecki and Rohman, *Virginia Woolf and the Natural World* (2011); Scott, *In the Hollow of the Wave* (2012); Swanson, ed. *Virginia Woolf Miscellany* (2013).
9. Scott, 'Virginia Woolf', 9.
10. Kostkowska, *Ecocriticism and Women Writers*, 12–28. For more detailed critique, see Wylie, 'Review'.
11. Woolf, *Congenial Spirits*, 298.
12. Tong, *Feminist Thought*, 246–77.
13. Gaard, 'Ecofeminism Revisited', 42. Going even further, contributors to Tsing et al., *Arts of Living on a Damaged Planet* (2018) question the very concept of the acculturated individual.
14. Gaard, *Ecofeminism*, 1–2.
15. Swanson et al. 'Bodies,' M7.
16. Woolf, *Diary*, 4:246.
17. Schreiner, *The Story of an African Farm*, 116–17, emphasis added.
18. Schreiner to Carpenter, 28 December 1887, OSLO.
19. Woolf, 'Mark on the Wall', 32–33.
20. Woolf, 'Mark on the Wall', 25–34.
21. Woolf, *Diary*, 3:196.
22. Woolf, *Room*, 5.

23. Woolf, *Waves*, 41.
24. Schreiner, 'Dawn', 209–12.
25. Schreiner to Havelock Ellis, 13 May 1890, *OSLO*.
26. Woolf, *Moments of Being*, 82.
27. Woolf, *Moments of Being*, 84.
28. Haraway, 'Symbiogenesis'.
29. Woolf, *Waves*, 7.
30. Schreiner, *The Story of an African Farm*, 118.
31. Haraway, 'Symbiogenesis', M27.
32. Schreiner, *The Story of an African Farm*, 118, Schreiner's italics.
33. Schreiner, 'Dawn', 212.
34. Schreiner, *From Man to Man*, 142, 143, 144.
35. Schreiner, *From Man to Man*, 144.
36. Schreiner to Lloyd, 29 October 1892, *OSLO*.
37. Woolf, *The Years*, 323.
38. Kissack and Titlestad, 'Secularisation'.
39. Schreiner to Pearson, 16 June 1886, *OSLO*, Schreiner's italics.
40. Schreiner to Lloyd, 29 October 1892, *OSLO*.
41. Knechtel, 'Schreiner's Pagan Animism', 260.
42. Taylor, 'From the Ground Up', 92.
43. Schreiner to Pearson, 10 July 1886, *OSLO*.
44. Schreiner to Havelock Ellis, 25 December 1884, *OSLO*.
45. Schreiner to Lloyd, 29 October 1892, *OSLO*.
46. Spencer, *First Principles*, 559.
47. Showalter, 'Introduction', 264.
48. Berkman, *Healing Imagination*, 124–45.
49. Berkman, *Healing Imagination*, 142.
50. Berkman, *Healing Imagination*, 128.
51. Berkman, *Healing Imagination*, 91.
52. Schreiner, *Words in Season*, 22.
53. Schreiner, *Words in Season*, 22.
54. Schreiner, *Words in Season*, 23.
55. Schreiner to Pearson, 10 September 1886; Schreiner to Pearson, 25 January 1887, *OSLO*.
56. Schreiner, 'Introduction to *A Vindication*,' 23.
57. Woolf, *Diary*, 4:264.
58. See Stevens, 'Human-Animal "Mother-Love"'.
59. Woolf, *Congenial Spirits*, 60.
60. For extended discussion see Wylie, 'Anthropomorphic Ethic'.
61. See Klopper, 'Between Man, Woman and Dog'.
62. Schreiner, *The Story of an African Farm*, 195.
63. Schreiner, *The Story of an African Farm*, 99.
64. Woolf, *Diary*, 1:176.
65. Schreiner, 'Dawn', 210.
66. Schreiner, 'Dawn', quoted in *Words in Season*, 210.
67. Schreiner, 'Dawn', 210.
68. Schreiner, 'Dawn', 210.
69. Schreiner, *From Man to Man*, 246.
70. Woolf, *Diary*, 1:131.

71. Woolf, *Diary*, 1:121; see Briggs, *Woolf*, 115.
72. Woolf, *Congenial Spirits*, 190.
73. Schreiner, *From Man to Man*, 174.
74. Schreiner, *From Man to Man*, 173, 175.
75. Haraway, 'Symbiogenesis', as well as other essays in Tsing et al., *Arts of Living*.
76. Beer, *Common Ground*, 42.
77. Woolf, *Congenial Spirits*, 90.
78. Woolf, *Congenial Spirits*, 117.
79. Woolf, *Waves*, 55.
80. Darwin, *Origins*, 125–6.
81. Darwin, *Origins*, 129.
82. Darwin, *Origins*, 116.
83. Darwin, *Origins*, 126.
84. Darwin, *Origins*, 429.
85. Schreiner, *From Man to Man*, 400.
86. Bedder, 'Olive Schreiner's *From Man to Man*', 103.
87. Schreiner, 'Dawn', 210.
88. Schreiner, 'Dawn', 210.
89. Tong, *Feminist Thought*, 277.
90. Schreiner, 'Dawn', 212.
91. Schreiner, *From Man to Man*, 183.
92. Scott, 'Virginia Woolf', 8.

Part II

Race and Anti-Racism

Chapter 4

Olive Schreiner and C. F. Andrews: Utopia and Paths to Anti-Racism and Decolonisation
Barnita Bagchi

This chapter discusses aspects of Olive Schreiner's writing and thought in relation to those of C. F. Andrews. Andrews was a British Christian writer and social actor, an anti-colonial, anti-racist and activist against the exploitation of indentured labourers in parts of the world ranging from South Africa to India and Fiji. He spent large parts of his life in India and is buried in a cemetery in Kolkata. Andrews was also a close friend of key Indian figures espousing decolonisation, including M. K. Gandhi and Rabindranath Tagore. In June 1928, Andrews published an article titled 'South Africa and India: Olive Schreiner's Message' in the Calcutta-based *Modern Review*.[1] Summarising Schreiner's pamphlet *Closer Union* (1909), Andrews's article also compares the struggle for racial unity in South Africa with that in India.

Isabel Hofmeyr notes that '[t]he idea of Olive Schreiner in Calcutta is not one we often think of, but it is a conjunction which holds out exciting possibilities'.[2] Hofmeyr's article is the starting point for this chapter, which analyses Schreiner and Andrews, each in their own way a social dreamer and critical of aspects of racism. Andrews is also a critic of racism as vitiating Christianity and of the exploitative practice of indentured labour; he played a major role in its legal abolition.[3] In what follows, I discuss questions of race, decolonisation, religion and spirituality, and the social dreaming of utopia, analysing a speculative parable in Schreiner's posthumously published novel *From Man to Man, Or Perhaps Only –* (1926), before discussing Andrews's writing (especially his 1932 autobiography, *What I Owe to Christ*) in relation to Schreiner, his visit to South Africa, their mutual South African friend and anti-racist activist Betty Molteno, and Gandhi. Schreiner, Andrews, Gandhi and other mutual associates such as W. W. (or Willie) Pearson, Molteno and Tagore, all invoked here, were engaged in utopian thinking, or what Lyman Tower Sargent calls social dreaming.[4] Three faces of utopianism – the literary utopia, utopian practice and utopian social theory – are all illuminated by my analysis of aspects of Andrews's and Schreiner's work.[5]

Utopia, a connotative term, names a mode of human imagination and practice. Although its origins are traced to Renaissance Europe, it has increasingly been theorised in non-Eurocentric ways,[6] seen as manifesting across times and cultures. Fictional and non-fictional writings by the figures in focus in this chapter imagine a better world, propose utopian practice and describe utopian intentional communities such as Santiniketan, founded by Tagore, and Phoenix Farm, founded by Gandhi. Literary utopia is not always fictional, and marginal genres such as modern religious autobiography (like Andrews's) need to be seen as part of utopian literature. Our theorising of utopian imagination, especially in relation to race, colonialism and transnational networks and solidarities, is deepened, I contend, by analysis of selected writing by Schreiner, Andrews, and mutual associates.

Speculative Fictions Critiquing Racialised Domination in *From Man to Man*

One of the heroines of Schreiner's posthumously published novel *From Man to Man, or Perhaps Only –*, a white South African woman named Rebekah, who lives and suffers in a marriage with a patriarchal and authoritarian man, offers her children a speculative parable. Towards the beginning of the chapter 'Fireflies in the Dark',[7] we encounter an evocation of fireflies that 'glinted' among the roses and lilies of Rebekah's garden 'like dim stars',[8] connoting glimmers of illumination in a world of racist settler colonialism. We go on to read about the child Sartje, 'a little, yellow-brown, frizzly-haired girl she [Rebekah] had adopted five years before as a little baby and treated in all ways as her own child, except that it was taught to call her mistress'.[9] Sartje is the daughter of Rebekah's husband, Frank, and a Black African female servant, Clartje.[10] Sartje calls Rebekah not mother, but mistress, though she is brought up by Rebekah as her own daughter, together with Rebekah and Frank's biological sons. By Frank's diktat, Sartje is allowed to dine with the couple's white children only when Frank is away. Rebekah takes risks to further Sartje's well-being, yet Sartje's story also shows the constraints of a white settler society on an independent-minded white woman questioning racism and patriarchy.

The occasion for Rebekah's speculative story is that Frank Junior declares that other boys had ridiculed him because he was walking with Sartje, 'a nigger-girl!'; he will never, he says, walk with Sartje again. Rebekah now tells the assembled children the story of 'a strange, terrible, race of people, coming from I know not where, perhaps from the nearest star'.[11] There is thus the quality of a science fiction tale to Rebekah's story too. This alien race of people have 'terrible white faces', with skin 'as white as driven snow,' and hair 'like thick threads of solid gold'.[12] With many kinds of advanced technologies in their possession, the aliens think of the inhabitants of the earth as 'Inferior Races'.[13] 'They broke down our little countries and our little governments and our little laws, they took all the earth', writes Schreiner.[14] In the tale, as it unfolds, the most terrible element of the colonisation and domination that the earthlings experience is their self-hate: '[b]ecause they [the colonisers] despised *us*, we began to despise ourselves'.[15] The result is that most of the colonised earthlings 'died' – both metaphorically and literally – '[a]nd the strange white people said, "See, they are an inferior race; they melt away before us"'.[16] But, 'the wisest' of the inhabitants of the earth refused to 'fade away'.[17] 'We will grasp the new life, and live!' they affirmed.[18] Rebekah's dream ends there, and in what she says next, Rebekah makes clear that the evolution and history of humanity is part of 'THE WORLD'S BOOK'.[19] Each particular historical and social context needs to be seen in a vast, unfolding panorama of the evolution of humanity, and according to this perspective, too, the norms and dogmas of the South Africa of Rebekah's and Schreiner's time seem limited.

The future can actually be very different, believes Rebekah, who tells her children that 'the day will come when you will regret utterly every slighting, every unkind word or act that you have ever given place towards Sartje'.[20] Even if Sartje is 'alone in the world', she 'shall walk with me,' Rebekah says.[21] To this, Hughie, another of Rebekah's sons, replies that he too will walk with Sartje. Through Rebekah's parable, which shows the utopia of the white-faced strangers as being almost wholly dystopian for the earthlings colonised by them, Schreiner obliquely critiques white settler colonialism, and vindicates the possibility of an alternative social future in which those dominated, colonised and oppressed people continue to endure, in which they do not allow themselves to be ashamed of their own strengths, and in which they work for a more just world. By telling her speculative tale, Rebekah thus opens out to her children an estranging and speculative critical perspective on racialised society.

C. F. Andrews's Critique of Racialised Colonialism in South Africa

Reading Andrews and/on Schreiner reveals shared anti-racist and anti-colonial thinking. Andrews, who died in India in 1940, is still known in India today by the respectful epithet of Deena-Bandhu or Friend of the Poor, and revered as an activist for social justice and a benevolent ally of India's struggle for decolonisation. Expanding Andrews's initials, Gandhi called him Christ's Faithful Apostle, again a token of the respect in which the former held the latter. In 1913, when Andrews and Pearson travelled to visit Gandhi in South Africa (Andrews's visit lasted through 1915), it was with Tagore's blessings.[22] Schreiner's friend Molteno spoke at a meeting on 4 January 1914 to welcome Andrews.[23] It was during the subsequent stay that Andrews and Schreiner met, though the date is uncertain.[24]

Schreiner's connection to India was not only through Andrews, however. In 1909, Schreiner and her sister Ettie had travelled to Cape Town to see Gandhi leaving for a trip to Britain. In defiance of the racist authorities, Schreiner shook hands with Gandhi and expressed sympathy for the Indian cause. Gandhi was thrilled.[25] He wrote about Schreiner as follows:

> Olive Schreiner was a gifted lady popular in South Africa and well known wherever the English language is spoken. Ever since she wrote the book, she became famous as the authoress of Dreams. Her love for all mankind was unbounded. Love was written in her eyes. Although she belonged to such a distinguished family and was a learned lady, she was so simple in habits that she cleaned utensils in her house herself. Mr. Merriman, the Moltenos and the Schreiners had always espoused the cause of the Negroes. Whenever the rights of the Negroes were in danger, they stoutly stood up in their defence. They had kindly feelings for the Indians as well, though they made a distinction between Negroes and Indians. Their argument was that as the Negroes had been the inhabitants of South Africa long before the European settlers, the latter could not deprive them of their natural rights. But as for the Indians, it would not be unfair if laws calculated to remove the danger of their undue competition were enacted. All the same they had a warm corner in their hearts for Indians.[26]

According to Gandhi (and Andrews), Schreiner believed that Black Africans had a greater claim to rights and equality than the Indians in South Africa, though both felt Schreiner's undoubted sympathy for them, too. Gandhi's warm admiration for Schreiner is evident in the passage, as is his attempt to represent without hostility Schreiner's views that Indians, not being original inhabitants of South Africa, could be subject to laws that limited their rights. Andrews characterises Schreiner as 'a fearless champion of the African races'.[27] He writes:

> Few outside South Africa have realised how brave this frail woman was in her defence of the rights of the Bantu races, whom she loved. To the Indian immigrants also, although she never came into close contact with them, she held out a hand of sympathy and welcome. Brought up in the very midst of deep colour prejudices and racial antipathies, her outstanding fearlessness was all the more remarkable and significant.[28]

He had bought a copy of Schreiner's *A Closer Union: A Letter on the South African Union and the Principles of Government* (1909), or 'Closer Union', in a second-hand bookshop in Cape Town, about twenty years after the book was published.[29] Andrews notes that though the book was ignored by the public, it was 'prophetic of the future', and unrivalled in 'living interest' among other pamphlets from South Africa.[30] 'Closer Union' is 'a very noble plea for the inclusion of the Bantu races in the Union as an organic member of the body politic'.[31]

Andrews writes in this essay, further, that:

> [Schreiner] rises to heights of splendid eloquence and fervent enthusiasm, as she comes to the one subject that interests her most deeply of all – 'the native question.' The word 'native' has still to be used in South Africa, unfortunately, because it is, in actual speech, the one common word for the African. But Olive Schreiner herself did very much indeed to introduce the true word, 'Bantu' in order to signify all Africans resident in the South.[32]

He continues that, 'in spite of the depth of race and colour prejudice on every side' Schreiner and her circle of likeminded friends held that 'Bantu races should not be trodden under foot by the more powerful civilization from the west, which was determined at any cost to assert itself and to possess the land, with all the diamonds and gold that lay beneath it'.[33] He quotes from 'Closer Union' Schreiner's ominous sense of a terrible future if the Black population of South Africa are treated only as tools to be exploited:

> If blinded by the gain of the moment, we see nothing in our Bantu people but a vast engine of labour; if to us the Bantu labourer is not a man, but only a tool; if he is dispossessed entirely of the land, for which he now shows that large aptitude for peasant proprietorship, for the lack of which among their masses many great nations are decaying; if we force him permanently in his millions into the locations and compounds and slums of our cities, obtaining his labour cheaper, only to lose what the wealth of all the gold reefs and diamond mines could not return to us. If, uninstructed in the highest forms

of labour, without the rights of citizenship, his own social organisation broken up ... we reduce this vast mass to the condition of a great seething, ignorant proletariat – then I would rather draw a veil over the future of this land.[34]

Andrews picks up the idea of South Africa as a heterogeneous nation from Schreiner in 'Closer Union', and views India in similar manner. Discussing a passage in 'Closer Union', where the leader of such a heterogeneous nation is seen as analogous to a mother who brings up her own children but also the children of her husband with other women, he writes:

> Towards the end of her essay, Olive Schreiner works out a very beautiful simile of the mother having younger children of her own by a husband, who has brought into the family other children by a former marriage. She uses this, as an illustration of the difficulties confronting a great ruler, who has to rule with fairness and equity, not only over his own people, but also over other races. I have never before seen this imagery used in literature with reference to the problem of racial unity. When I read it I felt very deeply indeed, that in the Hindu-Muslim unity problem it was, really this singular grace of character, this sensitive sympathy for others, this consideration of humanity that was needed, far more than anything else.[35]

The connection with *From Man to Man* is clear: in Schreiner's novel, Rebekah is a mother who adopts a child, Sartje, born of an exploitative union of her husband with a Black woman. Rebekah is a nurturing leader, prizing diversity. Andrews connects Schreiner's model of a feminised, maternal leader to an Indian leader able to nurture many different kinds of people in a country. Interestingly, he tropes Hindus and Muslims as different races in India, with the underlying idea that India is a diversity of categories of people; race, here, functions more as a category signifying hetereogeneity. Key leaders can unify such hetereogenerous peoples in a nurturing way, he argues. One thinks of Gandhi in this connection, as much as of Tagore, and Andrews does bring them up with great admiration in his piece on 'Closer Union'. But Andrews sees the Muslim leader Dr Mukhtar Ahmed Ansari as particularly exemplary of such recent Indian leaders, as he writes:

> In India itself, there are those who have learnt by birth and experience to set forth this higher type of human character. If wo leave aside for a moment such unique outstanding figures as Gandhi and Tagore, we may point with genuine pride to the President of the All-India National Congress, Dr Ansari. A country which can produce a character such as his, at the most critical time, need never despair.[36]

Ansari was a physician, educational leader and politician, who became President first of the Muslim League 1918–1920, and then of the Indian National Congress 1927. He was one of the founders of the Jamia Millia University (National Muslim University) in Delhi, a progressive educational institution with an explicit anti-colonial mindset (Chancellor 1928 to 1936, he is buried in the university precincts). According to Andrews, Indians have much to learn from the struggle for racial recognition of plurality and for unity that South Africa faces.

Race and Power in South Africa: Andrews's Religious Autobiography *What I Owe to Christ*

I devote the greater part of this chapter, starting at this point, to examining Andrews's religious autobiography *What I Owe to Christ* (1932), the sales proceeds of which went to benefit Tagore's utopian community at Santiniketan in Bengal in India. I read it as an important record of Andrews's engagement with Schreiner's work and with the race question in South Africa. This autobiography is the life-story of a deeply religious man seeking to fight against the colour bar, exploitative indentured labour and colonialism within the contexts and limits of his own time. While Schreiner is deeply critical of Christianity, and while Andrews is deeply Christian, both are critical of racism, and Andrews spends large sections of text expressing protest at the colour bar, and horror at how racism is allowed to vitiate Christianity. South Africa offers him the worst examples.

The periods Andrews spent in India after his arrival as an Anglican priest and lecturer at St. Stephen's College, Delhi in 1904, led to close friendships with figures like Sushil Rudra at St. Stephen's, and with Gandhi. Andrews soon turned against racism and colonialism and left formal missionary work. He went to South Africa at the earnest instigation of senior anti-colonial Indian National Congress politician G. K. Gokhale, who sent a telegram asking him to go and support Gandhi and the struggles of Indians, many of whom were indentured labourers. In his autobiography, Andrews lucidly connects indentured labour in South Africa to slavery, sees indentured labour as semi-slavery, and then offers extensive reflections on the viciousness of the colour bar penetrating Christian churches. Given this collection's focus on Schreiner's networks and global contexts, it seems to the present writer important to understand in some detail how their stay in South Africa affected figures such as Andrews, who wrote explicitly on Schreiner's writing and thought with admiration and in comparative consideration with other contexts such as India.

'It seemed to me an impossible position to observe, *as Christians*, racial and colour discriminations in human life. This would inevitably lead on to a new caste system,' wrote Andrews in *What I Owe to Christ*.[37] Pearson, Andrews's travel companion in South Africa, was also a Christian and a comrade of Andrews in his later voyage to investigate – and then campaign against – indentured labour to Fiji. Pearson was also a close associate of Tagore, accompanying him on his trips to Japan and the United States, and taught in Santiniketan. Pearson advocated Indian independence, and wrote a book arguing this in Japan.[38] In *What I Owe to Christ*, invoking the authority of St Paul, Andrews makes very clear the importance he places on the matter of Christianity's openness to different ethnic and racial groups.[39] Andrews sees St Paul going against racial exclusiveness, and urging the opening of the emerging Christian congregations to all, regardless of ethnic origins or whether free or bonded.[40] Andrews also criticises the Constitution of the South African Republic (the Transvaal), which stipulated: '[t]here shall be no equality between white and black either in Church or State'.[41] Andrews argues that, in contrast, Islam offers 'no racial barrier between its members'.[42]

He also offers telling anecdotes about racism within institutional Christianity in South Africa. When Pearson brought Gandhi to a church in South Africa where Andrews was preaching, the latter was ashamed to find out later that the churchwarden refused Gandhi entrance because he was a 'a coloured man and an Asiatic'.[43] Andrews recounts his experience of suggesting that he take Manilal, Gandhi's son, to a suburban church in Cape Town, where Andrews was about to preach. Even though the vicar was a great friend of the Indian community, and though the church itself had supported foreign missions in India for a long while, the vicar thought that his congregation would object to an Indian sitting side by side in Church with them. Eventually, Manilal was allowed to sit beside the vicar's wife in a back seat of the church near the door. Andrews also tells a moving story about his experience in celebrating the Holy Communion at St. George's Cathedral (Cape Town), 'where there never has been any colour bar'.[44] Here, after all the Europeans had returned to their seats, an elderly Black lady came up to receive communion: 'As I took the elements down to her while she knelt there in deepest reverence, it seemed to me that she represented the very soul of Africa, bowed down on account of the intolerable wrongs that Europe had committed'.[45] Andrews offered a fiery sermon about the two idols set up for worship in South Africa: gold and race prejudice.[46]

Soon after his indictment of the colour bar in South Africa, Andrews expresses his love and admiration for the Black population of South Africa, and for Schreiner and Molteno:

It was not long before the African Bantu people themselves, by their wistful faces telling of centuries of sorrow, won the fullness of my heart's sympathy and love. Olive Schreiner had taught me to understand the secret of Africa, and I was to learn it more fully from another South African lady, Miss Molteno. She, with Olive Schreiner, belonged to the company of those who had not bowed the knee to Baal. Her white hair and worn face revealed a life-long struggle for the oppressed.[47]

Molteno, also a friend of Gandhi's, met the latter in 1909 during a visit to England. In South Africa, too, Molteno visited the Gandhis regularly at their utopian settlement at Phoenix Farm, and lived for some time in a cottage built for her at the neighbouring Ohlange Institute. She spoke at meetings with Gandhi and mediated for him with key South African political figures such as General Louis Botha, seeing this work as equivalent to her advocacy for Black leaders and intellectuals such as John Dube, the first President of the African National Congress, and Sol Plaatje, its first General Secretary and later a celebrated author, and her support for their campaign for rights for Black South Africans.[48]

Andrews writes in his autobiography that Molteno told Indians at a meeting about three things that 'belonged to the very soil of Africa': music and song; the 'power of suffering' – suffering under the 'pain of Africa' – which had made African hearts 'softer' not 'harder'; and the 'moral power of woman'.[49] 'Woman had been always the burden-bearer, and, because the women of Africa had borne burdens as none others, they would come through the fire of suffering, pure and refined, as fine gold', Andrews reported Molteno saying.[50]

Andrews also writes of a farewell meeting arranged for him by the Indians of Durban, and his encounters with a large number of Black South Africans there. On that occasion, he had gone to the shop of an elderly Muslim man named Miankhan. Two 'Zulu leaders' also visited the shop and wished to ask Andrews a question.[51] This was translated, and the encounter is described in autobiography as follows:

'We have seen,' he answered, turning to me, 'by the look of your eyes when you speak to the Indians, that you are ready to die for the Indians. Are you ready to die for *us*?' Andrews answers, 'Yes, if the time comes, I am ready'.[52]

'For it came to me in a flash', Andrews writes, 'that in Christ's service there can be no thought of race at all; for all are one man in Him. There can only be one divine love wherein all the races of mankind are one'.[53] Andrews thus continually grapples with the racist injustice at the heart of white settler colonialism, and affirms repeatedly that the core of Christianity starkly goes against such racism.

It is in the same chapter on South Africa, too, that Andrews offer us accounts of his friendship with Gandhi, and how 'their hearts met from the first moment we met one another, and they have remained united by the strongest ties of love ever since'.[54] Having earlier written of racism, Andrews turns to vegetarianism, and Gandhi's argument to him that Christ's self-sacrifice proves that 'the divinest thing is to give life, not take it', thus critiquing the eating of slaughtered animals.[55] Gandhi's message for Andrews was that 'long-suffering and redeeming love is alone invincible'.[56] Andrews draws snapshots of times spent at Phoenix Farm in South Africa with the Gandhis. On one such evening, when Gandhi's wife and sons were still in prison, Gandhi had a baby girl from the untouchable castes in India in his arms, along with an ill Muslim boy, while a 'Zulu Christian' woman stayed to eat with them on her way to a Mission on the hill.[57] There was no animosity expressed against the British and the Boers. The picture offered by Andrews is thus of Gandhi's conviviality with people of different religions, as well as of Gandhi's anti-casteism and anti-racism. Andrews also creates a powerful sense of fellowship across races, genders, cultures and between public actors critical of racism.

Andrews saw the terrible consequences of indentured labour in Natal: he writes of how a man bound to indenture in Natal showed Gandhi the unhealed marks of lashes on his back. When the man sees Andrews, he 'started back with fear', as though Andrews might strike him.[58] 'That look of fear on his face as he saw me coming towards him haunted me for many days, and filled me with pity', writes Andrews.[59] Andrews was 'confronted by the very same questions of racial and religious exclusiveness which so deeply offended Christ and called forth His severest condemnation'.[60] In his stay in Santiniketan in India – the next episode of his life that he recounts after his South African experiences in his autobiography – he was able to ruminate and reflect further on Christianity and racism, along with other key questions relating to war. Just as Andrews's anti-racism and his Christianity synchronised, so did his pacifism and Christianity. He traced in British history a hardening colour prejudice and racial arrogance, going hand-in-hand with the consolidation of empire (with the 1880s seen as especially bad), and he pondered ways forward beyond such arrogant prejudice in his own time.[61] His next journey took him to Fiji with Pearson to campaign against indentured labour. Partly as a result of their campaign, the system of indenture was formally abolished on 1 January 1920. This date, Andrews writes, was commemorated as Abolition Day in the British colonies.[62]

Conclusion

Andrews's autobiography is the imaginative record of a deeply religious and radical man seeking to fight against the colour bar, exploitative indentured labour and colonialism, living in a lifeworld of mutual influence with key anti-colonial utopian actors such as Gandhi.[63] Andrews thought and acted, of course, within the contexts and limits of his own time. Reading his work as an integral part of the reception and afterlives of Schreiner's oeuvre and public action is illuminating on many fronts. Such reading is illuminating in understanding the depth and extent of Schreiner's influence on figures in, or with strong links to, India; in understanding Schreiner's speculations and criticality, with utopian and dystopian overtones, around questions of race, gender and settler colonialism in wider global and Global South contexts; and in understanding the results of comparing figures cognate to Schreiner, with the explicit realisation that Schreiner needs to be understood also in this global comparative context. While Schreiner and Andrews take centre-stage in this chapter, it also shows how important networks, solidarities and friendships across cultures and nations with figures such as Molteno, Pearson and Gandhi were to the social dreaming of Schreiner and Andrews.

Both Schreiner and Andrews are examples of white writers and public actors who were products of their own time, with undoubted socially and historically conditioned limitations to their attitudes to race and colonialism, yet both are deeply moving figures through which to understand the history of anti-racism and critiques of white settler colonialism.

Works Cited

'Elizabeth Maria Molteno'. *South African History Online: Towards A People's History*. Updated November 19 2020. https://www.sahistory.org.za/people/elizabeth-maria-molteno.

Andrews, C. F. 'South Africa and India: Olive Schreiner's Message'. *Modern Review*, 43, no. 6 (June 1928): 641–46.

—. *What I Owe to Christ*. London: Hodder and Stoughton, 1932.

Bagchi, Barnita. 'Transcultural Utopian Imagination and the Future: Tagore, Gandhi, Andrews, and India–Britain Entanglements in the Early 1930s'. *Utopian Studies: The Journal of the Society for Utopian Studies* 33, no. 2 (2022): 206–22.

Bhattacharya, Sabyasachi, ed. *The Mahatma and the Poet: Letters and Debates between Gandhi and Tagore 1915–1941*. New Delhi: National Book Trust, 1997.

Driver, Dorothy. 'Introduction to the New Edition'. In *From Man to Man or Perhaps Only –*, by Olive Schreiner, edited by Dorothy Driver, ix–xlvi. Claremont: University of Cape Town Press, 2015.
Dutta, Krishna, and Andrew Robinson. *Rabindranath Tagore: The Myriad-Minded Man*. London: Tauris Parke Paperbacks, 2009.
Dutton, Jacqueline. '"Non-western" Utopian Traditions'. In *The Cambridge Companion to Utopian Literature*, edited by Gregory Claeys, 223–58. Cambridge: Cambridge University Press, 2010.
Gandhi, Mohandas Karamchand. *The Collected Works of Mahatma Gandhi*, vol. 10. Delhi: Publications Division Government of India, 1963.
—. *The Collected Works of Mahatma Gandhi*, vol. 29. Delhi: Publications Division Government of India, 1968.
Hofmeyr, Isabel. 'The Black Atlantic Meets the Indian Ocean: Forging New Paradigms of Transnationalism for the Global South – Literary and Cultural Perspectives'. *Social Dynamics* 33, no. 2 (2007): 3–32: https://doi.org/10.1080/02533950708628759.
Pearson, W. W. *For India*. Tokyo: Asiatic Association of Japan, 1917.
Reddy, Enuga Sreenivisulu. 'Some Remarkable Women who Helped Gandhiji in South Africa'. *South African History Online: Towards a People's History*. Updated June 17, 2019. https://www.sahistory.org.za/archive/some-remarkable-women-who-helped-gandhiji-south-africa-e-s-reddy.
Sargent, Lyman Tower. *Utopianism: A Very Short Introduction*. Oxford: Oxford University Press, 2005.
Schreiner, Olive. *Closer Union: A Letter on the South African Union and the Principles of Government*. London: A. C. Fifield, 1909.
—. *From Man To Man, or Perhaps Only –*. London: Virago Modern Classics, 1982.
Tinker, Hugh. *The Ordeal of Love: C. F. Andrews and India*. New York: Oxford University Press, 1997.

Notes

1. Andrews, 'South Africa and India: Olive Schreiner's Message', 641–46.
2. Hofmeyr, 'The Black Atlantic', 21.
3. Tinker, *Ordeal of Love*, 131–33, 138–39, 142–43.
4. Sargent, *Utopianism: A Very Short Introduction*, 5.
5. Sargent, *Utopianism*, 5.
6. Dutton, '"Non-Western" Utopian Traditions', 223–32; Bagchi, 'Many Modernities and Utopia'.
7. Schreiner, *From Man to Man*, 416–23.
8. Schreiner, *From Man to Man*, 411.
9. Schreiner, *From Man to Man*, 411.
10. The name of the Black servant is not given in the published edition of *From Man to Man*, but was later discovered in a draft manuscript by Dorothy Driver. See Driver, 'Introduction', xxiv.
11. Schreiner, *From Man to Man*, 417–18.
12. Schreiner, *From Man to Man*, 418.
13. Schreiner, *From Man to Man*, 421.

14. Schreiner, *From Man to Man*, 421.
15. Schreiner, *From Man to Man*, 422.
16. Schreiner, *From Man to Man*, 423.
17. Schreiner, *From Man to Man*, 423.
18. Schreiner, *From Man to Man*, 423.
19. Schreiner, *From Man to Man*, 430.
20. Schreiner, *From Man to Man*, 439.
21. Schreiner, *From Man to Man*, 439.
22. Bhattacharya, *The Mahatma and the Poet*, 12. Andrews had brought about the meeting that led to a subsequent close friendship between Tagore and Gandhi. It was he who kept Tagore informed of Gandhi's South African activities and arranged for some of Gandhi's Phoenix Farm students in South Africa, and Gandhi himself, to visit Santiniketan, where Tagore and Gandhi met for the first time, in 1915. See Dutta and Robinson, *Rabindranath Tagore*, 196.
23. Reddy, 'Some Remarkable Women'.
24. Hofmeyr, 'The Black Atlantic', 21.
25. Gandhi, *Collected Works*, vol. 10, 270, 287.
26. Gandhi, *Collected Works*, vol. 29, 34. John X. Merriman served as Prime Minister of the Cape Colony from 1908 to 1910, before the Union of South Africa was formed.
27. Andrews, 'South Africa and India', 641.
28. Andrews, 'South Africa and India', 641.
29. Andrews, 'South Africa and India,' 641.
30. Andrews, 'South Africa and India', 642.
31. Andrews, 'South Africa and India', 641.
32. Andrews, 'South Africa and India', 642.
33. Andrews, 'South Africa and India', 643.
34. Schreiner, *Closer Union*, 50–51; quoted in Andrews, 'South Africa and India', 644–45.
35. Andrews, 'South Africa and India', 645.
36. Andrews, 'South Africa and India', 646.
37. Andrews, *What I Owe to Christ*, 238.
38. See Pearson, *For India*.
39. Andrews, *What I Owe to Christ*, 239.
40. Andrews, *What I Owe to Christ*, 239.
41. Andrews, *What I Owe to Christ*, 239.
42. Andrews, *What I Owe to Christ*, 240.
43. Andrews, *What I Owe to Christ*, 240.
44. Andrews, *What I Owe to Christ*, 241.
45. Andrews, *What I Owe to Christ*, 241–42.
46. Andrews, *What I Owe to Christ*, 242.
47. Andrews, *What I Owe to Christ*, 243.
48. 'Elizabeth Maria Molteno'.
49. Andrews, *What I Owe to Christ*, 243–44.
50. Andrews, *What I Owe to Christ*, 244.
51. Andrews, *What I Owe to Christ*, 245.
52. Andrews, *What I Owe to Christ*, 245.
53. Andrews, *What I Owe to Christ*, 245.

54. Andrews, *What I Owe to Christ*, 246.
55. Andrews, *What I Owe to Christ*, 246.
56. Andrews, *What I Owe to Christ*, 247.
57. Andrews, *What I Owe to Christ*, 247.
58. Andrews, *What I Owe to Christ*, 248.
59. Andrews, *What I Owe to Christ*, 248.
60. Andrews, *What I Owe to Christ*, 255.
61. See Andrews, *What I Owe to Christ*, 282.
62. Andrews, *What I Owe to Christ*, 291–92.
63. See Bagchi, 'Transcultural Utopian Imagination', 214–16.

Chapter 5

Turning Points: Olive Schreiner Changing Her Mind About Race Matters

Liz Stanley

Introduction

Olive Schreiner wrote that, when a young girl, she imagined she was Queen Victoria and commanded that Africa – the Africa of the 1850s – should be partitioned, with all the Black people on one side and all the white people on the other.[1] In later years, her race politics were different. She had been involved in a campaign countering the 'so-called black peril', supported the anti-pass law militancy of women traders in Bloemfontein, contributed money to the embryonic ANC, and defended strikes by dockworkers in Port Elizabeth (Gqeberha).[2] She had also, among other relevant work, written radical commentaries about race, describing it as a social construction and suggesting that everyone was actually 'mixed-race'.[3] How did such changes happen and what clues are there in the remaining sources?

Texts, both oral and written, fictional and factual, often deploy fictive devices of different kinds, artifices that help to shape rather than fabricate truths within them.[4] One of these is the use of epiphanies, which invoke major events or circumstances that signify change by marking departures and new beginnings. In doing so, they act as delineated pivot points in moving the action or characterisation forward.[5] Epiphanies are also retrospective assemblages, artful ways of drawing together and highlighting things that were not seen as momentous at the time but are perceived so retrospectively; with hindsight, they indicate something that became highly consequential.[6] This chapter is concerned with how Schreiner's changing ideas about race and racism came about. A number of relevant epiphanies appear in the different writings she produced when indicating her own, or a character's, changing frame of mind. Some of them have been discussed by Schreiner scholars, with a resonant example being a so-termed 'Bantu woman' who appears in a number of Schreiner texts and speaks of the universalism of women's oppression and why its yoke is borne.[7] As this example suggests, they often take on a condensed, quasi-allegorical form, and have pointed significance.

There are also examples of lower-key changes involving what one might call pre-assemblage and looser kinds of turning points, concerning events that act as markers of change but are part of a wider set of circumstances in which Schreiner's rethinking about race took place. These turning points were emergent, of their moment, and subject to Schreiner's ongoing enquiry. They are important in understanding Schreiner's changing ideas about race, but have largely escaped scholarly discussion. This chapter proposes that paying close attention to these instances is helpful in teasing out the detail of how Schreiner changed her mind, showing her complex responses to circumstances, and suggesting that it was not only sharply perceived epiphanies that influenced her re-evaluations of her thinking about race. Three such turning points are discussed below.

Turning points

Three instances have been chosen because they highlight key aspects of Schreiner's analytical thinking, in her emphasising the importance of the material world, countering essentialist ideas about race, and opposing white violent hegemony, respectively. They concern: first, the group of San, Khoisan and Xhosa workmen with whom Schreiner became friendly between March and July 1890, while living for extended periods in Matjiesfontein, soon after returning to South Africa from Britain;[8] second, Schreiner's acquaintance with Eliza Brown, married to a missionary and one of the granddaughters of the Rev James Read and his Khoisan wife Sara Elizabeth Valentyn, when staying in Taung in January 1894; and third, her encounter in October and November 1905 with the work of Black US sociologist W. E. B. Du Bois and recognition of its then-unparalleled epistemological position. As well as exploring how Schreiner writes about these experiences, the reasons why they did *not* become epiphanies in her wider writing will also be considered.

In the first example, taken from Schreiner's 1890 letters, she expresses her friendly affinity with the workmen around Matjiesfontein employed in building the hotel and outbuildings owned by railway entrepreneur James Logan. Schreiner was strongly attracted to this 'in between' place due to its Karoo landscape of grandeur and beauty, coupled with her alienation from the daily stream of railway visitors who dined in the hotel while their train halted and left without actually seeing the place. The workmen were a constant, and she writes of being friendly with them without being actually friends, combined with invoking the powerful effects on her of the untamed landscape.

The second example occurred in Taung, in early 1894, when visiting the Brown family. Schreiner wrote that Eliza Brown – not named in these letters – lamented her mixed-race status and wished she had not had children because of the prejudice she and they faced. Schreiner's empathy with Mrs Brown's outsider position comes across, and her perception of the lack of a distinct identity among mixed-race people at the time of writing is explored in an essay published subsequently.

The third example concerns the impact of Schreiner reading Du Bois's *The Souls of Black Folk*, given to her by visiting friends.[9] As well as closely identifying with his essay on the death of his son, what struck her, according to her letters from 1905 about the encounter, was that Du Bois did not need any well-meaning white liberal – she mentions herself and US author Harriet Beecher Stowe – to represent his experience for him. He did this in a powerfully effective way himself, from the inside, as a first-hand source of knowledge. For Schreiner, his work marked the development of a distinct epistemological position, of Black people analysing and representing their own situations.

Each of these turning points involved Schreiner, as noted earlier, as a kind of interlocutor of her own experiences, partly concerning the specifics of these examples, and partly the wider context of which they were part. As a result, they contributed to her rethinking her ideas. She comments explicitly on this in *Thoughts on South Africa*, that this was not the result of any training, but simply of an increased knowledge. But none of them became epiphanies in the retrospective assemblage sense. The questions arise: what kind of knowledge was this, and why not? In addition, separately and taken together, there is the wider question: what clues do they provide about how Schreiner's changes of mind on race occurred?

The men and the material things

Schreiner's strong reaction to landscape, and her almost mystical sense of a change in her being and self in the context of its material grandeur and import, has been frequently remarked on.[10] It is expressed in her allegories as well as the novels and essays. It also occurs in her letters, particularly those to close friends. One such occasion involves the first turning point for discussion: her encountering a group of workmen when staying in Matjiesfontein, a small Karoo village some 150 miles north of Cape Town. To Henry Havelock Ellis, an English friend who later became a pundit on sexual matters, she wrote on 25 March 1890:

> The sun is just rising the hilltops are dark purple. Over the way at the railway station the coloured boys are at work already digging the new foundations. I might be at Rattel Hoek as far as the sounds go [. . .] [s]uch a sense of wild exhilaration and freedom comes to me when I walk over the Karroo. [. . .] It is curious, & to me very attractive this mixture of civilisation & the most wild untamed freedom; the barren mountains & the wild Karroo & the railway train. [. . .] Wild stretch of Karroo in front of my door so glorious.[11]

This passage in Schreiner's letter begins with the sun only just rising. The implication is that she was already up and had started work herself, although her attention is on the group of men referred to as the 'coloured boys'. They were at work, so she will have observed or heard them digging the foundations. A parallel is drawn: she is at work and so are they. The foundations the men were digging were for the buildings being constructed in Logan's railway village, one of which was the cottage that would become Schreiner's base there. The sound of them at work, she writes, reminds her of being at Ratel Hoek, one of the farms where she worked as a governess and drafted what became the novels *Undine*, *The Story of an African Farm* and *From Man to Man*.[12] The implication is that she was also working on a writing project, something confirmed in other letters at this time.[13]

In this letter, Schreiner also comments to Ellis about the exhilaration she was experiencing, and links this to the mixture of civilisation and wild freedom that characterised the place, that she could revel in the untamed landscape but jump on a train if she wanted and go elsewhere. The 'coloured boys' appear as an undifferentiated group, and this means an ethnically mixed group, as this how she tended to use the word at the time. There are three notable things here: the parallel between her work and her observation of the men at work; her exhilaration at the mixture of untamed and wild and civilised; and the association made between the men and an extremely productive period in her writing life. Schreiner was at this time, early in 1890, engaged with the essays that eventually became *Thoughts on South Africa*, initially magazine-published as by 'A Returned South African'. Race matters were on her mind and they were also important in her life in other ways.

Related comments about the men also appear in other letters. For instance, a few weeks later, on 25 April 1890, Schreiner wrote again to Havelock Ellis:

But some how just now I feel more fit for practical work travelling, climing [sic] mountains &c I seem to drink in the external world through every little pore. Never before, never when I was a child, have I been able to live such an objective life, a life in which I feel not the least wish to give out to express, seem conscious of nothing but an alpowerful [sic] desire to drink in through my senses. I look & look at the skies & the bushes & the men & the material things as if I were just newborn, & was learning to know them.[14]

This letter makes a strong distinction between the period Schreiner had spent in Britain, in which she 'gave out', and her sense, on returning to South Africa, that she wanted to do 'practical work' and live an 'objective life' that engaged with the external world rather than the inner life of the imagination. This 'external world' is, as is often the case regarding Schreiner's engagement with landscape, a landscape with figures.[15] In *The Story of an African Farm*, for instance, while the farmhouse is alone in the landscape, there are the herdsmen and shepherds who silently come and go. And in this particular passage in her letter, she is not 'giving out' but drinking in through her senses, offering a litany of the skies, bushes, the men and material things. This locates the men in the landscape with a strong sense of renewal, for she is learning to apprehend the skies, the bushes, the men and other material things in a new way.

Another letter, also to a friend in Britain, the English socialist and early gay-rights campaigner Edward Carpenter, provides more information. Writing on 20 July 1890, after she had moved into the cottage built by the workmen, Schreiner comments: 'I hire the little cottage I live in by myself. No, I have no friends here, but I am very friendly with all the Bushman Hottentots Kaffers [sic] & I'm very well & very very happy'.[16] Here, Schreiner makes a distinction between friendship and being 'very friendly with' people. She has no friends in Matjiesfontein, whether Black or white, and those singled out (with whom she is 'very friendly') are the erstwhile 'coloured boys', the workmen, who, from the description in this letter and in contemporary nomenclature, were likely San, Khoikhoi, and Xhosa. The mixture of ethnic groups is interesting, as is her use of the then-liberal racial terminology, and her distinction between friendship and being friendly *with*; there is no sense that this is because of their ethnicity but that they are the only people there she finds sympathetic. It is telling that Schreiner mentions none of the white people working at the railway village, nor the visitors she entertained when their train stopped, including Cecil John Rhodes and Rudyard Kipling, among others.

Some observations can be drawn from these tantalising glimpses of Schreiner meeting the Matjiesfontein workmen. These events took place in the context of her powerful response to the landscape. Its impact on her was partly about the physical space as such, and partly that its untamed wildness marked the end of her immersion in the subjective world within and turn to the objective world and material things without. This is a peopled landscape, featuring people at work.

One highly cultured and intellectual woman

Schreiner returned to South Africa from Europe at the end of 1889 with a project in mind. This was the 'Returned South African' essays mentioned earlier, informed by her intention to travel all over southern Africa.[17] In addition to travels to the Eastern Cape and to Matjiesfontein, in December 1893 and January 1894, she set out with her sister Ettie northwards, by ox-wagon, to meet Ettie's husband John Stakesby Lewis, a mining engineer, in what was then Rhodesia. Ettie Stakesby Lewis, a well-known and high-ranking evangelist in the Good Templars organisation, also a Christian Scientist, possessed a religious fervour many regarded as magnetic. One of their stops was in Taung, north of Kimberley in present-day North West province. This was a visit to the household of missionary Rev John Brown and his wife Eliza Brown née Read. It is not known how they met, probably when both were younger and living in the Eastern Cape; as family letters testify, Mrs Brown was one of the people who saw Ettie as a religious leader.[18]

Schreiner's letters from the period, including one to Carpenter dated 19 January 1894, mentions the pleasures of the trip.[19] She later mentions the wagon, the heat and other matters, but not the people being visited. Meanwhile Mrs Brown's letters to her children describe the visit in religious terms. What is not conveyed is that Mrs Brown was a mixed-race woman; family photographs show that Mrs Brown had somewhat darker skin than her husband, as did her children. Her paternal grandmother was Sara Elizabeth Valentyn, a Khoisan woman who married the London Missionary Society missionary James Read Senior. Before marriage, Mrs Brown had been proactively involved in furthering the religious activities of her father, the Rev James Read Junior, in the Eastern Cape, close to where Schreiner's father, Gottlob Schreiner, had also been a missionary.[20] Schreiner had either started, or would soon begin, writing one of her 'Returned South African' essays on mixed-race groups, which raises a question about the omission from her correspondence or reference to her having met a mixed-race family during precisely the period she was writing about South Africa's mixed-race populations. The influence of this context, however, can be discerned in two ways.

First, it impacted on the content of Schreiner's third 'Returned South African' essay, and how she edited it subsequently when preparing the essays for book publication; second, it is considered in detail in a letter to the leading Cape liberal politician John X. Merriman on 29 June 1896, after this essay first appeared. This letter was Schreiner's response to one from Merriman commenting on her third 'Returned South African' essay, now entitled 'The problem of slavery' but originally called simply 'A Returned South African No. 3':[21]

> I do not think I over state the painful position of the Halfcaste [. . .] I could recount to you if there were time, several instances in which coloured women have poured out a flood of bitterness at their position. [. . .] I know also one highly cultured & intellectual woman, in a good social position who has one 8th of Hottentot blood. She has declared that if she had had any conception of what her children would have had to go through she would never have given one of them birth. Her hatred towards her grandfather for the misery he has caused his descendants is something almost savage! She certainly is the only person in upper ranks of life, who has ever spoken frankly to me of their position; but I have not the slightest doubt that thousands and do not speak, feel just as bitterly.[22]

The circumstantial details in the letter show that Schreiner's reference is indeed to Eliza Brown. She was cultured, intellectual and in a good social position; she did have one-eighth Khoisan heritage, and others of her letters mention – though without detail – her dislike of her paternal grandfather and his morals. The link between the Schreiners and the Browns was strong and continued over time, with one of Schreiner's favourite nieces marrying one of the younger sons of Mrs Brown.

Mrs Brown's bitterness is explained both by this letter and in more general terms by Schreiner's essay. She was certainly a woman of good social position but often not treated as such; she was 'between' and belonged to neither white nor Black populations. This is one of the overarching themes of Schreiner's essay, although it is less concerned with people in the position of Mrs Brown, and more with those further down the social hierarchy who were dependent on white patronage for employment and faced opprobrium from all sides. What this adds up to, Schreiner argues in the essay, is that the negative traits sometimes associated with mixed-race people came from social situation and the deculturation that characterised it. With hindsight, this was more likely to have been experienced by the Mrs Browns of the time, as the many mixed-race people further down the social structure were, or identified with and became, members of South Africa's Griqua people (a partly mixed-race population with a strong and distinctive culture).

106   Liz Stanley

During the 1910s, Olive Schreiner went back to her 'Returned South African' essays with the intention of revising them for a book. They were typeset by the publisher as proof copies, which she worked on editing.[23] One of the extant proofs, number 3, along with her edits, make for interesting reading. The original title is present, and it and the others appear as linked explorations of 'the problem of South Africa', rather than being confined to slavery (as resulted from Cronwright Schreiner's later editing). Passages insisting that households and 'our very persons' are composed by mixed race are present and highlighted. Also, a future in which reculturation will have taken place as part of the processes of change, appears in some of the reworking. Strong continuities exist across these different proof copies, from essays 1 through 3, regarding the emphasis on the social construction of race and ethnic categories. They also indicate that the processes of change continue to unfold, therefore considering the likely directions in which this will occur is important. Among other points, Schreiner also comments that negative responses to mixed-race people will not cease until everyone is in the same category.

This book from the heart of a black man

Schreiner felt very close to the British women's suffrage supporter Frederick Pethick-Lawrence. She had a more problematic relationship with his wife, Emmeline Pethick-Lawrence, for reasons not spelled out, although they became closer during the Great War because of their shared pacifism.[24] Schreiner first met and felt an affinity with Frederick Pethick-Lawrence when, as a newspaper editor, he visited South Africa at the start of the South African War in 1899. Subsequently, both Pethick-Lawrences came to stay with Schreiner in Hanover in October 1905. One of their gifts was *The Souls of Black Folk* by W. E. B. Du Bois. This had a great impact, which Schreiner comments on across a number of letters at this time, and which resurfaced in 1911, when she hoped to attend the Universal Races Congress in London.[25] This was in large part because of its content and who wrote it, but also because of the wider context, as the 1906 Bambatha Rebellion was starting to unfold in Natal and Schreiner was anticipating a wider bloodbath of white retaliation.[26] She comments in some detail about the gift from the Pethick-Lawrences in a letter to Carpenter dated 26 October 1905:

> They have given me a book called The Souls Of Black Folk by a coloured man Burghardt Du Bois. If you've not read it you must get it & read it

> at once. [. . .] Uncle Tom's Cabin or poor little Peter Halket are all very well [. . .] [b]ut this book from the heart of a black man can surely not be met so. [. . .] I can't even write of the book it touches me so. Of course it can't be <u>quite</u> the same to you who have not all your life been face to face, with persistent quiet oppression & humiliation which [the] white man deals out to dark. The book makes me feel so much that sometimes I can't look at it; it seems to come from within me.[27]

Across letters mentioning Du Bois's book, there is a sense of urgency in Schreiner enquiring if people have read it and encouraging them to do so. In a letter to Merriman discussed below, this is to the point of sending him her own copy to make sure. What struck her was that white, liberal literary accounts, such as her own *Trooper Peter Halket of Mashonaland* (1897) and Harriet Beecher Stowe's *Uncle Tom's Cabin* (1852), were 'all very well' but did not have the same impact. As she explains, this is because she has been waiting for something in which a Black person would represent their own lives as they actually experienced them, rather than in terms that white people would find acceptable.

There are other Schreiner letters on *The Souls of Black Folk* and its impact, and in particular the distinctiveness of what Du Bois had done in representing oppression and humiliation from the inside rather than how white sensibilities might like it put. In the letter to Merriman dated 31 October 1905, she comments:

> It's a book I have long been seeking & waiting for, in which some native should give true expression, not to what he feels it's polite & wise to express to white men, but what <u>he</u> really feels. This book is just what I have wanted. [. . .] I will send you my copy. I should much like to know how you feel to it.[28]

As Schreiner puts it, she had been waiting for a 'true expression' of what Black people felt. Given this, there is her oddly inappropriate use of the word 'native', which she usually reserved for describing people who remained living largely rural and tribal lives, rather than associating it with educated metropolitan people such as Du Bois. However, the impact of the book and the urgency with which she wants her correspondent to read it is apparent. While she did not think Carpenter, who had not visited South Africa, would understand her lifelong awareness of the oppression and humiliation of Black people, it is likely that she thought Merriman would realise this, even though his liberalism only went so far.

The impact of *The Souls of Black Folk* conveyed in these letters comes across clearly, including Schreiner's insight that what she had done in *Trooper Peter Halket of Mashonaland*, and Harriet Beecher Stowe had done in *Uncle Tom's Cabin*, were very different. They were 'all very well', as she puts it, but limited because emanating from amongst the people who had dealt out 'oppression & humiliation' and had not experienced this from the inside. Also, this was not a transitory response, limited to the period around first reading the book, and it influenced Schreiner's later eager response to an invitation from the Universal Races Congress in 1911, for she expected to meet Du Bois there. Self-representation was clearly a matter of great importance for her, and it was this that propelled her profound and lasting reaction to Du Bois's work.

Changes of mind

The three turning points discussed are interesting in their own right. They also throw light on how Schreiner's thinking about race changed over time, which allows us to reflect on what general themes emerge. The Matjiesfontein workmen are figures in the landscape, alongside whom Schreiner herself is at work. A notable aspect of how Schreiner writes about the impact of living in Matjiesfontein concerns the change in terminology regarding these men: they appear first as a generalised category, then in relation to their ethnic origins, and then as people she is very friendly with, leading to an increase in personalisation over a period of time. At the same time – and remembering here Schreiner's litany of the skies, the bushes, the men, the material world – they are figures in a landscape, and the detail provided concerns the impact of the material world on her frame of mind and activities. Bringing these together by mentioning the time she lived at the farm Ratel Hoek is charged, for this was an extremely productive period in her writing life, and what was going on in her sojourn in Matjiesfontein appears to have been very productive too. Not just the 'Returned South African' essays, not just a book on women, not just allegories, not just a return to the unfinished *From Man to Man*, but all of these were being engaged with.

The Matjiesfontein workmen appear in a shadowy way in later writing, silent witnesses to the effects of landscape on her. It is the power of landscape and its semi-mystical meaning that recurs and is seen in a deeply meaningful way. However, in Schreiner's writing about this it is associated with her own changing frame of mind, so that other people become largely invisible. In a sense, then, the men are absorbed into the power of landscape, with this appearing under the sign of the import of the material world.

It comes across clearly in her letter to Merriman that Schreiner feels for the plight of Mrs Brown. This is underlined by her speaking about this on the other woman's behalf, rather than giving her own interpretation. This is interestingly compared with how the question of mixed-race people is dealt with in the 'Returned South African' essays. Schreiner is concerned overall with what is referred to as 'the problem of South Africa', race oppression and its likely future outcomes. As noted earlier, in the third essay the question of racial mixing appears as the situation of a large mass of such people, who are further down the social hierarchy than the white South African minority. Thus, although Schreiner is concerned in the letter with what this 'intellectual and educated woman' had experienced, the third essay in a sense treats such experiences by default as not an important part of the problem being analysed in its argument, which concerns an entire population group. This leads to something of a contradiction in the position Schreiner is thinking through, for the plight of Mrs Brown was not particularly rare. Indeed, she writes as much in her letter to Merriman, that although Mrs Brown's remarks had not been spoken to her by anyone else before, she knew that similar feelings were felt by many.

This was certainly an experience that made a mark on Schreiner's thinking, but it did not become a major epiphany referred to in other writings. This is likely to have been partly for ethical reasons, in not wanting to identify the particular individual concerned. But in addition, there were wider things going on at this time, concerning the argument Schreiner was crafting in the 'Returned South African' essays about race and racialised groups in the South African population. This led her to the idea of deculturation and to the experiences of the majority of mixed-race people, rather than those of individuals.

Rather different but equally strong feelings were expressed by Schreiner in relation to the impact of *The Souls of Black Folk*. In letters to various correspondents, she invokes the importance of self-representation, explaining that this is why she responded in the way she did. Du Bois's book had a galvanising effect, but as her letters also comment, Schreiner was on tenterhooks because disturbing events connected with racial oppression were taking place in South Africa about which she had very strong feelings. In the background here are the first stirrings of the Bambatha Rebellion and Schreiner's concern that there would be a bloodbath of reprisals by white forces combining from across the different parts of South Africa. This Rebellion was to be a reaction in Natal to oppression and humiliation, and there were false rumours of a wider Black insurrection across southern Africa circulating among the white population. What particularly disturbed Schreiner was that white interests had combined to carry out devastating reprisals, rather than ameliorating the problems, so she was sure there would be worse to come.

She saw this as the trajectory of wider political changes happening in southern Africa and developed an analysis of it over the following years; it is the focus of her 1909-published *Closer Union*.[29]

Schreiner's interest in the work of Du Bois was not confined to this first encounter with his book, as noted earlier. In July 1911, the first Universal Races Congress took place in London, and both Schreiner and Du Bois were members of its general organising committee.[30] Schreiner was energised by thoughts of meeting Du Bois, as both were scheduled to speak at the Congress. In the event, her heart problems prevented her from travelling, so the meeting never took place. However, the address she had been asked to provide was dispatched with her brother Will Schreiner, who was due to attend the Congress.[31] He was also taking her greetings to Du Bois, explaining her annoyance when the latter failed to attend as planned. The three turning points explored here all concern galvanising experiences which Schreiner comments on with insight, and their reverberations were experienced incrementally over time. In addition, each of them occurred within a wider framework of unfolding events and circumstance related to race matters, which in part amplified and in greater part tempered their effects. The result was that they were not picked out in the epiphany sense, but were located in a more general trajectory of rethinking about race matters that Schreiner was engaged in.

Can a pattern be identified from these turning points and their differentiation from the idea of epiphanies to show how Schreiner's changes of mind about race matters occurred? In Schreiner's case, epiphanies are retrospective assemblages of an almost allegorical character that stand for ideas she wants to draw to her reader's attention. In a sense, they represent the culmination of her thinking about the issues involved, and act as condensed conclusions used to convey import to readers. The examples discussed in this chapter are different, and the observation in the introduction that Schreiner acted as an interlocutor of these experiences is germane here. These turning points show Schreiner in the midst of rethinking, with these specific events engaged with as part of a broader process. Certainly, they were important in the sense of reconsideration, but this was as components within a wider rethinking of issues concerning race, which (it is worth emphasising) Schreiner saw as 'the world's great question'.[32]

Overall, these turning points throw light on what was involved in Schreiner rethinking race matters. In brief, this involved her being confronted with new experiences and with the unexpected in race terms, particularly in meeting people who she identified with (in the Du Bois example, at a remove through writing, of course), around the effects of landscape, the sense of outsider fellow-feeling and the importance of self-representation. At the same time, these experiences were located within the wider changes happening that deeply engaged her. These wider circumstances tempered the specific events and led to them being perceived in the broader context, rather than taking on a sharper epiphanous character. The importance of the material world, developing a critique of essentialist thinking about race, and countering a white backlash against Black people's resistance to oppression and humiliation, were foregrounded in Schreiner rethinking race matters, while these turning points were part of the foundations underpinning it.

Acknowledgement

The Olive Schreiner letters project and the Whites Writing Whiteness project were funded by the ESRC. Both research projects have been drawn on in discussion here. The ESRC's support is gratefully acknowledged.

Works Cited

Eakin, Paul John. *How Our Lives Become Stories*. New York: Cornell University Press, 1999.
Denzin, Norman. *Interpretive Interactionism*. New York: Sage, 2002.
Du Bois, W. E. B. *The Souls of Black Folk*. Chicago: McClung, 1903.
London Missionary Society collection, South Africa/Cape. School of Oriental and African Studies. University of London, London.
Monsman, Gerald. *Olive Schreiner's Fiction: Landscape and Power*. Brunswick: Rutgers University Press, 1991.
Olive Schreiner Collection. National Library of South Africa. Cape Town.
Schreiner Hemming Collection. Manuscripts & Archives. University of Cape Town, Cape Town.
Schreiner, Olive. *Closer Union*. London: Fifield, 1909.
—. *From Man to Man*. London: T. Fisher Unwin, 1926.
—. *The Story of an African Farm*. London: Chapman & Hall, 1883.
—. *Thoughts on South Africa*. London: T. Fisher Unwin, 1909.
—. *Trooper Peter Halket of Mashonaland*. London: T. Fisher Unwin, 1897.
—. *Undine*. London: Ernest Benn, 1929.
—. *Woman and Labour*. London: T. Fisher Unwin, 1911.
Spiller, G. *Papers on Inter-Racial Problems communicated to the First Universal Races Congress*. London: P. S. King, 1911.
Stanley, Liz. 'More or Less White: Olive Schreiner's Address'. Whites Writing Whiteness. Accessed 2021. https://www.whiteswritingwhiteness.ed.ac.uk/blog/more-or-less-white/.

—. 'Olive Schreiner's Address to the Universal Races Congress'. Whites Writing Whiteness. Accessed 2021. https://www.whiteswritingwhiteness.ed.ac.uk/traces/schreineraddress/.
—. and Helen Dampier. '"I Just Express My Views and Leave Them to Work": Olive Schreiner as a Feminist Protagonist in a Masculine Political Landscape with Figures'. *Gender & History* 24, no. 3 (2012): 677–700.
—. and Andrea Salter (eds). *The World's Great Question: Olive Schreiner's South African Letters*. Cape Town: Van Riebeeck Society, 2014.
Stowe, Harriet Beecher. *Uncle Tom's Cabin*. Boston: John Jewitt, 1852.

Letters

Olive Schreiner to Edward Carpenter, 20 July 1890. *Olive Schreiner Letters Online*.
Olive Schreiner to Edward Carpenter, 19 January 1894. *Olive Schreiner Letters Online*.
Olive Schreiner to Edward Carpenter, 26 October 1905. *Olive Schreiner Letters Online*.
Olive Schreiner to Havelock Ellis, 25 March 1890. *Olive Schreiner Letters Online*.
Olive Schreiner to Havelock Ellis, 25 April 1890. *Olive Schreiner Letters Online*.
Olive Schreiner to John X. Merriman, 29 June 1896. *Olive Schreiner Letters Online*.
Olive Schreiner to John X. Merriman, 31 October 1905. *Olive Schreiner Letters Online*.
Olive Schreiner to Jan Smuts, 19 October 1920. *Olive Schreiner Letters Online*.

Notes

1. This remark appears in the Introduction to *Thoughts on South Africa* (1923), 15.
2. These all feature in Schreiner's letters. For the complete letters in a variorum edition, go to *Olive Schreiner Letters Online (OSLO)*. A selection is also provided with commentary in Stanley and Salter, *The World's Great Question*.
3. A differently edited version of this is in *Thoughts on South Africa*, as compared with its first appearance as one of Schreiner's 'A Returned South African' essays, and is discussed later in this chapter.
4. For a key discussion of fictive devices which stimulated much subsequent work, see Eakin, *How Our Lives Become Stories*.
5. See Denzin, *Interpretive Interactionism* for work on epiphanies that has influenced much subsequent research and theory.
6. A key example is in *From Man to Man*, 196. The door slams when Bertie returns from a party at which she is 'cast out' as a sexually loose woman. Ironically, her sister Rebekah is so immersed in great thoughts she does not register the sound, and nor does the reader recognise its significance until later in the novel.

7. A resonant example appears in the opening chapter of *Woman and Labour*, 13–14.
8. Schreiner's language on race is here retained, though 'Khoisan' is actually a collective term for two distinct ethnic groups who do not speak Bantu languages: the Khoikhoi and the San.
9. See Du Bois, *The Souls of Black Folk*.
10. Writings on Schreiner and landscape are now voluminous. Early work by Gerald Monsman, *Olive Schreiner's Fiction* has influenced discussion here.
11. Schreiner to Havelock Ellis, 25 March 1890, *OSLO*.
12. In addition to these novels, it is Schreiner embarked on other fictions as well.
13. Letters of the time indicate that Schreiner was working on a number of projects simultaneously: the 'Returned South African' essays, a book on women and allegories, as well as editing what became *From Man to Man*.
14. Schreiner to Havelock Ellis, 25 April 1890, *OSLO*.
15. See Stanley and Dampier, 'I Just Express My Views,' 677–700.
16. Schreiner to Carpenter, 20 July 1890, *OSLO*. 'Hottentot' and 'Kaffer' are now considered highly offensive racist terms, though at the time Schreiner considered them appropriate (if not entirely neutral) designators of different ethnic groups.
17. As noted earlier, there were other writing projects, too. See endnote 13.
18. The University of Cape Town's Schreiner Hemming Collection also holds many letters by and to Brown family members.
19. Schreiner to Carpenter, 19 January 1894, *OSLO*.
20. The Read sisters wrote letters relating to their father's work, which are now part of the regular letters sent by Cape missionaries to detail their activities, held in the London Missionary Society South African/Cape collection at the School of Oriental and African Studies (SOAS) in London.
21. As part of his often intrusive editing practices, Schreiner's estranged husband Cronwright Schreiner renamed this after Schreiner's death, when he was preparing outstanding manuscripts for publication.
22. Schreiner to Merriman, 29 June 1896, *OSLO*.
23. The proof copies are held in a number of Schreiner collections. Number 3 is in the National Library of South Africa Cape Town's Olive Schreiner collection.
24. As prominent members of the Women's Social and Political Union, information about the Pethick-Lawrences appears in many sources about the suffrage movement of the day.
25. Organisational papers from the Congress are in Spiller, *Papers on Inter-Racial Problems*. See also Stanley 'More or Less White', and 'Olive Schreiner's Address'.
26. The Bambatha Rebellion was sparked off by a hut tax increase but concerned a whole raft of long-term punitive measures. Its aftermath features in many Schreiner letters over this time. See *Olive Schreiner Letters Online*, topic collections on race and labour.
27. Schreiner to Carpenter, 26 October 1905, *OSLO*.
28. Schreiner to Merriman, 31 October 1905, *OSLO*.
29. *Closer Union* in 1909 resulted from an extended 1908 newspaper article that brought together Schreiner's thinking about the race politics underpinning

the retrograde political changes occurring in South Africa, which she predicted would increase if the four settler states (the Cape, Natal, Transvaal and Orange Free State) agreed to union rather than federation in the future. In the event they did, in 1910. And her prediction was correct.
30. See Spiller, *Papers on Inter-Racial Problems*.
31. See Stanley 'More or Less White' and 'Olive Schreiner's Address'.
32. Schreiner's letters frequently name race as a 'great question' for the whole world. This particular phrase is in Schreiner's letter to Smuts, 19 October 1920, *OSLO*; see also Stanley and Salter, *The World's Great Question*, 367–68.

Chapter 6

Olive Schreiner, Race and Black South Africa: #RhodesMustFall and a 'Prophetic Vision of the Future'
Janet Remmington

Of the many societal issues that Olive Schreiner took up and with which she has been associated, race is the most challenging with which to engage as a contemporary reader. It is also one of the most contested topics in critical assessments of Schreiner's life and work. Reasons for the complexity include her shifting views on the matter (and her uneven textual treatments of it over time); the asynchronous publication of some of her non-fiction in relation to its origination (especially *Thoughts on South Africa*, much of which was written in the 1890s though published posthumously in 1923); the range of strategies Schreiner used for addressing different audiences; and the fluid ways in which the term 'race' circulated in society and in which she applied the term.[1] The recuperation, analysis and historicisation of Schreiner's corpus of letters (not least those pertaining to South Africa from 1890s to 1920) – read in relation to her actions, publications and other articulations – have shed invaluable light on the extent to which her anti-racist views developed over the second half of her life.[2] Of 'the three great "Questions" of the age concerning "Labour", "Woman" and "the Native", or in today's terminology, class, sex and race', as Liz Stanley asserts, race increasingly came to the fore as a rallying point for Schreiner, inflected by gender and class dynamics.[3]

In the years following the South African (or 'Anglo-Boer') War (1899–1902), with imperial Britain, the former Afrikaner republics and the British colonies of the region prioritising white reconciliation and reconstruction at the expense of the Black majority, Schreiner accentuated the extent to which race would take centre stage.[4] In 1905, she wrote to a friend: 'Even the question of woman's emancipation comes second to it'.[5] More than a decade later, in 1920, in what would be the final year of her life, she positioned race in the boldest of terms as 'not only South Africa's, but the world's great question'.[6] Wielding this conviction, Schreiner confronted segregationist Prime Minister Jan Smuts about his lack of a 'broad & sane view' concerning the country's Black population.[7] Making connections with socio-economic and political developments of the era including the Bolshevik revolution, but focusing on South African specificities, Schreiner insisted that Smuts change his views and actions to embrace a more socially inclusive vision of modernity that disrupted historically entrenched, indeed intertwined, class and race structures:

> This is the 20th century; the past is past never to return, even in South Africa. The day of princes, & Bosses, is gone forever: one must meet the incoming tide & rise on it, or be swept away forever.[8]

In what follows, I examine Schreiner's mid-to-late life of varied antiracist activity, engaged public and private writing, and cross-racial interaction, while exploring how she was assessed and claimed by Black South Africans – and others – advocating for rights. The chapter opens with a focus on her changing, ultimately oppositional, relationship with archimperialist Cecil John Rhodes (1853–1902) and the public capital they each acquired for their positions, while it discusses resonances between Schreiner's anti-Rhodes advocacy and decolonial activism in the present (most particularly the #RhodesMustFall movement). It reflects too on complexities around how some Cape Africans invoked both Rhodes and Schreiner in particular ways for strategic purposes. The chapter then analyses Schreiner's energetic post-South-African-War involvement in Black causes, her increased linkages with Black political and press leaders, and her participation in wider conversations and interventions around race in the world. It uncovers perspectives on Schreiner from the Black press that have not featured strongly in analyses to date.

Schreiner, Rhodes and Race across Time and Space

In reflecting on a centenary since Olive Schreiner's death and on South Africa's commemorative recognition of Schreiner's 'commitment to the struggle for human rights and democracy', Jade Munslow Ong evokes the idea of Schreiner as an early #RhodesMustFall proponent.[9] There is much to be said for exploring the resonances between Schreiner's strident public censure from the late 1890s of Rhodes's capitalist imperial project and the #RhodesMustFall student movement in South Africa more than a century later. In fact, Lucy Graham compared Schreiner's anti-Rhodes activism and the movement's Rhodes-flagging decoloniality action in a valuable essay published the year after the emergence of the #RhodesMustFall movement.[10] In March 2015, in a moment that catalysed the protests in Cape Town and internationally, University of

Cape Town student Chumani Maxwele, the son of a miner and domestic worker, threw excrement at the statue of Rhodes on campus, calling out to the gathering crowd: 'Where are our heroes and ancestors?'. Weeks of campaigning followed to remove the statue: its white-supremacist symbolism, protesters argued, was an 'embodiment of black alienation and disempowerment'.[11] An important expression of #RhodesMustFall's activism was to use creative forms to deliver its messages, as Schreiner had done more than a century before.[12] In April 2015, to mark the statue's removal, Sethembile Msezane choreographed a performance piece in which she depicted the legendary Zimbabwean Chapungu bird bearing witness to the symbolic fall of Rhodes. Highly conscious of Rhodes's 'wrongful appropriation' of this emblematic bird from Great Zimbabwe to represent his imperialist creation of Rhodesia, Msezane could not let this historic moment of figurative encounter and retributive justice pass.[13] Elevated on her own plinth as the Chapungu bird, she lifted the artificial wings strapped to her arms in a profound gesture of ascent as Rhodes's statue was unceremoniously unseated. In claiming this public ceremonial space, Msezane reaffirmed the histories and lived realities of pre- and anti-colonial Zimbabwe and Africa more generally – not least of its women marginalised by the racial and gender hegemonies of colonialism.[14] All too aware 'that South Africa's memorialised public spaces are barren of the black female body', Msezane offered a highly attuned, historically significant response to #RhodesMustFall.[15]

While #RhodesMustFall made searing socio-political and economic connections in the present and precipitated an era-defining movement, it did not at the time specifically link its twenty-first century protest action to the vocal, multi-sited anti-Rhodes activism of the past, including that of Schreiner.[16] Counted among Rhodes's detractors during his lifetime, for example, was John Langalibalele Dube, educationist, journalist and missionary, who in 1912 would assume presidency of the nascent African National Congress (loosely becoming part of Schreiner's network). When Dube was studying and travelling as a young man in the United States during the 1890s, he wrote in the *Los Angeles Times* about the deadly hand of Rhodes in the region, registering a sense of how it implicated Black people across the region. He inscribed the collective 'us' into his analysis and invoked the shared status of oppression owing to race: 'Rhodes and the other officials of the South Africa Company, we have found by fearful experience, are trying to put all they can in their pockets by killing and plundering us'.[17] Dube railed against the violent 1896–97 seizures by Rhodes and his British South Africa Company of Shona and Matabele land north of the Limpopo, with brutal crackdowns on resistance. Indeed, representatives from across the Black diasporic world as well as those from all backgrounds in Britain and the Empire levelled criticism against Rhodes just as others lauded him. At the turn of the new century, the inaugural 1900 Pan-African Conference in London petitioned Queen Victoria about the 'degrading and illegal compound system of labour in vogue in Kimberley and Rhodesia' attributed to Rhodes's racial capitalism.[18] Prominent Black intellectual W. E. B. Du Bois, leader of the African American delegation to the 1900 Conference, was to have a direct influence on Schreiner with his exposition of the 'colour line' becoming the overarching issue of the twentieth century.[19]

Schreiner, who keenly observed socio-political developments on her return to South Africa from Britain in 1889 and who interacted with several Black leaders and thinkers over time, became one of most vociferous critics of Rhodes after her earlier, if short-lived, regard for the scope of his knowledge which she had experienced first-hand in Cape social circles. However, Rhodes's support for the 'Strop Bill', sanctioning the flogging of Black servants and workers under contract in the Cape, presented a stark turning point for her. As she wrote to her sister Ettie Stakesby-Lewis, she 'accepted no invitation to his house or had anything to do with him' once his brutal human dealings, hard-line segregationist policies, and networks of influence and corruption became irrefutably clear.[20] 'The perception of what his character really was in its inmost depths was one of the most terrible revelations of my life', she commented.[21]

In addition to public speeches, many press pieces, and her pamphlet *The Political Situation* (1896), Schreiner took Rhodes on through her piercing book-length allegory, *Trooper Peter Halket of Mashonaland* (1897), exposing his violent incursions in what became Rhodesia to annex territory and resources at great human cost. 'What an accursed spite it is that the two people of genius which South Africa has produced should be in opposite camps', wrote W. T. Stead, editor of the prominent British periodical *Review of Reviews*, who despite his great regard for Schreiner, touted Rhodes's grand vision until he later reversed his position.[22] The first edition of *Peter Halket*, featuring the startling and distressing photographic frontispiece of three executed Black men, hung as 'rebels' by their necks from a tree, sent shockwaves across London, the British Empire and beyond. We know that Cape African newspaper editor John Tengo Jabavu visited Schreiner on his return from investigating the Rhodes-backed atrocities north of the Limpopo, corroborating the colonial violence.[23] Published at the same time that the British Parliamentary Sub-Committee was investigating Rhodes's role in the scandalous 1895–96 Jameson Raid on the mineral-rich Transvaal Boer republic, an act that would contribute to the triggering of the South African War (1898–1902), *Trooper Peter* injected further energy into the public debate around the mining magnate-cum-politician's commercial exploits and complicities. Rhodes was not ultimately indicted for the bloody Mashonaland and Matabeleland invasions, but was forced to resign as Prime Minister of the Cape owing to his association with Jameson. Schreiner's horror over Rhodes's actions was such that she wrote later of *Peter Halket* as being her most important, if not her best, book. She wrote that the allegorical exposé would offer her a measure of 'comfort' on her deathbed.[24] It came at a great cost, however. Rhodes's backlash attempted to cripple her financially ('get his teeth fast into us'),[25] through a lawsuit his associate took out against Schreiner's husband, Samuel Cron Cronwright-Schreiner, and through other means such as hate mail and attacks in the white press.

In her time, Schreiner's denunciation of Rhodes was no less public condemnation and exhibition than #RhodesMustFall activism has been in the contemporary period. Furthermore, Schreiner's emphasis more than a century ago on the extent to which Rhodes both enabled and emerged from a system has been strikingly prescient of #RhodesMustFall's focus on the structural power of coloniality.[26] While Rhodes undoubtedly 'shap[ed] the world from beyond the grave', to borrow Hedley Twidle's words,[27] he could not thwart his detractors then or now. Interrogations

Figure 6.1 Performance artist Sethembile Msezane as the Zimbabwean Chapungu bird bearing witness to the dismantling of Rhodes's statue at the University of Cape Town. Her performance endured after the crowds dispersed. © David Harrison

of Rhodes's legacy, and the systemic nature of white privilege and 'institutional colonialism' more generally, show no signs of dissipating.[28] The twenty-first-century #RhodesMustFall campaign has powerfully inspired other Fallist movements, including #RMFOxford, while forging deep-seated solidarities with the #BlackLivesMatter social justice movement in the US and around the world.[29]

The Politics of Racial Exclusion, Equal Rights, and Closer Union

After Rhodes's forced resignation as Prime Minister of the Cape Colony, he nevertheless exerted significant influence through the media, corporate power, associates and allies. Along with Alfred Milner, Governor of the Cape and British High Commissioner for Southern Africa, Rhodes promulgated an unremittingly imperialist agenda, steering the region towards war to bring the greater region under British rule. In the closing years of the nineteenth century, Schreiner strongly counselled many – including her brother William (Will) Philip Schreiner, who had formerly worked as Attorney General in Rhodes's administration – to keep Rhodes at bay. In 1898, she wrote to Will, who together with liberals John X. Merriman and J. W. Sauer had associated themselves with the Afrikaner Bond after the Jameson Raid, urging that they distance themselves from Rhodes 'openly and forever'.[30] 'There [is] a certain class of human being, fortunately only a small one', she held, 'with whom the course is openly and avowedly to declare war against them'.[31] In the same letter, Schreiner set out her position in relation to the Rhodes-backed Gordon Sprigg government's proposed discriminatory Redistribution Bill, which had been designed to give more electoral weight to white imperial-leaning urban constituencies over rural Black and Afrikaner areas. 'I believe that every adult inhabiting a land irrespective of race, sex, wealth or poverty should have the vote', she articulated.[32] Will Schreiner would go on to issue a vote of no confidence in Sprigg, precipitating an election that would propel him into the position of leading the Cape government (1898–1900) into an unenviable period of war.

For years, Schreiner had steadily worked on steering her brother Will towards a 'more liberal position on the native question'.[33] Much was at stake for the Black majority across the region of South Africa, with British and proto-Afrikaner polities fighting for control of territory, resources and access to labour. In various forms, the Black educated classes interacting with traditional chiefdoms made increasing moves to organise themselves socio-politically to protect and progress their rights. In the Cape, with its long history of missionary education and the qualified African franchise since 1853, Black voters had a measure of influence at the ballot box as well as through other means, including the press, even as colonial pressures increased over time to raise the Colour Bar. In reality, Black voters and organisations had no easy choices in terms of political party alliances or guarantees that white representatives would heed their interests.

In the aftermath of the Jameson Raid, the first African independent newspaper, *Imvo Zabantsundu* (*Native Opinion*), founded by leading figure John Tengo Jabavu, changed its strategic allegiance from pro-British to Afrikaner Bond, following in the footsteps of 'friends of the natives' Merriman and Sauer. Although the Bond's position on native rights was far from reassuring, Jabavu's realignment was not illogical given that Rhodes and Sprigg of the pro-imperial South African League (later to become the Progressive Party) had a record of backing policies that undermined African rights.[34] However, the vast majority of the region's Black inhabitants had British loyalties and aspirations for further freedoms stemming from the logic of the Cape African franchise and the legacy of Victorian liberalism.[35] A rift in Cape African politics was thus created, with repercussions and complexities ensuing for decades. Olive and Will Schreiner interacted with leading figures of both Cape camps, although they had deeper and more personal ties with Jabavu. It was in this complex political context (personal and other issues notwithstanding) that a syndicate of Black professionals, opposed to Jabavu and greatly suspicious of Afrikaner intentions (the group included Mpilo Walter Benson Rubusana, a leading Xhosa missionary, educationist and political figure), set up a rival newspaper, *Izwi Labantu* (*Voice of the People*), under the auspices of the newly launched South African Native Congress (SANC), seeking capital from Rhodes to supplement its funds.[36] This appeal for funds aligned with Rhodes's interests in currying electoral favour for the League among enfranchised Black voters. Rubusana was not afraid to push against the parameters of white oversight, however. While thanking Rhodes in a letter of May 1900, Rubusana firmly set the operational boundaries to match the already established editorial independence of his paper. Taking exception to *Izwi*'s financial performance being 'wholly managed' by Rhodes's associate Mr C. P. Crewe, and calling out the latter's lack of transparency and cooperation, Rubusana insisted that there would be no compromise: 'the direction of the paper itself as well as the staff [must be left] in the hands of the Directors'.[37]

During Rhodes's lifetime and beyond, enfranchised Cape Africans sympathetic to the SANC (including Rubusana of *Izwi* and Solomon

(Sol) Tshekisho Plaatje, editor of northern Cape Setswana-English newspapers) made use of a resonant phrase attributed to Rhodes – 'Equal rights for all south of the Zambesi' – to appeal to an idealized version of inclusive British citizenship. Though Rhodes had used this phrase in a slippery, calculated way in an electioneering context, they deployed it for rhetorical strategic purposes more broadly.[38] As Bhekizizwe Peterson comments, Black reiterations of Rhodes's declaration were designed to condemn 'the increasing erosion of Victorian ideals and the Cape African franchise'.[39] In a similar vein, *Izwi*, on Rhodes's death, tactically featured the newspaper's role in collecting subscriptions for the mooted Rhodes Memorial in Cape Town. At the head of its English section on 6 May 1902, the newspaper announced the part it would play in memorialising this son of British soil, and its intention to convey fealty to Britain with the expectation, though not to be fulfilled, that native loyalty would be rewarded in a post-War future of shared non-racial Britishness.[40] While *Izwi* acknowledged Black 'suspicion' of Rhodes, it articulated that it was 'gratified in being entrusted with this duty [of collecting Memorial subscriptions to] bring our people into closer touch with the feelings and sentiments of the great British race – a bond of union'.[41] It is striking that immediately below this Rhodes Memorial article, *Izwi* featured an extended commentary on 'Native Land Tenure' that, from the outset, magnified Schreiner's support for Black land rights, referring to her views articulated in *The Political Situation*, and in contrast to Rhodes's policies. 'Olive Schreiner's words', the article claims, 'afford us the true perspective plane from which to approach what is called the Native Question'.[42] At the same time, *Izwi* was careful to distance itself from Schreiner's pro-Boer sentiments so as not to suggest any lack of support for the British at war.[43] With its nuances and caveats, *Izwi* thus invoked both Rhodes and Schreiner in very specific ways in service to its advocacy goals within the space of a column in this war-time edition. The newspaper, with its activist strapline 'for the [black] cause that lacks assistance', drew on these prominent figures to accentuate different points: Rhodes for his association with Britishness, Schreiner for her race advocacy. It performed a complex dance in bringing these oppositional figures into close quarters within its centrefold.

In the post-War years, it became clear to Black inhabitants through a series of developments that white South Africa was intent on keeping people of colour in check. The 1907 Selborne Memorandum triggered the envisaged unification of the former republics and the Cape and Natal colonies. The subsequent two years were spent hammering out its terms, culminating in the whites-only 1908–09 Convention in which a constitution would be drafted for imperial ratification. The draft constitution would come to promulgate a racially exclusive franchise, except for retaining the Cape's non-racial franchise as a concession, while codifying that only people of European descent could serve in the Union government. Throughout this period, Schreiner was an active commentator, agitator for the rights of people of colour and keen correspondent with a wide range of figures in the political landscape, while also pursuing her women's emancipation work. With a great sense of urgency, dread and responsibility, Schreiner wrote in 1904 to her sister:

> Remember it is not always ink one dips one's pen in; it may be blood in a country like South Africa. The majority of the people English & Dutch in this country want Closer Union because it will enable them to crush [. . .] the natives. [. . .] What there is a great opening for now, is private work, getting individuals of influence to try & see things in a generous & pure spirit.[44]

In addition to these energetic behind-the-scenes endeavours, Schreiner assumed a vocal public position on the Union Bill, advocating instead for a federation in order to dilute centralised power. She published a lengthy letter in the *Transvaal Leader* in 1908; it was subsequently issued in pamphlet form in London as *Closer Union* (1909). In this text, Schreiner painted a visionary picture of both opportunity and threat that depended on the response of white South Africa to race at this crucial moment:

> If it be possible for us out of our great complex body of humanity (its parts possibly remaining racially distinct for centuries) to raise up a free, intelligent, harmonious nation, each part acting with and for the benefit of the others, then we shall have played a part as great as that of any nation in the world's record.
> [. . .]
> But if we fail in this?—If, blinded by the gain of the moment, we see nothing in our dark man but a vast engine of labour; if to us he is not man, but only a tool [. . .] if we force him permanently in his millions into the locations and compounds and slums of our cities, obtaining his labour cheaper [. . .] without the rights of citizenship, his own social organisation broken up [. . .]; if we reduce this vast mass to the condition of a great seething, ignorant proletariat—then I would rather draw a veil over the future of this land.
> [. . .]
> I believe that an attempt to base our national life on distinctions of race and colour, as such, will, after the lapse of many years, prove fatal to us.[45]

With rhetorical flourish, Schreiner drew on points of principle and pragmatism in making her case for racial inclusion. In places she simulated the language of those she was trying to unsettle and persuade, on occasion evincing white paternalistic sentiments.[46] To drive the message home to her white audience, she set out in dramatic terms the repercussions of subjugating the Black majority, while also appealing to an aspirational vision of racial interdependence to achieve a stable, prosperous future South Africa. She tackled white fears by arguing for inclusive citizenship on the basis of the qualified Cape African franchise, arguing that not accommodating Black representation meaningfully at this juncture would lead to long-term insecurity and even race warfare, as well as economic consequences.[47] Privately, she expressed that '[if] the plans of this miserable convention are carried out we stand at the beginning of a long steady downward course [. . .]. There is no hope of even that little shred of justice to the natives there has been in years past'.[48]

Schreiner's *Transvaal Leader* and *Closer Union* interventions led to widespread, animated media coverage. Many white papers hit back, including the *Rand Daily Mail*, which dismissed her views and called for 'the new [white] national policy' to become 'a living force'.[49] In contrast, Black newspapers close to home and across the continent lauded her strong stand. The *Sierra Leone Weekly News* praised her 'farsighted "coloured" policy'.[50] Mohandas Gandhi's *Indian Opinion* wrote that 'Olive Schreiner's pen has not lost her cunning', and moreover that her writing delivered 'a statesmanlike grasp of the present situation and a prophetic vision of the future that compels one's attention'.[51]

In March 1909, the SANC convened a regionally inclusive, transethnic assembly, the South African Native Convention, in response to the National Convention from which people of colour were excluded. In anticipation of this event, and of the plans taking shape for a representative delegation to take the Black cause to imperial London, *Izwi* struck a defiant note. Rehearsing Rhodes's onetime electioneering slogan, *Izwi* insisted in its Editorial of 16 February 1909 that '"Equal rights for all south of the Zambesi" is the motto that will yet float at the masthead of this new ship of state which has been launched under the Union'.[52] *Izwi* went on to underscore that 'no other will be permanently substituted while there is one black or coloured man of any consequence or self-respect in the country, or any white man who respects the traditions of free Government – so help us God'.[53]

Later that year, with *Izwi* having ceased publication owing to insolvency, the rival *Imvo* reported on the multiracial delegation, which, in something of a breakthrough, featured the two great Cape African rivals associated with the two competing newspapers, Rubusana and Jabavu, on behalf of their respective organisations. They joined forces with a formidable host of other Black leaders from across the South African region, such was the outrage and concern about the tabled Bill of Union.[54] At the same time and in a similar spirit, if in parallel, Gandhi led a delegation of the Transvaal British Indian Association to London to address discriminatory legislation against South African Indians. Heading up the delegation to the imperial government was none other than 'the Hon. W P Schreiner', who Rubusana called 'that noble and true friend of the natives'.[55] Will Schreiner had by this time turned most of his attention to Black causes, in no small part owing to his sister's influence. Schreiner wrote to her brother in London to encourage him (and sending greetings in particular to Jabavu and to Dr Abdurahman, Cape-Town-based leader of the African Political Organisation), while also being clear-eyed that 'many will try to make the anti-native policy the point of Union'.[56] Unsurprisingly, the imperial government did not overturn the racial exclusions in the draft Bill of Union – in fact, these would 'set the tone and parameters of political contestation over

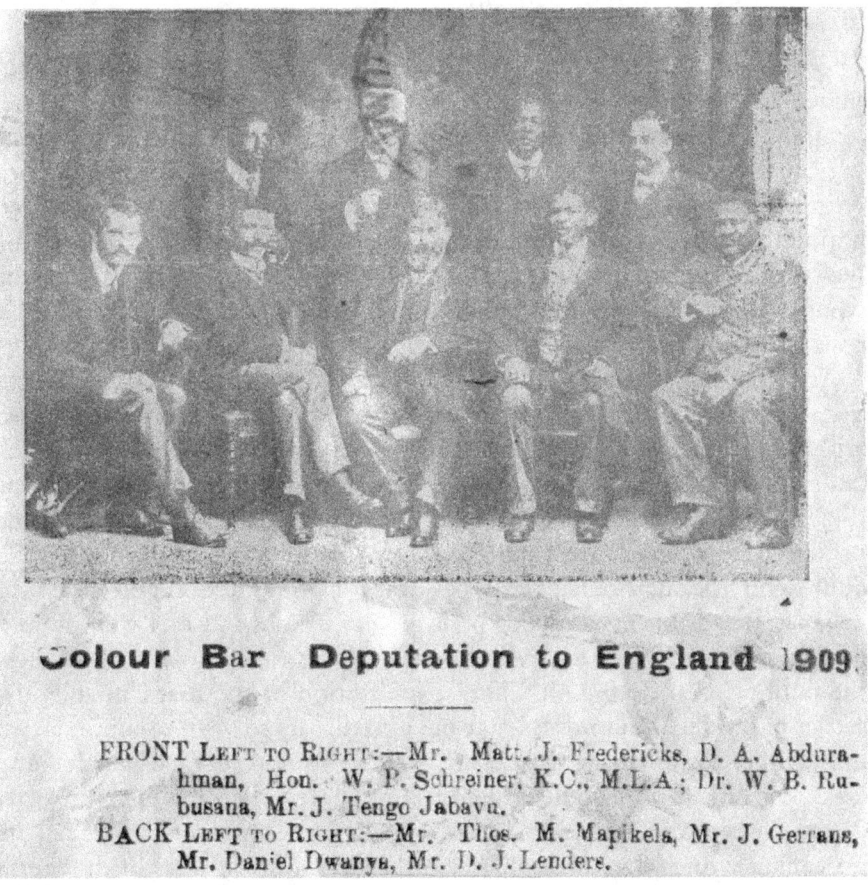

Figure 6.2 Colour Bar Deputation to England 1909. Photograph with annotation included in Mweli Skota's *African Yearly Register, Who's Who*. Courtesy of Wits Historical Papers.

the idea of South Africa for the large part of the 20th century' – but it did exclude the protectorates of Swaziland, Basotholand, and Bechuanaland from the Union's scope.[57] While the delegation could not dislodge fundamental tenets of the draft Constitution in the face of settler-colonial and imperial power, it represented a prominent cross-organisational endeavour of unity against the politics of racial exclusion and, among other things, it contributed to the 1912 founding of the organisation that would come to be known as the African National Congress, which would endure for a more than a century in the country's liberation struggle.

Race Advocacy, White South Africa, and Black Mobilisation of Schreiner

Though dealing with growing ill health in her later years, Schreiner continued her writing and campaigning in support of anti-racist, pacifist, feminist and socialist advocacy efforts. While contributing to intersecting causes and trying to find sufficient time and energy for her literary writing, Schreiner gave increasing attention to race in the heightened national milieu of the Union of South Africa inaugurated in 1910, in the regional context pertaining to Rhodesia, and in international circuits where longstanding power imbalances in the world order were being reassessed.

As white South Africa became emboldened in its new national identity, attitudes to race hardened. In May 1911, Olive Schreiner shared with her brother Will her distress at the social panic about alleged Black male predation of white women and children being popularised as the 'Black Peril'. '[I]t's White Peril that hangs over every black man', she protested.[58] In 1912, over half of the Witwatersrand's 100,000-strong adult white population signed a petition for police action and increased urban segregation as rumours of rape and sexual liaisons were amplified.[59] As was the case for earlier panics of this type in colonial settings, the public spectacle fed on white sexualisation of the Black male body, settler paranoia about miscegenation, and threats to a white supremacist, masculinist vision of society.[60] At the crossroads of race, gender and class, the 'Black Peril' phenomenon highlighted the fault lines in early twentieth-century South African society.[61] Olive Schreiner challenged the prevailing white view, aligning herself with Black critiques of the moral panic, especially highlighting the marginalised position of Black women. As she wrote to the General Missionary Commission set up to investigate the 'Black Peril': 'My feeling of course is that the peril which has long overshadowed this country is one which exists for all dark skinned women at the hands of white men'.[62] She stressed the plight of Black women 'triply oppressed' to apply Musa Dube's term – Black women subjugated by racism and by white and Black forms of patriarchy.[63] She did not budge in her belief that feminist activism should concentrate on all women being given the vote. In 1912, she resigned from the Cape Women's Enfranchisement League after it took a decision to shift its non-racial stance to achieve unity with the other branches across South Africa.

In public meetings and the press, Black South Africans were vocal in expressing their deep concerns about the 'Black Peril' accusations. Sol Plaatje, who Schreiner had known since Kimberley days in the 1890s, and who named his second daughter 'Olive' in honour of Schreiner, wrote of the dangers of the 'peril' propaganda and of white hypocrisy in relation to race-related violence. In a 1911 editorial in his newspaper *Tsala ea Becoana*, Plaatje echoed the words of Schreiner in commenting on the brutal beating of a Black servant, inverting the colonial discourse of savagery:

> ... some of the most barbarous human beings we ever saw prowl about the streets of Johannesburg [are] in white skins. Olive Schreiner never coined a more appropriate title than when she called the golden city Judasburg. What else could be expected of a community who are commendably keen on the spotlessness of white women and express specious indignation on what they term the 'black peril' when they are callously indifferent to the purity of their men who condone the white peril, another phase of the social pest.[64]

Half a year later, Plaatje published the message Schreiner prepared for the inaugural Universal Races Congress (see Figure 6.3), a humanist conference hosted in London with over two thousand representatives from fifty countries, including Du Bois, among other notable intellectuals, leaders and activists from far and wide. As Schreiner was unable to be present in person, she had asked her brother Will to read her contribution, while he would also deliver a lengthier speech as a senator in the Union's upper house representing Black views. She was upset that Will did not in the end give the full address to the gathering, but her text was published by the Black press in South Africa and elsewhere, including by Plaatje's newspaper and the *Lagos Weekly Record*, for example. In relation to this contribution and her other interventions and commentaries, Olive Schreiner acquired the status of a standard bearer for exposing 'brutal treatment dealt by colonials to the natives', as conveyed in the *Lagos Standard*.[65] Her message to the Congress

Figure 6.3 Olive Schreiner's message to the Universal Races Congress published in Sol Plaatje's *Tsala ea Becoana*, 28 October 1911. Courtesy of the National Library of South Africa, Cape Town.

struck a similar chord to that of her *Closer Union* message, as excerpted below:

> For us in South Africa the question [of] how ennobling and harmonious relations can be attained between the light and dark races which build up

our nations is not one of merely abstract intellectual interest, it is the root problem on the solution of which our whole future national life depends. [...] [If we] give to [the Native races] no place in the body politic of our national life, the future of South Africa [...] is one which we who are the children and lovers of South Africa cannot look forward to without dark foreboding.[66]

Gandhi's *Indian Opinion* reported too on a letter Schreiner sent to the press about the significance of the Congress in more general terms. The event, in her words, facilitated an 'increasing consciousness of kinship' in the context of 'minor differences of race and colour [uniting] all human creatures'.[67]

From late 1913 until shortly before her death in Cape Town in 1920, Schreiner lived in Europe. She had gone abroad for medical reasons, only to end up stranded in London during the World War. The build-up to, enactment of and fallout from South Africa's Natives Land Act of 1913, protecting white interests at the expense of Black South Africans, greatly exercised her. During the War years abroad, she would reconnect with and support Plaatje, who played a leading role in two protest delegations to imperial London against the Land Act (1914–17 and 1919–1923), while she associated also with other expatriate South Africans of colour including Gandhi, although she made it clear she took exception to their support of the War effort.

Striking a particularly low note before departing South Africa for Europe in 1913, Schreiner bemoaned the tragedy of two leading 'friends of the natives', Sauer and Merriman, in their respective ways selling out to white nationalist interests and enabling what Plaatje called the 'plague' Land Act.[68] In synchrony with Plaatje (and the nascent African National Congress of which he was founding General Secretary), Schreiner wrote to Merriman to convey her alarm and disappointment around this major piece of segregationist legislation. Indicting Merriman and Sauer by implication, she underlined that all that ultimately mattered in life was 'in however small a way [to fight] against injustice and oppression'.[69] In the next breath, she warned against the consequences of exclusionary politics:

A class or a sex or a race refused in a so-called democratic state under 20th century conditions the right to take its share in the government of the state will ultimately be driven [to] the lamentable use of force, & answer repression with resistance which must shake society to its foundations.[70]

In London three years later, with some support from Schreiner's networks, Plaatje would publish his landmark political book *Native Life in South Africa*, exposing the Land Act's dispossessions, while calling for imperial intervention to help the Black cause. He lamented that the Black population of South Africa found themselves in 'a state of affairs' that led them 'to depend solely on themselves to obtain redress – and that way rebellion lies'.[71] Resonating with Schreiner's discourse of reproach, appeal and warning in relation to racial injustice, Plaatje's book made a significant impact at the time on the public and press, as well as in parliamentary debate, while it remains relevant in addressing persistent issues related to Black life today.

A century before Msezane performed her feminist, decolonising act of representing the Zimbabwe bird rising against the backdrop of Rhodes falling, Plaatje described a scene in *Native Life* that surely would have struck Schreiner to the core given her focus on the long shadow of Black women's exploitation. Outraged by the course of the Land Act and other settler-colonial violations, Plaatje sounded retributive warnings reminiscent of Schreiner's. What would South Africa's future hold if structural and societal inequities around race, inflected by gender and class, were not addressed? In drawing *Native Life* to a close, he powerfully conjured Black women as the agents of reckoning:

> ... the only thing that stands between us and despair is the thought that Heaven has never yet failed us. We remember how African women have at times shed tears under similar injustices; and how when they have been made to leave their fields with their hoes on their shoulders, their tears on evaporation have drawn fire and brimstone from the skies.[72]

Conclusion: Schreiner as Agent and Icon

Overall, this chapter situates Schreiner as a key public figure in relation to race matters and advocacy on the South African stage, and in the international arena too as struggles over power, social organisation and resources played out in the imperial chambers, democratic outlets and labour frontlines of the early twentieth century. With regards to 'the world's great question', Schreiner called for racially injurious policies and practices to fall and a visionary future of racial interdependence to rise. In addition to her statements, speeches, publications and press articles provoking and influencing the courts of public opinion, as well as her targeted letters and conversations addressing leaders in circles of power, she exercised a notable shaping force over her powerfully positioned brother Will Schreiner. He significantly changed his socio-political views over the years that spanned the turn of the century, distancing himself from Rhodes's racial capitalism and from exclusionary racial politics, becoming increasingly active in efforts to secure Black rights, including accepting the role of heading the multiracial 1909 delegation to the imperial government. In taking up the position of South Africa's High Commissioner in London in his latter years, he articulated that 'nothing has been a greater wrench [than] to resign as one of the representatives of the native races in the Senate of the Union Parliament'.[73]

Without overlooking some complexities in relation to Schreiner and/ on race, the range of her weighty public and private contributions to race causes emerge in coverage in the Black press, and in the panoply of ways that she was assessed, conjured and mobilised by Black South Africans and other peoples of colour in the service of racial justice. Schreiner campaigned and showed support for diverse groups discriminated against on the basis of race (intersecting too with other factors), but she was leveraged by many far and wide, thus acquiring status and instantiations beyond her immediate reach, influence and awareness. In relation to race advocacy, Schreiner was both agent and icon.

Works Cited

'East and West in London'. *Lagos Weekly Record*, 2 September 1911.
'Editorial'. *Tsala ea Becoana*, 18 March 1911.
'Native Land Tenure'. *Izwi Labantu*, 6 May 1902.
'Olive Schreiner, Closer Union'. *Sierra Leone Weekly News*, 1909.
'Olive Schreiner in the Universal Races Congress'. *Tsala ea Becoana*, 28 October 1911.
'Olive Schreiner on the Unity of the Races'. *Indian Opinion*, 3 June 1909.
'Olive Schreiner's Pen Has Not Lost Its Cunning'. *Indian Opinion*, 2 January 1909.
'Race Assimilation: *Stray Thoughts on South Africa*'. *The Lagos Weekly Record*, 22 August 1896.
'Rhodes Must Fall Mission Statement' (2015). The Poor Print (Oriel College Student Newspaper). 28 April 2017. https://thepoorprint.com/2017/04/28/rhodes-must-fall-uct-mission-statement/.
'The Act of Union: Report of Native Delegates'. *Imvo Zabantsundu*, 2 November 1909.
'The New Year'. *Rand Daily Mail*, 1 January 1909.
'The People's Art: Chapungu – The Day Rhodes Fell'. Iziko Museums of South Africa. 14 March 2019. https://www.iziko.org.za/news/peoples-art-chapungu-day-rhodes-fell/.
Ahmed, A. Kayum. '#RhodesMustFall: How a Decolonial Student Movement in the Global South Inspired Epistemic Disobedience at the University of Oxford'. *African Studies Review* 63, no. 2 (September 2019): 281–303.
Anderson, David M. 'Sexual Threat and Settler Society: "Black Perils" in Kenya, c. 1907–30.' *The Journal of Imperial and Commonwealth History* 38, no. 1 (2010): 47–74.

Asante, Molefi K. *The History of Africa*. New York: Routledge, 2007.
Chigudu, Simukai. 'Rhodes Must Fall in Oxford: A Critical Testimony'. *Critical African Studies* 12, no. 3 (2020): 302–12.
Chrisman, Laura. *Rereading the Imperial Romance: British Imperialism and South African Resistance in Haggard, Schreiner, and Plaatje*. Oxford: Oxford University Press, 2011.
Clayton, Cherry. *Olive Schreiner*. Johannesburg: McGraw-Hill, 1983.
Dube, Musa W. 'Searching for the Lost Needle: Double Colonization & Postcolonial African Feminisms'. *Studies in World Christianity* 5, no. 2 (1999): 213–28.
Dubow, Saul. 'How British was the British World? The Case of South Africa'. *The Journal of Imperial and Commonwealth History*, 37, no. 1 (2009): 1–27.
—. *Scientific Racism in Modern South Africa*. Cambridge: Cambridge University Press, 1995.
Gill, Clare. 'I'm really going to kill him this time': Olive Schreiner, W. T. Stead, and the Politics of Publicity in the *Review of Reviews*'. *Victorian Periodicals Review*, 46, no. 2 (Summer 2013): 194–210.
Gordimer, Nadine. 'The Prison House of Colonialism: Review of Ruth First and Ann Scott's *Olive Schreiner*'. In *Olive Schreiner*, edited by Cherry Clayton, 97–98. Johannesburg: McGraw-Hill, 1983 [first published in the *Times Literary Supplement*, 15 August 1980].
Graham, Lucy. 'Olive Schreiner and Rhodes Must Fall'. *Bulletin of the National Library of South Africa* 70, no. 2 (December 2016): 199–212.
—. *State of Peril: Race and Rape in South African Literature*. Oxford: Oxford University Press, 2012.
Hughes, Heather. 'Remembering Rhodes' Detractors'. *The Round Table* 105, no. 2 (March 2016): 221–22.
Izwi Labantu, 16 February 1909.
Krebs, Paula M. 'Olive Schreiner's Racialization of South Africa'. *Victorian Studies* 40, no. 3 (Spring 1997): 427–44.
Lenta, Margaret. 'Racism, Sexism, and Olive Schreiner's Fiction'. *Theoria*, no. 70 (October 1987): 15–30.
Levine, Roger S. 'Revisiting the "Black Peril", South Africa, circa 1912: Popular Culture, Group Identity, and New Ways of Knowing.' *Safundi* 22, no. 4 (2021): 398–416.
Lewis, Simon Keith. 'Reading Olive Schreiner Reading W. E. B. Du Bois'. *Research in African Literatures* 45, no. 2 (Summer 2014): 150–67.
Luzipho, S. W. T. *U-Boni Buka Dr. Walter Benson Rubusana* [unpublished biography]. Rubusana Papers, School of Oriental and African Studies Special Collections. London: University of London.
Mahapa, Rambina. 'Rambina Mahapa on the Rhodes Must Fall Movement (2015).' YouTube. https://www.youtube.com/watch?v=uAeLJDqP2oI.
Msezane, Sethembile. 'Sethembile Msezane Performs at the Fall of the Cecil Rhodes Statue'. [Interview by Erica Buist]. *The Guardian*. 15 May 2015. https://www.theguardian.com/artanddesign/2015/may/15/sethembile-msezane-cecil-rhodes-statue-cape-town-south-africa.
Munslow Ong, Jade. *Olive Schreiner and African Modernism: Allegory, Empire and Postcolonial Writing*. New York: Routledge, 2017.

—. 'Remembering Olive Schreiner 100 Years After Her Death'. *Africa in Words*. 10 December 2020. https://africainwords.com/2020/12/10/remembering-olive-schreiner-100-years-after-her-death/.

Ngqulunga, Bongani. 'Towards a Closer Union: Race, Citizenship and the Contested Idea of South Africa'. In *The Contested Idea of South Africa*, edited by Sabelo J. Ndlovu-Gatsheni and Busani Ngcaweni, 32–50. Abingdon: Routledge, 2021.

Nyamnjoh, Francis B. *#RhodesMustFall: Nibbling at Resilient Colonialism in South Africa*. Bamenda: Langaa, 2016.

Odendaal, André. *The Founders: The Origins of the ANC and the Struggle for Democracy in South Africa*. Johannesburg: Jacana, 2012.

Peterson, Bhekizizwe. 'Modernist at Large: The Aesthetics of *Native Life in South Africa*'. In *Sol Plaatje's Native Life in South Africa: Past and Present*, edited by Janet Remmington, Brian Willan and Bhekizizwe Peterson, 18–36. Johannesburg: Wits Press, 2016.

Piquet, A. Chessel. 'The First Universal Races Congress'. *Indian Opinion*, September 1911.

Plaatje, Sol T. *Native Life in South Africa, Before and Since the European War and the Boer Rebellion*. London: P. S. King & Son, 1916.

—. *The Mote and the Beam: An Epic on Sex-Relationship 'twixt White and Black in British South Africa*. New York: The Author, 1921.

Plaut, Martin. 'A Menu for Change – the South African Deputation to London, 1909'. *Quarterly Bulletin of the National Library* 67, no. 2 (2013): 64–68.

Rhondda Williams, Thomas. 'Prize Fight Stopped. What Next?' *Lagos Standard* 11, no. 3, 7 (November 1911). [Republished from the *Christian Commonwealth*].

Remmington, Janet. 'Interrogating the Imperial Factor and Convoking Black South Africa: Cape African Newspaper *Izwi Labantu* (1897–1909)'. In *Edinburgh Companion to British Colonial Periodicals*, edited by Caroline Davis, David Finkelstein, and David Johnson. Edinburgh: Edinburgh University Press, forthcoming.

Saunders, Chris. 'African Attitudes to Britain and the Empire before and after the South African War'. In *The South African War Reappraised*, edited by Donal Lowry, 140–49. Manchester: Manchester University Press, 2000.

Schreiner, Olive. *A Closer Union: A Letter on the South African Union and the Principles of Government*. London: A. C. Fifield, 1909.

—. *Thoughts on South Africa*. Parklands: A. D. Donker, 1992.

—. *Trooper Peter Halket of Mashonaland*. Teddington: Echo Library, 2009.

—. Schreiner, Olive, and C. S. (*sic*) Cronwright-Schreiner. *The Political Situation*. London: Unwin, 1896.

Stanley, Liz. *Reintroducing Olive Schreiner: Decoloniality, Intersectionality and the Schreiner Theoria*. Abingdon: Routledge, 2022.

—. 'The Reader, the Text and the Editor: On the Making of Olive Schreiner's Letters Online and The World's Great Question'. *English in Africa* 42, no. 1 (2015): 59–76.

Stanley, Liz, and Helen Dampier. '"I Trust That Our Brief Acquaintance May Ripen into Sincere Friendship": Networks across The Race Divide in South Africa in Conceptualising Olive Schreiner's Letters 1890–1920'. Working Paper, Olive Schreiner Letters Project (2010): 1–76.

Stanley, Liz, and Andrea Salter. *The World's Great Question. Olive Schreiner's South African Letters 1889–1920*. Cape Town: Van Riebeeck Society, 2014.

Schreiner, W. P. 'South Africa and the War'. *Journal of the Royal African Society* 14, no. 54 (Jan 1915), 117–22.

Twidle, Hedley. 'To Spite His Face. What happened to Cecil Rhodes's nose? Letter from Cape Town.' *Harper's* (December 2021): 37–47.

Walters, Paul, and Jeremy Fogg. 'The Short Sorry Tale of *Trooper Peter Halket of Mashonaland* and its Frontispiece'. *English Studies in Africa* 53, no. 2 (2010): 86–101.

Letters

Olive Schreiner to Edward Carpenter, 19 February 1909, Archives & Local Studies. Sheffield Archives, Sheffield.

Olive Schreiner to Mr. J. Henderson, 26 December 1911, Cory Library. Rhodes University, Makhanda.

Olive Schreiner to John X. Merriman, 3 April 1897, Special Collections. National Library of South Africa, Cape Town.

Olive Schreiner to John X. Merriman, 20 July 1913, Special Collections. National Library of South Africa, Cape Town.

Olive Schreiner to Betty Molteno 18 September 1897, Manuscripts and Archives. University of Cape Town, Cape Town.

Olive Schreiner to Betty Molteno, November 1987, Manuscripts and Archives. University of Cape Town, Cape Town.

Olive Schreiner to Betty Molteno, 16 December 1897, Manuscripts and Archives. University of Cape Town, Cape Town.

Olive Schreiner to Caroline Murray née Molteno, 9 December 1907, Manuscripts and Archives. University of Cape Town, Cape Town.

Olive Schreiner to Henrietta ('Ettie') Schreiner, 25 May 1896. *Olive Schreiner Letters Online*.

Olive Schreiner to Henrietta ('Ettie') Schreiner, January 1904, Manuscripts and Archives. University of Cape Town, Cape Town.

Olive Schreiner to William Philip ('Will') Schreiner, 12 June 1898, Manuscripts and Archives. University of Cape Town, Cape Town.

Olive Schreiner to William Philip ('Will') Schreiner, 10 May 1908, Manuscripts and Archives. University of Cape Town, Cape Town.

Olive Schreiner to William Philip ('Will') Schreiner, 27 July 1909, Manuscripts and Archives. University of Cape Town, Cape Town.

Olive Schreiner to William Philip ('Will') Schreiner, 25 May 1911, Manuscripts and Archives. University of Cape Town, Cape Town.

Olive Schreiner to Jan Smuts, 19 October 1920, National Archives Repository. Pretoria, South Africa.

Notes

1. Critical assessments of Schreiner in relation to race have varied greatly. Krebs' 'Olive Schreiner's Racialization of South Africa', 427–44, places her in the

evolutionist camp. Dubow's *Scientific Racism in Modern South Africa*, 72, refers to her 'curious blend of progressive and social evolutionist thought'. Gordimer's 'The Prison House of Colonialism', 97–98 critiques her focus on gender above race. Lenta's 'Racism, Sexism, and Olive Schreiner's Fiction', 15–30, and Munslow Ong's *Olive Schreiner and African Modernism*, 101–42, highlight the extent to which her fictional treatment of race developed, with her late novel *Man to Man* offering an intersectional vision. Stanley analyses her changing conceptions of race and growing commitment to anti-racist activity in *The World's Great Question* and *Reintroducing Olive Schreiner*, 65–101; see also Stanley and Dampier's 'I Trust That Our Brief Acquaintance May Ripen into Sincere Friendship', 1–76.
2. See Stanley and Salter, *The World's Great Question*.
3. Stanley, 'The Reader, the Text and the Editor', 66.
4. 'Black' is used in this chapter primarily as an inclusive political category in the South(ern) African context, taking into account peoples of colour historically disadvantaged by colonialism.
5. Schreiner to Caroline Murray née Molteno, 9 December 1907, BC16/Box3/Fold6/1907/33.
6. Schreiner to Jan Smuts, 19 October 1920, A1/207/185.
7. Schreiner to Jan Smuts, 19 October 1920, A1/207/185.
8. Schreiner to Jan Smuts, 19 October 1920, A1/207/185.368, emphasis in original.
9. Schreiner was posthumously awarded South Africa's Order of Ikhamanga in Gold in 2003. See Munslow Ong, 'Remembering Olive Schreiner 100 Years After Her Death'.
10. Graham, 'Olive Schreiner and Rhodes Must Fall', 199–212.
11. 'Rhodes Must Fall Mission Statement.' Originally published on 'Rhodes Must Fall' Facebook page.
12. Graham, 'Olive Schreiner and Rhodes Must Fall', 206.
13. Msezane, 'Sethembile Msezane Performs at the Fall of the Cecil Rhodes Statue'.
14. 'The People's Art: Chapungu – The Day Rhodes Fell'.
15. Msezane, 'Sethembile Msezane Performs at the Fall of the Cecil Rhodes Statue'.
16. Hughes, 'Remembering Rhodes' Detractors', 221.
17. Dube quoted in *Los Angeles Times* (30 June 1896), 1; quoted in Hughes, 'Remembering Rhodes' Detractors', 222.
18. '1900 Pan African Conference Petition to Queen Victoria', quoted in Asante, *The History of Africa*, 160.
19. Stanley this volume; Lewis, 'Reading Olive Schreiner Reading W. E. B. Du Bois', 2014.
20. Schreiner to Henrietta ('Ettie') Schreiner, 25 May 1896, *Olive Schreiner Letters Online (OSLO)*.
21. Schreiner to Henrietta ('Ettie') Schreiner, 25 May 1896, *OSLO*.
22. W. T. Stead, quoted in Gill, 'I'm really going to kill him this time', 201.
23. Schreiner to Betty Molteno, 16 December 1897, BC16/Box1/Fold4/1897/25.
24. Schreiner to Will Schreiner, 10 May 1908, BC16/Box4/Fold1/1908/29.
25. Schreiner to Betty Molteno, November 1987, BC16/Box1/Fold4/1897/23.

26. 'If [Rhodes] passed away tomorrow there still remains the terrible fact that something in our society has formed the matrix which has fed, nourished, and built up such a man!' Schreiner wrote to John X. Merriman, 3 April 1897, MSC 15/1897:17. See also Chrisman, *Rereading the Imperial Romance*, 130, and 'Rhodes Must Fall Mission Statement'.
27. Twidle, 'To Spite His Face. What happened to Cecil Rhodes's nose?' 40.
28. Mahapa, 'Rambina Mahapa on the Rhodes Must Fall Movement'.
29. Nyamnjoh, *#RhodesMustFall*; Ahmed, '#RhodesMustFall,' 281–303; Chigudu, 'Rhodes Must Fall in Oxford'.
30. Schreiner to Will Schreiner, 12 June 1898, BC16/Box1/Fold5/1898/10.
31. Schreiner to Will Schreiner, 12 June 1898, BC16/Box1/Fold5/1898/10.
32. Schreiner to Will Schreiner, 12 June 1898, BC16/Box1/Fold5/1898/10.
33. Schreiner to Betty Molteno, 18 September 1897, BC16/Box1/Fold4/1897/17.
34. Odendaal, *The Founders: The Origins of the ANC*, 149–50.
35. Saunders, 'African Attitudes to Britain', 140–49.
36. Remmington, 'Interrogating the Imperial Factor and Convoking Black South Africa' (forthcoming).
37. Rubusana, quoted in Luzipho, *U-Boni Buka Dr. Walter Benson Rubusana*, 18–19.
38. Beinart, 'Cecil Rhodes: Racial Segregation in the Cape Colony and Violence in Zimbabwe', 4.
39. Peterson, 'Modernist at Large: The Aesthetics of *Native Life in South Africa*', 27.
40. On the concept of inclusive Britishness, see Dubow, 'How British was the British World? The Case of South Africa'.
41. 'The Rhodes Memorial', 3.
42. 'Native Land Tenure', 3.
43. *Izwi*'s rival *Imvo* was forced to cease operations under court martial August 1901 to October 1902 for its critical stance towards the war.
44. Schreiner to Henrietta ('Ettie') Schreiner, January 1904, BC 1080 A1.7/72.
45. Schreiner, *A Closer Union*, 46, 50, 17.
46. At times, Schreiner used language that suggested developmentalist views about people of colour – she held, for instance, that education was essential to Black advancement and true sharing in South Africa's future, but her vision remained one of racial mutuality. See Bock, 'From Words to Deeds', 127.
47. 'As long as nine-tenths of our community have no permanent stake in the land, and no right or share in our government, can we ever feel safe?', she asked, continuing: 'in the commercial sense, will it pay us in the direction of manufacture and trade if [black labouring classes] remain in the mass mere hewers of wood and drawers of water?' Schreiner, *A Closer Union*, 52, 51.
48. Schreiner to Edward Carpenter, 19 February 1909, 359/94.
49. 'The New Year', *Rand Daily Mail*.
50. 'Olive Schreiner, Closer Union', 9.
51. 'Olive Schreiner on the Unity of the Races', 2.
52. *Izwi Labantu*, 16 February 1909.
53. *Izwi Labantu*, 16 February 1909.
54. Plaut, 'A Menu for Change – the South African Deputation to London, 1909', 64–68.

55. 'The Act of Union: Report of Native Delegates', *Imvo Zabantsundu*.
56. Schreiner to Will Schreiner, 27 July 1909, BC16/Box4/Fold2/1909/39.
57. Ngqulunga, 'Towards a Closer Union', 33.
58. Schreiner to Will Schreiner, 25 May 1911, BC16/Box4/Fold4/1911/10.
59. Levine, 'Revisiting the "Black Peril", South Africa', 399.
60. Anderson, 'Sexual Threat and Settler Society'.
61. See Lucy Graham, *State of Peril*.
62. Schreiner to Mr. J. Henderson, 26 December 1911, Folder 25, MS 14, 847/2.
63. Dube, 'Searching for the Lost Needle', 213–28.
64. 'Editorial', *Tsala ea Becoana*, 18 March 1911. See also Plaatje's pamphlet *The Mote and the Beam: An Epic on Sex-Relationship 'twixt White and Black in British South Africa* (1921) dedicated to this topic.
65. Rhondda Williams, 'Prize Fight Stopped. What Next?' 7.
66. See 'Olive Schreiner in the Universal Races Congress', 2. Schreiner's contribution to the Universal Races Congress was thought to be lost. It was, however, reported verbatim by the Black press, which I discovered in doing research for this chapter. A transcription is now included under 'New Materials' of *OSLO*.
67. 'Olive Schreiner on the Unity of the Races', 2; see too Piquet, 'The First Universal Races Congress', 350.
68. Plaatje, *Native Life in South Africa, Before and Since the European War and the Boer Rebellion*, 201.
69. Schreiner to John X. Merriman, 20 July 1913, MSC 15/1913:134.
70. Schreiner to John X. Merriman, 20 July 1913, MSC 15/1913:134.
71. Plaatje, *Native Life in South Africa*, 217.
72. Plaatje, *Native Life in South Africa*, 365.
73. W. P. Schreiner, 'South Africa and the War', 121.

Chapter 7

The Influence of Olive Schreiner on Howard Thurman and, through Thurman, on Martin Luther King, Jr.
Heidi Barends

As a student at a retreat in Pawling, New York, a young Howard Thurman (1899–1981) – later a noted writer, philosopher, political activist and educator – first encountered the writing of Olive Schreiner (1855–1920). It was 1925, and the text of Schreiner's that was being read to him was 'The Hunter', an allegory about the quest for truth and higher human consciousness. In Thurman's autobiography, he writes that this initial encounter with Schreiner 'led [him] into a wonderland of the spirit and imagination', sparking what would become a lifelong interest in reading all of her works.[1] While several scholars have acknowledged the posthumous relationship between Thurman and Schreiner, few have provided an in-depth consideration of her impact on his thought and writing.[2] Schreiner's writing did more than just inspire Thurman creatively, or encourage him to think about women's position in society – it helped to shape Thurman's social vision, and his conception of the unity of life. Considering the relationship between Thurman and Schreiner within the context of recent Schreiner scholarship enriches an understanding of Schreiner's profound influence on Thurman's thinking and writing. Furthermore, considering Schreiner's influence on Thurman has an impact on how we might understand Schreiner's influence on the famous Civil Rights leader, Martin Luther King, Jr. (1929–1968).

Situating Schreiner, Thurman and King

Schreiner was an avid letter writer, and the large body of correspondence to recipients across the world are amongst the most illuminating artefacts for the purposes of this chapter. As a literary, historical and sociopolitical figure, Schreiner is difficult to categorise within any particular canon; she has been labelled a feminist, a socialist, a racist, an anti-racist, a pacifist, a mystic literary-philosopher and more. As Liz Stanley and

Andrea Salter note, Schreiner cannot be 'pigeon-holed' as any particular '-ist'.[3] We might more accurately refer to Schreiner as a white South African intellectual whose words and deeds engaged creatively, radically and interconnectedly with social, political, biological, metaphysical and existential issues in South Africa, England and the world.

Thurman is a similarly difficult figure to categorise as his influence has spanned various spheres and disciplines. Born in Daytona, Florida, in 1899, nearly fifty years after Schreiner, he became known as an author, philosopher, academic, theologian, preacher, political theoriser, mystic, educator and Civil Rights leader and is arguably one of the most influential African American intellectuals of the twentieth century. Thurman established the first interracial, non-denominational and interfaith church in the USA – The Church for the Fellowship of all Peoples – in 1944. He published over twenty books, including the well-known *Jesus and the Disinherited* (1949) and *Meditations of the Heart* (1954). The majority of his books are spiritual writings, with the exception of *A Track to the Water's Edge* (1973) – an editorial homage to Schreiner. Thurman played a considerable 'behind-the-scenes' role in the Civil Rights movement, introducing the concept of nonviolent protest to the African American cause after meeting with Mohandas Gandhi and leading a delegation to India in 1935, and mentoring many major religious and political figures of his time, such as Jesse Jackson, Vernon Jordan and Otis Moss, Jr. Most notably for the purposes of this chapter, he also mentored King, who was enrolled at Boston University when Thurman became Dean at the university's Marsh Chapel.

As an independent figure, King is iconic and needs little introduction. He is well-known for his anti-racism and nonviolent activism in the pursuit of civil rights for all Americans, and was awarded the Nobel Peace Prize in 1963 (the youngest person to ever receive it). His conceptualisation and advocacy of the beloved community – that is, his 'dream' of the ultimate realisation of a society that is built on a foundation of love and care that is evident in, and worked out through, social and economic justice – is one of his greatest religious, political and philosophical legacies.[4] King's notion of the beloved community was inspired by multiple figures, writings, movements, places and events, ranging from the philosophy of Josiah Royce, to the Black Church tradition to Gandhi and the *satyagraha* movement in India.[5]

King's relationship with Thurman had a long history, stemming from King's father's days at Morehouse College, where Thurman and Martin Luther King Sr. were classmates. While studying for his doctoral degree in Theology, King would attend chapel service and take notes while Thurman preached. King obtained his doctoral degree in Systematic

Theology in 1955, the same year that he led the peaceful bus boycott in Montgomery that would launch his political career and accelerate the Civil Rights movement. In the days leading up to the Montgomery boycotts, King carried a copy of Thurman's *Jesus and the Disinherited* with him for political and religious inspiration.[6] While Thurman and King did not have a close personal relationship, Thurman mentored King at key moments in his political career, and King borrowed extensively from Thurman's writings in his own works.[7] There is no doubt that Thurman had a profound influence on King's spiritual and political views, and thus a consideration of the impact of Schreiner's work on Thurman in the context of his influence on King is pertinent.

Thurman's intellectual and creative reverence for Schreiner has long confounded Thurman scholars, primarily because of the seeming disparities between the two figures in terms of gender, race and nationality. Mozella G. Mitchell writes that it 'is phenomenal ... that this white, female, South African writer, daughter of English missionaries to South Africa, should have such a profound and lasting influence on a black, male, religious scholar and preacher in America'.[8] Schreiner's influence on Thurman was prolific – indeed, in Thurman's own words, 'profound' – and far reaching.[9] The earliest textual evidence of Schreiner's influence on Thurman appears in his graduate thesis: 'The Basis of Sex Morality: An Inquiry into the Attitude toward Premarital Sexual Morality among Various Peoples and an Analysis of its True Basis' (1926). Thurman scholar Peter Eisenstadt describes the thesis as 'sweepingly, outspokenly, and in places, incandescently, feminist'.[10] It may seem unsurprising that Schreiner, who has been popularised and is perhaps primarily known as a feminist (although she herself never used this term), should have influenced Thurman's early written treatment of gender and sexuality. However, her influence on him extended well beyond the woman question.

Differently put, Thurman's interest in the woman question was but one in a greater scheme of interrelated questions and issues concerning the unity of life. As Eisenstadt argues, this early thesis 'undergirded much of [Thurman's] later thought, and not merely about sexuality or feminism but also about ... a self-knowledge that the "good life" is the "unified life, the undivided life"'.[11] In subsequent years, Thurman often quoted from Schreiner's writing (especially her allegories) in his writings and sermons, using them to preface or conclude his own thoughts, and her views on women (and subsequently, relations between strong and weak) are mentioned explicitly in a chapter on 'Deception' in *Jesus and the Disinherited*.[12] Schreiner's literary style, too, informed Thurman's own. Both Eisenstadt and Mitchell have noted that Thurman's meditations – his 'lucid' prose-poems written in a lyrical, dream-like fashion – are evocative of Schreiner's allegories, but the style and substance of her novel writing may be seen in Thurman's writing, too.[13] In *Jesus and the Disinherited*, for example, the passage preceding Thurman's mention of Schreiner is directly comparable to passages in Schreiner's posthumously published, *From Man to Man, or Perhaps Only* – (1926). Thurman uses examples from nature to explain social relations in a prosaic and allegorical way, in many ways evoking the novel's protagonist, Rebekah's, philosophical monologues and musings in the novel.[14] In *Jesus and the Disinherited*, Thurman writes:

> The techniques of deception seem to be a part of the nervous-reflex action of the organism. The cuttlefish, when attacked, will release some of the fluid from his sepia bag, making the water around him murky; in the midst of the cloudy water he confuses his attacker and makes his escape. [. . .] Consider the behavior of the birds a few feet away as they see the shadow. I have seen them take little feet full of dried grass or leaves, turn an easy half somersault, and play dead. The hawk blinks his eyes, thinks he has had an optical illusion, and goes on.[15]

In *From Man to Man*, Rebekah regularly uses this imagery of 'organisms' (that is, natural or biological analogies) to explain social phenomena and segment her arguments for gender and racial reform.[16] For example, in contestation of the notion of 'survival of the fittest' as a precursor to 'beauty, strength and unfolding in sentient life', Rebekah writes: 'From every cave and den and nest, from the depths of the sea, from air and earth, from the recesses of the human breast, rises but one great "No!" that refutes you'.[17] She goes on to list examples of the 'sea lion who carries his young in the bag on his own person' and the 'ostrich' whose male 'take[s] his house of brooding on the nest to keep the eggs warm' as proof that strong need not dominate weak, similar to Thurman's use of the 'cuttlefish' and the 'hawk' in relaying his thoughts on deception.[18]

Most significantly, Schreiner influenced Thurman's conceptualisations of the 'unity of life'.[19] It was the articulation of a distinct 'unity of life' that Thurman observed across Schreiner's works, and that formed the basis of his selections in *A Track to the Water's Edge*. Here Thurman attests to the impact of Schreiner's work on his social vision:

> [Schreiner] possessed what comes through to me as an innate, instinctual sense of the unity of all of life. It was this emphasis in her writing that was the first external confirmation of what had always been an active ingredient in my own awareness of life. As a boy in Florida, I walked along the beach of the Atlantic in the quiet stillness that can only be completely felt when the

murmur of the ocean is stilled and the tides move stealthily along the shore. I heard my breath against the night and watched the stars etch their brightness on the face of the darkened canopy of the heavens. I had the sense that all things, the sand, the sea, the stars, the night, and I were *one* lung through which all of life breathed. Not only was I aware of a vast rhythm enveloping all, but I was a part of it and it was a part of me. It was not until I read Olive Schreiner that I was able to establish sufficient psychological distance between me and the totality of such experiences to make the experience itself an object of thought. Thus it became possible for me to move from primary experience, to conceptualizing that experience, to a vision inclusive of all life. The resulting creative synthesis was to me *religious* rather than *metaphysical*, as seems to have been true in Olive Schreiner's case.[20]

Scholars who have analysed this passage have tended to focus on the 'confirmation', rather than inspiration or consolidation, that this instance brought for Thurman. For example, Walter Fluker argues that Schreiner did not offer Thurman anything 'new' in her ideas of 'oneness', but rather 'confirmed' what Thurman already knew, while Mitchell argues that Schreiner helped Thurman 'articulate' the vision of unity that he had always possessed.[21] However, the latter part of the excerpt juxtaposes confirmation with 'creative synthesis'. Thurman explains that Schreiner not only 'confirmed' these thoughts for him, but helped him make the significant move from experience, to conceptualisation, to building a 'vision inclusive of all of life'. In these terms, Thurman broadly yet clearly attributes the powerful impact of his creative and intellectual engagements with Schreiner to the realisation of his own broader social vision.[22]

Schreiner and Race

Thurman's 'intellectual coup de foudre' (to use Eisenstadt's wonderfully apt term) with Schreiner was not, however, without its difficulties.[23] Upon discovering that Schreiner was a white South African, Thurman 'became immediately suspicious and felt guilty that [he] was so affected by her'. He wrote:

[m]y initial investigation in an effort to find who she was and 'how come' was urgent. I had to answer the critical question, How could a white woman born and reared in South Africa think as she thought and feel about man as she felt?[24]

In pursuit of his answer, he read all of Schreiner's works, and all works about her he could find in the United States, becoming somewhat of a Schreiner scholar over the course of his life. Greater knowledge about

Schreiner and a larger awareness of her writing had a twofold effect: he continued to be 'profoundly moved and stirred by the power of her creative imagery', but nevertheless 'had to overcome certain well-grounded prejudices that screened everything [he] read from her life'.[25] For Thurman, Schreiner was a gifted writer and visionary, 'but when [he] placed her in her setting, [his] problems arose'.[26] His description of Schreiner echoes those of many Schreiner scholars today: '[s]he was, by endowment and philosophy, a universalist in outlook and feeling, while, at the same time, being a child of her times as a member of the exploiting and colonizing community'.[27] Thurman was appalled by Schreiner's use of racial epithets, a topic that requires deeper analysis given its frequent treatment by scholars. Thurman writes:

> I shall never forget my shock and anger when, in some of her stories or other writings, the word *nigger* was used. I do not refer to the times when she is quoting someone like Rhodes, or when it is a part of the language of one of the characters in her story, as in *Trooper Peter Halket*. Even though such a term was a part of the common language of the Boer and the English, for Olive Schreiner to be guilt of such insensitivity seemed to me inexcusably obscene. To the reader, this may seem undue sensitiveness on my part. So be it.[28]

Schreiner's use of racial terminology has been a topic of considerable debate amongst Schreiner scholars for many years. Much of Schreiner's work, and her non-fiction in particular, is peppered with racial epithets. Some scholars, such as Simon Lewis, argue that Schreiner's racial terminology (and her use of 'Kaffir' in particular) 'was probably not intended as derogatory'; Dorothy Driver notes, through meticulous analysis of Schreiner's published works and archive, that her language of race was uncertain and constantly changing as she grew in awareness, and that 'indications are that Schreiner would in due course have developed the political sensitivity she now lacked'.[29] Stanley and Salter, in their pioneering work on Schreiner's South African letters, explain that the term 'nigger'

> came to South Africa via white miners from the United States, and theirs was from the outset a contemptuous usage. Schreiner's first use of it came in the context of her time in the New Rush in the 1870s, so mining was almost certainly its source for her. In her letters, Schreiner uses the term to stand for 'black people generally', she uses it only when writing to specific people; and on three occasions, she uses it ironically when expressing the views of other people which she thought reprehensible.[30]

It does seem curious to me that Schreiner was not more aware of the offence her language might cause at the time she was using it.

Many Black persons vocalised the offence caused by commonly employed racial terms at the turn of the century, and there seems to have been an international awareness of the derogatory nature of particular terms (such as 'Kaffir') as well.[31]

Nevertheless, while Schreiner's racial terminology should be addressed and analysed, the revolutionary nature of her thinking and writing should not, I contend, be dismissed as a result thereof. Paul Harvey, in his book *Howard Thurman and the Disinherited*, comments that '[i]t remains one of the great curiosities of Thurman's life that a South African writer who was occasionally given to racial epithets in her writing should have exercised such an influence, but she did'.[32] Like Fluker, Harvey goes on to argue that 'Schreiner's influence came not so much from generating new ideas for Thurman as from clarifying and supporting ideas that Thurman in effect already had'.[33] Rather than attempting to understand how the use of racial epithets and a view of the unity of life could (or could not) co-exist (a phenomenon which Thurman himself endeavoured to understand in his study of Schreiner), such accounts dismiss the evidence of Schreiner's significant and, in many ways, novel influence on Thurman on the basis of Schreiner's assumed racial politics.

In this vein, there is a tendency to view Schreiner's use of racial epithets as indicative of her antipathy towards Black liberation. In Eisenstadt's analysis of Schreiner and Thurman, for example, he calls Schreiner 'Thurman's casually racist white South African soulmate', and comments that 'although [Schreiner] was, for her time, forward-thinking about the future of South Africa's native peoples, they were never central to her politics'.[34] Recent Schreiner scholarship indicates that this is not accurate.

As Stanley and Salter document impressively, Schreiner's South African letters show that from 1890, Schreiner was increasingly involved in activities related to 'South Africa's native peoples'. She was a powerful influence in the development of a 'radical third force in Cape political life'; she championed the plight of full adult suffrage (rejecting distinctions based on race or sex) with the Cape Women's Enfranchisement League; and she voiced her opposition to increasingly racialised policies and practices that were implemented after the Union of South African in 1910. Stanley and Salter further explain that Schreiner

> actively supported black causes and political activism around 'native' rights and the franchise, intervened publicly regarding Chinese labour, rebutted 'so-called black peril' claims being orchestrated to legitimate repressive legalisation, supported Gandhi and Indian protest activities in the Transvaal, and opposed the Native's Land Act of 1913.[35]

Additionally, Schreiner supported two South African National Native Congress (SANNC) delegations to Europe against the Land Act and the curtailment of Black rights in 1916 and 1919. Indeed, Stanley and Salter write that, shortly before her death in 1920, Schreiner professed in a letter to J. C. Smuts, a South African statesmen and former Boer General, that 'race' had become not just South Africa's, but 'the world's great question'.[36]

Thurman himself provided an extended account of his view on Schreiner's racial politics in *A Track to the Water's Edge*. He did not view Schreiner as 'an avowed', 'messianic', or 'religious racist' (in fact, he does not refer to her explicitly as a 'racist' at all), but he does note the stark paradox between her views on race and her views on the unity of life.[37] Thurman argued that Schreiner 'identified acutely with Africans on a personal, individual level', and that he could 'as a black man, deal with her attitude with integrity' because she 'did not love the Africans for Christ's sake'.[38] While he detected 'sentimentality' in her writing, he wrote that 'in all her utterances, she seemed to escape the necessity of thinking of the African in abstract rather than in concrete terms'.[39] Schreiner's attitude toward Africans in her writing remained, for Thurman (and perhaps for present-day Schreiner scholars, too), an 'unresolved conflict'.[40] He concluded that despite Schreiner's 'fundamental affirmation about the unity of life and the resultant compassion for all of life which it inspired, it was not easy for her to translate these into the terms of a primary attitude toward the individual African'.[41] Thurman's statement does not claim that the individual African was not a primary concern of Schreiner's, but rather highlights the clear difficulty Schreiner experienced in articulating a vision of the unity of life that productively encompassed racial justice.

It must be noted that Schreiner's thinking on race evolved over the course of her life, as evidenced by the key 'turning points' in Schreiner's thinking about race that are traced by Stanley in her chapter in this collection. Indeed, many scholars have noted the shifts and nuances that can be read across Schreiner's *oeuvre* in line with her burgeoning awareness of the oppressions of racism.[42] A moment of particular relevance with regard to a discussion of Thurman and Schreiner is Schreiner's reading of W. E. B. Du Bois's *The Souls of Black Folk* in 1905. In an oft-quoted letter to Edward Carpenter (English socialist and gay rights activist), Schreiner wrote that *Souls* was what she had 'for years & years longed for' – that is, an encounter with a 'book from the heart of a black man', rather than a book written by white authors about Black men, such as her own *Trooper Peter Halket* (1896) or Harriet Beecher Stowe's *Uncle Tom's Cabin* (1852). Du Bois's book affected her on a personal and emotional level, as well as politically. She wrote:

> I can't even write of the book it touches me so. Of course it can't quite be the same to you who have not all your life been face to face, with persistent quiet oppression & humiliation which white man deals out to dark. The book makes me feel so much that sometimes I can't look at it; it seems to come from within me.[43]

Schreiner then goes on to say:

> [b]efore us here looks a terrible thing, a great desolating native war, in which Boers & British will combine to wipe out the black man's freedom, take his land, his franchise, where he has it, as in the Cape Colony & gain cheap labour.[44]

Du Bois was a contemporary of Thurman, and made several appearances at Morehouse College during Thurman's time there. One thinks of Thurman's remarks when he first heard Schreiner's 'Hunter' that '[i]t seemed that all my life long I was being readied for such an encounter', and one wonders what incredible, radical, perspective-altering conversations could have occurred had Schreiner read the works of Thurman.

The Influence of Schreiner, through Thurman, on Martin Luther King, Jr.

Despite ample scholarly considerations of Schreiner's influence and reception in America, and the influence of Du Bois and African American thought on Schreiner's racial politics, very little attention has been paid to Schreiner's influence on African American intellectual thought and history. In the recently published Broadview Edition of Schreiner's *Dreams*, the editors provide a comprehensive introduction to Schreiner and write of her influence on socialists and suffragettes in America, most notably on Charlotte Perkins Gillman.[45] No mention, however, is made of Schreiner's influence on Thurman, and there seems to be little (if any) real evidence of a consideration of Schreiner and Thurman by Schreiner scholars.[46] This is despite the fact that Thurman is one of the few authors to have published an anthology of Schreiner's works. The lack of scholarly consideration of Thurman's anthology in Schreiner scholarship is somewhat strange.

Thurman's anthology, *A Track to the Water's Edge: An Olive Schreiner Reader*, gains its title from a line in Schreiner's allegory 'Three Dreams in a Desert' (1890). The anthology is prefaced with an excerpt from 'Three Dreams in a Desert', and also includes a longer excerpt from the allegory within the book itself, signalling its conceptual importance. 'Three Dreams in a Desert' speaks directly to the nature of positive influence, and Schreiner's influence on Thurman in particular. Like the locust who 'comes down to the water-edge, and is swept away', and whose body piles up with others to build a bridge that 'the rest pass over', Schreiner's social vision and her views on the interconnections and unity of life made a track to the water's edge upon which Thurman could build. Schreiner's influence on Thurman was not singular – and influence rarely is. As Thurman wrote of Schreiner:

> It is difficult to identify precisely the influences that shape and fashion the life of the individual. The enigma is the process at work in the private world of an individual that finds its expression in the thoughts, words, and actions that ultimately emerge. It has been aptly said that the time and place of a man's life is the time and place of his body, but the meaning and significance of a man's life is as creative, as vast, and as far-reaching as his gifts, his dreams, and his response to his times can make them. This was certainly true of Olive Schreiner.[47]

This was just as true of Thurman, who was influenced – to what extent we shall never know – by various figures, including George Cross, Mohandas Gandhi, W. E. B. Du Bois, William James, Josiah Royce, Alain Locke, Rufus Jones and others.[48] As a white South African woman, Schreiner does stand out as an oddity if added to this list. However, it is imperative that she be included in discussions on Thurman because Thurman's social vision, acutely aware as he was of the realities and oppressions of the colour line, may be seen as extending, expanding and perhaps even transforming Schreiner's social theory on the unity of life.

The notion of the unity of life, and that of community, are intricately linked. Walter Fluker explained that community, for Thurman,

> refers to wholeness, integration and harmony. For him, all life is interrelated and involved in goal-seeking. In each particular manifestation of life, there is the potential for it to realize its proper form, and the actualization of potentiality in any form of life is synonymous with community. 'Community' as 'actualized potential' is true at all levels of life: in tiny cells and in human society.[49]

'[W]holeness, integration and harmony' may be read as synonymous with a sense of the 'unity of life' and, if we acknowledge the synthesis in life that reading Schreiner helped Thurman perceive (that is, as Thurman professed to recognising after reading Schreiner, that 'all things, the sand, the sea, the starts, the night and I were *one* lung through which life breathed') then it is highly probable that Schreiner influenced Thurman's conceptualisation of community.[50]

Thurman's conceptualisation of community, and the beloved community in particular, may be seen as linked to King's conceptualisation. Kipton Jensen and Preston King write:

> For King and Thurman and [Josiah] Royce, though each expressed it in his own way, the notion of the beloved community signaled a loyal commitment to radical because unconditional love, social justice, and an acknowledgement of the inviolable dignity of persons.[51]

We might also read the thread of the 'unity of life' in the beloved community. As Fluker explains, for King: 'all human life is *interrelated* and must be seen as a *single process* culminating in the beloved community'.[52]

It is commonly accepted by Fluker and others that King's idea of the beloved community 'represents a synthesis from a wide range of thinkers' (Thurman included), although Schreiner has not yet been considered within this context.[53] Perhaps the overtly Christian nature of King's philosophical and political views may make a link between himself and Schreiner (and Schreiner and Thurman too, for that matter) unlikely, as Schreiner rejected orthodox Christianity from an early age and considered herself a 'Free-thinker'.[54] She also never expressly used the term 'beloved community' in her writing, although intertextual affinities are certainly present. For King, the 'theological dimension of the "beloved community" is primary' as is 'the idea of a personal God, who is a creative force who works for universal wholeness, informs his philosophical and ethical claims'.[55]

It must be said that Schreiner was deeply influenced by the Bible, and though she rejected conventional notions of Christianity, she undoubtedly believed in a unifying metaphysical life force.[56] In a letter to J. T. Lloyd, Schreiner wrote that she did not take much from the teachings of Jesus, and Christ is a core aspect of both Thurman's and King's visions of the Beloved Community.[57] But what Thurman identifies as Schreiner's 'basic social philosophy' is in fact put forth by a Christ-figure in her novella, *Trooper Peter Halket of Mashonaland* (the so-called 'Stranger') who professes:

> Love your enemies; do good to them that hate you. Walk ever forward, looking not to the right hand or the left. Heed not what men shall say of you. Succour the oppressed; deliver the captive. If thine enemy hunger, feed him; if he is athirst, give him a drink.[58]

If we add to the Stranger's profession above, consideration of the importance of community through oneness in life associated with Waldo in *The Story of an African Farm*, and which is also a concept that Thurman and King extended theologically and politically in their own ways, then the link between Schreiner and the sense of a beloved community perhaps becomes more tangible. Waldo attests:

> For the little soul that cries aloud for continued personal existence for itself and its beloved, there is no help. For the soul which knows itself no more as a unit, but as a part of the Universal Unity of which the Beloved also is a part; which feels within itself the throb of the Universal Life; for that soul there is no death.[59]

It is only through reconciliation with the whole of 'Universal Life' – of a beloved community – that a liberated life can be achieved.

To reduce Schreiner's influence, relevance and, relatedly, her literary and historical importance to the scope of her identity position (white, female, colonial South African) is a historical inaccuracy. In *Imperialism, Labour and the New Woman*, Stanley notes that Schreiner was a

> major intellectual presence for other circles and collectivities of people, in South Africa, Britain, North America, Japan, Russia and elsewhere as well as for many individual people who came across her work and felt their ideas and lives changed by it.[60]

In this sense, a link from Schreiner to Thurman, and through Thurman to King, makes almost perfect sense. Kipton Jensen, in an analysis of the influence of Josiah Royce on Thurman and King, writes that while influence is often subject to 'many significant factors or variables in a complex confluence of sociohistorical and philosophical' factors, this does not make it 'nontrivial' as a matter of study.[61] Jensen goes on to say that 'while the genius of Thurman or King cannot be reduced to the ideas of their predecessors, whether Royce and Du Bois, whether intellectual or cultural ... something valuable is gained by revisiting this history'.[62]

The 'something valuable' that is gained by considering Schreiner in terms of her influence on Thurman, and through Thurman on King, is the widening of historical lineages to include figures who may not conventionally seem to pass on ideas across race, space, gender or time. Influence does not equal ownership; I am by no means arguing that King's Beloved Community originated with Schreiner. However, I am arguing for Schreiner to be included in discussions on the influences on King, particularly in terms of his conceptualisation of the Beloved Community. Where Schreiner struggled to conceive of the language and methodology to meaningfully include the vision of racial equality she so longed to see realised within her wider social vision, Thurman drew from, and built upon, Schreiner's genius in ways that were 'strange and defiant' to him and others, but which were nevertheless, in his words, 'profound'.[63] In serving as a mentor and key influence to King, Thurman's indebtedness to Schreiner must be considered in terms of Thurman's influence on King.

In the final stanza of 'Three Dreams in a Desert', Schreiner writes:

And I dreamed a dream.
　I dreamed I saw a land. And on the hills walked brave women and brave men, hand in hand. And they looked into each other's eyes, and they were not afraid.
　And I saw the women also hold each other's hands.
　And I said to him beside me, 'What place is this?'
　And he said, 'This is heaven.'
　And I said, 'Where is it?'
　And he answered, 'On Earth.'
　And I said, 'When shall these things be?'
　And he answered, 'In the FUTURE'.[64]

King outlined his political dream for society in his iconic speech in 1963, transforming the notion of the American Dream into a tactile vision of the Beloved Community. It was a dream that Thurman, in his obituary of King, claimed to share as a 'fellow pilgrim'.[65] Nearly four decades after Schreiner's death, King's dream of the beloved community may be read as a radical advance of the justice that Schreiner's allegory saw appearing in the 'FUTURE'. For as Waldo professed in *The Story of an African Farm*: 'so age succeeds age, and dream succeeds dream, and of the joy of the dreamer no man knoweth but he who dreameth. Our fathers had their dream; we have ours; the generation that follows will have its own'.[66]

The dreams of social change that each of these three figures nurtured and espoused are thus interlinked and interconnected. Their ideas on the unity of life spanned race, place, gender, nationality, religion and generation, infusing, cross-pollinating and stretching each other in ways that may confound and perplex us as modern scholars. Considering the influence of Schreiner on Thurman, and through Thurman on King, allows us to widen our understandings of Schreiner's influence and impact within the context of the Civil Rights era.

Works Cited

Barends, Heidi. '"The Dream Ends There": Transnational Feminist Negotiations in the Lives and Works of Pauline E. Hopkins and Olive Schreiner'. PhD diss., University of Cape Town, 2018.

Berkman, Joyce Avrech. *The Healing Imagination of Olive Schreiner: Beyond South African Colonialism*. Amherst: University of Massachusetts Press, 1989.

Black, Barbara, Carly Nations, and Anna Spydell. 'Introduction.' In *Dreams*, edited by Barbara Black, Carly Nations, and Anna Spydell, 13–48. Peterborough: Broadview Press, 2020.

Dorrien, Gary. *Breaking White Supremacy: Martin Luther King Jr. and the Black Social Gospel*. New Haven: Yale University Press, 2018.

Driver, Dorothy. 'Introduction to the New Edition.' In *From Man to Man or Perhaps Only–*, edited by Dorothy Driver, ix–xlvi. Claremont: University of Cape Town Press, 2015.

Eisenstadt, Peter. *Against the Hounds of Hell: A Life of Howard Thurman*. Charlottesville: University of Virginia Press, 2021.

First, Ruth, and Ann Scott. *Olive Schreiner*. New York: Schoken Books, 1982.

Harvey, Paul. *Howard Thurman and the Disinherited: A Religious Biography*. Michigan: William B. Eerdmans Publishing Company, 2020. E-book.

Fluker, Walter. 'They Looked for a City: A Comparison of the Idea of Community in Howard Thurman and Martin Luther King Jr'. *The Journal of Religious Ethics* 18, no. 2 (1990): 33–55.

Jensen, Kipton. 'The Growing Edges of Beloved Community: From Royce to Thurman and King'. *Transactions of the Charles S. Peirce Society* 52, no. 2 (2016): 239–58.

—. Jensen, Kipton, and Preston King. 'Beloved Community: Martin Luther King, Howard Thurman and Josiah Royce.' *AMITY: The Journal of Friendship Studies* 4, no. 1 (2017): 15–31.

King Jr, Martin Luther. 'I Have a Dream Speech'. *Washington DC* (August 28 1963).

Lewis, Simon. *White Women Writers and Their African Invention*. Gainesville: University Press of Florida, 2003.

Massey, James. 'Howard Thurman and Olive Schreiner on the Unity of All Life: A Bibliographical Essay'. *Journal of Religious Thought* 34, no. 2 (1977/1978): 29–33.

Mitchell, Mozella G. 'Howard Thurman and Olive Schreiner: Post-modern Marriage Post-mortem'. *Journal of Religious Thought* 38, no. 1 (1981): 62–72.

Schreiner, Olive. *The Story of an African Farm*. Boston: Roberts Brothers, 1888.

—. 'The Story of an African Farm'. In *A Track to the Water's Edge: An Olive Schreiner Reader*, edited by Howard Thurman, 1–12. New York: Harper & Row, 1973.

—. *From Man to Man, or Perhaps Only –*, edited by Dorothy Driver. Claremont: UCT Press, 2015.

—. 'Three Dreams in a Desert'. In *A Track to the Water's Edge: An Olive Schreiner Reader*, edited by Howard Thurman, 53–56. New York: Harper & Row, 1973.
Stanley, Liz. *Imperialism, Labour and the New Woman: Olive Schreiner's Social Theory*. Durham: Sociologypress, 2002.
—. Stanley, Liz, and Andrea Salter. 'Introduction: Olive Schreiner, a Life'. In *The World's Great Question: Olive Schreiner's South African Letters 1899–1920*, edited by Liz Stanley and Andrea Salter, xii–xliv. Cape Town: Van Riebeeck Society, 2014.
Thurman, Howard. *Jesus and the Disinherited*. Boston: Beacon Press, 1996.
—. *A Track to the Water's Edge: The Olive Schreiner Reader*. New York: Harper & Row, 1973.
—. *With Head and Heart: The Autobiography of Howard Thurman*. New York: Harcourt Brace & Company, 1979.

Letters

Olive Schreiner to Edward Carpenter, 26 October 1905. *Olive Schreiner Letters Online*.
Olive Schreiner to Henry Havelock Ellis, 25 November 1880. *Olive Schreiner Letters Online*.
Olive Schreiner to J. T. Lloyd, 29 October 1892. *Olive Schreiner Letters Online*.

Notes

1. Thurman, *With Head and Heart*, 255.
2. Eisenstadt, *Against the Hounds of Hell*, 91–96, 357–59; Mitchell, 'Post-Modern Marriage Post-Mortem', 63; Massey, 'Howard Thurman and Olive Schreiner on the Unity of All Life', 29–33.
3. Stanley and Salter, *The World's Great Question*, xxxiii.
4. King Jr, 'I Have a Dream Speech'.
5. Fluker, 'They Looked for a City', 37–39. Fluker writes: 'King's conception of the "beloved community" represents a synthesis of from a wide range of thinkers', but Olive Schreiner has yet to be considered within this range.
6. Thurman, *With Head and Heart*, 255.
7. Dorrien, *Breaking White Supremacy*, 171.
8. Mitchell, 'Post-Modern Marriage Post-Mortem', 63.
9. Thurman, *A Track to the Water's Edge*, xi.
10. Eisenstadt, *Against the Hounds of Hell*, 93. Eisenstadt provides an excellent analysis of this thesis and one of the best contextual considerations of Schreiner's general influence on Thurman within Thurman scholarship.
11. Eisenstadt, *Against the Hounds of Hell*, 95.
12. Massey, 'Howard Thurman and Olive Schreiner', 32; Thurman, *Jesus and the Disinherited*, 64.
13. Eisenstadt, *Against the Hounds of Hell*, 92; Mitchell, 'Post-Modern Marriage Post-Mortem,' 63.
14. Schreiner, *From Man to Man*, 140–88.

15. Thurman, *Jesus and the Disinherited*, 58.
16. Thurman, *Jesus and the Disinherited*, 58.
17. Schreiner, *From Man to Man*, 171.
18. Schreiner, *From Man to Man*, 172. Notably, the sections of *From Man to Man* that are excerpted in *A Track to the Water's Edge* all relate to Rebekah's intellectual musings, highlighting their importance to Thurman (Thurman, *A Track to the Water's Edge*, 151198).
19. Schreiner's understanding of the 'unity of life' was, in turn, inspired by the work of Herbert Spencer and Ralph Waldo Emerson.
20. Thurman, *A Track to the Water's Edge*, xxvii–xxviii.
21. Fluker, 'They Looked for a City', 38; Mitchell, 'Post-Modern Marriage Post-Mortem,' 63.
22. Thurman, *A Track to the Water's Edge*, xxviii.
23. Eisenstadt, *Against the Hounds of Hell*, 91.
24. Thurman, *A Track to the Water's Edge*, xi–xii.
25. It must be noted that prior to *A Track to the Water's Edge*'s publication in 1973, the sources that Thurman had access to included Schreiner's published works, and Cronwright-Schreiner's biography and severely bowdlerised edition of his wife's letters. It does not seem that Thurman had access to Schreiner's wider archive, including her extensive body of letters not published in Cronwright-Schreiner's edition, nor any of her unpublished works, such as the 'Introduction to the Vindication'. Thurman wrote: 'Systematically I sought and found all of her works available in the United States in the late twenties and early thirties: *The Story of an African Farm*; *Undine*; *From Man to Man*; *Dreams, Stories and Allegories*; *Trooper Peter Halket of Mashonaland*; *Dream Life and Real Life*; *Woman and Labour*; and "The Dawn of Civilisation," a rather extensive article that appeared in *The London Nation and Atheneum* in 1921. Then I secured the two volumes edited by her husband, Cronwright-Schreiner: *Life of Olive Schreiner* and *The Letters of Olive Schreiner*. Only recently was I able to acquire *Thoughts on South Africa*; *Closer Union, a Letter by Olive Schreiner*; *A Letter on the Jew*'. See Thurman, *A Track to the Water's Edge*, xii. He also obtained copies of Schreiner centennial writings in the 1950s, and described Vera Buchanan-Gould's biography as noteworthy. See Thurman, *A Track to the Water's Edge*, xviii.
26. Thurman, *A Track to the Water's Edge*, xxvii.
27. Thurman, *A Track to the Water's Edge*, xx.
28. Thurman, *A Track to the Water's Edge*, xxix.
29. Lewis, *White Women Writers*, 202; Driver, 'Introduction', xi.
30. Stanley and Salter, 'The World's Great Question', xlii–xliii.
31. See Barends, 'The Dream Ends There', 79–80.
32. Harvey, *Howard Thurman and the Disinherited*.
33. Harvey, *Howard Thurman and the Disinherited*.
34. Eisenstadt, *Against the Hounds of Hell*, 93.
35. Stanley and Salter, 'The World's Great Question', xxxiii.
36. Stanley and Salter, 'The World's Great Question', xxxiii.
37. Thurman, *A Track to the Water's Edge*, xxv.
38. Thurman, *A Track to the Water's Edge*, xxv.
39. Thurman, *A Track to the Water's Edge*, xxv.

40. Thurman, *A Track to the Water's Edge*, xx.
41. Thurman, *A Track to the Water's Edge*, xxix.
42. See Stanley and Salter 'The World's Great Question', xxxiv; Driver, 'Introduction', xxx; Barends, 'The Dream Ends There', 62–65.
43. Schreiner to Carpenter, 26 October 1905, *Olive Schreiner Letters Online* (*OSLO*).
44. Schreiner to Carpenter, 26 October 1905, *OSLO*.
45. Black, Nations and Spydell, 'Introduction', 37.
46. Ruth First and Ann Scott, in their biography of Schreiner, mention Thurman's shock at Schreiner's racial terminology in a footnote. See *Olive Schreiner*, 23n.
47. Thurman, *A Track to the Water's Edge*, xix.
48. Fluker, 'They Looked for a City', 38.
49. Fluker, 'They Looked for a City', 38. The quote from Thurman comes from his book, *The Search for Common Ground: An Inquiry Into The Basics of Man's Experience of Community*.
50. Thurman, *A Track to the Water's Edge*, xxvii.
51. Jensen and King, 'Beloved Community', 15.
52. Fluker, 'They Looked for a City', 39, emphasis added.
53. Fluker, 'They Looked for a City', 39.
54. Schreiner to Havelock Ellis, 25 November 1880, *OSLO*. This letter is a copy of Schreiner's application to study nursing at the Edinburgh Royal Infirmary, and is marked for the attention of the 'Lady Superintendent of Nurses'. Schreiner gives the answer 'Free-thinker' in response to the question 'Of what religious denomination?'
55. Fluker, 'They Looked for a City', 39.
56. For an in-depth account of Schreiner's views on religion, see Joyce Avrech Berkman's *The Healing Imagination of Olive Schreiner*, 43–73.
57. Schreiner to Lloyd, 29 October 1892, *OSLO*.
58. Thurman, *A Track to the Water's Edge*, xxiv.
59. Schreiner, *The Story of an African Farm*, 360–61.
60. Stanley, *Imperialism, Labour and the New Woman*, 18.
61. Jensen, 'The Growing Edges', 240.
62. Jensen, 'The Growing Edges', 240.
63. Thurman, *A Track to the Water's Edge*, xi.
64. Schreiner, *Three Dreams in a Desert*, 58.
65. Thurman, *With Head and Heart*, 255.
66. Schreiner, *The Story of an African Farm*, 362.

Part III

Print, Publishing and Translation

Chapter 8

Dreaming of Liberty: Olive Schreiner's Ambivalent Anarchism
Clare Gill

Writing in the *Novel Review* in 1892, the socialist journalist and novelist Margaret Harkness asserted that Olive Schreiner's politics should be categorised as anarchist, a claim that Schreiner herself refuted as 'untrue'.[1] Schreiner's rejection of the anarchist label is certainly in keeping with scholarly assessments of the major currents of her intellectual and political preoccupations during the time she spent in England in the 1880s. Given her friendships with leading socialists and radicals including Eleanor Marx, Havelock Ellis and Edward Carpenter, and her engagement with intellectual organisations such as the Fellowship of the New Life, the forerunner of the Fabian Society, and the Men and Women's Club, a radical discussion group that debated issues relating to sex and the 'Woman Question', scholarly accounts of Schreiner's placement within the chequered landscape of British radical politics in this period have focused attention on her engagements with, and influence on, the women's movement and socialism. Schreiner's letters from and about her time in England in the 1880s reveal her embeddedness within the political networks and activities of the Left in particular. She witnessed and was inspired by the possibilities of mass action suggested by the London Dock Strike of 1889; she attended the inaugural meeting of the women's branch of H. M. Hyndman's Marxist-inspired Democratic Federation (later the Social Democratic Federation); she made regular visits to Edward Carpenter's home at Millthorpe, near Sheffield, where she observed and was greatly inspired by Carpenter's practical anti-capitalism, including his commitment to agrarian self-sufficiency. When Schreiner reflected on this period of her life in a letter to her brother William Schreiner in 1912, she listed such political activities and alliances from her time in England as evidence of her socialist credentials, informing him, with clear pride, that the 'Socialist[s] do look upon me as one of their folk'.[2]

Schreiner clearly thought of herself as a comrade of the British Left, but as for many radicals in this period, particularly undoctrinaire political thinkers like Schreiner, such an identification did not necessarily – or always – exclude anarchism. Certainly, Schreiner's wider radical network in Britain in the 1880s and 1890s brought her into contact with a range of anarchist proponents and exposed her to anarchist writings and ideas. She was friends, for example, with Charlotte Wilson, the feminist and anarchist who, in 1886, co-founded the anarchist newspaper *Freedom* with the exiled Russian prince, Peter Kropotkin. In addition to reading Wilson's journalism on subjects such as anarchism and marriage, Schreiner also requested in 1890 that a copy of *Dreams* be forwarded to Wilson for review in *Freedom*, indicating not only her engagement with, but also her desire to be a part of, anarchist print culture.[3] Even Carpenter, who is often associated with an idealised form of dreamer socialism, has been more accurately characterised as having drifted between the ideological poles of socialism and anarchism in his lifetime.[4] While he was heavily involved in organised socialism and virulently opposed the violent tactics preferred by some anarchists, Carpenter was ultimately a proponent of a voluntary and decentralised social system – what he referred to as a 'non-governmental society' – and described himself in 1892 as 'more of an anarchist than anything else as regards government'.[5] Carpenter always insisted that anarchists belonged to the wider family of the labour movement, a view shared by Schreiner. In May 1892, the same month that Schreiner denied Harkness's claim that she was an anarchist, she wrote to Carpenter to sympathise with him about the 'anarchist troubles' he faced from a violent contingent within the Sheffield Socialist Society and to express regret that *'our people* could do such things'.[6] In spite of her disapproval of the violent methods of the Sheffield anarchists, her sense of anarchism's ideological placement within the broader landscape of radical politics in the 1890s remained intact.

Schreiner's disgruntlement at being labelled an anarchist in print was no doubt fuelled by anarchism's growing image problem in the final decades of the nineteenth century, which resulted from its association with dynamite and other forms of violent direct action. Yet, as both a political ideology and a social movement, anarchism's remit was expansive and diverse; its followers aligned with a dizzying array of organisational subdivisions and ideological permutations, from egoism and individualism to anarchist communism, mutualism, collectivism and syndicalism. Schreiner's complex political philosophy did not map onto any one school of anarchist thought, nor was it comfortably accommodated by any other single political framework or taxonomy. Part of her power as a political thinker was located in her capacity to move amongst various ideological formations and 'great world movement[s]' of the day without 'bind[ing]' herself dogmatically to any of them.[7]

For Schreiner, the issues of labour and class debated by the socialists were inseparable from the ideological terrain of the 'Woman Question', and all were complicated further by her understanding of the ways in which metropolitan models of social justice failed to engage with questions of race and nationality, or to account for the particular forms of oppression and injustice that flourished under imperial capitalism. It is not my intention in this chapter to argue that Schreiner was, in fact, an anarchist. While she was, as Carolyn Burdett notes, 'non-committal' in her view of the role of the state, Schreiner tended to favour parliamentary solutions to the political struggles and causes with which she was actively involved in her lifetime, a position that places her askance to most of the major currents of anarchist thinking in respect of government.[8] Yet, as this chapter will reveal, Schreiner's fiction of the 1880s and 1890s struck a chord with anarchist readers internationally, many of whom registered an anarchistic cadence in the appeals to liberty and fantasies of perfect freedom contained within her allegorical short fiction in particular.

Schreiner's influence was especially pronounced in American anarchist print media, including *Liberty*, the Boston individualist anarchist newspaper edited by Benjamin R. Tucker, where she was championed for her freethinking and radical questioning of nineteenth-century orthodoxies regarding sex, love and marriage. By tracing Schreiner and her works through the pages of *Liberty* and outwards through the paper's publishing offshoots, the ideological importance of her work and politics for individualist forms of anarchism that were developing on both sides of the Atlantic in this period will become clear and, with it, the proximity of aspects of her writing and ideas to elements of anarchism's wider intellectual and ideological purview. This chapter will also cast light on the anarchic distribution practices of American anarchists such as Tucker, *Liberty*'s founder and editor, and Sarah E. Holmes, a key contributor, who both put out editions of Schreiner's works in formats and through channels that circumvented mainstream publishing networks. Schreiner's ambivalent anarchism will therefore be situated within broader debates about copyright, including a consideration of piracy, a practice that bypasses – and yet also curiously recreates – the structures of what Schreiner herself described as the 'capitalist rings' of publishing and bookselling.[9]

Individualist Anarchism and *Liberty*

The individualist tradition was deeply entrenched within American political culture, taking root, according to David Goodway, in the 'values of the American Revolution and Jeffersonian democracy', budding under the influence of the philosophical individualism of Emerson and Thoreau, and flowering in the 1880s and 1890s with the activities of the so-called Boston anarchists, spearheaded by Benjamin Tucker and the anarchist network clustered around his periodical *Liberty*.[10] Unlike in Europe at the end of the nineteenth century, where communist anarchism sounded the dominant note, individualist and communist strains of anarchism co-existed in the United States. While public debates between American proponents of the two broad strands of anarchism was often adversarial, they nevertheless shared a number of common basic principles, such as an opposition to capitalism, a commitment to freedom and an understanding of the state as coercive and functioning as an instrument of oppression. One of the key areas of dissent was in their conception of property and attendant political economy. Where anarchist communists sought the abolition of private property and a redistribution of wealth in accordance with need, individualists, as Peter Ryley has noted, 'advocated the right of possession through use and labour, together with a freely negotiated system of exchange and trade'.[11] This partial defence of private property and advocacy of free trade – elements more often understood as cornerstones of capitalism rather than features of radical thought – help to explain why individualist forms of anarchism occupy a distinctive and contested placement within anarchist historiography, and why some scholars refute that individualism can be considered a form of anarchism at all.

This reservation was not shared by Benjamin Tucker, individualist anarchism's most significant and galvanising voice in the United States in the final two decades of the nineteenth century. Fully assured of individualism's position within the ideological pantheon of radicalism, Tucker enthusiastically embraced the label of anarchist, making him, according to the historian Peter Marshall, 'the first American thinker to call himself an anarchist with pride'.[12] Tucker was supplied with an early model of productive anti-authoritarianism via his Quaker upbringing in mid-century Massachusetts, but the flame of his radicalism was truly ignited by his encounters in the 1870s with veteran individualist radicals such as Josiah Warren and William B. Greene, as well as the anarchist and labour reformer Ezra Heywood. Tucker's career as an anarchist journalist was set in motion when he was hired as the associate editor of Heywood's anarchist-feminist periodical, *The Word*, in 1875, but it was with his periodical *Liberty* that he established himself as a political force within anarchism, not only in terms of the intellectual high bar set within the pages of the paper, but also in respect of its crucial role in the articulation and dissemination of individualist anarchist thought in the United States and beyond. Founded in Boston in 1881, *Liberty* functioned as the principal organ for American individualism until its cessation in 1908. Tucker's own brand of anarchism formed the spine of the periodical, and he made no effort to conceal his editorial interventions or his attempts to influence the opinion of its readers. His candid pronouncement in the first number that the periodical 'will be edited to suit its editor, not its reader', it being 'published for the very definite purpose of spreading certain ideas', is characteristic of both Tucker's interventionist editorial style and his propagandic intentions for the paper.[13]

Liberty therefore articulated and advocated for a particular strain of individualist anarchism, one shaped by its editor's unique roster of political and intellectual influences. At its heart, the ideology espoused by *Liberty* balanced the general anarchist call for the abolition of the state with the individualist defence of the unfettered freedom of the individual. Under the influence of the egoism of Max Stirner, whose work *The Ego and His Own* was published in translation by Tucker, *Liberty* promoted the concept of self-ownership, defined by Tucker as 'the mainspring of conduct' under which 'the ego is supreme'.[14] Stirner's extreme individualist philosophy preached the primacy of the self and the individual's self-interest and thus was antithetical not only to the collectivism of anarchist communism and socialism, but also to the widespread calls for altruism and sympathy that punctuated the work of many socialist writers in this period, including Schreiner's.[15] If Stirnerite egoism provided Tucker with a philosophical scaffolding for his belief that there should be no external limits imposed on individual autonomy, it was the economic mutualism of Proudhon and the model of voluntary cooperation provided by Josiah Warren that undergirded Tucker's political economy and that enabled him, in spite of his fidelity to free-market logic, to categorise his economic framework as socialist. In *Liberty*, Tucker promoted a vision of a future stateless society in which capitalism has been disbanded, every form of economic monopoly eradicated, and the full value of labour returned to the labourer. The anti-capitalist basis of the individualist political economy espoused by Tucker provides a context for the ideological harnessing of Schreiner's late-Victorian fiction, and especially of her socialist allegories in the pages of *Liberty*.

While Tucker was an omnipotent editorial presence in *Liberty*, the periodical was more than a unitary mouthpiece for its editor – and far from myopic in terms of content. *Liberty* showcased contributions from and responses to most of the leading voices within American anarchism, charting the news and activities of individuals and organisations associated with anarchism's offshoots and the variety of other radical currents with which *Liberty*, its contributors and readers were affiliated. All of this gave *Liberty* a distinctly homespun flavour, yet the periodical's content and character were also shaped by its editor's cosmopolitan vision. As Wendy McElroy has demonstrated, Tucker's 'embrace of international anarchism' was reflected in the foreign news and causes highlighted within the pages of his flagship periodical: from its coverage of the trial of the French anarchist Louise Michel to the 'plights of Russian nihilists and Irish tenants'.[16] Tucker also translated into English the works of a number of major Russian and European anarchists, including Kropotkin, Bakunin and Proudhon, and these translations, in keeping with Tucker's wider strategy as an anarchist publisher and bookseller, were heavily advertised within *Liberty*. Tucker's cumulative efforts as a translator, editor and publisher of anarchist print culture were instrumental to the importation of international anarchist thought to the United States, but his influence (and that of *Liberty*) was certainly not landlocked. The periodical drew readers and correspondents from Australia, Russia and across Europe, including Britain, where Tucker's brand of anarchism is known to have asserted a powerful influence over a growing core of individualists, many of whom became contributors to the paper.[17] The web of connections established between its international readership and contributor pool made *Liberty* a significant vehicle for the formation of national and transnational radical networks, as well as a conduit for the border-crossing flow of anarchist propaganda, culture and ideas. Thus, when Schreiner was introduced to the pages of *Liberty*, the author and her writings were enmeshed in a ready and complicated network of radicalism and disseminated through the far-reaching tentacles of the periodical's publishing and circulation channels, attracting new political audiences in the United States, Europe and beyond.

Allegorical Anarchism

The first mention of Schreiner in *Liberty* came not with a reference to the author's celebrated debut novel, *The Story of an African Farm* (1883), but with the republication of her allegorical short story 'Three Dreams in a Desert' in October 1887. Tucker's embrace of Schreiner's allegorical fiction echoed a contemporaneous trend within radical print media in Britain, which saw Schreiner's allegories reprinted in the papers associated with the various schisms of socialism and the women's movement.[18] The early emphasis on Schreiner's short fiction in *Liberty* is also reflective of the wider ideological resonance of her allegorical writing within American anarchism more generally. Leading voices from across the various factions of late-nineteenth-century anarchism similarly attested to the aesthetic power of Schreiner's allegories to speak to their particular mutation of anarchist thought. For the anarchist-feminist Voltinaire de Cleyre, 'Three Dreams in a Desert' provides a trenchant defence of the necessary 'suffering of Now' on the basis that it will form 'the gateway' to a future 'Land of Freedom', while for the communist-anarchist Emma Goldman, Schreiner's allegories embody the 'inexorable, implacable Power of the Ideal'.[19]

The capacity for Schreiner's allegorical idealism to appeal across the ideological battle lines of American anarchism can be traced to the nuanced texture of the author's response to the varieties of socialism with which she was intellectually and practically immersed throughout the 1880s in Britain. Schreiner's views took shape in response to the collectivist model of socialistic labour supplied by her close involvement with the Fellowship of the New Life and through her sharpening resistance to Karl Pearson's roadmap for authoritarian state socialism.[20] As she put it in a letter to the Fabian socialist Beatrice Webb in 1888, Schreiner was engaged at this point with 'working out what seems to me the reconciliation of Socialism & Individualism'.[21] This combination, which Ruth Livesey has described as Schreiner's 'espousal of both communalism and the vital force of expressive individualism', undergirds the emancipatory visions of perfect freedom imagined in her allegories from the 1880s and helps to explain the political power those stories held for both collectivists such as Goldman and individualists like Tucker.[22]

Originally published in the London journal the *Fortnightly Review* in August 1887, 'Three Dreams in a Desert' was one of a series of allegories written by Schreiner and published in the British press throughout the 1880s before being gathered in the short fiction collection *Dreams* (1890). When the allegory was reproduced in full in *Liberty*, it was accompanied by a candid acknowledgement of its publishing provenance in the *Fortnightly Review*. In addition to underscoring the periodical's cosmopolitan cadences, Tucker's sanguine attitude to the appropriation of copy from other sources also aligned *Liberty* with the broader cultural practice of reprinting then endemic in the radical press during this period.[23] Whether obtained through formalised editorial exchange arrangements, or – as was the case with *Liberty* – through largely unofficial means, the transportation of content from one publishing context to another, what Ryan Cordell has described as a process of 'cultural repetition and remediation', necessarily transformed how a given text was encountered and understood by its various audiences.[24] By extracting 'Three Dreams in a Desert' from its point of origin in a British literary journal and implanting it within the pages of *Liberty*, Tucker aimed not only to aid the diffusion of Schreiner's story, but also to circulate that text – including in Britain, where *Liberty* is known to have been distributed – as one framed ideologically as anarchist.

Writing in his editorial leader on the first page of the number in which Schreiner's allegory was reproduced, Tucker advises that 'Three Dreams in a Desert' 'is as remarkable for wisdom and insight as for beauty' before issuing readers of *Liberty* with the following succinct instruction: 'Read it'.[25] The 'wisdom' Tucker valued in Schreiner's allegory has been more commonly viewed as feminist, socialist or a combination of the two; it is not difficult, however, to see why the story's emancipatory appeals and rousing rhetorical language held particular forms of ideological significance for anarchists, too. In the story's first dream, the unnamed woman, who carries the 'great burden' of historic subjection on her back, lies inert and suffering in the sand, shackled to a man who cannot help her. The details of Schreiner's allegory – from the woman's self-reliant capacity to 'struggle until she is strong' and stagger 'on to her knees' together with the second dream's metaphoric casting-off of 'the mantle of Ancient-received-opinions' during the woman's journey to the 'Land of Freedom' – connect the story to some of Tucker's favourite themes: pursuit of individuation, resistance to orthodoxy and the overthrow of oppression as a necessary condition of liberty.[26]

The allegory's famed central symbol of sacrifice in the name of progress – a bridge constructed of the bodies of women, 'piled up' so that the 'rest pass over' – would have held a particular resonance for the readers of *Liberty* in the winter of 1887.[27] Published one month before the execution of four of the seven anarchists who had been convicted, on spurious evidence, for involvement with the bombing at a labour rally in Haymarket Square in Chicago the previous year, 'Three Dreams in a Desert', with its dramatisation of womanly sacrifice, became entangled with the real-world martyrdom of the Chicago anarchists. Tucker's emotive reflection in *Liberty* on 'the tragedy just enacted at Chicago' closes with a quotation from Proudhon that, in its emphasis on death as a necessary constituent of social progress, bears a striking similarity to the corporeal violence on which Schreiner's bridge of human bodies is reliant: 'the Revolution advances, with sombre and inevitable tread, over the flowers with which its devotees strew its path, through the blood of its champions, and over the bodies of its enemies'.²⁸ While neither Schreiner nor Tucker were revolutionaries and both were consistent in their opposition to violence as a political strategy, they nevertheless shared a sense that the path to a future 'Land of Freedom' would inevitably be paved with human suffering.

The framing of Schreiner's allegory as anarchist was further facilitated by the story's dialogic encounters with the surrounding content in this issue of *Liberty*. 'Three Dreams in a Desert' appeared alongside the periodical's usual summary reports of local and international anarchist news and activities, as well as a variety of articles and extracts which ruminate on various aspects of the economic inequities of capitalism. This includes an article entitled 'How Capitalists "Make" Their Capital', attributed to George Bernard Shaw, and a lengthy extract from Stephen Pearl Andrews's book *The Science of Society*, which expounds on Josiah Warren's economic principle of 'cost the limit of price', a version of the labour theory of value. Schreiner's allegory is therefore folded within a larger economic argument for the downfall of capitalism from which it is distinguished, as Tucker acknowledges, by its aesthetic 'beauty'. Through its visualisation of a future 'heaven' on earth, a transformed world where men and women 'walk hand in hand' and 'were not afraid', 'Three Dreams in a Desert' provided the readers of *Liberty* with a powerfully affective vision of a future society in which the anarchist dream of equal freedom has been realised.²⁹

While much of the literary content reprinted in *Liberty* was ephemeral, the resonance of Schreiner's allegory with its readers led to the formalisation of the story's status as anarchist propaganda. In December 1887, two months after the allegory's first publication in *Liberty*, Tucker announced that 'in response to a demand created by its recent appearance in Liberty', Schreiner's story had been issued as a standalone pamphlet by feminist-anarchist and *Liberty* contributor Sarah E. Holmes.³⁰ Tucker's framing of the pamphlet as anarchist was unequivocal: readers are advised that they can purchase a copy, along with the leading individualist-anarchist Victor Yarros's pamphlet 'Anarchism: its Aims and Method', at the next meeting of the Anarchists' Club. In keeping with the informal, counter-cultural publishing and distribution methods deployed by many of the radical factions and organisations that mushroomed in this period, members of the Anarchists' Club are encouraged not only to read but also to disseminate Holmes's pamphlet, according to the following terms: 'Persons who desire to distribute this pamphlet can procure it at the very low rate of three cents a copy, if they will take a hundred copies'.³¹ The intimate connection between publishing and propaganda, and the significant placement of Schreiner's allegory within the *Liberty* canon of anarchist literature, are highlighted by Tucker: 'these additions to the Anarchistic propaganda will greatly increase its efficacy'.[32]

Although not officially a *Liberty* publication, Holmes's self-published pamphlet was heavily promoted in the periodical in regular advertisements, as well as through editorial prompts from Tucker, and was therefore extensively framed as buttressing the ideological agenda of that periodical. When Holmes announced – in an advertisement in *Liberty* – her intention to publish a 'de luxe' edition of the pamphlet in 1897, Tucker devoted the opening section of his front-page editorial leader to encouraging his readers to support Holmes's venture:

> Read the advertisement on the eighth page wherein the publisher of Olive Schreiner's 'Three Dreams in a Desert' announces her intention of issuing an *edition de luxe* of that booklet, and asks for cooperation. There must be not a few among Liberty's readers who will desire to take advantage of her advance offer of ten copies for a dollar, as this remarkable work in new and dainty dress will make a pretty and appropriate souvenir for presentation to friends who can appreciate it.[33]

While it is impossible to quantify sales figures for the various editions of the pamphlet, its enduring presence in *Liberty* suggests the significance of 'Three Dreams in a Desert' for the readers of that periodical and to the propaganda efforts of the individualist anarchists more generally. Certainly, the informal publishing and dissemination practices of Holmes and her *ad hoc* band of anarchist distributors were sufficiently effective to attract the attention of the author herself. In a letter composed in Italy in December 1888, Schreiner noted, with some pride, that the 'small article I wrote in the Fortnightly some months ago' had been 'three times reprinted in America, & is now published in a pamphlet form in Boston'.[34]

Holmes's pamphlet was also promoted within and circulated by American anarchist periodicals other than *Liberty*, including by the Chicago-based anarchist-feminist newspaper *Lucifer, the Light Bearer*, which advertised the 1897 'edition de luxe of this charming pamphlet' for sale from the *Lucifer* office at the rate of '25 cents a copy or five copies for $1'.[35] Its framing of the pamphlet places emphasis on the story's feminist significance ('no work of the present century has done more to arouse women to thought concerning their dependence upon men than Olive Schreiner's '"Three Dreams in a Desert"') and also on the brilliance of Holmes, who is described as 'one of the brightest radical women in America'.[36] In addition to casting light on Holmes's significance to radical forms of feminism in this period, the endorsement of her pamphlet and her politics within *Lucifer* also helped to draw Holmes out from the shadow of the garrulous male anarchists who dominated *Liberty*'s pages. While Holmes was given the space to write about women's sexuality and marriage in *Liberty*, where she contributed under the pseudonym Zelm, anarchism's practical and ideological entanglement with the 'Woman Question' remained a minor current rather than a dominant stream within that periodical. For Tucker and for those male anarchists who ventured into the terrain of the 'Woman Question' in *Liberty*, the problems associated with issues such as marriage, female sexuality, domestic labour and childrearing raised by anarchist-feminists like Holmes, would largely be tended to by the macro forms of freedom promised for all in a future anarchist society.

While Holmes agreed with the broader *Liberty* support of free love and denunciation of marriage, she also recognised the male anarchists' failure, as Margaret Marsh puts it, to 'connect their condemnation of "women as property" with the realisation that the domestic relationship that made women economically dependent was at least partly responsible for their social, legal, and civic inequality'.[37] Like Schreiner, Holmes believed that women's economic independence from men was a necessary precondition of women's emancipation, and she also shared with Schreiner an understanding of the fundamental role that productive labour would play in attaining that goal. 'Three Dreams in a Desert', with its specific focus on a woman's journey to the Land of Freedom, and the feminised forms of suffering and sacrifice endured in order for her to achieve freedom on the same terms as men, therefore spoke in clear terms to the gap Holmes perceived as inherent within masculinist conceptions of liberty.

Liberty's Library

Tucker failed to imagine how women's historically constituted ties to the domestic sphere, if left unchecked, would ultimately recreate women's economic dependence on men in a free society and therefore undermine their liberty. Nonetheless, his vision of future relations between the sexes under anarchism was a radical one. Tucker's ideal involved the dissolution of the institution of marriage and the implementation of free love, which he defends along individualist lines.[38] Unshackled from the tyranny of marriage and in keeping with the individualist principle of self-sovereignty, men and women would become autonomous sexual agents, who are free to 'love each other for as long or as short a time as the can, will, or may'.[39] Tucker's sense of marriage as an 'absurdit[y]' that imposes oppressive limits to sovereignty and to the individual's capacity to exercise sexual freedom necessarily has implications for his understanding of the family. In his essay 'State Socialism and Anarchism', delivered as a lecture and reprinted in *Liberty* in March 1888, Tucker cites the antithetical models of the family imagined under anarchism and state socialism as one of the many features distinguishing the two systems of thought. Where state socialism would, according to Tucker, be economically dependent upon the nuclear 'State family', created through a system of stirpiculture (or eugenic-based breeding), anarchism, contrastingly, would allow 'every individual, whether man or woman' to be 'self-supporting' in an 'independent home of his or her own', with the children born of free unions living 'exclusively with the mothers until old enough to belong to themselves'.[40] The key elements of Tucker's blueprint for sexual freedom in a free society – the dissolution of marriage and the bourgeois family, the implementation of free unions – not only rendered his sexual politics anarchistic but also formed the basis for his interpretation and avid promotion of Schreiner's novel, *The Story of an African Farm*, in *Liberty*'s pages.

Tucker valued *African Farm* for its radical non-conformity, one that takes shape, according to his précis of the novel, in its expression of 'advanced ideas on religious and social questions' and through its characters' intellectual growth 'from orthodoxy to rationalism'.[41] Certainly, Tucker would have seen his own views on sex reflected back at him in Lyndall's scornful diatribes against marriage and her advocacy of free love as a viable alternative. When she refuses to marry her stranger because she 'cannot be tied', Lyndall instead openly proposes that they embark on a free sexual union in terms reminiscent of the phlegmatic accounts of free love published in *Liberty*: 'if you wish, you may take me away with you, and take care of me; then when we do not love any more we can say good-bye'.[42] Lyndall's principled commitment to free love, which comes at great personal cost, would have appealed to Tucker given his own tendency to obduracy in upholding the 'plumb-line principle' of anarchism.[43] This dogmatic fidelity to his individualist philosophy regularly led him into disputatious waters including, for example, in relation to the thorny issue of the legal age of sexual consent.

Liberty broadly rejected calls to raise the age of consent on the basis that such a move would contravene the principle of 'liberty of sexual association'.[44] Tucker's 'plumb-line' take on this issue led to widespread consternation in the press, including the charge by the *Journal of United Labour* that 'Anarchy asks liberty to ruin little girls'.⁴⁵ Writing in *Liberty* in 1891, Tucker enlists the example of Schreiner to further defend his ground in the enduring debate about the age of consent on individualist principles. He asks how the 'individuality of the girl who wrote "The Story of an African Farm"' could be denied by 'send[ing] to prison for twenty years, as guilty of rape, any man with whom she might have freely chosen, at the age when she began to write that book, to enter into sexual relations'.⁴⁶ In Tucker's example, Schreiner becomes imbricated with the sexual philosophy of Lyndall, and her intellectual exceptionalism is harnessed to heighten Tucker's sense of the injustice of the consent laws in denying adolescent girls 'the right of choice'.⁴⁷ While Schreiner's views on female sexuality and desire were certainly progressive, Tucker's deployment of the author as a signifier of anarchic sexual radicalism within *Liberty* is not without its problems, not least because of the public support Schreiner had given W. T. Stead during his campaign to raise the sexual age of consent in Britain in 1885. Schreiner was deeply critical of the sexual double standard and the economic basis of women's dependence on men. However, unlike Tucker, she was not intrinsically opposed to marriage, and nor did she advocate free love.⁴⁸ Nevertheless, Tucker's attempt to graft Schreiner's sexual politics to the anarchism of *Liberty* continued in the 1890s through Tucker's dedicated promotion and dissemination of his own 'Liberty's Library' edition of *African Farm*.

While Schreiner viewed the international reprints of the allegories that had been published in the British press throughout the 1880s as a sign of their evolving stature, her attitude to the proliferation of pirated editions of her book-length publications in America was more complex. Prior to entering into an exclusive publishing arrangement with the American publisher Roberts Bros around 1890, Schreiner had received welcome remuneration in the form of 'large yearly cheques' from 'about nine' of the estimated 'sixteen American publishers' who had published editions of *African Farm* in the years preceding her agreement with Roberts Bros.⁴⁹ As Schreiner acknowledged in a letter to the American publisher Little, Brown, & Co. in 1900, the payment she received from the publishers who had issued pirated editions of her first novel was 'in no way logically and only in honour bound' given that the text, first published in Britain in 1883, was not protected under copyright law in the United States.⁵⁰ Having bestowed Roberts Bros with the 'exclusive right to act as my publisher of an <u>African Farm</u> in America', Schreiner considered it a 'matter of honour' that unofficial editions of her novel cease to be published.⁵¹ She claims to have petitioned American publishers directly as part of her efforts to diminish sales of these, even taking out advertisements in American newspapers announcing her official arrangement with Robert Bros. While pirated editions of *African Farm* continued to be sold, including one produced as part of Tucker's 'Liberty's Library' series, the royalty cheques she had previously received from publishers other than Roberts Bros soon dried up. The diminishing returns from sales of her novel in the United States resulted in a sharpening of the author's views on piracy and copyright. Consequently, Schreiner kept a vigilant eye on the progression of the International Copyright Act of 1891 and was confident that the protections it promised would see her 'flowing in riches' following the publication of any new works in the United States.[52]

Tucker's edition of *African Farm* was announced by the editor on the front page of *Liberty* in September 1888 when Schreiner's novel was not protected by international copyright laws. Described in uncharacteristically fawning terms by Tucker as '[o]ne of the bravest and most truthful, one of the rarest and most original, one of the finest and most artistic works of fiction that have seen the light for many a day', the text would go on to occupy a prominent position within Tucker's 'Liberty's Library' book list, and advertised within *Liberty*, until 1897.[53] While it is unclear if Schreiner had counted Tucker's edition as among the nineteen pirated versions of *African Farm* circulating in the United States in the 1880s, it is certainly the case that Tucker would not have been one of the nine publishers recompensing Schreiner for American sales of her novel. Tucker's position on copyright diverged sharply from Schreiner's increasingly protectionist stance. As McElroy observes, Tucker 'flatly rejected the idea that legal copyright was compatible with anarchism', a view he steadfastly and often provocatively defended in an enduring debate about the issue in *Liberty*.[54] In addition to his belief that 'there can rightfully be no such thing as the exclusive ownership of an idea', he also reverted to market logic to defend his anti-copyright position from the point of view of the author.[55] In a free society in which capitalism, monopoly and all forms of authority have been eradicated, the author (Tucker argues) would fare better under a post-capitalist system of *laissez-faire* competition and individual self-interest than they would within the capitalist structures of commercial publishing. According to Tucker:

> [W]hen labor is left in possession of the capital which it produces unburdened by usury or taxation, the author and the inventor will not have to appeal to the rich in order to put their product on the market, but will be able to do so directly, and the start which they will naturally have of all competitors will secure them an equitable reward of their labor.[56]

Through his energetic contributions to the enduring debate about intellectual property and copyright in *Liberty*, Tucker not only supplied an individualist-anarchist rationale for his anti-copyright stance but simultaneously defended the culture of reprinting upon which his *Liberty* book lists and wider work as a publisher and bookseller were dependent.

Tucker's edition of *African Farm* capitalised on the success of 'Three Dreams in a Desert' with *Liberty*'s readers, who were, according to the editor, 'hungry' for additional works from the 'author of that allegory'.[57] Schreiner's novel was framed by Tucker as buttressing 'radical' principles, particularly in terms of its 'attitude towards love and marriage'; however, it was the edition's placement within Tucker's 'Liberty's Library' series that more explicitly aligned the novel with anarchism. The list was curated by Tucker and advertised in *Liberty*, and the books and pamphlets it featured were published and disseminated by *Liberty*'s publishing offshoot. In addition to functioning as a practical catalogue of works available for sale, 'Liberty's Library' was also very much a repository of Tucker's own reading tastes and interests. Here Schreiner's novel rubbed shoulders with classic works of anarchism including Bakunin's *God and the State* and Proudhon's *What is Property?*, both translated by Tucker, as well as more perceptibly anarchist literary works such as *Bombs: the Poetry and Philosophy of Anarchy* by William A. Whittick, and Nikolay Chernyshevsky's novel *What is to be Done?*, which clearly foregrounds its radical themes in its subtitle: 'A Nihilistic Romance. Written in Prison. Suppressed by the Czar'.

When he added *African Farm* to 'Liberty's Library', Tucker was, from the outset, unequivocal about his intention to harness the novel in the service of anarchism, stating: 'I have determined to include it in Liberty's propaganda, and will supply it, bound in cloth, post-paid, at sixty cents a copy'.[58] While individual titles moved in and out of 'Liberty's Library', *African Farm* was a mainstay in the advertising back matter of *Liberty* until 1897. As a further sign of the text's popularity in anarchist circles, Tucker also issued the novel in a cheap paperback edition retailing at 25 cents. A principled rejection of copyright and advocacy of piracy notwithstanding, Tucker's approach to the business of bookselling actually mimicked many of the basic techniques of the same commercial publishing structures he sought to bypass: from periodical advertising and publisher's lists to subscription services and the creation of a plurality of editions of texts available at different price points. His propaganda machine was thus fuelled by the mechanisms of mainstream publishing to achieve radical effects.

Conclusion

Tracing Schreiner through the pages of *Liberty* and outwards through the periodical's publishing and distribution networks demonstrates how her fiction was not only sold *by* anarchists, it was sold *as* anarchist, generating a classification for Schreiner's work and politics that the author herself was known to have repudiated. The ideological framing of her work as buttressing individualist conceptions of free thought, free love and freedom without limits created new political audiences for *African Farm* and for her allegorical short stories throughout the United States – and beyond – in the final decades of the nineteenth century. Schreiner's short fiction in particular registers the author's own attempts, in the 1880s, to formulate a political vocabulary that grafted the best elements of the collectivist models of socialism she encountered through her associations with the socialist and labour movements in Britain to her profoundly individualistic demands for personal autonomy and social, economic and artistic freedom. While Schreiner failed to settle on a single taxonomy that might accommodate her nascent intersectional political philosophy, a reading of *Liberty* demonstrates that anarchists such as Tucker and Holmes were more assured of Schreiner's political classification and of her work's alignment with anarchism. Anarchists valued Schreiner's freethinking, her questioning of nineteenth-century social, political and religious orthodoxies, and the anti-capitalist current running through her work. For her part, Schreiner would undoubtedly have admired the individualists' defence of personal autonomy, their repudiation of monopoly in any form, and aspects of their radical reimagining of sexual desire and the relations between the sexes. She also converged with the individualists' understanding of the economic basis for woman's historic subjugation, and with feminist individualists like Holmes she shared an intractable belief in the necessity of women's economic independence in order to safeguard their liberty.

Nevertheless, and in spite of these ideological crosscurrents, anarchism, much like socialism, did not provide the solutions to the constellation of social and political problems with which Schreiner was engaged in the 1880s. For Schreiner, the *laissez-faire* underpinnings of Tucker's individualistic political economy, with its privileging of self-interest over cooperation, would inevitably reproduce the same social and economic inequities realised under capitalism. Her belief that 'human nature will assert itself under Socialism as elsewhere' shows how socialists, too, fell short of imagining the kind of wholesale renovation of the self and human relationships required to reach the 'Land of Freedom'.[59] The idealist vision of freedom imagined in works like 'Three Dreams in a Desert' held great affective power for late nineteenth-century anarchists, but Schreiner's ethical insistence on sympathy and altruism as necessary constituents of social, economic and sexual transformation was missing from the materialist blueprint for freedom provided in *Liberty*.

Works Cited

'Advertisement'. *New-York Daily Tribune*, 3 November 1892.
Berkman, Joyce Avrech. 'Possessing Women in Olive Schreiner's *From Man to Man or Perhaps Only –*.' *Journal of Commonwealth Literature* 56, no. 1 (2021): 28–43.
Burdett, Carolyn. *Olive Schreiner and the Progress of Feminism. Evolution, Gender, Empire*. Basingstoke: Palgrave, 2001.
Cordell, Ryan. 'Viral Textuality in Nineteenth-Century US Newspaper Exchanges'. In *Virtual Victorians. Networks, Connections, Technologies*, edited by Veronica Alfano and Andrew Stauffer, 29–56. Basingstoke: Palgrave Macmillan, 2015.
De Cleyre, Voltairine. 'American Progress'. *The Open Court, a Quarterly Magazine* 5, no. 223 (3 December 1891): 3040.
Gill, Clare. 'Reading the Religion of Socialism: Olive Schreiner, the Labour Church and the Construction of Left-Wing Reading Communities in the 1890s'. In *The History of Reading, Volume 2: Evidence from the British Isles, c. 1750–1950*, edited by Katie Halsey and W. R. Owens, 48–63. Basingstoke: Palgrave Macmillan, 2011.
Goldman, Emma. 'The Power of the Ideal'. *Mother Earth* 7, no. 1 (March 1912).
Goodway, David. *Anarchist Seeds Beneath the Snow. Left-Libertarian Thought and British Writers from William Morris to Colin Ward*. Liverpool: Liverpool University Press, 2006.
Harkness, Margaret. 'Olive Schreiner'. *Novel Review* 1, no. 2 (May 1892): 112–15.
Kissack, Terence. *Free Comrades. Anarchism and Homosexuality in the United States, 1895–1917*. Oakland: AK Press, 2008.
'Liberty's Library'. *Liberty* 12, no. 3 (13 June 1896).
Livesey, Ruth. *Socialism, Sex, and the Culture of Aestheticism in Britain, 1880–1914*. Oxford: Oxford University Press, 2007.
Marsh, Margaret S. *Anarchist Women*. Philadelphia: Temple University Press, 1981.
Marshall, Peter. *Demanding the Impossible. A History of Anarchism*. London: Harper Perennial, 1992.
McElroy, Wendy. 'Benjamin Tucker, "Liberty", and Individualist Anarchism'. *The Independent Review* 2, no. 3 (Winter 1998): 421–34.
—. *The Debates of Liberty. An Overview of Individualist Anarchism, 1881–1908*. Lanham: Lexington Books, 2003.

Mutch, Deborah. *English Socialist Periodicals, 1880–1900: A Reference Source*. Aldershot: Ashgate, 2005.

Ryley, Peter. 'Individualism'. In *The Palgrave Handbook of Anarchism*, edited by Carl Levy and Matthew S. Adams, 225–36. Basingstoke: Palgrave, 2019.

—. 'Individualist Anarchism in late Victorian Britain'. *Anarchist Studies* 20, no. 2 (Autumn 2012): no pages.

Schreiner, Olive. 'Three Dreams in a Desert'. *Liberty* 5, no. 5 (8 October 1887).

—. 'Three Dreams in a Desert'. *Lucifer, the Light Bearer* 1, no. 51 (22 December 1897).

—. *The Story of an African Farm*. Broadview: Ontario, 2003.

Tucker, Benjamin. 'Anarchy and Rape'. *Liberty* 5, no. 17 (31 March 1888).

—. 'Drops of Cold Water'. *Liberty* 8, no. 9 (17 October 1891).

—. *Instead of a Book. By a Man Too Busy to Write One*. New York: Benj. R. Tucker Publishers, 1897.

—. 'On Picket Duty'. *Liberty* 1, no. 1 (6 August 1881).

—. 'On Picket Duty'. *Liberty* 5, no. 5 (8 October 1887).

—. 'On Picket Duty'. *Liberty* 5, no. 11 (31 December 1887).

—. 'On Picket Duty'. *Liberty* 6, no. 4 (29 September 1888).

—. 'On Picket Duty'. *Liberty* 8, no. 8 (1 August 1891).

—. 'On Picket Duty'. *Liberty* 13, no. 4 (July 1897).

—. 'Plumb-Line or Cork-Screw, Which?' *Liberty* 4, no. 1 (17 April 1886): 4–5.

—. 'The Reward of Authors'. *Liberty* 7, no. 19 (10 January 1891).

—. 'To the Breach, Comrades'. *Liberty* 5, no. 8 (19 November 1887).

Letters

Olive Schreiner to Edward Carpenter, 23 May 1892. *Olive Schreiner Letters Online*.

Olive Schreiner to William H. Dirks, December 1888. *Olive Schreiner Letters Online*.

Olive Schreiner to Havelock Ellis, 29 March 1885. *Olive Schreiner Letters Online*.

Olive Schreiner to Havelock Ellis, 16 October 1888. *Olive Schreiner Letters Online*.

Olive Schreiner to Havelock Ellis, 30 August 1890. *Olive Schreiner Letters Online*.

Olive Schreiner to Hudson Findlay, 10 October 1900. *Olive Schreiner Letters Online*.

Olive Schreiner to Little, Brown & Co, 5 October 1900. *Olive Schreiner Letters Online*.

Olive Schreiner to Mary Sauer, July 1892. *Olive Schreiner Letters Online*.

Olive Schreiner to William Schreiner, January 1891. *Olive Schreiner Letters Online*.

Olive Schreiner to William Schreiner, 21 April 1912. *Olive Schreiner Letters Online*.

Olive Schreiner to Beatrice Webb, October 1888. *Olive Schreiner Letters Online*.

Notes

1. Harkness, 'Olive Schreiner', 115; Schreiner to Mary Sauer, July 1892, *Olive Schreiner Letters Online* (OSLO).
2. Schreiner to William Schreiner, 21 April 1912, *OSLO*.
3. Schreiner to Havelock Ellis, 16 October 1888, *OSLO*.
4. On Carpenter and libertarian socialism, see Marshall, *Demanding the Impossible*, 168–71. For a discussion of Carpenter and anarchism, see Goodway, *Anarchist Seeds*, 35–61.
5. Goodway, *Anarchist Seeds*, 57, 55.
6. Schreiner to Edward Carpenter, 23 May 1892, *OSLO*.
7. Schreiner to William Schreiner, 21 April 1912, *OSLO*.
8. Burdett, *Olive Schreiner*, 186.
9. Schreiner to Hudson Findlay, 10 October 1900, *OSLO*.
10. Goodway, *Anarchist Seeds*, 98.
11. Ryley, 'Individualist Anarchism'.
12. Marshall, *Demanding the Impossible*, 389.
13. Tucker, 'On Picket Duty', 1881, 1.
14. Tucker, 'Drops of Cold Water', 3.
15. For a succinct overview of Stirner's influence on nineteenth-century individualism, see Ryley, 'Individualism', 227–28. For a more specific account of the impact of Stirner on Tucker and *Liberty* see McElroy, 'Benjamin Tucker', 426–28.
16. McElroy, 'Benjamin Tucker', 429.
17. See Ryley, 'Individualist Anarchism'.
18. For a discussion of the significance of Schreiner's allegories within the British socialist press see Gill, 'Reading the Religion of Socialism', 48–63.
19. De Cleyre, 'American Progress', 3040; Goldman, 'Power', 24.
20. Two excellent accounts of Schreiner's intellectual sparring with Pearson are given in Livesey, *Socialism*, 79–85 and Burdett, *Progress*, 50–54.
21. Schreiner to Beatrice Webb, October 1888, *OSLO*.
22. Livesey, *Socialism*, 76.
23. For examples of literary texts reprinted in the British socialist press, see Mutch, *English Socialist Periodicals*.
24. Cordell, 'Viral Textuality', 50.
25. Tucker, 'On Picket Duty', October 1887, 1.
26. Schreiner, 'Three Dreams', 7.
27. Schreiner, 'Three Dreams', 7.
28. Tucker, 'To the Breach', 4.
29. Schreiner, 'Three Dreams', 7.
30. Tucker, 'On Picket Duty', December 1887, 1.
31. Tucker, 'On Picket Duty', December 1887, 1.
32. Tucker, 'On Picket Duty', December 1887, 1.
33. Tucker, 'On Picket Duty', July 1897, 1.
34. Schreiner to William H. Dirks, December 1888, *OSLO*.
35. 'Three Dreams', *Lucifer*, 406.
36. 'Three Dreams', *Lucifer*, 406.
37. Marsh, *Anarchist Women*, 84.

38. For a full discussion of Tucker's radical views on sex, see Kissack, *Free Comrades*.
39. Tucker, *Instead*, 15.
40. Tucker, *Instead*, 15.
41. 'Liberty's Library', 8.
42. Schreiner, *African Farm*, 229.
43. Tucker, 'Plumb-Line', 4–5.
44. Tucker, 'Anarchy and Rape', 4.
45. Tucker, 'Anarchy and Rape', 4.
46. Tucker, 'On Picket Duty', 1891, 1.
47. Tucker, 'On Picket Duty', 1891, 1
48. For analysis of Schreiner and free love, see Berkman, 'Possessing', 39.
49. Schreiner to Little, Brown & Co, October 5 1900, *OSLO*. Schreiner refers to a planned publishing arrangement with Roberts Bros in a letter from 1890 to Havelock Ellis. See Schreiner to Ellis, August 30 1890, *OSLO*. Roberts Bros publicised their status as Schreiner's authorised publisher in the United States in advertisements for their edition of *Dreams*. See, for example, 'Advertisement', 8.
50. Schreiner to Little, Brown & Co, 5 October 1900, *OSLO*.
51. Schreiner to Little, Brown & Co, 5 October 1900, *OSLO*.
52. Schreiner to William Schreiner, January 1891, *OSLO*.
53. Tucker, 'On Picket Duty', 1888, 1.
54. McElroy, *Debates of Liberty*, 85.
55. Tucker, quoted in McElroy, 86.
56. Tucker, 'The Reward of Authors', 1887.
57. Tucker, 'On Picket Duty', 29 September 1888, 1.
58. Tucker, 'On Picket Duty', 29 September 1888, 1.
59. Schreiner to Havelock Ellis, 16 October 1888, *OSLO*.

Chapter 9

The Reception of Olive Schreiner's Work and Thought in the Dutch Press
Małgorzata Drwal

Introduction

Browsing the digitalised Dutch press archive Delpher.nl, one might easily conclude that Olive Schreiner enjoyed the status of a well-known writer and intellectual in the Netherlands. Her name appears numerous times in the periodical press and daily papers, mostly between the 1890s and the 1930s, corresponding to the period between the 1892 publication of the Dutch translation of Schreiner's *The Story of an African Farm* (1883) as *Op een Hoeve in Afrika*, until about ten years after the author's death.

The Dutch press landscape at that time reflected the pillarisation of society, that is, its division into relatively autonomous spheres based on religious and political worldviews (Dutch: *verzuiling*), a characteristic of late-nineteenth-century Dutch political formation that encompassed all spheres of social life. Schreiner appears in press titles representing all four pillars (*zuilen*) – Catholic, Protestant, Socialist and Liberal – yet the frequency and number of mentions vary. Her thought was referred to in various contexts, even to support conflicting opinions. This chapter sets out to examine the contexts in which Schreiner and her work are referenced, and the public image of her that was shaped by the press. The analysis – of archival material including book reviews and announcements of publications, reprinted excerpts from Schreiner's works, as well as references to her as a writer and progressive intellectual – focuses on the correspondence between the political, religious, social and cultural leanings of a publication and the way in which her thought was quoted and commented on in it. I ask: what causes were supported by her views? How did papers' profiles contribute to shaping Schreiner's public persona? Finally, I assess Schreiner's impact on the Dutch public, explaining how the context in which her text or thought was referred to influenced its interpretation, and the implications this had for her public persona in the Netherlands.

Public persona

Mineke Bosch's discussion of scholarly or scientific personae offers some useful insights into how the public image of an intellectual is shaped. Even though Schreiner was a writer and political commentator (rather than a scholar), the creation of her public image relied on similar procedures. Bosch defines a scholarly persona as an 'embodied performance of scholarly or scientific identity that makes use of cultural and scientific repertoires of conduct in order to convince professional peers and the wider audience of the scholar's or scientist's reliability and credibility'.[1] A persona (mask in Latin) is 'a collective identity that mediates between the private person and the public institution'.[2] This mask, however, is not only worn to perform professional tasks: it shapes and cultivates what Paul Herman describes as 'certain dispositions (attitudes, character traits, abilities) that can never be detached from their possessor'.[3] Consequently, 'the identity of individuals making assertions', writes Steven Shapin, and the 'credibility of those assertions', are intertwined, while the authority of a figure is constructed from such components as trustworthiness and reliability, which come from what Bosch identifies as 'repertoires [of] the disciplinary virtues and skills'.[4]

A public persona is a relational identity that emerges as a result of an 'ongoing, collective, fragmented, cultural and contextual process'.[5] Fomichenko suggests that the audience plays an important role in this process by contributing to the 'author-function'.[6] The author-function, as defined by Michel Foucault, emphasises the importance of the author's name in validating or authorising the source of a particular discourse: it is the author's name that 'group[s] together a number of texts and thus differentiate[s] them from others'.[7] Texts are linked by the name of an author to create relationships of homogeneity, filiation, reciprocal explanation and authentification. The author's name comes to describe a particular discourse, whereas the culture in which this discourse circulates defines its status and reception. While scientific texts need an author to attest to their reliability, the value of literary texts tends to be determined by the public recognising and associating the author's name with their other works, Foucault contends.[8]

Dutch archival press material reflects (roughly speaking) four facets to Schreiner's author persona: a socially engaged writer, an 'English-South African' expertly commenting on the social and political situation in South Africa,[9] an ethical thinker and a feminist. In order to understand the contexts in which these facets appeared in print, we need to appreciate the extent to which the Dutch press of the late-nineteenth-century was organised in a reflection of Dutch society.

Pillarisation in the Dutch press

Pillarisation is a term used to describe the 'compartmentalisation' of Dutch society, coinciding with modernisation and industrialisation from around 1880 (although the term has only been in use since the 1930s).[10] Four pillars, which 'to an increasing extent, disagreed on pretty much everything', are understood to have emerged,[11] each including institutions that encompassed diverse spheres of social life, such as education and culture, as well as the press. Not all pillars, however, provided for all social functions of their members. For example, Catholics set up their own educational and healthcare institutions, while Socialists did not. The Socialist pillar had clear links with trade unionism, and was particularly antagonistic towards Catholics' hierarchical, theocratic and conservative approach to social order. This clearly contrasted with the Socialists' vision of change which sought the move to a classless society.[12]

Some Dutch historians, however, have questioned the very concept of the pillars, which had no uniform basis.[13] The Catholic and Protestant pillars were confessional in character; the Socialist pillar focused on the needs of one social stratum, namely the working-class; while the Liberal pillar had an even more doubtful basis as it incorporated a range of diverse worldviews that could be described as progressive. In fact, only Catholics formed one clearly delineated pillar, while among the Protestants there was internal division: the *Christelijk-Historisch Unie* (Christian Historical Union) and the members of the *Hervormde Kerk* (Reformed Church) on the one hand, and the *Anti-Revolutionaire Partij* (Anti-Revolutionary Party) and the members of the *Gereformeerde Kerk* (Orthodox Reformed Church), on the other. Despite the drawbacks of the concept, pillarisation offers a framework to discuss the progress and emancipation of Dutch society against the background of economic and religious differences. Faith was employed to solve certain conflicts that resulted from modernisation and shifts in economic relations. These conflicts concerned oppositions between liberals and conservatives, and workers and capitalists, as well as issues around gender inequality.[14]

The media played a vital role in pillarisation by expressing political sentiments and promoting certain visions of social life, thereby contributing to the solidification of distinct communities. Amongst the periodicals in which Schreiner was featured, the Catholic pillar is represented by the daily *De Tijd* (*The Time*) (1845–1974) and the popular periodical *Katholieke Illustratie: Zondags-lektuur voor het Katholieke Nederlandsche Volk* (*Catholic Illustration: Sunday Read for the Catholic Dutch People*) (1867–1967). The Protestant pillar included the daily *De Standaard* (*The Standard*) (1872–1944) and *De Blijde Wereld: Christen Socialistisch Weekblad* (*The Joyful World: Christian-Socialist Weekly*) (1902–1915); the latter is particularly interesting since it propagated a Protestant take on social issues and competed for readership with socialist periodicals.

The socialist press, in turn, directly addressed industrial workers and encouraged trade unionism. Schreiner's name appears in *De Fabrieksbode; Weekblad der Nederlandsche Gist- en Spiritusfabriek* (*The Factory Messenger: Dutch Yeast and Spirits Factory Weekly Paper*) (1882–2001), welcoming the reader with the slogan 'factory for all – all for the factory' (de fabriek voor allen – allen voor de fabriek) and *De Arbeider; Socialistisch Weekblad voor de Provincie Groningen* (*The Worker; Socialist Weekly for the Groningen Province*) (1892–1940). Among socialist periodicals there were those with a specifically cultural focus, including *Morgenrood: Zondagsblad Gewijd aan Wetenschap, Kunst en Letteren* (*Daybreak: Sunday Magazine for Science, Art and Letters*) (1888–1900). This was a supplement to *Recht voor Allen* (*Right for All*) (1879–1900), which had been established by prominent socialist politician, Ferdinand Domela Nieuwenhuis. *De Proletarische Vrouw* (*The Proletarian Woman*) (1905–1940) was a periodical aimed at working-class women, and was co-founded by editor Carry Pothuis-Smit with other female members of the *Sociaal-Democratische Arbeiderspartij* (Social Democratic Workers' Party).

The Liberal pillar is represented by the dailies *Algemeen Handelsblad* (*General Trade Newspaper*) (1828–1970), *Nieuwe Rotterdamsche Courant* (*New Rotterdam Newspaper*) (1843–1970) and *Het Vaderland – Staat- en Letterkundig Nieuwsblad* (*The Fatherland – Political and Literary Newspaper*) (1869–1982). The feminist press formed a separate category, which was pillarised as Liberal and progressive. These publications advocated broad access to education for women and included: *Maandblad van de Vereeniging voor Vrouwenkiesrecht* (*Monthly of the Society for Women's Suffrage*) (1899–1909), *De Vrouw. Veertiendaagsch Blad Gewijd aan de Onderlinge Opvoeding der Vrouwen* (*The Woman. Fortnightly for the Mutual Education of Women*) (1895–1900), and another biweekly, *Belang en Recht; Orgaan van het Comité tot Verbetering van den Maatschappelijken Rechtstoestand der Vrouw in Nederland, van den Vrouwenbond te*

Groningen en van de Vereeniging "Thugatêr" te Amsterdam (Interest and Right; Organ of the Committee for the Improvement of the Social Legal Situation of the Woman in the Netherlands, of the Women's Association in Groningen, and of Society "Thugatêr" in Amsterdam) (1896–1918). The most radical feminist publication in the period was *Evolutie: Veertiendaagsch Blad voor de Vrouw* (*Evolution: Biweekly for Women*) (1893–1926), edited by Wilhelmina Drucker and Dora Schook-Haver. This publication was notorious for controversial articles criticising gender inequalities and was particularly scathing about religion and custom. Another example of a liberal periodical was *Het Kind; Veertiendagsch Blad voor Ouders en Opvoeders* (*The Child; Biweekly Paper for Parents and Teachers*) (1900–1955), which was edited by Jan Gunning, a modern pedagogy scholar from the University of Utrecht. The magazine propagated a liberal and progressive vision of education, including the Montessori approach. Finally, there were popular dailies aimed at broad audiences across all sections of society, including *De Telegraaf* (*The Telegraph*) (established in 1893) and *Rotterdamsch Nieuwsblad* (*Rotterdam Newspaper*) (1878–1991). Wijfjes estimates that in 1939 up to 57 per cent of the daily press in the Netherlands had no direct affinity to any particular pillar.[15]

A socially engaged writer

The first mentions of Schreiner in the daily press correspond to the appearance of the Dutch translation of *The Story of an African Farm*. For example, on 9 February 1892, the progressive liberal paper, *Het Vaderland*, announced the publication of *Op den Hoeve in Afrika*, translated by Ms. G. Willeumier and published by Van Druten te Sneek. This was described as 'no usual little novel' (geen gewoon romannetje) and a work in which the talented author created intriguing characters and plot with peculiar humour.[16]

It was *Dreams*, however, that earned Schreiner a reputation as an exceptional writer of great sensitivity. This collection of allegories was unanimously praised in all reviews regardless of the political profiles of the paper. In the 18 July 1893 issue of *Algemeen Handelsblad*, the Dutch edition (*Droomen*, translated by Guilette Willeumier) is described as a register of Schreiner's personal reflections: 'short allegories in prose, the thoughts of a young woman who has suffered and loved and thought a great deal' (korte allegorieën in proza, de gedachten van een jonge vrouw, die veel leed en liefhad en veel heeft nagedacht).[17] The reviewer assures readers that the new book is original and 'finely touches on what moves the human soul and so truthfully reflects it, that her books are hugely fascinating, especially for the young' (fijn voelt het geen de menschenziel beweegt en zoo ongekunsteld geeft zij dit weer, dat haar boeken grote bekoring hebben, vooral voor het jonge geslacht).[18]

The socialist literary magazine *Morgenrood* recommended *Dreams* because of its 'peculiar, sometimes touching form' (eigenaardigen, soms aangrijpenden vorm).[19] The critic was clearly impressed, and having quoted a couple of passages, concludes: 'beautiful, isn't it' (schoon, niet waar).[20] This edition, from Amsterdam publishers De Veldt, cost 1.90 gulden, so the reviewer adds: 'the price is high but the content is worth it' (De prijs is wel wat hoog, maar de inhoud is goed).[21] Indeed, *Morgenrood* continued to publish excerpts from *Dreams* for many years after this first edition. For example, issue 19, published on 19 March 1897, includes the chapter 'Drie Dromen' ('Three Dreams' originally published as 'Three Dreams in a Desert'), and issue 45 (25 December 1920) prints a translation of 'The Lost Joy' as 'De verloren vreugd'. Another socialist publication, *De Arbeider*, also printed a positive review in their 13 October 1900 issue. The enthusiastic reviewer G. F. Lindeijer stresses that *Dreams* tells 'beautiful and truthful fairy tales from a happy land' (mooie reine sprookjes uit 'n gelukkig land), deploys 'no idle pretty words' (geen ijdele woordenpraal), and conveys 'in clear, comprehensible language high and elevated thoughts' (in klare, duidelijke woorden hoog verheven gedachten).[22]

Another of Schreiner's works, the allegorical novella *Trooper Peter Halket of Mashonaland* (1897), received positive reviews in socialist magazines. Schreiner was profiled as an important commentator on current affairs, and her calls for a social change meant that she was often categorised as belonging to a group of eminent socially and politically engaged writers, both Anglophone and Dutch. Thus, *Morgenrood* compared *Trooper Peter Halket* to both Harriet Beecher Stowe's *Uncle Tom's Cabin* (1852), and to *Max Havelaar* (1860) by the renowned Dutch writer Multatuli (Eduard Douwes Dekker). The reviewer stressed the shared aim of all three, which was to criticise the so-called 'civilising mission' of the white man.[23] Quoting *Hollandse Revue*, the reviewer states that, by exposing the hypocrisy of colonial reality, Schreiner demonstrates her exquisite literary talent so that her compassionate approach to suffering exceeds the work of both other writers: her work is above Stowe's when it comes to artistry, and above Multatuli's when it comes to the 'human dimension' (menschelijk oogpunt).[24] For this reviewer, Schreiner's work emerged out of sympathy for others and was therefore not motivated by purely personal reasons.

In the years following her death in 1920, Schreiner remained a source of inspiration for many Dutch socialists. *Dreams* and *Trooper Peter Halket* were included in socialist clubs' reading lists, recommended for purchase by workers' libraries,[25] and read at various group meetings. *De Proletarische Vrouw* regularly reported that excerpts from *Dreams* were discussed at gatherings held by local branches of socialist clubs in the late 1920s and 1930s.[26] Thanks to *Dreams*, Schreiner was recognised in the socialist milieu as on par with such well-known Dutch poets as Herman Gorter and Adama van Scheltema, who were also actively propagating socialist ideals through literature.[27]

The liberal *Algemeen Handelsblad* was more critical of the literary value of *Trooper Peter Halket*. In a review published on 4 July 1897, the book is described as 'unsympathetic' (onsympathiek) and tendentious, marked by poor plot and overt didacticism: 'This kind of preaching is seldom pleasant to read, especially when the thoughts expressed are hardly new' (Preeken als deze zijn zelden aangenaam om te lezen, allerminst wanneer de daarin verkondigde denkbeelden zoo weinig nieuw zijn).[28] The review closes with the remark that Schreiner must learn from Multatuli how to write an exciting *tendenzroman* (novel of purpose).[29] Equally unimpressed was the reviewer from the newspaper *De Telegraaf*, who on 13 July 1897 assessed *Trooper Peter Halket* as 'efficient journalism, without pretence to literary achievements' (vlotte journalistiek, zonder aanspraak op letterkundige verdinste).[30] The description of the novella as 'another Uncle Tom's Cabin of Mashonaland' (een andere Negerhut van Oom Tom van Mashonaland)[31] once again emphasised a perceived lack of originality in Schreiner's approach.

For the general public in the Netherlands, Schreiner was a recognisable, even celebrity, author. This can be inferred from the way in which *Algemeen Handelsblad* announced the publication of Schreiner's biography, which was written by her husband, S. C. Cronwright-Schreiner. The announcement described the book as containing 'very thrilling anecdotes' (zeer pakkende anecdotes) from the life of the writer who was 'also in our country so well-known and celebrated' (ook in ons land zoo bekende en gevierde).[32]

'An English South African': a political commentator

Although during the Anglo-Boer War (1899–1902) the Netherlands had no territorial claims to South Africa, the cultural links remained strong. Dutch was still the official written language in the Boer republics of the Transvaal and Orange Free State, even though inhabitants spoke various dialects which gave rise to the Afrikaans language. Dutch sympathies for South Africa were based on the colonial history and on a construct of 'stamverwantschap', a kind of 'racial and cultural kinship'.[33]

The Dutch pillarised press unanimously expressed their support for the Boer cause, even though before the war the attitudes towards the Boer republics varied. For example, the Catholics were sceptical of the Boers' strong Calvinism, while socialists tended to see the republics as conservative feudal states.[34] Yet during the war, similar reports were published in the politically neutral *Algemeen Dagblad* and Catholic *De Tijd*. The Netherlands had no independent network of undersea telegraph cables and so the press was dependent on foreign agencies for information.[35] This meant that items were repeated by several papers, often including unconfirmed news and rumours.

Schreiner was seen as a specialist on South African social and political complexities. Her pro-Boer sympathies and critical stance on British politics were sentiments shared by the Dutch. The Liberal pillar represented by *Algemeen Handelsblad*, profiled her as an advocate of the Boer cause. Shortly before the outbreak of the conflict, the paper printed translations of excerpts from her essay 'An English-South African's View of the Situation' as 'De Zuidafrikaansche quaestie. Door een Engelsch-Afrikaansche'.[36] On 5 April 1896, the paper announced that it would publish a series of Schreiner's 'Losse Gedachten' ('Loose Thoughts'), translations of her contributions to *Fortnightly Review*, pointing out that Dutch audiences should be well informed about the growing tensions between the British and the Boers in South Africa. Schreiner was described as a uniquely competent source to discuss these issues because she was

> the writer of *Dreams* and *The Story of an African Farm* [who] for years has lived among the Boers, has participated in their everyday life, understands their language, and has discovered a more finely crafted heart under their rough shell. So she took to these people. ('De schrijfster van *Dreams* en *The Story of an African Farm* heeft jaren lang onder de Boeren gewoond, heeft deelgenomen aan hun dagelijksch leven, verstaat hun taal en heeft onder den ruwen bolster de fijner bewerktuigde kern ontdekt. Zoo heeft zij het volk liefgekregen').[37]

The 29 July 1896 issue presented a translation of Schreiner's *Fortnightly Review* contribution on the ethnic diversity of South Africa and the consequences of slavery. As the Dutch commentator introducing Schreiner's thoughts explained, her writings 'provide a better insight into the youth of the [South African] state, into the impossibility of applying European ways of thinking to South African conditions' ([haar geschriften] geven een beter begrip van de jongheid van het land, van de onmogelijkheid om onze Europeesche denkbeelden te willen toepassen op Zuidafrikaansche toestanden).[38] According to the article's author, Schreiner's essay elaborates on the 'half-blood-question and the slavery problem' (half-bloedquaestie en het slavenvraagstuk)[39] by explaining that slavery remained a thorny issue in South Africa, whilst for Europe it was in the past. Though the slave trade was officially abolished in South Africa in 1834, the problem of 'the half caste'[40] is described by Schreiner as a most pressing issue and a very hard one to solve. She stresses that both the Boers and the English used to be slave owners and thus both white races are guilty of the creation of the 'half-blood'. She shares her expert insider knowledge on the origin and diversification of African people by describing the differences in appearance and ways of life of the San (then called the Bushmen) and the Khoi (Hottentots), who – applying social Darwinian terminology – she calls 'eternal children'.[41] To characterise the Bantus, in particular the Zulus, she refers to political theory. Admitting that their social structure is complex and was well-developed before the Europeans came, she calls them communists and tough negotiators, strongly attached to cryptic laws and customs. In social Darwinist terms, she explains that both white and Black people have their pride and a rightful place in the world since they are God's creation, while people of mixed race are ostracised by all other ethnic groups in South Africa.[42]

Across a variety of publications, Schreiner emerges as a reliable authority on late nineteenth-century sciences, demonstrating a vast knowledge of African history that she analyses and interprets using the latest European scientific theories. When *Losse Gedachten* was launched in book form by the H. D. Tjeenk Willink & Zoon Haarlem publishing house in 1900, both the confessional and liberal press published announcements. On two consecutive days, 6–7 March 1900, the liberal *Het Vaderland*[43] and the Catholic *De Tijd*[44] each recommended a translation by Mr. J. A. Bientjes of a 'sympathetic English woman's' (sympathieke Engelsche vrouw) writings 'that no one must leave unread these days' (dat niemand in deze dagen ongelezen mag laten).[45]

For the Protestant *De Standaard*, Schreiner's thought served to support their condemnation of British imperialist greed. When on 16 September 1898 the paper quoted an article from the South African *Randpost* about the Black people in erstwhile Rhodesia being sold as slaves, it drew a comparison with the situation that Schreiner described in *Trooper Peter Halket*. Shortly after the outbreak of the Anglo-Boer war on 6 November 1899, *De Standaard* reprinted a telegram that had been published in the *New York Journal*, in which Schreiner explained the causes of the conflict as economic. She characterised the war as the 'shameful business of the gold-chasers' (schandzaak der goudjagers),[46] rather than as a nation-based conflict between the English and the 'African Hollanders'.[47] Moreover, she claims that the British press had been lying to the global public about the Transvaal government, profiling it as discriminatory and abusive towards the English. Interestingly, Schreiner is introduced here not only as a renowned writer but also as the sister of the eminent politician and Prime Minister of the Cape Colony, William Schreiner. In this case, her authority as political commentator rests also on her direct connections with a progressive South African statesman.

Similarly, the politically neutral *Rotterdamsch Nieuwsblad* saw Schreiner as a competent political commentator. The article 'Nieuws uit het Oorlogsterrein' ('News from the War Terrain')[48] quotes a letter from Schreiner to W. T. Stead, who, as editor of *War against War*, was similarly critical of the Anglo-Boer conflict. In the letter, Schreiner writes that the war led to the death of 'heroic Transvaalers' (heldhaftige Transvalers) and 'brave English soldiers' (dappere Engelse soldaten) in the interest of 'miserable packs of blood suckers and money makers' (ellendige benden bloedzuigers en geldmakers).[49] She expresses a straightforwardly pacifist message: 'War is a terrible thing. But a war that started to serve capital and to smother freedom is hell' (Oorlog is een verschrikkelijk ding. Maar als hij in dienst van het kapitaal wordt begonnen, om de vrijheid te worgen, is bij een hel).[50]

On 18 April 1900, *Algemeen Handelsblad* elaborated on Schreiner's political role as a member of a reconciliation committee formed by influential English-speaking South Africans and Britons. In the first phase of the war, this body strove to improve the relationships between the Afrikaans and English-speaking South Africans by spreading reliable information and supporting both parties' justified claims.[51] A more radical image of Schreiner emerges from an article from the 5 November 1900 issue of the newspaper.[52] It quotes Reuter's report that during a women's meeting in the small Eastern Cape town of Somerset East, a letter by Schreiner was read in which she called the English the oppressor ('verdrukker'), condemned their actions in South Africa, and expressed the wish that the republics regain their independence. The Dutch paper reports that *Cape Argus* reacted 'furiously' (woedend),[53] accusing Schreiner of breaking the loyalty that she owed to Britain. The *Cape Argus* reporter even suggested that she was guilty of a treason, even though – as he patronisingly puts it – her words were read only at a women's meeting: 'Women can be granted a measure of leniency, but treason is treason, even at a women's meeting' (Aan dames moge een mate van toegeeflijkheid zijn toegestaan, meenen wij; doch verraad is verraad, zelfs op een vrouwenvergadering).[54]

The gossip that Schreiner was arrested by the British as a result of this speech was reported in all Dutch newspapers, which only confirms how recognisable a figure she had become during the war. For example, the news appears on the front page of the morning issue of *Algemeen Handelsblad* on 17 July 1901, and in *De Standaard* the following day. In both cases, Schreiner is introduced as 'the brave English woman' ([d]e moedige Engelsche vrouw)[55] who was not afraid to expose British wrongdoings in South Africa. Drawing on a source in *Daily News*, *De Standaard*[56] published quotes by the English novelist Ouida (Maria Louise Rame) and English publisher Thomas Fisher Unwin. Ouida, who like Schreiner was fiercely anti-war, claimed that Schreiner had been detained due to her sympathy for the Boers, even though she had not been charged with a crime; she is presented as 'a writer with original visions ... [whose] words have moved many to tears over the poor, the lonely' (een schrijfster met oorspronkelijke denkbeelden ... woorden hebben velen doen weenen over de armen, de eenzamen).[57] Ouida appeals to people of influence to protest against the mistreatment of a woman and writer whose only crime was speaking her mind. She also expresses her outrage at the British for the cruelty and greed of their war policy in South Africa, and for their untruthful war reports. The war, Ouida concludes, was a stain on England's honour because the government's decisions meant that 'the British people are disrespected in the world's eyes and tarnish the English name' (verlagen het Britsche volk in de oogen der wereld en brengen schande over de Engelschen naam).[58]

The 17 July 1901 evening issue of *Algemeen Handelsblad* once again mentions Schreiner. Drawing on comments made by Fisher Unwin in the *Westminster Gazette*, the *Algemeen Handelsblad* reports that Schreiner was in good physical shape, but her works and papers had been destroyed in a fire. The Dutch contributor observes that Schreiner, who had 'loved and honoured' (liefhad en vereerde) England, 'came relatively late to the realisation that in South Africa a struggle is taking place between English domination and Holland's love of freedom' (tamelijk laat is ze tot inzicht gekomen dat daar in Zuid-Afrika een worsteling plaats had tusschen Engelssche overheersching en Hollandschen vrijheidszin).[59] The reference to 'Holland's love of freedom' points to the key feature of Dutch national identity as defined by the Batavian myth, and underscores the kinship between the Dutch and 'South African Hollanders' (Zuid-Afrikaansche Hollanders).[60] The journalist is critical of Schreiner's reflections in *Words in Season* (1899), in which she had claimed that many South African Hollanders who were educated in Europe and worked in the Cape administration were as close to Great Britain as the English themselves. He concludes the article on a dramatic note by portraying Schreiner as a martyr for the Boer cause: 'Truly, England procures martyrs from whom the seed of South Africa's independence will shoot!' (Voorwaar, Engeland kweekt de martelaren waaruit het zaad van Zuid-Afrika's onafhanklijheid zal opschieten!).[61]

On 19 July 1901, the *Algemeen Handelsblad* printed an article in which Schreiner's husband, Cronwright-Schreiner, denied Ouida's words. He explains that Schreiner was not imprisoned but had travelled to Hanover in the Cape for health reasons. The rumours about her being denied a permit to leave remained unconfirmed, though it was reported that she still lived 'under the "rule of terror"' which had been in force in a great part of South Africa' (onder het 'schrikbewind' dat over een groot deel van Zuid-Afrika is ingesteld).[62]

A moral authority and progressive intellectual

On 16 March 1904, the evening issue of the liberal paper *Algemeen Handelsblad* reported the establishment of the Amsterdam branch of the Erasmus Society for the 'promotion of international spiritual life' (bevordering van international geestelijk leven).[63] The society planned to hold lectures by international intellectuals from various domains ranging from literature, religion and ethics, to hygiene, healthcare, sociology and politics. The list of invited speakers begins with Schreiner, followed by the renowned anti-war writer Bertha von Suttner, Belgian author Maurice Maeterlinck, German novelist Gustav Frenssen, German philosopher Friedrich Paulsen, influential English anti-war journalist William (W. T.) Stead and French poet and writer Anatole France among others.

The Dutch confessional press, in turn, profiles Schreiner as a moral authority – primarily as a result of her anti-colonialism. The Protestant paper *De Standaard*[64] recommends *Trooper Peter Halket* as an important narrative of protest against British imperialism, and a reminder of the 'duty of civilised humankind towards Africa's black race' (plicht der beschaafde menschheid tegen Afrika's zwarte ras).[65] This facet of Schreiner's public persona emerges also in *De Telegraaf*, which on 13 July 1897 published a discussion of *Trooper Peter Halket* on the front page. Here, the novella is described as providing a sharp critique of colonisation as exposing the worst qualities in men. Though full of admiration for Schreiner's idealism, the reviewer nevertheless remarks that such literature will not help to effect great change.[66] A more optimistic tone appears in a contribution by Ida Heijermans in the women's periodical *De Vrouw*.[67] She recommends the book for its universal dimension, message of love and protest against oppression of the weak.

It seems that *Dreams*, due to its focus on spirituality and references to religious topics, contributed most to Schreiner's public persona as a moral thinker in the confessional press. Both Protestants and Catholics found passages they deemed representative of their worldviews. The Protestant *De Blijde Wereld*, which was edited by the predikants S. K. Bakker, S. Winkel and J. A. Bruins Jr., announced meetings that took as their primary topic Schreiner's visions of heaven and hell.[68] This weekly, established in 1902, was aimed at 'liberal Protestants' and sought to reconcile the ideals of socialism and Christianity with the intent of retaining at least some workers in the confessional pillar.[69] Schreiner's *Trooper Peter Halket* is presented as corresponding with the paper's view: it is a work that exposes 'the opposition between capitalism and Christianity' (de tegenstelling tusschen kapitalisme en christendom).[70] *De Blijde Wereld* was evidently greatly inspired by Schreiner's theological reflections, as it also published a contribution entitled 'In hell' ('In de hel'), by J. A. B. (Bruins, Jr.) with the acknowledgement: '[a]ccording to a vision of Olive Schreiner' (Naar een visioen van Olive Schreiner).[71] The article is in fact a translated excerpt from Schreiner's allegory 'The Sunlight Lay Across My Bed', which was published in *Dreams*. Moreover, several issues from 1915 and 1916 advertised 'Religious-socialist meetings' (Religieus-socialistische bijeenkomsten) with proposed discussion topics that included Schreiner's views on heaven and hell. The magazine also printed adverts about new publications in the series 'Blijde Wereldpreekjes' ('Joyful World Sermons') with Ds. A. van de Heide's contributions entitled 'Olive Schreiner on Hell' ('Olive Schreiner over de hel') and 'Olive Schreiner on Heaven' ('Olive Schreiner over de hemel').[72]

On the Catholic side, passages from *Dreams* were reprinted in *De Katholieke Illustratie*, with the aim of providing audiences with morally uplifting and instructive reading in their spare time. The periodical was established in 1867 and was in its initial phase strongly anti-Protestant, though it later became less radical.[73] It published a Dutch translation of the allegory 'In a Ruined Chapel' (In een verwoeste kapel)[74] from *Dreams*, which teaches about forgiveness and was therefore likely thought to convey a universal Christian message.

The pedagogical press saw Schreiner as an authority and instructor in matters of education. The 21 September 1912 issue of the biweekly *Het Kind* (*The Child*) recommends a couple of texts that provide guidance on how to raise children so that they become valuable members of society. The editor, Jan Gunning, promoted modern approaches to pedagogy, and believed that an individual was most useful in a community when given an opportunity to fully develop their talents. Schreiner's *Woman and Labour* is quoted as supporting the view that girls should be included in educational processes, so that in their future roles as mothers they would become spiritual guides for their children, and thus contribute to modern society.[75] Gunning identifies Schreiner as an important progressive voice and considers her contributions alongside the work of educational reformers. These include Jan Ligthart (1859–1916), who based his approach on Christian values, and John Dowey (1859–1952), Professor at the University of Chicago and advocate of a progressive education that encompassed such principles as learning by doing, critical thinking, problem solving and shaping social-responsibility awareness.

An important feminist voice

An article on the growing popularity of women's clubs in London was published in the literary supplement of the liberal daily, *Rotterdamsch Nieuwsblad*, on 18 January 1894.[76] It presented the Pioneer Club, whose members were fierce advocates of female suffrage, and comprised various educated women, including doctors, journalists and popular New Woman writers such as Schreiner and Sarah Grand, who, the journalist observes, were already known to Dutch readers. Feminist biweekly *De Vrouw* also lists Schreiner as an internationally renowned progressive woman writer, and places her alongside Charlotte Perkins Stetson, Lily Braun and Ellen Key as a leading advocate of female emancipation.[77]

Schreiner's *Woman and Labour* (1911) was undoubtedly the book that feminist circles in the Netherlands discussed most widely. Interestingly, even before the publication of Aletta Jacobs's Dutch translation, parts of the text found their way to the country. In 1900, *Belang en Recht* published extensive excerpts over three issues of the magazine, which were translated from English to Dutch by Ms Dyserinck-Bok.[78] The publication describes Schreiner as a supporter of women's access to education and jobs, and the selected passages argue for the importance of securing socially useful and meaningful work for women in the context of changing living conditions due to industrialisation.

The publication of *Woman and Labour* in Dutch translation was announced by various liberal papers, including *Nieuwe Rotterdamsche Courant* on 8 May 1911, and *Het Vaderland* on 14 May 1911. The morning edition of the latter introduced Schreiner as 'well-known amongst the cultured public, no less familiar in the modern woman's world' (een goede bekende bij het beschaafde publiek, niet het minst in de moderne vrouwenwereld) and as an undaunted defender of the oppressed during the Anglo-Boer war: 'the energetic woman who during the South African war so bravely stood up for the oppressed' (de energieke vrouw, die tijdens den Zuid-Afrikaanschen oorlog zoo dapper partij trok voor de verdrukten).[79] The article explains that *Woman and Labour* is not about working-class women or any particular path of education that women should follow, but about the 'need for labour for women [which is] the essence of the modern women's movement' (noodzakelijkheid van arbeid voor de vrouwen [which is] de kern van de hedendaagsche vrouwenbeweging).[80] The reviewer also mentions the leading Dutch suffragist and pioneer female doctor Jacobs, and presents Schreiner as her ally in working towards female emancipation.

Press articles published in the period during and after World War I refer to Schreiner as a feminist and pacifist voice of authority, and her work was often quoted by Jacobs in her public speeches. On 27 January 1915, *Het Vaderland* published a lengthy report on the meeting of the *Vereeniging voor Vrouwenkiesrecht* (Association for Women Suffrage), whose President was Jacobs. The article summarises Jacobs's anti-war speech, in which she condemns militarised countries for promoting the view that the sole role of women was to provide soldier-sons. The speech also makes a reference to a number of prominent feminists, including Schreiner, Bertha van Sutner, Carrie Chapman Catt and Rev Anna Shaw, all of whom claimed that the enfranchisement of women would prevent future conflicts and support the rebuilding of society after the end of the First World War.[81]

Unsurprisingly, *Woman and Labour* was positively received by the feminist press. The biweekly *Evolutie* published two issues (24 May 1911 and 8 June 1911) that discussed the main points in Schreiner's book. Schreiner is praised as 'a woman with a clear vision, who sees things in their entirety, [and] does not measure the world according to the little circle around her' (zij is een vrouw met helderen blik, die de dingen overziet in hun geheel, niet de wereld afmeet naar het kringetje, dat om haar cirkelt).[82] In a review published in *Maandblad van de Vereeniging voor Vrouwenkiesrecht*, J. Van Landschot Hubrecht (J. v. L. H) refers to *Woman and Labour* as 'a revelation' (een openbaring), and Schreiner as 'a splendid guide' (een uitstekenden gids), able to enlighten those unaware of existing gender inequalities and aims of the suffrage movement.[83] The periodical describes how Schreiner's work was regularly read during suffragists' meetings.[84]

The socialist women's press was far less enthusiastic about *Woman and Labour*. *De Proletarische Vrouw* published a disparaging review on 15 December 1911, in which the reviewer, H. M., admitted the book's merit for the feminist movement but argued that it expressed a bourgeois point of view unrelated to the actual plight of the working classes.[85] Thus the reviewer paints Schreiner as what Jansz describes as a 'bourgeois feminist', which can in part be attributed to her association with her book's Dutch translator, Jacobs.[86] The varied reception of *Woman and Labour* thus reflects the tensions between feminist and socialist circles in the Netherlands.[87]

In 1921, however, *De Proletarische Vrouw* published articles that discussed Schreiner in a much more favourable manner. For example, a lengthy fragment from 'Three Dreams in a Desert' ('Drie droomen in een woestijn')[88] was accompanied by a commentary by the feminist activist Mathilde Wibaut, in which she vehemently protested the Dutch government's bill proposing that married women be banned from working. Wibaut also criticised the prioritising of domestic duty over education for girls. She argued that if they remain unmarried or became widows, their financial situation would become difficult, because they would have limited job opportunities, would be forced to live on charity, or otherwise have to work as prostitutes. Schreiner is described by Wibaut as 'one of the first women who woke women up to no longer be dependent on others but to free themselves' (een der eerste vrouwen die de vrouwen opwekte niet langer afhankelijk te zijn, maar zichzelf te bevrijden).[89]

Conclusion

This chapter described the major contexts in which Schreiner's thought appeared in the Dutch press, which roughly correspond with her four public personae: socially concerned novelist, expert on South African politics, humanist thinker and feminist. Press publications representing all four Dutch pillars acknowledge her literary talent and see her as sharing her approach with Stowe and Multatuli. All pillars also emphasised her expertise on South Africa, her opinions drawing on (then-)modern science, sociology and anthropology. Moreover, she emerges as embodiment of a pro-Boer attitude,[90] which struck a chord with Dutch readers who saw the Boers as kin.

Not all publications, however, were equally enthusiastic about her feminist writings. Confessional (Catholic and Protestant) periodicals do not mention her efforts in the struggle for female franchise. Instead, when quoting *Dreams*, they choose only such passages that they consider communicate a Christian, ethical message. The Protestant press in particular accentuated Schreiner's moral vision and contempt for imperialist greed. Socialists, in turn, were critical of Schreiner's advocacy for female emancipation through professional jobs (as she proposes in *Woman and Labour*), since they believed that she shared this approach with the 'bourgeois feminist' Jacobs. At the same time, *Woman and Labour* was praised by feminist, liberal and the politically neutral press as an important and clear text that outlines the principles of a modern society in which genders are equal. Paradoxically, socialists sceptical about Schreiner's views in *Woman and Labour* frequently quoted *Dreams* and *Trooper Peter Halket* as mandatory reading for exposing social and colonial abuses in the capitalist world. Moreover, in the 1930s, Schreiner's name began to be mentioned in the same breath as prominent Dutch socialist writers – so that posthumously she gained a reputation as a socialist writer. Different audiences approached Schreiner's writings differently; the contexts in which her work appeared in print – differently directed according to the social and political circumstances each periodical addressed, and reinforced – determined the versions of Schreiner that circulated in the Netherlands. The same, of course, is true in any regional, linguistic, or national context. It is the task of the scholar to continue to draw attention to these contexts and consequences.

Acknowledgement

This research was funded by the Polish National Science Centre (NCN) SONATA 14 grant (grant no. 2018/31/D/HS2/00131: 'White South African New Women and cultural mobility in the first half of the 20th century').

Works Cited

'Boekaankondigingen'. *De Tijd*, 7 March 1900.
'Boekbeoordeling. Peter Halket van Mashonaland door Olive Schreiner'. *De Telegraaf*, 13 July 1897, 1.
'Boekbespreking'. *Morgenrood: Zondagsblad Gewijd aan Wetenschap, Kunst en Letteren* no. 34 (1899): 271.
'Buitenlandsche Kroniek'. *Algemeen Handelsblad*, 19 July 1901.
'Buitenlandsch Overzicht'. *Algemeen Handelsblad*, 17 July 1901.
'Clubberichten'. *Proletarische Vrouw* 33, no. 1188 (22 June 1938): 13.
'De vrouw en arbeid'. *Evolutie* 19, no. 4 (24 May 1911): 28–30.
'Een vrouwenvergadering'. *Algemeen Handelsblad*, 5 November 1900.

'Erasmus'. *Algemeen Handelsblad*, 16 March 1904.
'Gemengde meedeelingen. Onschadelijk gemaakt'. *De Standaard*, 18 July 1901.
'Jezus Christus in Zuid-Afrika'. *Morgenrood: Zondagsblad Gewijd aan Wetenschap, Kunst en Letteren*, no. 19 (1897): 151–52.
'Kunst en Letteren: *Droomen*'. *Algemeen Handelsblad*, 18 July 1893.
'Kunst en Letternieuws'. *Het Vaderland*, no. 33 (9 February 1892).
'Kunst en Wetenschappen'. *Algemeen Handelsblad*, 4 July 1897.
'Losse gedachten over Zuid-Afrika'. *Algemeen Handelsblad*, 5 April 1896.
'Nog een getuigenis'. *De Standaard*, 6 November 1899.
'Olive Schreiner'. *Algemeen Handelsblad*, 27 February 1924.
'Olive Schreiner krijgsgevangen'. *Algemeen Handelsblad*, 17 July 1901.
'Recensiën: *Peter Halket van Mashonaland*'. *De Standaard*, 1 June 1903.
'Transvaal en Oranje-Vrijstaat'. *Het Vaderland*, 6 March 1900.
'Uit onze afdelingen'. *Maandblad van de Vereeniging voor Vrouwenkiesrecht* 9, no. 8 (15 March 1915): 7–8.
'Van verre en nabij'. *De Blijde Wereld* 7, no. 6 (27 November 1908).
'Vereen. voor Vrouwenkiesrecht'. *Het Vaderland*, no. 27 (January 1915).
'Vrouwenclubs in Londen: "The Pioneer"'. *Rotterdamsch Nieuwsblad: Letterkundig Bijvoegsel* 16, no. 210 (18 January 1894).
Bosch, Mineke. 'Scholarly Personae and Twentieth-Century Historians: Explorations of a Concept'. *BMGN – Low Countries Historical Review* 131, no. 4 (2016): https://doi.org/10.18352/bmgn-lchr.10263.
Bossenbroek, Martin. *Holland op zijn breedst: Indië en Zuid-Afrika in de Nederlandse cultuur omstreeks 1900*. Amsterdam: Bakker, 1996.
Bruins, J. A. 'In de hel'. *De Blijde Wereld* 1, no. 46 (11 September 1903).
De fabrieksbode. Weekblad der Nederlandsche Gist- en Spiritusfabriek 20, no. 7 (16 February 1901).
De fabrieksbode. Weekblad der Nederlandsche Gist- en Spiritusfabriek 49, no. 9 (1 March 1930).
De Rooy, Piet. *A Tiny Spot on the Earth: The Political Culture of the Netherlands in the Nineteenth and Twentieth Centuries*. Amsterdam: Amsterdam University Press, 2015.
Drwal, Małgorzata. 'The Feminism of Olive Schreiner and the Feminism of Aletta Jacobs: The Reception of Schreiner's *Woman and Labour* in the Netherlands.' *Dutch Crossing* 45, no. 1 (2021): https://doi.org/10.1080/03096564.2019.1693200.
Ferf, A. 'Voor dames: Een mooi boek en een mooi tijdschrift'. *Het Vaderland*, no. 114 (14 May 1911).
Fomichenko, Anna. 'Oscar Wilde's Long Afterlife: Victorian Celebrity and Its Transformations in Modern Culture'. In *(Extra)Ordinary? The Concept of Authenticity in Celebrity and Fan Studies*, edited by Jade Alexander and Katarzyna Bronk, 77–92. Leiden: Brill Rodopi, 2018.
Foucault, Michel. 'What is an Author?' In *Aesthetic, Method and Epistemology*, edited by James Faubion, 205–22. New York: The New Press, 1998.
Gonzalez Sanchez, Sergio. 'Deconstructing Myths, Constructing History. Dutch National Identity: Formulation and Evolution of the Batavian Myth'. *Archeological Review from Cambridge* 27, no. 2 (2012): 85–110.
Gunning, Jan. *Het Kind* 13, no. 19 (21 September 1912): 159.

Heijermans, Ida. 'Een zonderling boek'. *De Vrouw* 2, no. 24 (26 July 1902): 189–91.
—. 'Lectuur. Uitgaven van 't Nut'. *De Vrouw* 26, no. 3 (19 October 1918): 47–8.
Herman, Paul. 'What is a Scholarly Persona? Ten Theses on Virtues, Skills, and Desires'. *History and Theory* 53, no. 3 (2014): https://doi.org/10.1111/hith.10717.
H. M. 'De Vrouw en Arbeid door Olive Schreiner'. *De Proletarische Vrouw* 7, no. 4 (15 December 1911).
Jansz, Ulla. 'Women Workers Contested: Socialists, Feminists, and Democracy at the National Exhibition of Women's Labour in the Hague, 1898'. *Yearbook of Women's History* 35 (2015): 69–85.
Klooster, Rienk. *Het vrijzinnig protestantisme in Nederland*. Kampen: Uitgeverij Kok. 2006.
Kuitenbrouwer, Vincent. *War of Words. Dutch Pro-Boer Propaganda and the South African War (1899–1902)*. Amsterdam: Amsterdam University Press, 2012.
Krebs, Paula M. 'Olive Schreiner's Racialization of South Africa'. *Victorian Studies* 40, no. 3 (1997): 427–44.
—. *Gender, Race and the Writing of the Empire. Public Discourse and the Boer War*. Cambridge: Cambridge University Press, 1999.
Lindeijer, G. F. 'Over lectuur'. *De Arbeider. Socialistisch Weekblad voor de Provincie Groningen* 10, no. 41 (13 October 1900).
Schreiner, Olive. 'De Zuidafrikaansche quaestie. Door een Engelsch-Afrikaansche'. *Algemeen Handelsblad*, 13 July 1899.
—. 'De Zuidafrikaansche quaestie. Door een Engelsch-Afrikaansche'. *Algemeen Handelsblad*, 14 July 1899.
—. 'De Zuidafrikaansche quaestie. Door een Engelsch-Afrikaansche'. *Algemeen Handelsblad*, 15 July 1899.
—. 'Der vrouwen vraag'. *Belang en Recht* 4, no. 82 (1 March 1900): 80–81.
—. 'Der vrouwen vraag'. *Belang en Recht* 4, no. 83 (15 March 1900): 91–92.
—. 'Der vrouwen vraag'. *Belang en Recht* 4, no. 85 (15 April 1900): 106–7.
—. 'In een verwoeste kapel'. *De Katholieke Illustratie* 37, no. 32 (1903): 257–58.
Sengers, Eric. *'Al zijn we katholiek, zijn wij Nederlanders'. Opkomst en verval van de katholieke kerk in Nederland sinds 1795 vanuit rational-choice perspectief*. Delft: Eburon, 2003.
Shapin, Steven. *A Social History of Truth: Civility and Science in Seventeenth-Century England*. Chicago: The University of Chicago Press, 1994.
Van Landschot Hubrecht, L. 'Vrouw en Arbeid'. *Maandblad van de Vereeniging voor Vrouwenkiesrecht*, 15 July 1915, 7–8.
Wibaut, Mathilde. 'Feuilleton: Fragment uit "Drie dromen in een woestijn" van Olive Schreiner.' *De Proletarische Vrouw* 16, no. 20 (6 August 1921): 3.
Wijfjes, Huub. *Journalistiek in Nederland 1850–2000*. Amsterdam: Boom, 2004.
Wijfjes, Huub, Gerrit Voerman and Patrick Bos. 'Meten van verzuilde politiek in de media: Een digitale benadering van katholieke en sociaaldemocratische dagbladen, 1918–1967'. *BMGN – Low Countries Historical Review* 136, no. 3 (2021): https://doi.org/10.51769/bmgn-lchr.6916.

Notes

1. Bosch, 'Scholarly Personae and Twentieth-Century Historians', 35.
2. Bosch, 'Scholarly Personae', 37.
3. Herman, 'What is a Scholarly Persona?' 355.
4. Shapin, *A Social History of Truth*, 126; Bosch, 'Scholarly Personae', 54.
5. Bosch, 'Scholarly Personae', 54.
6. Fomichenko, 'Oscar Wilde's Long Afterlife', 216.
7. Foucault, 'What is an Author?' 210.
8. Foucault, 'What is an Author?' 211.
9. This is how Schreiner described herself in her three-part essay 'An English South African's View of the Situation' (1899), see Schreiner, 'An English-South African's View of the Situation: Words in Season', *South African News*, 1, 2 and 3 June 1899.
10. De Rooy, *A Tiny Spot on the Earth*, 194.
11. De Rooy, *A Tiny Spot on the Earth*, 224.
12. Wijfjes, Voerman and Bos, 'Meten van verzuilde politiek in de media', 71.
13. Wijfjes, Voerman and Bos, 'Meten van verzuilde politiek in de media', 64–5.
14. Sengers, '*Al zijn we katholiek, zijn wij Nederlanders*', 22.
15. Wijfjes, *Journalistiek in Nederland 1850–2000*, 149.
16. 'Kunst en Letternieuws', *Het Vaderland*, 9 February 1892.
17. 'Kunst en Letteren: *Droomen*', *Algemeen Handelsblad*, 18 July 1893.
18. 'Kunst en Letteren: *Droomen*', *Algemeen Handelsblad*, 18 July 1893.
19. 'Boekbespreking', *Morgenrood*, 271.
20. 'Boekbespreking', *Morgenrood*, 271.
21. 'Boekbespreking', *Morgenrood*, 271.
22. Lindeijer, 'Over lectuur', *De Arbeider*, 13 October 1900.
23. 'Jezus Christus in Zuid-Afrika', *Morgenrood*, 151.
24. 'Jezus Christus in Zuid-Afrika', *Morgenrood*, 152.
25. See for example library catalogues printed in *De Fabrieksbode* 20, no. 7 (1901) and 49, no. 9 (1930).
26. Reports from the club's local branches informed about the readings from Schreiner's work as part of meetings; see for example *Proletarische Vrouw* 23, no. 667 (1928) or 25, no. 775 (1930).
27. 'Clubberichten', *Proletarische Vrouw*, 22 June 1938, 13.
28. 'Kunst en Wetenschappen', *Algemeen Handelsblad*, 4 July 1897.
29. *Max Havelaar or The Coffee Auctions of the Dutch Trading Company* (Dutch: *Max Havelaar, of De koffi-veilingen der Nederlandsche Handel-Maatschappy*) (1860) by Multatuli (Eduard Douwes Dekker) was hugely successful, although it covered the controversial issue of the exploitation of the colonial population of Dutch East Indies. This partly autobiographical novel (based on Douwes Dekker's own experiences as a colonial civil servant in Java) can be described as a novel of purpose, since it was written to condemn the corruption and abuse of power by the Dutch colonial administration. The book ends with Multatuli's appeal to King William III of the Netherlands to intervene.
30. 'Boekbeoordeling', *De Telegraaf*, 1.

31. 'Boekbeoordeling', *De Telegraaf*, 1.
32. 'Olive Schreiner', *Algemeen Handelsblad*, 9.
33. Kuitenbrouwer, *War of Words*, 20.
34. Kuitenbrouwer, *War of Words*, 20.
35. Bossenbroek, *Holland op zijn breedst*, 201–02.
36. See *Algemeen Handelsblad* 13 July 1899, Morning Issue, 1; 14 July 1899, Evening Issue, 7; 15 July 1899, Evening Issue, 7.
37. 'Losse gedachten over Zuid-Afrika', *Algemeen Handelsblad*, 5 April 1896.
38. 'Halfbloed en wilde stammen in Zuid-Afrika', *Algemeen Handelsblad*, 29 July 1896.
39. 'Halfbloed en wilde stammen in Zuid-Afrika', *Algemeen Handelsblad*.
40. 'Halfbloed en wilde stammen in Zuid-Afrika', *Algemeen Handelsblad*.
41. See Krebs, *Gender, Race and the Writing of the Empire*, 119.
42. Schreiner discusses racial mixing as a consequence of white man's violence and exploitation of people of colour. In her view, those with dual heritage are seen as inferior by white people and as alien by Black people. If the races were equal in South Africa, then she would not object to interracial relationships, and even describes mixed-race people as potentially more evolutionarily advanced than either the separate white and Black races. See Schreiner, 'The Problem of Slavery', in *Thoughts on South Africa*, 106–47.
43. 'Transvaal en Oranje-Vrijstaat', *Het Vaderland*, 6 March 1900.
44. 'Boekaankondigingen', *De Tijd*, 7 March 1900.
45. 'Transvaal en Oranje-Vrijstaat', *Het Vaderland*, 6 March 1900.
46. 'Nog een getuigenis', *De Standaard*, 6 November 1899.
47. 'Nog een getuigenis', *De Standaard*.
48. 'Nieuws uit het oorlogsterrein', *Rotterdamsch Nieuwsblad*, 6 December 1899.
49. 'Nieuws uit het oorlogsterrein', *Rotterdamsch Nieuwsblad*.
50. 'Nieuws uit het oorlogsterrein', *Rotterdamsch Nieuwsblad*.
51. 'Het Verzoeningscomite', *Algemeen Handelsblad*, 19 April 1900.
52. 'Een vrouwenvergadering', *Algemeen Handelsblad*, 5 November 1900.
53. 'Een vrouwenvergadering', *Algemeen Handelsblad*.
54. 'Een vrouwenvergadering', *Algemeen Handelsblad*.
55. 'Olive Schreiner krijgsgevangen', *Algemeen Handelsblad*, 17 July 1901.
56. 'Gemengde meedeelingen. Onschadelijk gemaakt', *De Standaard*, 18 July 1901.
57. 'Olive Schreiner krijgsgevangen', *Algemeen Handelsblad*, 17 July 1901.
58. 'Olive Schreiner krijgsgevangen', *Algemeen Handelsblad*.
59. 'Buitenlandsch Overzicht', *Algemeen Handelsblad*, 17 July 1901.
60. The Batavian myth occupies a central place in the Dutch national mythology. It is a reference to the freedom-loving ancient tribe of the Batavians who opposed the Roman Empire, and provided the foundation for many seventeenth- to nineteenth-century political narratives designed to shape the idea of the Dutch nation. See Gonzalez Sanchez, 'Deconstructing Myths', 94–6.
61. 'Buitenlandsch Overzicht', *Algemeen Handelsblad*, 17 July 1901.
62. 'Buitenlandsche Kroniek', *Algemeen Handelsblad*, 19 July 1901.
63. 'Erasmus', *Algemeen Handelsblad*, 16 March 1904, 1.
64. 'Recensiën', *De Standaard*, 1 June 1903.

65. 'Recensiën', *De Standaard*.
66. 'Boekbeoordeling', *De Telegraaf*, 13 July 1897, 1.
67. Heijermans, 'Lectuur. Uitgaven van't Nut', 47.
68. See ads that appeared in all October and November 1915 issues of the periodical.
69. Klooster, *Het vrijzinnig protestantisme in Nederland*, 54.
70. 'Van verre en nabij', *De Blijde Wereld*, 27 November 1908.
71. Bruins, 'In de hel', 11 September 1903.
72. A. van de Heide, 'Olive Schreiner over de hel', no. 1, series 6 (5 November 1915) and 'Olive Schreiner over de hemel', no. 2, series 6 (7 January 1916).
73. Sengers, *Al zijn we katholiek, zijn wij Nederlanders*, 82.
74. Schreiner, 'In een verwoeste kapel', 257–8.
75. Gunning, *Het Kind*, 159.
76. *Rotterdamsch Nieuwsblad: Letterkundig Bijvoegsel*, 18 January 1894.
77. Heijermans, 'Een zonderling boek', 191.
78. Excerpts from Schreiner's *Woman and Labour* appeared under the title 'Der vrouwen vraag' (The Woman's Question) in *Belang en Recht* 4, no. 82 (1 March 1900), 80–1; no. 83 (15 March 1900), 91–2; no. 85 (15 April 1900), 106–7.
79. Ferf, 'Voor dames', 14 May 1911.
80. Ferf, 'Voor dames'.
81. 'Vereen. voor Vrouwenkiesrecht', *Het Vaderland*, 27 January 1915.
82. 'De vrouw en arbeid', *Evolutie*, 24 May 1011, 29.
83. Van Landschot Hubrecht, 'Vrouw en arbeid', 8.
84. For example, during an open meeting of Den Burg division on 26 February 1915. See 'Uit onze afdelingen', *Maandblad van de Vereeniging voor Vrouwenkiesrecht*, 5 March 1915, 8.
85. H. M., 'De Vrouw en Arbeid door Olive Schreiner', 15 December 1911.
86. Jansz, 'Women Workers Contested', 72.
87. See also Drwal, 'The Feminism of Olive Schreiner and the Feminism of Aletta Jacobs', 84.
88. 'Drie droomen in een woestijn,' *Proletarische Vrouw*, 6 August 1921, 3.
89. Wibaut, 'Feuilleton', 3.
90. Schreiner's view on the Boers was, however, much more complex. Although she defended their political rights to the land, she was aware of their mistreating the African population – in which respect they were no better than the British. Moreover, she denied them the sophistication that she attributed to the British, portraying the Boers as a simple folk, strongly attached to the land, and limited by their language (Afrikaans, then referred to as 'the Taal'). See Krebs, 'Olive Schreiner's Racialization of South Africa', 444.

Chapter 10

The Reception of Olive Schreiner in the Swedish Press, 1890–1920

Sanja Nivesjö

In December 1888, Olive Schreiner wrote to her friend, the socialist and writer Edward Carpenter: 'Do you know I should like to go to Sweden. I love those simple child natures so, the Swedish people, have a somewhat of the child & nature in them that others have lost.'[1] The comment is prompted by Schreiner's encounter at Hotel du Pavillon in Mentone, France with a Swedish man who claimed he wanted to marry her. Schreiner did not marry the man and, as far as we know, she never made it to Sweden (though her brother, the barrister and politician William Schreiner, did travel to Norway in 1911). Although Schreiner's letters reveal that she read some literature by Norwegian authors and she herself compares her novel *From Man to Man* to a novel by an unnamed Swedish author, there is no evidence of any correspondence or engagement with Swedish intellectuals.[2] Nevertheless, Schreiner's writings and her ideas travelled to Sweden. Her books were available in Swedish translation soon after the English originals were published; they were frequently advertised and reviewed in Swedish newspapers, and her ideas were featured in news reports and used to prompt debates. This chapter explores the reception of Schreiner and her work in the Swedish mainstream press in Schreiner's own time, from the publication of the Swedish translation of *The Story of an African Farm* in 1890 until Schreiner's death in 1920.

In the late nineteenth and early twentieth centuries, news stories, and with them ideas and knowledge, circulated internationally in newspapers through what Isabel Hofmeyr and Derek R. Peterson describe as an 'exchange system' that saw papers reprinting material by mutual consent.[3] This meant that news stories could be culled from foreign papers and reprinted or adapted for the local press, 'produc[ing]', in Hofmeyr and Peterson's words, 'webs of interpenetrating periodical matter that carpeted the globe'.[4] In an English-language context, these 'textual commons' were 'delimited by language and form',[5] but translation ensured that news also spread across linguistic barriers. This did not mean that news was simply copied, presented and received in the exact same manner everywhere, however. As Bernhard Fabian points out in discussing the reception processes of eighteenth-century English authors in Europe, reception is 'a deliberate act of absorption and assimilation' rather than 'an act or process of acceptance'.[6] Nevertheless, as Johan Jarlbrink explains, during this early moment in mass-media print culture, the idea prevailed that 'everything that was real and worth knowing was on paper' (allt som var verkligt och värt att veta fanns på papper), the spread of news items meant that everyone from schoolboys to office workers were interested in 'what was occuring in other places' (vad som tilldrog sig på andra platser), and thus 'opinions and events worth noting became in fact identical to those reported by the newspapers' ([o]pinioner och händelser värda att ta notis om blev i och med det identiska med dem som tidningarna rapporterade om).[7] This chapter shows how, within this context of circulation, Swedish newspapers made Schreiner part of that which was 'worth knowing' in Sweden. Swedish newspapers responded to translations of her books, picked up on Schreiner's presence in public debate and in the press in other countries, and then incorporated these elements into their own textual fabrics.

This chapter makes use of the Swedish newspaper archive 'Svenska dagstidningar', digitalised by the National Library of Sweden.[8] This covers more than 1,500 titles from 1645 to the present day.[9] The first mention of Schreiner in the Swedish mainstream press appears in *Öresundsposten* in 1889, with a translation of her allegory 'Three Dreams in a Desert'. A search for 'Olive Schreiner' in the press archive 1889–1920 returns 334 hits.[10] The papers in which she is most frequently mentioned are the largest national papers, such as *Aftonbladet* (34 hits), *Svenska Dagbladet* (28 hits), *Göteborgs Handels- och Sjöfartstidning* (26 hits) and *Dagens Nyheter* (24 hits). During these thirty-one years, she is mentioned in 106 mainstream Swedish newspapers from the largest to the smallest; although, in fifty-two of these her name is only mentioned once.[11] Nevertheless, this spread of national, regional and local newspapers indicates that Schreiner was positioned as being of interest to a wide section of the Swedish reading population. Looking at the years with the most hits, the mentions of Schreiner in the Swedish press can be grouped around three key years and events: 1897, the publication of *Dreams*; 1900, the South African War; and 1911, the publication of *Woman and Labour*.[12] More than half of the hits (219 or 66 per cent), occur between the crucial years 1896–1901. It is, however, important to keep in mind that digitalisation is often not complete, as is the case with

'Svenska dagstidningar', which is an ongoing project. Thus, mentions of Schreiner and her work might appear in more Swedish newspapers from 1890 to 1920 than the ones discussed here. Furthermore, digitalisation can at times introduce 'digital noise' – distortions that happen in the digitalisation process.[13] As such, Johan Jarlbrink and Pelle Snickars liken digitalisation to the nineteenth-century exchange system in that content might be transformed to fit its medium.[14] Nevertheless, large-scale newspaper digitalisation makes possible the study of circulation and reception that I pursue here.

'Depictions from foreign continents': *The Story of an African Farm*

The glaring omission in the significant years listed above is the year 1890, when the Swedish translation of *The Story of an African Farm* was published. Translated by 'K. B-n' as *Under Afrikas himmel: historien om en farm i Kaplandet*,[15] and published by Hugo Gebers Förlag, the cover bore the name Ralph Iron (the pseudonym under which the original novel was published), with 'Olive Schreiner' entered in brackets underneath. Schreiner was then known by her pseudonym, and indeed one of the reviews of the novel refers to the author using only male pronouns.[16] A search for 'Ralph Iron' during the period 1889–1920 results in eighty-seven hits, of which the vast majority (66) occur during 1890. This indicates that after the publication of *Under Afrikas himmel* Schreiner quickly became known by her real name.[17] That in fact makes 1890 the year with the most hits related to Schreiner's work. The vast majority of the references are small and simple advertisements for the novel. These start to appear in May 1890 and continue into 1891 and beyond. However, there were also thirteen reviews of varying length, ranging from one sentence to two pages, with most about a paragraph long. These appeared mainly in medium-sized regional or national papers. The social-democratic newspaper *Arbetet* also ran excerpts of the novel in seven issues.[18]

Generally, the newspaper reviews were very positive, praising the book's originality, psychological portrayals and in-depth depiction of what was, for many Swedes, an unknown place with unknown social conventions.[19] Schreiner's use of humour and mysticism was commented on in *Arbetet*, which found the character of Tant Sannie amusing,[20] and similarly, *Skånska posten* commented on the author's wit and found that the use of pessimism and mysticism enhanced the book further.[21] Two reviews were more negative, however. The ideologically conservative

Nya Dagligt Allehanda thought the novel humourless, dull, slow and unrealistic, and thought that the narrative 'overindulged in religious mysticism' (förätit sig på religiös mystic).[22] A male reviewer in *Nya Wermlands-tidningen* found the book's messages on women and religion unpalatable.[23] Otherwise, the potentially contentious feminist and religious elements seem to have been well accepted across the Swedish press.

The point about the lack of realism raised by the anonymous reviewer in *Nya Dagligt Allehanda* is of particular interest, as the reviewer notes that they can accept as realistic that a farm in Africa populated by 'Boers' would result in 'crudeness in manner and material interests taking precedence' (råhet i sätt och materiella intressen taga öfverhand), but sees as fanciful the idea that there would be children in such a place 'who research, think and speculate on spiritual matters' (som forska, fundera och spekulera på andliga ting).[24] Elements of fascination with the perceived exoticism of Africa and its landscape, as well as of the 'Boer people', are clearly present in the Swedish reception of *The Story of an African Farm*. Overwhelmingly, though, this reception seems driven by ignorant curiousness rather than malevolent prejudice, with Schreiner described as 'the author famous for romanticised depictions stemming from foreign continents' (den för romantiserade skildringar från främmande verldsdelar berömda författarinnan).[25]

Dreams and Schreiner as 'the priestess of modern idealism'

In the decade following the Swedish publication of *The Story of an African Farm*, many of Schreiner's allegories were translated and published in national, regional and local newspapers. In fact, several of the allegories from Schreiner's collection *Dreams* were published in newspapers before the Swedish translation of the collection came out. In 1891, Gustaf F. Steffen wrote a passionate 'Literature Letter from England' on the remarkable qualities of *Dreams* (then newly published in London), which also includes his translations of two of the allegories: 'I Thought I Stood' and 'Life's Gifts'.[26] After this, other allegories were translated and published in mainstream newspapers, including 'The Lost Joy', 'The Gardens of Pleasure', 'In a Far-Off World' and 'In a Ruined Chapel'.[27] Most of these appeared in several regional newspapers around the same time, and would thus presumably have reached a wide audience throughout Sweden. Translations of other stories, such as 'The Woman's Rose', appeared in *Jämtlandsposten* and

Bärgslagsposten in 1897 and 1900 respectively.[28] The allegories continued to appear in the press long after the translation of *Dreams* was published. For example, 'In a Far-Off World' was printed in *Arbetet* as late as 22 January 1921.

The first Swedish-language version of *Dreams* (*Drömmar*) was published in 1897. Its reception shows that the publication of the translation of *The Story of an African Farm* and various allegories in newspapers throughout the 1890s had not yet made Schreiner a well-known name in Sweden (even to newspaper book reviewers). Although some reviews refer to her earlier work, and one writer claims she is much spoken about at the current moment, more than one reviewer calls her either unknown, or claims that her writing has not previously been translated into Swedish.[29]

Although *Dreams* received around the same number of reviews as *The Story of an African Farm*, they were more mixed. Descriptions of the allegories as original, rich in imagination, atmospheric, sensitive and deep of thought contrasted with other reviews that described them as depressing, tedious, uninspiring and too abstract.[30] In one of the longest reviews, *Dreams* is compared unfavourably to works by the well-known Swedish poet Victor Rydberg. The reviewer notes that they deal with similar topics, but where Rydberg manages to convey hope, Schreiner's collection is pessimistic, and even has a 'flavour of fanaticism' (anstrykning av fanatism).[31] The reviewer, nevertheless, finds the book's content valuable enough to recommend it as deserving of readerly attention.

The Swedish edition of *Dreams* was translated by Ingeborg Kleen, and richly illustrated by her sister, the Swedish symbolist artist Tyra Kleen. The illustrations constituted Kleen's artistic debut, and several newspapers report on an art exhibition held by the woman's organisation Nya Idun, at which Kleen's illustrations were shown.[32] *Dreams* was widely advertised in all major newspapers, not least due to the illustrations.[33] The lavish edition further featured in a Christmas advertisement by the publisher C. & E. Gernandts, together with another richly illustrated book by a Swedish author, as the publisher's two 'praktverk' (*pièces de résistance*, magnificent artists' books or *livres d'art*).[34] The following Christmas, the publisher readvertised both again, this time as decorative coffee table books.[35] Many of the newspaper reviews mention specifically how the book is materially a beautiful or magnificent object.[36]

Because *Drömmar* was sold as much on the merit of Kleen's illustrations, and the book as a decorative object, as on Schreiner's writing, the reception of Kleen's work also became a basis for the reception of the book as a whole. Practically all reviewers comment on the conjunction of Schreiner's text and Kleen's illustrations, and all see the images as well suited to the text. Kleen used an art nouveau style that was not common in Sweden at the time (see Figures 10.1 and 10.2). A reviewer of *Dreams* likens the style to that of German artist Max Klinger and English artist Walter Crane.[37] As such, Kleen's drawings were viewed as being at the forefront of a new modern style, and it was together with Schreiner's allegories that this art style first appeared in Sweden.[38] The translator, Ingeborg Kleen, indicated that an epithet given to Schreiner – the 'priestess of modern idealism' (den moderna idealismens prästinna) – was applicable not only to her politics but also to her poetics.[39] Accordingly, *Drömmar* became representative of a new, modern style.

Figure 10.1 Full-page illustration by Tyra Kleen from 'Nöjets Lustgård' (The Gardens of Pleasure). Schreiner, *Drömmar*, 22. Reproduction: National Library of Sweden.

Figure 10.2 Illustration by Tyra Kleen from 'Jag tyckte jag stod . . .' (I Thought I Stood). Schreiner, *Drömmar*, 49. Reproduction: National Library of Sweden.

Schreiner 'Goes Viral': The South African War

The turn of the century represents Schreiner's moment in Swedish press. Recall that more than half of all hits on her name in the press archive occur between 1896–1901. Hofmeyr and Peterson's application of a twenty-first century digital term to the early mass-media print landscape is therefore pertinent here, as they explain how the exchange system and access to an inexpensive and extensive postal system meant that 'in a time before digitised communication, apparently unremarkable publications could go viral'.[40] Schreiner's 'viral moment' is intimately tied to her writings on the South African War (also known as the Second

Anglo-Boer War or the Second Boer War), which broke out in October 1899 and lasted until 1902.

During this time, Schreiner's fiction continued to play an important role in how she was made part of that which was 'worth knowing', in Jarlbrink's words, in the Swedish press. The first part of her anti-imperialist, anti-Cecil Rhodes screed, the allegorical novella *Trooper Peter Halket of Mashonaland* was translated and serialised in one of the largest newspapers in Sweden, *Aftonbladet*, in 1897 (the same year as the original was published).[41] However, the story did not receive further treatment in the press until it was published as a book in the midst of the war in 1901 with the title *Soldaten Peter Halket: en berättelse från Sydafrika* (*The Soldier Peter Halket: a Story From South Africa*).[42] Ads for the new book 'by the famous Afrikaner author Olive Schreiner' (af den berömda afrikanderförfattarinnan Olive Schreiner) appeared in a number of papers.[43] I will return to the epithet 'Afrikaner' given to Schreiner here; but for now, let us just note that she is by this point in 1901 labelled 'famous'. The book received three short but very positive reviews that praised its gripping and captivating content and heartfelt language, as well as its topicality in relation to the war, ardent indignation towards English exploitation in South Africa and its emphasis on Christian love.[44] The local paper *Hessleholmstidningen* wrote that 'in these days of sympathy for the Boers we also predict that the book will have an enormous reach, which it richly deserves' (i dessa boersympatiernas dagar spå vi också boken en enorm spridning, ty det är den verkligen förtjent af).[45]

The many mentions of Schreiner in the years 1899 to 1901 are generally related to her non-fictional writings on, and opposition to, the South African War. Apart from *Trooper Peter Halket*, other of Schreiner's politically relevant writings were culled from British papers and published during this time. A short parable criticising the supposed greatness of Cecil Rhodes was taken from *The Review of Reviews* and was published in *Göteborgs-posten* in February 1896, with an introduction explaining that it was written by one of his 'most acrimonious political enemies' (bittraste politiska fiender).[46] It was published again in a new translation once the war began.[47] In the lead up to the outbreak of war in late summer and autumn 1899, Schreiner's written anti-war protests were much mentioned and summarised.[48] References to Schreiner's essay, 'An English-South African's View of the Situation', as well as other unspecified pamphlets and manifestos appeared in the newspapers. It is probably fair to assume that 'The Political Situation' was one of these sources, as many of the reports make mention of Schreiner's strong anti-Rhodes sentiments. 'A Message to the English

People', which was printed by the Johannesburg correspondent in *The Manchester Guardian*, was also translated and reprinted in full by two major newspapers.[49] In November 1900, at least nineteen newspapers reported on, and summarised, Schreiner's 'Speech on the Boer War', which she sent to the Somerset East Women's Meeting on 12 October 1900. Some newspapers also published shorter or longer excerpts, again collected from *The Manchester Guardian*.[50] This flurry of publications ended with *GHT* following up their earlier publication on 'Speech on the Boer War' with an extensive report on the Somerset East meeting, including excerpts from eyewitness accounts from women on the terrrible treatment of 'Boer' families, taken from *The Manchester Guardian*.[51] There were also reports lifted from *South African News* about the formation of a committee of South African women against the war, which included Schreiner as the only member mentioned by name.[52]

In the lead-up to the war, when the Swedish press increasingly wrote about 'the peculiar country' South Africa (det egendomliga landet), they showed a great deal of exoticising fascination with the 'Boer' people, who were described in *Göteborgs-Posten* as 'this remarkable people' (detta märkliga folkslag).[53] Schreiner, through her fictional and non-fictional writings, was often named as an insightful authority on the 'Boers' and the South African political situation. The tendency to call upon Schreiner as an expert on race relations and population groups in South Africa continued in later years too; for example, in an virulently racist 1906 article on the so-called Black peril, as well as in a 1909 article on the potential for racial co-existence in South Africa.[54] However, the Swedish press was at times confused about Schreiner's position in South African ethnic and political groupings. Schreiner was born in South Africa to a German father and an English mother. This heritage together with the fact that her mother tongue was English, designated her a so-called English South African, at a time when white South Africans were seen as belonging to two sides of the war, either English or Afrikaner/'Boer'. As mentioned above, Scheiner was referred to as 'the famous Afrikaner author' in advertisements for *Trooper Peter*. This was not an isolated incident. In an article warning of possible revolution in South Africa, and which outlined South African colonial and 'Boer' history, Schreiner is again mentioned as a 'Boer author' (boersk författarinna) who depicts her countrymen's lives.[55] Swedish news media's understanding of the complex population groupings in South Africa seems to have been rather rudimentary at times, complicated by the fact that Schreiner wrote against English imperialism and for the 'Boer' cause.

Through the frequent publication of, and references to, Schreiner's writings and opinions on the South African War, a distinctly anti-English image was created, which generated great sympathy for the poor treatment of the white Afrikaans-speaking population. When the war ended in 1902, one newspaper claimed that the English would have to contend with 'the testimonial' for the 'Boer' cause 'of among many others such a prominent Afrikaner as the author Olive Schreiner' (vitsordet af bland många andra en så framstående afrikander som författarinnan Olive Schreiner).[56] Schreiner was thus positioned as one of the leading voices on the war, who seemingly helped shape Swedish mass media views on the conflict. The national paper *SvD* even ran an article in 1899 titled 'Transvaal and Its Leading Men' (Transvaal och dess ledande män) with pictures of Oom Paul, Sir Alfred Milner, and 'Mrs Cronwright-Schreiner (Olive Schreiner)'.[57]

As far as I can tell, the image accompagning 'Transvaal and Its Leading Men' in *SvD* was the first portrait of Schreiner published in the mainstream Swedish press. Jarlbrink points out that at the turn of the century, portraits and interviews in newspapers served to make 'faces recognisable and names renowned' (ansikten igenkända och namn ryktbara), and that some readers might even cut out these images to save in their own private collections.[58] That Schreiner's fame in the Swedish mainstream press reached new levels in 1899 is further illustrated by the fact that the regional paper *Södermanlands Dagblad* published a profile on her, complete with a portrait specifically drawn for the occasion (Figure 10.3).[59]

Under the title 'Transvaal's Most Remarkable Woman' (Transvaals märkligaste kvinna), Schreiner was described as the 'world famous author' (öfver hela världen berömda författarinnan) who rose to prominence with *The Story of an African Farm*, and in Sweden with the translation of *Dreams*. The profile mentions that Schreiner had lately been writing against the 'Anglo Boer War', and ends by excitedly sharing the rumour that Schreiner will be visiting England to continue her pacifist campaign.[60] In the end, it was Schreiner's husband, Samuel Cron Cronwright-Schreiner, who went to England, whilst Schreiner remained in South Africa. Papers reported on Cronwright's anti-war speeches, which he delivered in various locations around England in 1900, explaining that he was the 'husband of the well-known author Olive Schreiner' (man till den bekanta författarinnan Olive Schreiner).[61] Schreiner is also mentioned in the press in relation to her brother William, especially in relation to his stepping down as Prime Minister of the Cape Colony.[62]

The peak of Schreiner's fame during the South African War came with reports on her supposed imprisonment by the English. In July

Figure 10.3 Profile of Schreiner including a portait drawn by Ivar Jonsson for the newspaper, *Södermanlands Dagblad*, 5 December 1899. Reproduction: Svenska Dagstidningar, National Library of Sweden.

1901, the top news for 'The War in South Africa' (Kriget i Sydafrika) was the item: 'Olive Schreiner in Captivity' (Olive Schreiner i fångenskap). The article drew on reports from the *Daily News* that claimed that Schreiner had been imprisoned, deprived of visits from her husband, had her manuscripts burnt and had not been allowed light at night.[63] This report is repeated, but also declared as false, in an article published in *GHT* the following day.[64] Nevertheless, the news continued to spread across various publications over the next few days. For example, on 27 July 1901, *Sundsvalls-Posten* ran an effusive article on Schreiner's prescient writings on the war, reported her imprisonment once more and described her as a martyr. The rapid and seemingly uncontrollable spread of rumours in 1901 might be interpreted as the moment when Schreiner properly 'goes viral' in Swedish news reporting, and this was made possible by her developing public presence over the preceding two years that had primed and established an audience for news of her life and works.

Schreiner, the Literary Model

Although the Swedish press focused on her political writings and her political persona at the turn of the century, Schreiner was also seen as intimately connected to, and knowledgeable about, literature. A talk given by Professor Ribbing at the Heimdall society for literature, culture, politics and social questions described Schreiner as 'a representative of modern colonial literature and colonial politics' (en representant för modern kolonial literatur och kolonial politik).[65] Several papers report that Schreiner was one of the few foreign authors to garner votes for inclusion in 'Les Annales politiques et littéraires' in France.[66] She was also called upon as an illustrative point of comparison in several reviews of other books. In a review of a Swedish book she is (incorrectly) grouped with Rudyard Kipling and Robert Louis Stevenson as example emigrant authors who write about their home nation, England.[67] In another review of a book by a Swedish author (who was also opposed to the South African War), Schreiner's depictions of nature are described as an obvious influence.[68] Schreiner's work is held up as the measure and model of quality South African literature in a review of a Swedish translation of Perceval Gibbon's *Vrouw Grobelaar and Her Leading Cases*.[69] In an obituary of the Irish-Greek-Japanese writer and translator, Lafcadio Hearn, Schreiner is described as the person who introduced South Africa to Europe's 'spiritual scene' (andliga scen), just as Kipling introduced India, and Hearn introduced Japan.[70] She is also mentioned in an entertaining piece reprinted from an English newspaper, in which she is described as an example of an exceptionally slow writer, who took five years to produce her novel.[71] Although attention had shifted from her fiction to her political writings during the war, she was still seen as an important and influential literary figure.

Transnational Feminism: *Woman and Labour*

Finally, the last significant impression that Schreiner leaves in Swedish mainstream press is with the translation by Hanni Flygare of *Woman and Labour* as *Kvinnan och arbetet* in 1911 (the same year as the original). The book was reviewed in five of the major national newspapers.[72] *Lantarbetare-Bladet*, the monthly supplement to the Social Democrat newspaper *Arbetet*, published a three-page extract.[73] The book was frequently advertised, and the adverts often noted that the first edition sold out in a couple of months. The reviews of *Women and Labour* were overwhelmingly positive. In *DN*, the book was praised for its depth of thought; the new light it sheds on old questions; the new issues it raises in relation to the woman question; its enthusiasm and warmth; and its 'wise and fine propositions and observations' (kloka och fina satser och iakttagelser).[74] A review in *Arbetet* commented approvingly on Schreiner's ability to speak openly about women's parasitism,[75] and the review in *DN* described *Woman and Labour* as 'law, gospel and prophecy' (lag, evangelium och profetia).[76] What is particularly interesting with these reviews, compared to the often shorter and anonymously published ones that Schreiner's previous work received in mainstream press, is that they are typically long, in-depth reviews, written by female journalists who were part of the women's movement.

In various press articles, Schreiner's ideas are compared to a range of Swedish and Scandinavian thinkers. Swedish author and feminist Anna Maria Roos, for example, compares Schreiner's view of sex parasitism – simplified, the idea that married women who are not allowed to work become parasites who pay with sex for economic upkeep from their husbands – with that of Swedish author August Strindberg, but comments that Schreiner's view is 'more apt, because it is free from one-sidedness and from injustice' towards women (mer träffande, emedan den är fri från ensidighet och från orättvisor).[77] An anonymous reviewer, on the other hand, compares Schreiner's ideas with those of Swedish feminist Fredrika Bremer, and opines that in comparison, Schreiner's book seems 'a bit outdated' (en smula förlegad).[78]

Although well-received, *Woman and Labour* was variously seen as relevant or not for a Swedish context. An anonymous reviewer commented that the book delivers a timely message for Swedish men about women's rights to well-paid work, and notes that the 'New Man' has yet to be seen in Sweden.[79] However, in a long review, 'Devinez' (the pseudonym of Swedish feminist Elin Wägner) argued that women's parasitism was a larger problem in the United Kingdom than in Sweden.[80] This was because the United Kingdom, unlike Sweden, had wealth accumulated through colonialism which enabled a larger middle-class and, thus, more women who were left without useful labour in a context where education and the professions were closed to them and household work was performed by servants.[81] Maria Cederschiold, under the signature 'M. C.', made the same argument in *Aftonbladet*.[82] 'Devinez' further claims that because of the lack of colonial riches, Scandinavian women have made more determined entries into new areas of work; an opinion that is echoed by the *GHT* reviewer.[83] Nonetheless, *Woman and Labour* was still seen as an important work within the broader women's movement.

With the publication of *Woman and Labour* and the end of the South African War, Schreiner's profile in the Swedish press shifted from that of an expert on South Africa and the Afrikaans-speaking people, to a prominent voice in the women's movement. This was particularly because the Sixth Conference of the International Woman Suffrage Alliance, which met in Stockholm 12–17 June 1911, coincided with the Swedish publication of *Woman and Labour*. In an article from 12 June, Swedish author and feminist Roos draws together the conference and Schreiner to make her argument for the relevance of women's suffrage to society in general.[84] The transnational aspects of the women's movement at the time, and Schreiner's place in it, were further illustrated by a front page report in *DN*. The article describes a visit by the American minister and leader of the suffrage movement, Anna Shaw, to the Gustav Vasa Church during the Congress, and reports on Shaw's use of one of Schreiner's allegories in one of her sermons.[85]

Schreiner is mentioned on multiple occasions throughout the 1910s in relation to women's suffrage and the broader women's movement.[86] One particularly notable reference to Schreiner in this context appears in a highly sarcastic and hilarious take-down of various powerful and sexist Swedish men (including ministers, actors, school inspectors and politicians). In the article, by social democract feminist, Elma Danielsson, she wonders sarcastically if a minister she criticises has read Schreiner's bible of the women's movement (*Woman and Labour*), and notes that if 'the minister does not learn from life, he should read books' (pastorn inte lär av livet, bör han läsa i böcker).[87]

Interest in Schreiner in the Swedish mainstream press was thus focused around *The Story of an African Farm* and *Dreams*, her opinions on the South African War, and the publication of *Woman and Labour*. After 1911, the mentions of Schreiner in the Swedish press dropped off quickly and remain sparse and infrequent. At the time of her death in 1920, only two newspapers published obituaries.[88] *GHT*, in a short and rather dry obituary, pinpointed *The Story of an African Farm* and *Woman and Labour* as Schreiner's two great works, with the former establishing her literary credentials, and latter as the one that brought her international fame. *SvD* drew a richer and more laudatory picture of her life's work, identifying her fame in Sweden as resting on *Woman and Labour*, which it calls 'one of the most beautiful and sympathetic contributions to the struggle to raise consciousness among women of the woman's task' (ett av de vackraste och mest sympatiska bidragen i kampen att väcka hennes eget kön till insikt om kvinnans uppgifter).[89]

Schreiner's Legacy in Sweden Today

Schreiner is not generally well-known in Sweden today. When *The Story of an African Farm* came out in a new translation in 1944, press reviewers were not aware that the novel had previously been translated into Swedish.[90] This is the only of Schreiner's works to be given a new translation. A cursory search in the catalogues of municipality and university libraries shows *The Story of an African Farm*, together with *Woman and Labour*, as the only Schreiner texts somewhat readily available in 2022.

Nevertheless, Schreiner pops up in Swedish press every now and then, and although she disappears almost entirely during the 1960s and 1970s, she has been 'revived' several times. As early as 1927, Schreiner was 'rediscovered' in *Arbetet* by 'Lei.', who, in reminiscing about the women's movement, picks up her well-read copy of *Woman and Labour* to realise that it is still relevant today, and goes on to produce a long explanatory article on the work in two later issues.[91] In 1960, *Expressen* summarises and praises Schreiner's life and work to be able to appoint Margaret Ballinger – white representative on the Native Representatives Council 1937–1960 and the first president of the Liberal Party of South Africa – as her worthy successor in feminist and anti-racist work in South Africa.[92] The most significant revival happens in 1981 with the reissue of the 1944 translation of *The Story of an African Farm*.[93] This is also the only one of Schreiner's works to have been reissued in Swedish. A few more articles crop up in the 1990s and 2000s, largely but not exclusively thanks to Stefan Helgesson, a literary scholar reawakening Schreiner's presence in the Swedish press through the culture pages of the national paper *DN*.[94]

In earlier newspaper mentions, Schreiner appears as the *only* well-known South African author and, as time passes, she is more frequently named *one of* the well-known South African authors, but in both cases her fame is almost always established in relation to *The Story of an African Farm*.[95] The blurb on the 1981 reprint of *The Story of an African Farm* indicates that her legacy in Sweden, such as it is, is not centred on her fiction, but her politics and her feminism: '[s]he published a few more books [after *The Story of an African Farm*], but she became best known for her opposition to the Boer War and colonial politics and above all for her struggle for women's rights' (Hon gav ut ytterligare några böcker, men mest känd blev hon för sin opposition mot boerkriget och kolonialpolitiken och framför allt för sin kamp för kvinnans rättigheter).[96] If Schreiner is remembered in any particular context in Sweden today, it is probably within the history of the women's movement. Certainly, there remains great scope for further work on Schreiner's literary and feminist influences in Sweden.

Acknowledgement

The research was conducted with funds from the Swedish Research Council (project number 2020-06436).

Works Cited

Ahlberg, Jonas. 'Kort om databasens innehåll'. Svenska dagstidningar. National Library of Sweden. Modified 30 March 2022. https://feedback.blogg.kb.se/forums/topic/kort-om-databasens-innehall/.

Anonymous. 'Character Sketch: Cecil Rhodes of Africa'. *The Review of Reviews* (February 1896): https://www.proquest.com/historical-periodicals/character-sketch/docview/3895443/se-2.

Fabian, Bernhard. 'The Reception of British Writers on the Continent: Principles and Problems'. *Hungarian Journal of English and American Studies* 13, no. 1/2 (2007): 7–21.

Hofmeyr, Isabel, and Derek R. Peterson. 'The Politics of the Page: Cutting and Pasting in South African and African-American Newspapers'. *Social Dynamics* 45, no. 1 (2019): 1–25.

Jarlbrink, Johan. *Informations- och avfallshantering: Mediearkeologiska perspektiv på det långa 1800-talets tidningar*. Lund: Mediehistoria and Lund University, 2019.

Jarlbrink, Johan, and Pelle Snickars. 'Cultural Heritage as Digital Noise: Nineteenth Century Newspapers in the Digital Archive'. *Journal of Documentation* 73, no. 6 (2017): 1228–43.

Kleen, Ingeborg. 'Olive Schreiners diktning'. *Ord och Bild* 6, no. 11 (1897): 521–24.

Schreiner, Olive. *Drömmar (Dreams)*, translated by Ingeborg Kleen and illustrated by Tyra Kleen. Stockholm: C. & E. Gernandts Förlag, 1897.

—. *Farmen i Afrika (The Farm in Africa)*, translated by Gurli Hertzmann-Ericson. Stockholm: Natur och kultur, 1944. Reprint, Stockholm: Trevi, 1981.

—. *Kvinnan och arbetet (Woman and Labour)*, translated by Hanni Flygare. Stockholm: Hugo Gebers Förlag, 1911.

—. *Soldaten Peter Halket: En berättelse från Sydafrika (Trooper Peter Halket of Mashonaland)*, translated by Walborg Hedberg. Stockholm: Albert Bonniers Förlag, 1901.

—. *Under Afrikas himmel: historien om en farm i Kaplandet (The Story of an African Farm)*, translated by K. B–n. Stockholm: Hugo Gebers Förlag, 1890.

Letters

Olive Schreiner to Edward Carpenter, 15 December 1888. *Olive Schreiner Letters Online*.
Olive Schreiner to Samuel Cron Cronwright-Schreiner, 25 February 1907. *Olive Schreiner Letters Online*.
Olive Schreiner to Henry Havelock Ellis, 28 March 1884. *Olive Schreiner Letters Online*.
Olive Schreiner to Henry Havelock Ellis, 6 July 1888. *Olive Schreiner Letters Online*.
Olive Schreiner to John Hodgson, 19 February 1919. *Olive Schreiner Letters Online*.

Newspapers

Aftonbladet
Arbetet
Bärgslagsposten
Borås Tidning
Brand
Dagens Nyheter (DN)
Expressen
Figaro
Göteborgs Aftonblad
Göteborgs Handels- Och Sjöfartstidning (GHT)
Göteborgs-Posten
Hallandsposten
Handelstidningens Veckoblad
Helsingborgs Dagblad (HD)
Hemlandsposten Halvveckoupplagan & Veckoupplaga
Hernösands-Posten
Hessleholmstidningen
Jämtlandsposten
Lantarbetare-Bladet (montly supplement to *Arbetet*)
Morgonbladet
Nerikes Allehanda
Norrbottens-Kuriren
Norrbottens Nyheter
Nya Dagligt Allehanda
Nyaste Kristianstadsbladet
Nyaste Öresunds-Posten
Nya Wermlands-tidningen
Nya Wexiö-Bladet
Skånska posten
Södermanlands Dagblad
Stockholms Dagblad
Stockholms-tidningen
Sundsvalls-Posten
Svenska Dagbladet (SvD)

Sydsvenska Dagbladet Snällposten
Tjenstebladet
Trelleborgs-Tidningen
Upsala Nya Tidning
Vesternorrlands Allehanda
Wärmlandsberg
Westerbottens-Kuriren
Westgöten
Öresunds-posten
Östergötlands-södermanlands Annonsblad

Notes

1. Schreiner to Edward Carpenter, 15 December 1888, *Olive Schreiner Letters Online* (*OSLO*).
2. Schreiner read Henrik Ibsen's plays *Nora* (later *A Doll's House*) and *The Lady from the Sea*, as well as Johan Bojer's *The Great Hunger*. See Schreiner to Havelock Ellis, 28 March 1884, *OSLO*; Schreiner to Havelock Ellis, 6 July 1888, *OSLO*; Schreiner to John Hodgson, 19 February 1919, *OSLO*. Schreiner briefly describes the similarities between her novel *From Man to Man* (1926), and a novel by an unnamed Swedish author, in Schreiner to Cronwright-Schreiner, 25 February 1907, *OSLO*. The editors of *OSLO* note that: 'The extracts here are all on small slips of paper in Cronwright-Schreiner's handwriting, taken from Olive Schreiner letters which he then destroyed. Most have also been edited by him as well. Considerable caution should therefore be employed in referring to their content.' It is not known which novel Schreiner is referring to. Searches were made in the *OSLO* archive for the following terms: 'Sweden' (18 March 2021) with two returns: one letter to do with the Swede at Hotel du Pavillon and one letter to do with rights of translation of Schreiner's novella, *Trooper Peter Halket of Mashonaland* (1897) in Sweden; 'Swedish' (18 March 2021) with two returns: one letter to do with *From Man to Man*, and one to do with Ibsen's *Nora*; 'Swede' (7 February 2022) with five returns: four letters to do with the Swede at the Hotel du Pavillon, Mentone, France, dating 10, 15, 17, 23 December 1888, and one letter dated 6 March 1914 from Florence, Italy; 'Stockholm' (19 March 2021) with two returns; 'Norway' and 'Norwegian' (19 March 2021) with six returns to do with William Schreiner's trip and with Bojer's *The Great Hunger*; well-known Swedish turn-of-the-century feminists 'Benedictson', 'Wägner' and 'Wagner', 'Bremer' and 'Ellen Key' returned nothing; 'Danish', 'Denmark', 'Finland', 'Finnish', 'Iceland', 'Icelandic', and 'Island' returned no relevant results.
3. Hofmeyr and Peterson, 'The Politics of the Page', 2.
4. Hofmeyr and Peterson, 'The Politics of the Page', 4.
5. Hofmeyr and Peterson, 'The Politics of the Page', 21.
6. Fabian, 'The Reception of British Writers', 10.
7. Jarlbrink, *Informations- och avfallshantering*, 110, 164. All translations from Swedish to English are my own. The translation is placed in

the running text to aid flow of reading, while the original is placed in brackets.
8. All newspapers are accessed through the Swedish digitalised press archive 'Svenska dagstidningar' by the National Library of Sweden: https://tidnin gar.kb.se/. 'Svenska dagstidningar' covers, according to the latest information (Ahlberg, 'Kort om databasens innehåll'), about three quarters of all Swedish newspaper publications 1645–1906; a smaller selection 1906–2014; and all publications from 2014 onwards.
9. Ahlberg, 'Kort om databasens innehåll'.
10. Search performed on 10 March 2022: https://tidningar.kb.se/?q=olive%20 schreiner&from=1889-01-01&to=1920-12-31. If the search is extended from 1889 to 2022, 410 hits are generated. All material in this chapter relating to mainstream Swedish newspapers is taken from the digitalised Swedish press archive, unless otherwise noted.
11. At times there might also be contaminations in the results, to the effect that it is not Olive Schreiner or her work that is referred to, but very few of these instances have been identified.
12. The greatest number of mentions are located in the years 1896 (30 hits), 1897 (63 hits), 1900 (40 hits), 1901 (49 hits) and 1911 (38 hits).
13. Jarlbrink and Snickars, 'Cultural Heritage', 1229.
14. Jarlbrink and Snickars, 'Cultural Heritage', 1240.
15. I translate this as: *Under Africa's Sky: the Story of a Farm in the Cape Country*.
16. *Helsingborgs Dagblad*, 11 October 1890. All references to primary material culled from the archive 'Svenska dagstidningar' is according to newspaper and date published. The 'works cited' contains a list of newspapers consulted.
17. Search performed 10 March 2022: https://tidningar.kb.se/?q=%22Ralph %20Iron%22&sort=asc&from=1889-01-01&to=1920-12–31. If the search is extended to 2022, only three more hits are generated.
18. *Arbetet*, 18, 19, 22, 24, 25, 26 and 27 September 1890.
19. *Nya Wexiö-Bladet*, 3 June 1890; *Helsingborgs Dagblad*, 11 October 1890; *Vesternorrlands Allehanda*, 9 June 1890; *Skånska posten*, 3 June 1890; *Öresunds-posten*, 21 June 1890; *Svenska Dagbladet*, 25 June 1890; *Arbetet*, 4 August 1890.
20. *Arbetet*, 4 August 1890.
21. *Skånska posten*, 3 June 1890.
22. *Nya Dagligt Allehanda*, 29 July 1890.
23. Carl Carlsson, *Nya Wermlands-tidningen*, 19 June 1890.
24. *Nya Dagligt Allehanda*, 29 July 1890.
25. *Aftonbladet*, 14 July 1897.
26. *Göteborgs Handels- Och Sjöfartstidning*, 14 March 1891. *Morgonbladet* (18 March 1891) also published 'I Thought I Stood'; the source is given as 'From *Dreams* by Olive Schreiner' (Ur *Drömmar* af Olive Schreiner), but considering that *Dreams* had not been translated as a whole yet, it is reasonable to assume that this is Steffen's translation being republished. 'Life's Gifts' also appears in *Nyaste Öresunds-Posten* (10 February 1892) with no translator credited.
27. 'The Lost Joy': *Stockholms Dagblad*, 1 January 1893. This allegory was advertised in the 31 December 1892 issue of *Stockholms Dagblad*. It was

also published by *Norrbottens Nyheter,* 22 March 1893. 'The Gardens of Pleasure': *Tjenstebladet,* 15 July 1896. Translated by the signature 'A. G.' with the title 'Lustgårdarne'. The story was subsequently published in many more newspapers during the month of July. A different translation, with a different title, 'Lyckans trädgård', was published in *Nerikes Allehanda* on 25 September 1896. 'In a Far-Off World': *Wärmlandsberg,* 29 September 1896. Translated by Sixten Rönn, for the newspaper, with the title 'I en värld långt borta'. 'In a Ruined Chapel': *Östergötlandssödermanlands Annonsblad,* 31 October 1896. Translated by 'Fingal', with the title 'I kyrkoruinen'.

28. Translated by 'Nina W-n' in *Jämtlandsposten* with the title 'Hennes ros', and with the title 'Rosen' by 'A. T-dh' in *Bärgslagsposten.* Many other newspapers also printed it during the year 1900.
29. For the former, see *Sydsvenska Dagbladet Snällposten,* 28 December 1897; for the latter, see *Aftonbladet,* 22 December 1897; *Helsingborgs Dagblad,* 24 December 1897.
30. For the former, see *Stockholms-tidningen,* 17 December 1897; *Hallandsposten,* 23 December 1897; *Helsingborgs Dagblad,* 24 December 1897; *Figaro,* 25 December 1897. For the latter, see *Dagens Nyheter,* 18 December 1897; *Sydsvenska Dagbladet Snällposten,* 21 December 1897; *Aftonbladet,* 22 December 1897.
31. *Sydsvenska Dagbladet Snällposten,* 21 December 1897.
32. For example, *Aftonbladet,* 6 December 1987; *Dagens Nyheter,* 7 December 1897.
33. For example, *Aftonbladet,* 14 December 1897; *Svenska Dagbladet,* 15 December 1897; *Göteborgs Handels- Och Sjöfartstidning,* 16 December 1897; *Sydsvenska Dagbladet Snällposten,* 16 December 1897.
34. The other book is *En gyldenne book* by Swedish cartoonist, artist and author Albert Engström: https://litteraturbanken.se/f%C3%B6rfattare/Engstr%C3%B6mA/titlar/BiblosOxymorotaton/sida/I/faksimil. This is a humorous book with rich typography and illustrations parodying sixteenth- and seventeenth-century religious books, such as *En gyllende book, om den andeliga högfärden, och thet diupa okända och förborgade onda, uti alla menniskors hierta: samt huru herren Gud, genom kors och anfäcktning, utrotar then innerliga högfärden* . . . originally in German by Alberto Dranckmeister and published in Swedish in 1724: https://digital.ub.umu.se/relation/347455?preview=329855%2F122%2Fsimple%2F0. It is interesting to note a pairing of a parodic book with Schreiner's serious allegories but that both tackle religious topics.
35. For example, *Dagens Nyheter,* 19 December 1898.
36. *Stockholms-tidningen,* 17 December 1897; *Sydsvenska Dagbladet Snällposten,* 21 December 1897; *Upsala Nya Tidning,* 24 December 1897; *Helsingborgs Dagblad,* 24 December 1897.
37. *Sydsvenska Dagbladet Snällposten,* 21 December 1897.
38. *Sydsvenska Dagbladet Snällposten,* 21 December 1897; *Aftonbladet,* 22 December 1897; *Figaro,* 25 December 1897.
39. Kleen, 'Olive Schreiners diktning', 521.
40. Hofmeyr and Peterson, 'The Politics of the Page', 6.
41. *Aftonbladet,* 13–14 July 1897.

42. The book was published in Swedish translation without the controversial frontispiece of the original which depicts the hanging of three Black men from a tree.
43. *Aftonbladet*, 14 March 1901; *Svenska Dagbladet*, 14 March 1901. A few pages are now also serialised in northen Swedish regional *Westerbottens-Kuriren* in a specially commissioned translation by Alida Jakobson (9 April 1901).
44. *Helsingborgs Dagblad*, 14 April 1901; *Aftonbladet*, 18 April 1901.
45. *Hessleholmstidningen*, 2 November 1901.
46. *Review of Reviews* February 1896, 117–18. *Göteborgs-posten*, 24 February 1896; this is a summarised part of the longer 'The Salvation of a Ministry', reprinted in Olive Schreiner, *Words in Season* (2005).
47. *Brand*, 3 February 1900.
48. See *Svenska Dagbladet*, 13 August 1899; *Borås Tidning*, 21 September 1899; *Göteborgs Handels- Och Sjöfartstidning*, 22 September 1899; *Westgöten*, 22 September 1899; *Öresunds-posten*, 25 September 1899; *Norrbottens Nyheter*, 28 September 1899.
49. *Sydsvenska Dagbladet Snällposten*, 22 September 1899; *Göteborgs Handels- Och Sjöfartstidning*, 25 September 1899.
50. Some that published longer excerpts were: *Göteborgs Handels- Och Sjöfartstidning*, 21 November 1900; *Handelstidningens Veckoblad*, 24 November 1900; *Hernösands-Posten*, 26 November 1900; *Vesternorrlands Allehanda*, 26 November 1900; *Hemlandsposten Halvveckoupplagan*, 27 November 1900 and *Veckoupplaga*, 29 November 1900.
51. *Göteborgs Handels- Och Sjöfartstidning*, 10 December 1900.
52. *Aftonbladet*, 27 June 1901 and others.
53. *Svenska Dagbladet*, 13 August 1899; *Göteborgs-Posten*, 29 April 1896.
54. *Norrbottens-Kuriren*, 29 July 1906; *Göteborgs Aftonblad*, 27 February 1909.
55. *Arbetet*, 3 January 1896.
56. *Göteborgs Handels- Och Sjöfartstidning*, 2 June 1902.
57. *Svenska Dagbladet*, 13 August 1899. 'Oom Paul' refers to Paul Kruger, President of the South African Republic and the face of the 'Boer' side. Sir Alfred Milner was Governor of the Cape Colony, and proponent of the war from the British side.
58. Jarlbrink, *Informations- och avfallshantering*, 150.
59. *Södermanlands Dagblad*, 5 December 1899.
60. *Södermanlands Dagblad*, 5 December 1899.
61. *Aftonbladet*, 27 March 1900.
62. *Stockholmstidningen*,18 June 1900.
63. *Aftonbladet*, 19 July 1901.
64. *Göteborgs Handels- Och Sjöfartstidning*, 20 July 1901.
65. *Sydsvenska Dagbladet Snällposten*, 6 March 1899.
66. For example, *Aftonbladet*, 9 January 1902.
67. *Göteborgs Handels- Och Sjöfartstidning*, 21 December 1898.
68. *Göteborgs Handels- Och Sjöfartstidning*, 7 June 1901.
69. *Göteborgs Handels- Och Sjöfartstidning*, 20 December 1907.
70. *Göteborgs Aftonblad*, 8 October 1904.
71. *Svenska Dagbladet*, 23 August 1909.

72. *Aftonbladet*, 24 March 1911; *Dagens Nyheter*, 16 May 1911; *Arbetet*, 10 June 1911; *Svenska Dagbladet*, 17 June 1911; *Göteborgs Handels- Och Sjöfartstidning*, 19 June 1911; *Aftonbladet* 17 September 1911.
73. *Lantarbetare-Bladet*, 15 August 1911.
74. *Dagens Nyheter*, 16 May 1911.
75. *Arbetet*, 10 June 1911.
76. *Dagens Nyheter*, 16 May 1911.
77. *Svenska Dagbladet*, 17 June 1911.
78. *Göteborgs Handels- Och Sjöfartstidning*, 19 June 1911.
79. *Aftonbladet*, 24 March 1911.
80. *Dagens Nyheter*, 16 May 1911.
81. *Dagens Nyheter*, 16 May 1911.
82. *Aftonbladet*, 17 May 1911.
83. *Dagens Nyheter*, 16 May 1911; *Göteborgs Handels- Och Sjöfartstidning*, 19 June 1911.
84. *Svenska Dagbladet*, 12 June 1911.
85. *Dagens Nyheter*, 12 June 1911.
86. See for example, *Göteborgs Handels- Och Sjöfartstidning*, 12 June 1911; *Arbetet*, 7 December 1911; *Göteborgs Aftonblad*, 11 April 1912; *Aftonbladet*, 6 June 1912; *Arbetet*, 17 March 1913; *Svenska Dagbladet*, 16 August 1913; *Aftonbladet*, 31 August 1913; *Stockholms-Tidningen*, 4 December 1913; *Göteborgs Handels- Och Sjöfartstidning*; 19 April 1915, *Jämtlandsposten*, 18 June 1917; *Göteborgs Handels- Och Sjöfartstidning*, 7 July 1917.
87. *Arbetet*, 7 December 1911.
88. *Göteborgs Handels- Och Sjöfartstidning*, 17 December 1920; *Svenska Dagbladet*, 18 December 1920.
89. *Svenska Dagbladet*, 18 December 1920.
90. It was re-translated by Gurli Hertzman-Ericson as *Farmen i Afrika* (*The Farm in Africa*). See Elin Brandell's review in *Dagens Nyheter*, 25 September 1944 and Olof Lagercrantz's review in *Svenska Dagbladet*, 16 October 1944.
91. Lei, *Arbetet*, 2, 9 and 23 July 1927.
92. *Expressen*, 6 June 1960.
93. *Dagens Nyheter*, 4 May 1981 and many more.
94. *Dagens Nyheter*, 6 May 1991; *Dagens Nyheter*, 15 October 1991; *Dagens Nyheter*, 22 December 1994; *Dagens Nyheter*, 26 April 2000; *Dagens Nyheter*, 23 September 2010.
95. *Trelleborgs-Tidningen*, 1 November 1933; *Dagens Nyheter*, 18 January 1954; *Dagens Nyheter*, 6 April 1955; *Dagens Nyheter*, 23 September 2010; *Aftonbladet*, 5 January 2015.
96. See Schreiner, *Farmen i Afrika*.

Part IV

Antipodean Schreiner

Chapter 11

Olive Schreiner and the New Women of New Zealand: Feminist Solidarities Across the Southern Colonies
Emma Barnes

Introduction

In February 1908, Olive Schreiner wrote to her friend, the socialist, writer and activist Edward Carpenter, to lament that 'South Africa is quite 80 years behind Europe; and a century behind Australia & New Zealand'.[1] Less than three months later, Schreiner expressed to another friend, the anti-war activist and social reformer, Emily Hobhouse, her wish for South Africa to follow Australia's 'recognition of woman's citizenship, & her duty towards the nation'.[2] At the time this correspondence took place, women in New Zealand had been able to own property for nearly thirty years, and all women had been able to vote since 1893; whilst in Australia, women gained the right to vote in 1902. In Schreiner's South Africa, however, women's suffrage was not progressing at the same speed as its southern colonial counterparts, hence Schreiner's frustration. Schreiner's transnational and transcontinental comparison of women's suffrage across South Africa, Aotearoa New Zealand and Australia implies that, although geographically diverse, these polities possessed similar political and social fabrics, implicating them within a framework of relationality. It is these structural similarities, effected by broadly similar experiences of colonialism, that have prompted Sarah Comyn and Porscha Fermanis to unite these countries under the rubric of 'the southern archive'.[3] Such categorisation allows for the cultural distinctiveness of South Africa, New Zealand and Australia, whilst indicating that their shared colonial and political landscapes still facilitated a very locally specific literary production during the nineteenth century.

This chapter develops a uniquely gendered understanding of the exchange of ideas and forms within the southern archive by examining political and aesthetic connections between white women writers of South Africa and New Zealand, specifically those whose works constituted

New Woman fiction. As a literary and cultural construct of the *fin de siècle*, the 'New Woman' simultaneously encapsulated progressive ideas relating to the emerging economic and sexual freedoms of white middle-class women, as well as associated anxieties about female moral decline. Although the term 'New Woman' was first used in 1894 by British writer Sarah Grand in her essay, 'The New Aspect of the Woman Question', the New Woman was not an exclusively British phenomenon.[4] The rise of the New Woman coincided with widespread migration across the colonies, as Cecily Devereaux explains: 'the New Woman and this New World both, simultaneously, took shape within the expansionist discourses of the New Imperialism in the last two decades of the 19th century'.[5] The New Woman, therefore, was as much a colonial figure as she was a feminist one,[6] with Schreiner's *The Story of an African Farm* often cited as the first example of New Woman literature (with the character Lyndall in starring role).[7] This chapter offers preliminary investigations into the ways in which the southern archive can help to account for the development of New Woman fiction by analysing the transnational influence of Schreiner's writings on two examples of New Zealand New Woman fiction: *A Daughter of the King* (1894) by Louisa Alice Baker (Alien), and *The Story of a New Zealand River* (1920) by Jane Mander (Manda Lloyd). Drawing the constituent colonies of South Africa together with Aotearoa New Zealand in terms of the trajectories of their feminist politics gives rise to a new dimension of the southern archive as the site of emerging networks of feminist, settler, literary cultures.

New Zealand women writers often acknowledged Schreiner's literary and feminist influences on writing and readerships in the colony. In correspondence with South African novelist, Sarah Gertrude Millin, New Zealand-born modernist Katherine Mansfield remarked that 'the only way to live as a writer is to draw upon one's real *familiar* life – to find the treasure in that as Olive Schreiner did'.[8] In the New Zealand newspaper *Otago Witness*, for which Baker also wrote, novelist Edith Searle Grossmann specifically named Schreiner as a writer able to 'open up fresh ground' and from whom 'that real creative force comes now'.[9] In reviews of New Zealand literature, Schreiner's work became the standard against which other novels were measured; a glowing review of Baker's *Wheat in the Ear* in *The Dawn* stated that the work 'is worthy to stand beside "The Story of an African Farm"'.[10] In another column 'To The Editor', the same book was invoked as a 'forerunner' to Baker's *A Daughter of the King*.[11] Schreiner was clearly a writer whose impact was not limited to her own political and literary networks, but was foundational to the development of feminist thinking and literary cultures across New Zealand.

Despite Schreiner's mentions in New Zealand newspapers and by other nineteenth- and twentieth-century New Zealand writers, her transnational influence in the southern colonies has only recently emerged as a scholarly line of enquiry.[12] Rebecca Burns was the first to acknowledge that Grossmann's short stories derived aesthetic pointers from Schreiner's use of Christian symbols and religious allegories.[13] Kirstine Moffat then developed this in her 2019 article on the polemical and autobiographical nature of writing by Grossmann, Baker and Mander, in which she also traced their allusions to Schreiner. More recently, in their introduction to the 'preoccupations of the Australian novel', Louis Klee and Nicholas Birns invite a transnational analysis of *African Farm* alongside 'equivalent novels' from the southern colonies, yet they do not pursue this themselves.[14] Though there is a great body of evidence to show how New Women writers from the southern colonies drew upon formal, political and extratextual elements to allude to Schreiner's writing, I confine myself here to one particular line of enquiry: I demonstrate how Schreiner's use of natural imagery to depict and support expressions of female agency and rebellion is connected to corresponding aesthetics and arguments that appear in novels by Baker and Mander. Like Schreiner, Baker draws upon the image of the rose to express her feminist politics relating to marriage in *A Daughter of the King* (1894); and Mander's overt references to Schreiner's *African Farm* and parallel title of *The Story of a New Zealand River*, are enriched further by the inclusion of water imagery also featured in Schreiner's short stories 'Three Dreams in a Desert' (1887) and 'Dream Life and Real Life: A Little African Story' (1885). Through intertextual and comparative close readings, this chapter makes the case that early New Zealand New Woman novels by Baker and Mander are indebted to the global reach of Schreiner's politics and aesthetics, and that it is their relationship with Schreiner's work that implicates them within a transnational and literary feminist exchange unique to the southern colonies.

Gender and the Southern Archive

For Comyn and Fermanis, the similarities amongst South Africa, New Zealand and Australia stem from the fact that they collectively contrast the 'slavery-driven capitalist modernity of the Black Atlantic' and 'the plantation economies of the Caribbean and American South' due to their focus on settlement rather than extraction of Indigenous labour.[15] As well as the focus on settlement, the historical and structural parallels of the southern colonies are characterised by the social and economic contexts that caused and facilitated migration to and between these spaces in the nineteenth century. Migration, in this context, refers to 'missionary circuits, settler and Indigenous entanglements, carceral geographies, and free and indentured labour migrations across transoceanic and transimperial spaces'.[16] It is largely the operationalisation of labour within global capitalism that drove migration to and between the southern colonies and shaped analogous socio-political systems. Opportunities to benefit from gold rushes or undertake agricultural labour meant that it was predominantly men who were globally mobile. The labour market produced what Paul Callister, Robert Didham and Richard Bedford dub a 'gendered migration flow' to New Zealand, a point further elucidated by Charlotte MacDonald, who explains that New Zealand Company ships 'set out with more men than women' so that by 1864, censuses revealed that 61.9 per cent of the settler population of New Zealand was male, and, between 1840 and 1870, there were 140 male for every 100 female migrants.[17] Therefore, the labour upon which colonial expansion relied was a predominantly male venture and, at present, it is this that draws together Comyn and Fermanis's conception of the southern colonies and the southern archive.

There were, however, thousands of young, single women who voluntarily migrated to New Zealand throughout the late nineteenth century. As Macdonald explains, many of these women were part of organised immigration programmes designed to provide the colony with government workers, domestic servants or to balance 'the disproportion of the sexes' in the settler population.[18] Although the reasons for migration were various, what is clear is that some female immigration was voluntary rather than obligatory, largely because movement to the colonies 'held out the prospect of improvement, of a better future'.[19] Many women migrants – and their reasons for migrating – have not, however, been officially documented, as 'the realms in which most women spent their lives tended not to be the realms which drew the attention of historians'.[20] This means that their movements cannot be accounted for under the categories of indentured labour, carcerality or missionary work.[21] This is not to say that women of the colonies did not perform labour – rather, that their unpaid or cheap (and predominantly domestic) labour cannot neatly fit into existing paradigms of the southern archive.

As imperial subjects who at once benefitted from colonial expansion, yet were still subject to the logics of patriarchy, white women who migrated across the empire simultaneously experienced the privilege of global mobility and the isolation that came with reproducing English domesticity outside of England. Diane Archibald encapsulates this figure as the 'angel of the bush', who 'will never have a true "home" while they live out of sight of English shores'.[22] Mandy Treagus further explains how the complex position of white, middle-class settler women in the southern colonies contributed to a specific form of literary production:

> They are colonials, removed from and overlooked by the imperial Centre; they are women in an entrenched patriarchy; they are intellectuals and writers in pragmatic emerging cultures in which the arts are feminised and disregarded. They are also members of invading/settling groups, usurping the indigenous occupants of their lands; they are part of the largest empire on earth, and thereby the beneficiaries of the imperial dividend; they are middle-class, educated, mobile and white. As both Othered and Othering, colonised and colonising, these writers produce fictions which reflect these complex subjectivities.[23]

In turning to the dialogue that emerges between the works of Schreiner, Mander and Baker, this chapter foregrounds the creation of a south-south knowledge exchange that is located in white, middle-class, feminist ideas and experiences. Taking into consideration the way that the southern archive as a methodological framework seeks to 'prioritize the thematic, structural, and generic similarities or parallels between the literary cultures of the southern colonies', this chapter reveals thematic, structural and aesthetic parallels that stem from Schreiner's fiction, and subsequently characterise the production of New Woman literature from New Zealand.[24]

Dreams and Allegory in Louisa Alice Baker's *A Daughter of the King* (1894)

After listening to Schreiner speak in London in 1914, Baker described her in 'the Ladies' Page' of *Otago Witness* as 'one of the pioneers of the advanced women's movement'.[25] Twenty years earlier, Baker also alluded to the importance of Schreiner's influence upon her debut novel, *A Daughter of the King*. In the Tennyson Neely edition, the novel's subtitle, 'An answer to "The Story of an African Farm"', conveys a direct engagement with Schreiner's fiction, whilst the edition published by Hutchinson and Co. begins with an epigraph from the same novel:

> A great soul draws, and is drawn, with a more fierce intensity than any small one. By every inch we grow by intellectual height, our love strikes down its roots deeper, and spreads out its arms wider. It is for love's sake yet more than for any other that we look for that new time.[26]

This epigraph is taken from one of the most poignant parts of *African Farm*, the 'Lyndall' chapter, in which Schreiner most clearly articulates her New Woman politics. This quotation encapsulates Schreiner's belief that women will continue to be worthy of love outside of the heteronormative roles of wife and mother.[27] Lyndall describes the need for liberation from sundering inequalities within marriage – a message that also drives the narrative of Baker's novel and motivates the feminist politics of her protagonist, Florence. Like Lyndall, Florence challenges conventional views regarding marriage and the expectations placed upon women in their role as wives and mothers, as she purposefully casts doubt over the paternity of her child as a means of escaping from her marriage.

Beyond overt allusions to Schreiner's work, *A Daughter of the King* draws upon floral imagery used by Schreiner, specifically the rose, to establish transnational expressions of white feminist solidarity. The rose is a recurrent motif across Schreiner's works, including in the feminist allegory, 'The Woman's Rose' (1891). According to Schreiner, this story is about 'how one woman gives another woman a rose',[28] an act read by Graham Pechey as the women's initiation into 'social sisterhood'.[29] The exchanging of roses between women is also seen in Schreiner's first (abandoned) novel, *Undine*, as the young female character Diogenes nurtures a rose that she gifts to the eponymous heroine. Roses also feature in another short story, 'Dream Life and Real Life: A Little African Story', first published in *New College Magazine* in 1885, within the context of a dream.

Analysis of the rose is, according to Dorothy Driver, 'a new topic in Schreiner criticism',[30] most recently explored by Driver herself, as well as Jade Munslow Ong, Valerie Stevens and Stephanie Eggermont, all of whom read Schreiner's roses as expressions of her feminist politics. In their respective readings of Schreiner's allegory, 'The Woman's Rose', Munslow Ong argues that the flower is 'a symbol of female solidarity'; Eggermont argues that the allegory privileges the values of solidarity and trust over individualism and rivalry; and Laura Chrisman describes the rose as enabling a 'critique of patriarchal/colonial commerce'.[31] I probe these claims further by arguing that Schreiner and Baker are concerned more particularly with the articulation of *white colonial* feminism, and it is through the rose that this exclusionary mode of feminism can be represented. As Sanja Nivesjö and Heidi Barends note with reference to Schreiner's final novel, *From Man to Man*, 'Schreiner explores the rights of white women as owners and managers of property' but she 'does not take the same critical interest in the position of Indigenous men and women *as* property'.[32] Moffat similarly argues that Baker's feminist views are centred upon the experiences of white, Pākehā women and the subsequent obfuscation of Indigenous women:

> the predominant silence regarding the indigenous population in the New Zealand New Woman novels points to the ambivalent position of white settler women in an invader settler nation; preoccupied with their own predicament as an oppressed gender, most of these authors fail to acknowledge their complicity as imperial subjects in the subjugation of Māori people.[33]

Baker's incorporation of Schreiner's rose motif into *A Daughter of the King* reveals her own 'complicity' in the foregrounding of a feminist politic that speaks only to the concerns and experiences of white women in the colonies. As Helen Tiffin notes, literary representations of flowers – including the rose – constitute a '(re)constructed landscape in which, through a dialogic process of image making, the *entangled* history of colonized and coloniser is invoked and reworked'.[34] In relation to the southern archive then, the rose in Schreiner and Baker's fiction represents the 'entangled history' of colonial women across the southern colonies.

Analysing Schreiner and Baker's roses as motifs to represent white, colonial feminism stems from the rose's cultural and ecological significance in colonial histories. Tiffin explains that the rose has 'acquired a lengthy and complex symbolic history in the European and English traditions' and has attained the 'symbolic or iconic status as quintessentially English'.[35] The cultural association of the rose with colonial histories is compounded by its ecological history and its introduction to the southern colonies. Introduced to New Zealand in 1800,[36] the sweet briar rose also 'colonizes dry areas of South America, New Zealand, South Africa, and Australia'.[37] In both cultural and ecological discourses, the rose is associated with colonisation, and the transplanting of 'Englishness' into a colonial landscape. The rose thus becomes a useful image for women of the southern colonies to incorporate into their New Woman fiction, as it signifies a form of white, middle-class femininity that is attempting to 'bloom' in a new environment.

Baker's chapter 'Climbing the Mountain' is particularly evocative of Schreiner's allegory 'The Gardens of Pleasure', which was published in *Dreams* in 1890. In this short story, a woman is finding joy in gathering flowers, but is then obliged by a male figure named 'Duty' to repeatedly cast them away until she has 'nothing left to give'.[38] Cherry Wilhelm interprets Schreiner's narrative as an allegory for 'the renunciation of pleasure', as women must always 'yield to Duty'; and Chrisman makes the case that the narrative depicts 'the process of a woman achieving autonomy through the renunciation of pleasure'.[39] In 'Climbing the

Mountain', Baker presents an similar narrative through a literary aesthetic closely associated with Schreiner: the dream.

Baker's dream narrative, which operates as an allegory, mimics the formal and aesthetic elements of 'The Gardens of Pleasure' to convey Florence's personal journey as she loses, and then tries to regain, her own autonomy within her marriage. It also maps onto a key narrative thrust of the novel in which Florence tries to divorce her husband. The dream takes place after Florence has been coerced into marrying her adopted brother, Claude. She does so believing him to be on his deathbed. Florence's adoptive mother, Mrs Arnold, encourages Florence to return to her childhood home at the Bay after she has given birth to an unwanted child so she can be under her care and 'regain her roses' (here used in a metaphorical sense to refer to her health).[40] Read in dialogue with Schreiner's 'The Gardens of Pleasure', Baker's dream-narrative represents the subjugation women experience in their roles as wives and mothers. Prior to falling asleep, Baker describes Florence's existence as a mother and wife as comparable to living 'in captivity', and invokes language associated with chattel slavery: 'she was not a slave, therefore she protested against her bonds' (language that Schreiner also later used in *Woman and Labour*).[41]

The dream occurs during Florence's first night away from her husband and begins in a very similar manner to Schreiner's 'The Gardens of Pleasure'. Schreiner's protagonist begins her journey stood 'among the flowers'.[42] She 'gathered her hands full of flowers' and stood 'with her hands full'.[43] Around her a 'sweet rich scent arose'.[44] An almost identical image is presented by Baker: Florence dreams that she is 'stood in a valley of roses' and 'with both hands full'.[45] The sensory element is also evoked as Florence is surrounded by 'the perfume of the flowers'.[46] Where Schreiner uses the flowers as a metaphor for pleasure, Baker's flowers draw on long-standing cultural and literary associations with female innocence. Baker establishes this connection earlier in the novel. Upon Florence's arrival to the Bay as a child, she sees 'gardens' that were 'a blaze of flowers' with 'wild roses', and her childhood bedroom is 'sweet with the scent of briar roses, growing round the open window'.[47] Baker makes a direct link between childhood, feminine innocence and the roses as she 'seemed to bring her sweetness in from the fields, the gorse bloom, and briar roses', and her adoptive mother Mrs Arnold notes that 'the roses seemed to belong to the children' as she 'looked back longingly to her time of flowers'.[48] In the dream, then, Florence's possession of roses represents the possession of her own childhood innocence.

Both stories follow a similar structure, as the women begin their journeys surrounded by flowers before being coerced into discarding them.

In 'The Gardens of Pleasure', the woman 'ceased from gathering' when she becomes the object of the male gaze, and so 'dropped the fairest of the flowers she had held'.[49] In 'Climbing the Mountain', Florence realises 'that she must not linger among the perfume of the flowers' and is 'obliged to let go of her roses'.[50] For both characters, this is an act that causes distress. Schreiner's character 'looked back at the sunlight on the faces of the flowers, and wept in anguish', and Florence is 'in sorrow and crying'.[51] For Schreiner, the personified masculine 'Duty' with 'his white clear features' and 'his still white face', compels the woman to cast away her blooms.[52] Similarly, for Baker, the obligation to 'let go' of her roses represents the renunciation of autonomy through her 'duty', a patriarchal form of control that underpins Florence and Claude's marriage. Prior to the dream, when asked by Claude what the marriage means for Florence, she responds: 'To do my duty', and upon agreeing that Florence can return home to live with her mother, Claude states that 'I shall claim from you your duty'.[53] Immediately after marrying Claude, Florence sees only 'withered roses', 'yellow leaves' and a 'dismal' garden that contrasts with the blooming gorse of her childhood.[54] The loss of Florence's flowers and the 'withered rose' enact a euphemistic 'deflowering' (an obvious reference to the loss of Florence's virginity). Baker thus incorporates Schreiner's rose imagery as a means to express the ways the institution of marriage forces Florence to relinquish her female autonomy.

Baker also invokes Schreiner's depiction of female resistance to marriage and motherhood as both stories depict the women attempting to keep possession of some flowers, and thus, in Florence's case, the attempt to retain some of the autonomy she possessed prior to marriage. Schreiner writes that 'in her hand she held of the buds she had gathered', but then upon seeing the 'death-like face', she 'unbent the fingers, and let the flowers drop out, the flowers she had loved so'.[55] Florence also attempts to reclaim some flowers, as 'she loitered, and gathered lovely flowers', before she was again 'compelled to cast away her flowers'.[56] This part of the dream functions as an allegory for the way Florence attempts to retain a sense of self in marriage. Before her dream, Claude reprimands Florence, stating that she 'means to defy' him, and in a later letter to her, Claude writes that 'the emotional instincts of women' were 'too rash to maintain standards upon which our civilization rests in those hours when desire and self-interest are weighed against duty'.[57] In his letter, Claude implies that Florence chooses her own self and livelihood over her 'duty' as a wife, even though Claude knows that Florence did not enter their marriage out of love, but out of obligation. Like with Schreiner's character, Florence's attempt to gather flowers once again in the dream narrative indicates her trying to retain her sense of self and 'self-interest' that she possessed prior to her coercion into marriage.

Attending to the thematic and structural concerns shared between Baker's and Schreiner's writing offers a powerful way of attending to feminist solidarity between South African and New Zealand New Woman writers, and provides a way of nuancing the southern archive to encompass distinctly female concerns. Evoking 'The Woman's Rose', in which a bloom is passed from one woman to another in an act of female solidarity, Baker's incorporation of Schreiner's rose motif gestures towards a form of female solidarity that is expressed specifically through the shared aesthetics of New Woman writing. Schreiner does more than offer Baker a rose: she offers her a representational means through which to articulate her New Woman politics.

Migration and Liberation in Jane Mander's *The Story of a New Zealand River* (1920)

Jane Mander was born in Auckland, Aotearoa New Zealand, in 1877, but did not remain there for long. As Philip Steer notes, Mander's family moved to different parts of New Zealand at least twenty-nine times, and at age thirty Mander moved across the water to Sydney, Australia.[58] There she worked as a freelance journalist under the pseudonym Manda Lloyd, and thus became part of what Comyn and Fermanis term the 'intercolonial traffic' between New Zealand and Australia.[59] Her debut novel, *The Story of a New Zealand River*, depicts women travelling across these southern colonies, and represents mobility between rural and metropole locations as generative for the creation of New Womanhood.

As the title indicates, Mander's novel takes inspiration from Schreiner's *African Farm*, particularly in the way that Asia possesses unconventional attitudes towards marriage and transgresses sexual norms like Schreiner's protagonist, Lyndall. As well as the title, Mander makes overt reference to Schreiner in the narrative, as Mrs Brayton welcomes Asia's mother to Pukekaroro by offering her 'a wonderful new novel called *The Story of an African Farm*, by an Olive Schreiner'.[60] As Diane Long Hoeveler notes, however, Mander was a 'a devoted reader of all of Schreiner's writings', and it is therefore likely that Mander was also familiar with Schreiner's short stories 'Three Dreams in a Desert' (1887) and 'Dream Life and Real Life: A Little African Story' (1885).[61] In 'Three Dreams in a Desert', the river allegorises progress, so that the female protagonist must cross the river to reach the 'Land of Freedom'.⁶² Similarly, in 'Dream Life and Real Life: A Little African Story' the enslaved protagonist Jannita reaches freedom by traversing a river. Critical attention to Schreiner's use of water is limited to the very recent work of Maria Geustyn, who examines her oceanic imagery in *From Man to Man* and *African Farm*, as well as a chapter by Deborah Shapple Spillman, who briefly traces Schreiner's 'ecological vision' in *Trooper Peter Halket of Mashonaland*.⁶³ Early New Zealand writers were quicker to realise Schreiner's use of river-crossing as an allegory for progress and liberation. As such, Mander uses the river as a means to rework Victorian associations of water with sexually 'deviant' women, and newly present women's movement along rivers as conducive to the realisation of a sexually liberated New Womanhood. While Mander does not invoke Schreiner's uniquely allegorical mode of representation, she does present the subject of the title, 'the New Zealand river', as central to the attainment of women's sexual autonomy, and to the destigmatisation of female sexuality.⁶⁴

By invoking an association between female freedom and rivers, Mander subverts conventional Victorian interpretations of the relationships between bodies of water and the figure of the 'Fallen Woman'.⁶⁵ Both a cultural and literary figure, the 'Fallen Woman' represented social and moral decline associated with female sexual transgressions. Her relationship with water stemmed from a sombre reality: women who became pregnant out of wedlock would often commit suicide by drowning rather than be ostracised and thrust into poverty and homelessness.⁶⁶ Bodies of pregnant women were frequently found in the River Thames, so much so that the drowned woman became an icon in Victorian literature and art. As Martha Patterson explains: 'associating water with dangerous feminine desire is a defining aspect of fin-de-siècle culture', and it is the image of the drowning woman in particular that pervades discussions of female sexual transgression in nineteenth-century literary cultures.⁶⁷

In Schreiner's 'A Little African Story', Jannita travels via the river so 'they would not be able to find her footmarks'; in *The Story of a New Zealand River*, the Wairoa river conceals Alice's past and allows her to escape social scrutiny.⁶⁸ Mander's protagonist Alice recalls how upon becoming pregnant out of wedlock in Australia, she is encouraged to travel to New Zealand to begin a new life under the guise of a widow. When reflecting on her secrets, Alice considers the river to be the place where she can '[l]et them die', so that she can possess a clear conscience moving forwards.⁶⁹ The way that it is impossible to know 'where all the water comes from and where it goes' also parallels the way that the Alice's movement between the colonies enables her history to remain unknown.[70] As well as facilitating Alice's movement between the southern colonies, the Wairoa also enables Alice to begin a 'new' life free from judgement, as '[e]very bend in the river meant a fearful look forward'.[71] The association of the river and new beginnings is reiterated throughout the novel, as Mander writes: '[a]s she walked home in the fresh morning air, and looked down upon the sun-specked river dancing its way to sea, the natural vitality in Alice reasserted itself, and she realized once more that she could begin again'.[72] Reminiscent of the ways that Schreiner's protagonist must cross the 'dark flowing river' in 'Three Dreams in a Desert', the New Zealand river is associated with Mander's protagonist reaching her own 'land of Freedom' in which she is no longer ostracised.[73] For Mander, the river no longer ends the lives of fallen women, instead becoming the means through which sexually 'deviant' women can begin new lives.

Mander presents Alice's journey along, and subsequent relationship with, the river as representative of her own personal journey. During Alice's initial journey to Pukekaroro, Mander describes how '[e]very bend in the river meant a fearful look forward', and in this way, she allegorises Alice's movement along the river as movement through life, the 'forward' movement of personal progress.[74] Later in the novel, Alice sees her changes as allied to the continuous flow of the river:

> she had begun to question the verities. If you live beside a river sooner or later you have to. You can't help sitting beside it, and listening to it, and watching the water go by. And then you wonder idly where all the water comes from and where it goes, and when it began to run and why, and if it will ever end and why. And your thoughts run with it and change with it.[75]

In associating her proximity with the river with her question of 'verities', Alice associates the flowing river with the realisation of truth and meaning. This again recalls elements of Schreiner's 'Three Dreams in a Desert', in which 'Truth' is revealed to the protagonist upon preparing to cross the river.[76] The river also enables Alice to realise her own sense of self. Just as waterways shape gullies, the Wairoa metaphorically 'shapes' Alice's mind, as her thoughts 'run with it and change with it'.[77] Rather than her views being static and unchanging, living in Pukekaroro enables Alice to become more receptive to changing social landscapes. Mander ends the novel by reiterating the ways that Alice's growth has been underpinned by her relationship with the river, as she writes: 'they knew, even when the gap had cut it all out of sight, that they had not left the river and the hills behind them'.[78] Mander indicates that they cannot 'leave' the Wairoa because it has enabled their personal and moral growth during their time in Pukekaroro, and is therefore something that will stay with them on their new journey back to Australia.

Mander presents the river as a friend and teacher to Alice, and thus as complicit in Alice's ability to realise her own autonomy. Mander notes that 'it seemed to Alice the friendliest river she had ever seen', and describes Alice as 'learning the language that belonged to the mountain and the river', therefore attributing to the river typically human qualities that can welcome her into the space.[79] The concept of Alice as learner and the river as teacher is echoed upon her leaving Pukekaroro for Australia, as Alice remarks that 'I am bringing away all it has taught me'.[80] Here, Mander refers to Alice's acceptance of her 'scandalous' past, and her ability to embrace love beyond the confines of marriage. The notion of the river as an agent of forgiveness is also alluded to earlier by Mander, as Alice reflects that 'it was the hand of God she saw in that night, in that mountain, that bush and that river' upon her arrival to Pukekaroro.[81] In referring to the river and surrounding landscape as the 'hand of God', Mander implies that the river is a mighty force that has acted on behalf of her God in giving her a second opportunity at living with a husband and children. Rather than presenting drowning in the river as the only and inevitable end for the fallen woman, Mander presents the river and its facilitation of a new life as an alternative way for God to absolve fallen women from sin.

Mander's New Zealand river is also associated with Alice's daughter, Asia. Asia embraces a sexually liberated lifestyle, in which she cannot quantify or name the 'various men' with whom she has sexual relationships outside of marriage, and they appear in a list identified only by town, nation and/or employment: 'an Kaiwaka curate, a surveyor, an English derelict working on the gum fields, and others'.[82] Mander uses the river to foreshadow Asia's 'fall', as she literally 'falls' into the Wairoa on her journey to Pukekaroro:

> Alice moved round just as [Asia] lost her balance, clutched vainly at the taut connecting the rope, and went down. Before she could even utter a sound Bruce, who had seen it coming, shot over the stern of the tow-boat, and dived at the sinking blue bonnet. There was an eternal moment of silence when Alice knew they were both somewhere underneath the punt. Then she heard a splash toward the rear. [. . .] Bruce struggled in, pulled the rope, and handed Asia, who was spluttering and coughing, but otherwise unhurt and unafraid, over the end of the punt.[83]

As the novel progresses, Alice associates all of Asia's transgressions with her near-drowning in the river. For example, after an altercation in which Alice reprimands Asia for going 'into the bush' with a 'coarse, rough boy', Asia escapes to Mrs Brayton's house, leaving Alice fearful for her daughter.[84] Alice exclaims '[d]o you realize that my child may be lying drowned in the river?' and laments that '[s]he ran away – she may be drowned', repeating 'she may be drowned' to another neighbour.[85]

In surviving the fall and submersion into the river, Asia is a character through whom Mander reworks the associations between sexually deviant women and death by drowning. Describing Asia as returning from the water 'unhurt' and 'unafraid', Mander indicates that Asia is able to survive the depths of the river and does not view the water as a dangerous space.[86] Like Schreiner, Mander invokes the river as a liberatory force for her female characters. Mander later notes that 'no water was too deep for Asia, who had more than a nodding acquaintance with deep waters'.[87] Her eventual love interest Ross notes that Asia sails 'like one who belongs to the river', and she is elsewhere compared to a 'water sprite', which Emily Alder explains was often associated with 'sexual and ontological transgression'.[88] Mander therefore subverts the association between sexually 'deviant' women and water; more than being able to survive the river, the river welcomes Asia as an 'acquaintance', and is a space where Asia 'belongs'.[89] As a 'water sprite' figure, Asia is simultaneously coded as sexual and as a being who thrives and makes a home in the water. Like Schreiner, who uses the river to reach freedom, Mander uses water imagery to signal a form of female, sexual freedom, wherein Asia's sexually liberal lifestyle is not condemned, but celebrated.

Whereas the Wairoa enabled Alice to leave Sydney, the site of her 'fall', for Asia the Wairoa facilitates her travel to Sydney, the site of her liberation. It is in Sydney that Asia feels 'the effects of the city upon herself', and enjoys 'adventures with men', specifically Ross, a married man with whom she later cohabits.[90] Asia takes up smoking, an image associated with the New Woman,[91] feels 'emancipat[ed] from the old-fashioned ways of her mother's generation', and learns about modernist art and thought.[92] Migration across the water is therefore of vital importance for Asia's liberation from her isolated life at the logging village, and from her mother's Puritanism. Asia's narrative reflects in some ways Schreiner's 'Three Dreams in a Desert'; she is able to reach a land on which 'walked brave women and brave men, hand in hand. And they looked into each other's eyes, and they were not afraid'.[93] By travelling along the river and ocean to live in Sydney, Asia and Ross are able to walk 'hand in hand' and 'love each other in freedom' without fear of scrutiny from the village, particularly from Alice.[94] Mander, therefore, presents this female, voluntary migration between the southern colonies as a means to achieve and realise New Womanhood.

The scope of the southern archive is greatly extended by considering the movement of women between the southern colonies. Both Schreiner's and Mander's works represent a form of 'intercolonial traffic' that is not structured by trade and commerce, but by the emancipation of white colonial women from oppressive social conventions. Mander's novel suggests that movement between the southern colonies produces a liberatory form of New Womanhood that may otherwise not be achieved in Britain, and therefore offers a new way for the southern archive to decentre Britain 'as the dominant identificatory category in the relationship between colonies and metropoles'.[95]

Expanding the southern archive

Reading the literary relationships amongst Schreiner, Baker and Mander in the context of the southern archive gives rise to the consideration of hemispheric and transnational relations between white, middle-class women in particular, and expands the scope of the southern archive by de-centring the role of involuntary and predominantly male labour as the primary factors in establishing relationality between the colonies. By analysing literary depictions of the New Woman in the context of systems of settler colonialism and patriarchy, this chapter gestures towards a southern archive that attends not only to the 'shared history and structural similarities of the southern settler colonies' that relate to settler colonialism, but also to patriarchal structures.[96] Considered together, South African and New Zealand New Woman literatures appear as part of interconnected systems that engender complex and varied experiences for women who are simultaneously privileged subjects of empire and oppressed subjects of patriarchy, thus facilitating new understandings of a shared literary tradition. For New Women of the southern colonies, including Schreiner, Mander and Baker, it is this south-south relationality that produces a literary aesthetic through which to represent new forms of feminist solidarity.

Works Cited

'A Daughter of the King'. *Otago Witness*. 4 October 1984.
Alder, Emily. '"A Thing of Dreams and Desires, a Siren, a Whisper, and a Seduction": Mermaids and the Seashore in H. G. Wells's 'The Sea Lady: A Tissue of Moonshine'. *Shima* 15, no. 2 (2021): 85–100.

Alexander, Lynn. '"Hearts as Innocent as Hers": The Drowned Woman in Victorian Literature and Art'. In *Beauty, Violence, Representation*, edited by Lisa Dickson and Maryna Romanets, 79–96. Oxon: Routledge, 2013.

Alien [Baker, Louisa Alice]. 'Alien's Letters from England'. *Otago Witness*. 18 February 1914.

Archibald, Diana. *Domesticity, Imperialism and Emigration in the Victorian Novel*. Columbia: University of Missouri Press, 2002.

Baker, Louisa Alice. *A Daughter of the King*. London: Hutchinson & Co, 1894.

Burns, Rebecca. 'Rediscovered: Two Short Stories by Edith Searle Grossmann'. *Kōtare: New Zealand Notes and Queries* (2011): 1–11.

Callister, Paul, Robert Didham and Richard Bedford. 'Changing Sex Ratios in New Zealand: Real Change or a Statistical Problem?' *New Zealand Populations Review* 32, no. 1 (2006): 21–33.

Chrisman, Laura. 'Allegory, Feminist Thought and the Dreams of Olive Schreiner'. *Prose Studies* 13, no. 1 (1990): 126–50.

—. 'Colonialism and Feminism in Olive Schreiner's 1890s Fiction'. *English in Africa* 20, no. 1 (1993): 25–38.

Comyn, Sarah and Porscha Fermanis. 'Rethinking Nineteenth-century Literary Culture: British Worlds, Southern Latitudes and Hemispheric Methods'. *The Journal of Commonwealth Literature* 0, no. 0 (2021): 1–18.

Devereux, Cecily. 'New Woman, New World: Maternal Feminism and the New Imperialism in the White Settler Colonies'. *Women's Studies International Forum* 22, no. 2 (1999): 175–84.

Driver, Dorothy. 'Invoking Indigeneity: Olive Schreiner and the Poetics of Plants'. *The Journal of Commonwealth Literature* 56, no. 1 (2021): 61–76.

Eggermont, Stephanie. '"The Method of Life we all Lead": Olive Schreiner's Short Fiction as Challenge to the Stage Method'. In *Writing Women of the Fin de Siècle: Authors of Change*, edited by Adrienne Gavin and Carolyn Oulton, 43–54. London: Palgrave MacMillan, 2016.

Elaine, 'Books – New and Old'. *The Dawn*. 1 March 1900.

Gadzinowska Joanna, Agnieszka Ostrowska, Katarzyna Hura, Michał Dziurka, Bożena Hura, Pawłowska, and Tomasz Hura. 'Physiological Traits Determining High Adaptation Potential of Sweet Briar (Rosa Rubiginosa L.) at Early Stage of Growth to Dry Lands'. *Scientific Reports* 9, no. 1 (2019): 1–10.

Gadzinowska, Joanna, Michał Dziurka, Agnieszka Ostrowska, Katarzyna Hura and Tomasz Hura. 'Phytohormone Synthesis Pathways in Sweet Briar Rose (Rosa Rubiginosa L.) Seedlings with High Adaptation Potential to Soil Drought'. *Plant Physiology and Biochemistry* 154 (2020): 745–50.

Geustyn, Maria. 'Olive Schreiner's Oceanic Imaginary and the Question of Deep History'. *English in Africa* 48, no. 1 (2021): 53–72.

Grand, Sarah. 'The New Aspect of the Woman Question'. *The North American Review* 158, no. 448 (1894): 270–76.

Grossman, Edith. 'Spare Half Hours: Genius and Talent in the Colony'. *Otago Witness*. 19 July 1894.

Heilmann, Ann. *New Woman Strategies: Sarah Grand, Olive Schreiner, and Mona Caird*. Manchester: Manchester University Press, 2004.
Hetherington, Naomi. 'Feminism, Freethought, and the Sexual Subject in Colonial New Woman Fiction: Olive Schreiner and Kathleen Mannington Caffyn'. *Victorian Review* 37, no. 2 (2011): 47–59.
Hodge, Merton. *Story of an African Farm: A Play in Three Acts*. London: William Heineman Ltd, 1938.
Jusová, Iveta. *The New Woman and the Empire*. Columbus: Ohio State University, 2005.
Klee, Louisa and Nicholas Birns. *The Cambridge Companion to the Australian Novel*. Cambridge: Cambridge University Press, 2023.
Le Gay Brereton, John. *The Song of Brotherhood: And Other Verses*. London: George Allen, 1896.
Long Hoeveler, Diane. 'Silence, Sex, and Feminism: An Examination of "The Piano"'s Unacknowledged Sources.' *Literature/Film Quarterly*, 24, no. 3 (1998): 303–22.
Macdonald, Charlotte. *A Woman of Good Character: Single Women as Immigrant Settlers in Nineteenth-Century New Zealand*. New Zealand: Bridget Williams Books Ltd, 2015.
Mander, Jane. *The Story of a New Zealand River*. London: Forgotten Books, 2018.
Mitchell, Dolores. 'The "New Woman" as Prometheus: Women Artists Depict Women Smoking.' *Woman's Art Journal* 12, no. 1 (1991): 3–9.
Moffat, Kirstine. '"Devoted to the Cause of Women's Rights": The New Zealand New Woman Novel'. *Women's Writing* 26, no. 3 (2019): 304–27.
—. 'Louisa Alice Baker'. *Kōtare: New Zealand Notes & Queries* 7, no. 1 (2007): 10–18.
Montgomerie, Deborah. 'New Women and Not-So-New Men Discussions About Marriage in New Zealand, 1890–1914'. *New Zealand Journal of History* 51, no. 1 (2017): 36–64.
Munslow Ong, Jade. *Olive Schreiner and African Modernism: Allegory, Empire and Postcolonial Writing*. London: Routledge, 2018.
Nivesjö, Sanja, and Heidi Barends. 'Current Perspectives on Olive Schreiner's *From Man to Man or Perhaps Only—*',*The Journal of Commonwealth Literature* 56, no. 1 (2021): 44–60.
'Olive Schreiner'. *The Australian Worker*. 6 January 1921.
Patterson, Martha. *Beyond the Gibson Girl: Reimagining the American New Woman, 1895–1915*. Chicago: University of Illinois Press, 2008.
Paxton, Nancy L. 'The Story of an African Farm and the Dynamics of Woman-to-Woman Influence'. *Texas Studies in Literature and Language* 30, no. 4 (1988): 562–82.
Pechey, Graham. '"The Woman's Rose": Olive Schreiner, the Short Story and Grand History'. *Critical Survey* 11, no. 2 (1999): 4–17.
Schreiner, Olive. 'Dream Life and Real Life: A Little African Story'. Boston: Roberts Brothers, 1893.
—. 'The Gardens of Pleasure'. In *Dreams*, 53–55. London: T. Fisher Unwin, 1891.
—. *The Story of an African Farm*. Oxford: Oxford University Press, 1998.

—. 'Three Dreams in a Desert'. In *Dreams*, 67–85. London: T. Fisher Unwin, 1891.
—. *Undine: A Queer Little Child*. New York: Johnson Reprint Company, 1929.
Shapple Spillman, Deborah. 'Waste Lands and Preserves: Olive Schreiner's Ecological Allegories and Colonial Zimbabwe'. In *The Economics of Empire*, edited by Maureen E. Ruprecht Fadem and Michael O'Sullivan, 122–40. New York: Routledge, 2020.
Steer, Philip. 'Jane Mander'. *Kōtare: New Zealand Notes & Queries* 7, no. 1 (2007): 37–54.
Tiffin, Helen. '"Flowers of Evil, Flowers of Empire": Roses and Daffodils in the Work of Jamaica Kincaid, Olive Senior and Lorna Goodison'. *Span* 46, no. 1 (1998): 58–71.
Treagus, Mandy. *Empire Girls: The Colonial Heroine Comes of Age*. South Australia: University of Adelaide Press, 2014.
—. and Alex Sutcliffe and Nicholas Jose. 'The Story of an Australian Farm'. In *Olive Schreiner in the World*, edited by Jade Munslow Ong and Andrew van der Vlies, 244–65. Edinburgh: Edinburgh University Press, 2023.
Wilhelm, Cherry. 'Olive Schreiner: Child of Queen Victoria Stories, Dreams and Allegories'. *English in Africa* 3, no. 1 (1976): 63–69.

Letters

Katherine Mansfield to Sarah Millin, 1 March 1922. *Katherine Mansfield Society*.
Olive Schreiner to Edward Carpenter, 24 February 1908. *Olive Schreiner Letters Online*.
Olive Schreiner to Emily Hobhouse, 29 May 1908. *Olive Schreiner Letters Online*.
Olive Schreiner to Mary Sauer, March 1981. *Olive Schreiner Letters Online*.

Notes

1. Schreiner to Carpenter, 24 February 1908, *Olive Schreiner Letters Online* (*OSLO*).
2. Schreiner to Hobhouse, 29 May 1908, *OSLO*.
3. Comyn and Fermanis, 'Rethinking', 2.
4. Grand, 'The New Aspect of the Woman Question', 270–76.
5. Devereaux, 'New Woman, New World', 176.
6. See also Jusová, *New Woman and Empire*; Treagus, *Empire Girls: The Colonial Heroine Comes of Age*.
7. Heilmann, 'New Woman Strategies', 3; Hetherington, 'Feminism, Freethought and the Sexual Subject', 47.
8. Mansfield to Millin, 1 March 1922, *Katherine Mansfield Society*.
9. Grossmann, 'Spare Half-Hours: Genius and Talent in the Colony', 47.
10. Elaine, 'Books – New and Old', 21.
11. Anonymous, 'To the Editor', 35.

12. See for example the poetry collection, *The Song of Brotherhood: And Other Verses* by Australian poet John Le Gay Brereton, which includes the poem 'To Olive Schreiner' that includes the praise: 'a cry of thanks to thee' (61). Also, in 1938, New Zealand actor and playwright H. E. Hodge, better known as Merton Hodge, transformed Schreiner's debut novel *The Story of an African Farm* into a play entitled *Story of an African Farm: A Play in Three Acts*. Articles on Schreiner's feminist politics also appear in a host of examples across the New Zealand press, with Deborah Montgomerie explaining that newspapers could report on Schreiner without needing 'to provide her with a lengthy introduction' (43). In 'Devoted to the Cause of Women's Rights', Moffat also identifies the impact of Schreiner on New Zealand New Women writers Edith Searle Grossmann and Elsie Story.
13. Burns, 'Rediscovered', 8.
14. Klee and Birns, *A Cambridge Companion*, 4.
15. Comyn and Fermanis, 'Re-thinking', 4.
16. Comyn and Fermanis, 'Re-thinking', 4.
17. Callister, Didham and Beckford, 'Changing Sex Ratios', 25; MacDonald, 'A Woman of Good Character', iv.
18. MacDonald, 'A Woman of Good Character', 5.
19. MacDonald, 'A Woman of Good Character', 5.
20. MacDonald, 'A Woman of Good Character', 6.
21. Comyn and Fermanis, 'Re-thinking', 2.
22. Archibald, 'Domesticity, Imperialism and Emigration', 93.
23. Treagus, *Empire Girls*, 243–44.
24. Comyn and Fermanis, 'Rethinking', 10.
25. Alien, 'Alien's Letters from England', (67).
26. Schreiner, quoted in Baker, 'A Daughter of the King', ii.
27. Nancy Paxton, 'Dynamics of Woman to Woman Influence', 574.
28. Schreiner to Mary Sauer, March 1891, OSLO.
29. Pechey, 'The Woman's Rose', 6.
30. Driver, 'Invoking Indigeneity', 62.
31. Nivesjö and Barends, 'Interview with Angelo Fick, Jade Munslow Ong and Valerie Stevens', quoted in Nivesjö and Barends, 'Current Perspectives on Olive Schreiner', 58; Eggermont, 'The Method of Life we all Lead', 50; Chrisman, 'Colonialism and Feminism in Olive Schreiner's 1890s Fiction', 29.
32. Nivesjö and Barends, 'Current Perspectives on Olive Schreiner', 51, emphasis added.
33. Moffat, 'Devoted to the Cause of Woman's Rights', 307.
34. Tiffin, '"Flowers of Evil, Flowers of Empire"' 59.
35. Tiffin, '"Flowers of Evil, Flowers of Empire"' 60.
36. Gadzinowska et al., 'Physiological traits', 1.
37. Gadzinowska et al., 'Phytohormone synthesis pathways in sweet briar rose', 745.
38. Schreiner, 'The Gardens of Pleasure', 55.
39. Wilhelm, 'Child of Queen Victoria', 64; Chrisman, 'Allegory, Feminist Thought', 140.
40. Baker, *A Daughter of the King*, 132.

41. Baker, *A Daughter of the King*, 138.
42. Schreiner, 'The Gardens of Pleasure', 53.
43. Schreiner, 'The Gardens of Pleasure', 53.
44. Schreiner, 'The Gardens of Pleasure', 53.
45. Baker, *A Daughter of the King*, 138.
46. Baker, *A Daughter of the King*, 138.
47. Baker, *A Daughter of the King*, 24, 35.
48. Baker, *A Daughter of the King*, 43, 50.
49. Schreiner, 'The Gardens of Pleasure', 54.
50. Baker, *A Daughter of the King*, 139.
51. Baker, *A Daughter of the King*, 139.
52. Schreiner, 'The Gardens of Pleasure', 53.
53. Baker, *A Daughter of the King*, 105, 106.
54. Baker, *A Daughter of the King*, 92.
55. Schreiner, 'The Gardens of Pleasure', 54.
56. Baker, *A Daughter of the King*, 141.
57. Baker, *A Daughter of the King*, 161.
58. Steer, 'Jane Mander', 37.
59. Comyn and Fermanis, 'Re-thinking', 2.
60. Mander, *The Story of a New Zealand River*, 38.
61. Long Hoevelor, 'Silence, Sex, and Feminism', 111.
62. Schreiner, 'Three Dreams in a Desert', 76.
63. Geustyn, 'Olive Schreiner's Oceanic Imagery', 55; Shapple Spillman, 'Waste Lands and Preserves', 122.
64. Mander, *New Zealand River*, 11.
65. Examples can be found in Elizabeth Gaskell's *Ruth* (1853); Charles Dickens' *David Copperfield* (1849–50) and *Dombey and Son* (1846–48); and George Eliot's *Adam Bede* (1859).
66. See Alexander, 'Hearts as Innocent as Hers', 74.
67. Patterson, 'Reimagining the American New Woman', 19.
68. Schreiner, 'A Little African Story', 20.
69. Mander, *New Zealand River*, 430.
70. Mander, *New Zealand River*, 112.
71. Mander, *New Zealand River*, 25.
72. Mander, *New Zealand River*, 247.
73. Schreiner, 'Three Dreams in a Desert', 76.
74. Mander, *New Zealand River*, 25.
75. Mander, *New Zealand River*, 112.
76. Schreiner, 'Three Dreams in a Desert', 78.
77. Mander, *New Zealand River*, 112.
78. Mander, *New Zealand River*, 431.
79. Mander, *New Zealand River*, 64, 248.
80. Mander, *New Zealand River*, 430.
81. Mander, *New Zealand River*, 27.
82. Mander, *New Zealand River*, 217.
83. Mander, *New Zealand River*, 18.
84. Mander, *New Zealand River*, 124.
85. Mander, *New Zealand River*, 119–21.
86. Mander, *New Zealand River*, 18.

87. Mander, *New Zealand River*, 223.
88. Mander, *New Zealand River*, 255; Alder, 'Mermaids and the Sea Shore', 85.
89. Mander, *New Zealand River*, 255.
90. Mander, *New Zealand River*, 285.
91. See Mitchell, 'The "New Woman" as Prometheus', 3.
92. Mander, *New Zealand River*, 285.
93. Schreiner, 'Three Dreams in a Desert,' 84.
94. Mander, *New Zealand River*, 329.
95. Comyn and Fermanis, 'Rethinking', 2.
96. Comyn and Fermanis, 'Rethinking', 2.

Chapter 12

The Story of an Australian Farm: Olive Schreiner in Australia
Nicholas Jose, Alex Sutcliffe and Mandy Treagus

Olive Schreiner never visited Australia. But soon after its London publication in 1883, with the author's identity known, *The Story of an African Farm* was debated by Australian readers and inspired Australian writers. The literary presence of Schreiner in Australia in her lifetime and thereafter is the subject of this essay. Surprisingly perhaps, it has not been explored in detail before. While a comprehensive, book-historical account is beyond our scope, we offer a preliminary overview. Part one focuses on the influence of *African Farm* on significant novels produced by Australian writers during Schreiner's lifetime. Part two reads Patrick White's key modernist novel *The Aunt's Story* (1948) through the lens of *African Farm*, the source of two of its epigraphs. The critic Dorothy Green called *African Farm* a 'fertilising novel' for Henry Handel Richardson.[1] This essay aims to show Schreiner's work as 'fertilising' for Australian literature more generally.

When A. B. 'Banjo' Paterson interviewed Schreiner in Cape Town in 1900, the Australian war correspondent and poet, most famous as the author of 'Waltzin' Matilda', wrote that 'The authoress of "The Story of an African Farm" needs no introduction to Australians [...] Yet they will be surprised by her forthright views'.[2] 'You Australians and New Zealanders and Canadians', Schreiner told him, 'I cannot understand it at all, why you come here light-heartedly to shoot down other colonists of whom you know nothing – it is terrible. Such fine men too [...] You Australians do not understand'.[3] Paterson would come to share her views. The sense of colonial commonality evident in his report recurs in later Australian tributes, including after her death, when one former commander in the South African campaign recalled her life behind barbed wire under his charge at Hanover, when his job included censoring material she sent out. They parted 'with a friendly grasp of the hand', he wrote; Schreiner was 'a patriot', fired up by 'imagined wrongs' to her country and people.[4]

At the end of the nineteenth century, *The Story of an African Farm* was among the most popular of all novels with 'farm women' in Australia, according to one Perth bookseller.[5] It continued to be influential for women writers, as Susan Sheridan notes in *Along the Faultlines: Sex, Race and Nation in Australian Women's Writing 1880s–1930s*.[6] She identifies Capel Boake's novel *Painted Clay* (1917) as clearly in Schreiner's debt. At a key moment, Helen, the protagonist, turns to her artist friend Walter to say:

> You remember in the 'Story of an African Farm' Lindall [sic] says to Waldo—'I like talking to you, Waldo, it's like talking with a spirit,' that is how I feel with you [. . .] I suppose it is your art and your singlemindedness of purpose that makes the difference.[7]

By the time of her death Schreiner had become a beacon for Australian women, as is evident in the obituary by 'Bay Ash' in the *Australian Worker* on 6 January 1921:

> Perhaps the position of women was never so clearly stated, and the plea for equality so calmly urged as in this book [*African Farm*], written by a girl of eighteen. Many sex barriers have fallen since then. [. . .] And Olive Schreiner's share in this great achievement is enshrined forever [. . .] She is dead, but in the minds of thousands of women all over the world she will always live in grateful remembrance.[8]

Her 'purpose' for many Australians from then on encompassed spiritual wisdom as well as anti-imperialist and feminist commitments, and her literary reputation.[9] A shared, although very different, colonial situation and the literary potential of south-south connection make Schreiner's life and afterlife in Australia an important dimension of the global circulation through which this collection re-evaluates her achievement.

1. Olive Schreiner in Australia

Catherine Helen Spence and Catherine Martin

'The New Woman appeared in Australia, tamely enough, when Catherine Spence reviewed [*The*] *Story of an African Farm*', writes historian Susan Magarey.[10] Reformer, feminist, educator and novelist, Catherine Helen Spence (1825–1910) critiques Schreiner's novel in an unsigned piece in the *South Australian Register* in 1889 titled 'Why Do Women Wilt!'. Responding to the debate ignited in London the previous year by novelist Mona Caird's article 'Is Marriage a Failure?', Spence is here concerned with the treatment of marriage in contemporary fiction, including in Caird's novel *The Wing of Azrael* (1889) and Schreiner's *African Farm*. Identifying Caird as the granddaughter of a South Australian colonist and extending a comparable familiarity to Schreiner as a colonial sister, Spence commends Schreiner's originality while calling *African Farm* 'a strange book to come from such a nest of missionaries as she was reared in'.[11] She observes that '[a]s a novel the book is nowhere, as an expression of revolt it is everywhere',[12] and adds wryly that when Schreiner's sister Helen toured Australia, 'the religious booksellers [who] had stacks of the cheap edition of the "African Farm" on their counters [. . .] evidently did not know the character of the book they wished to circulate'.[13] Spence's commentary is likely to have been read by her friend Catherine Martin, author of the celebrated *An Australian Girl* (1894). The two women, both childhood emigrants from Scotland, met in Adelaide in 1876 and became close friends, with Spence acting as a literary mentor to the younger woman. Though Spence shows some sympathy for Schreiner's critique of marriage, her review is not altogether favourable; Martin takes this critique more seriously in her own first novel, *An Australian Girl*. (There is no conclusive record of Martin owning *African Farm*, but given her friend and mentor Catherine Spence's engagement with Schreiner's novel, it is difficult to believe that she did not read it).[14] Published anonymously as a three-decker in London in 1890, *An Australian Girl* was reissued as an abridged single volume the following year, with a further Australian version in 1894.[15]

At first reading, *An Australian Girl* seems a long way from *The Story of an African Farm*. For one thing, the tone is notably different: Martin's novel contains extended passages of amusing dialogue, some of it quite satirical; the characters, especially Stella, are not marginalised orphans, but well-to-do members of Adelaide and Melbourne societies. Stella marries, and the final part of the narrative takes place after her marriage. This was something of a novelty in much Victorian fiction and certainly not Lyndall's choice or experience in *African Farm*. Stella also has a Christian conversion experience and resolves to live a productive and self-sacrificing life, a trajectory that seems at odds with that of either Waldo or Lyndall. Despite these apparent differences, however, the appearance of *African Farm*, and its preoccupations with the chief drivers of the nineteenth-century *Bildungsroman*, vocation and romance, created a space in which Catherine Martin could write a deeply serious novel about life in colonial Australia that addressed just those same issues, albeit with varied outcomes and resolutions.

One element of *African Farm* that is shared by Martin's work is the reference to an Indigenous presence. While this might seem unsurprising, given that First Nations people were present and visible in colonial society in Australia, it was unusual in the fiction produced during the period, which tended to sustain the myth of *terra nullius*. Martin represents the stories of several Indigenous characters, though they are admittedly minor and tend to be imbued with the dying race discourse so prevalent at the time.[16] It was only in her later novel, *The Incredible Journey* (1923), that Martin would bring such characters to the fore in a sympathetic portrayal of Aboriginal motherhood. This has its own ambivalences, however; Allen and Sheridan show how this sympathy is also reflective of the 'work of recuperation for the white project of colonisation' through an 'assimilation discourse'.[17] Similarly, Schreiner portrays the endemic racism of her society, but is not immune from it herself.[18]

The entry on Martin's novel in the *Oxford Companion to Australian Literature* notes that *An Australian Girl* is 'often described as a conventional nineteenth-century, genteel romance with the standard preoccupation with love and courtship', but also observes that this is an inaccurate view.[19] It is full of debate about marriage and contains plenty of critique of it as an institution, mostly delivered by the heroine Stella but also by virtue of how the plot plays out for various women. Since that time, the novel has received greater and more serious attention. Martin, like many novelists in the decade following the publication of *African Farm*, entered into debates about gender roles, especially about marriage, *because* Schreiner had brought them into the public sphere, and had done so through her fiction. As soon as *African Farm* appeared, *The Englishwoman's Review* quoted a large section of Lyndall's speech likening the marriage contract to prostitution, a concept that became widespread in late-nineteenth-century feminism and was enlarged upon in Schreiner's 'The Woman Question' and *Woman and Labour* as 'sex-parasitism'.[20] Likewise, Martin makes the economic reality of marriage for women clear. An example of this is the young woman Stella encounters at her brother Hector's station, Julia Morton; she is seen calculating the necessity of marrying one of the three possibly available men in her orbit, before realising that she might need to make a play for the unattractive, ageing yet wealthy neighbour she had previously rebuffed.[21] While such elements might form part of light-hearted standard romance, such novels would not contain the expression of sentiments like Stella's, in a series of jokes about marriage. In one, hearing that an older man planned to marry a woman who 'had been his intimate friend for over twenty years', she quips: 'Is it not dreadful to spoil so tried a friendship in this ruthless way?'.[22] There are enough of these comments to confirm a view in those around her that Stella is against the institution; it is not just fodder for humour. There are also minor plot lines about women who marry abusive men, spendthrifts or drunkards, so placing themselves and their children in danger.

That such things were in the air, and potential subjects for fiction, is due in large part to Schreiner. Her novel was transformative for many, as a young student at Cheltenham Ladies College wrote: 'Girls smuggled in *African Farm*, then just out. The whole sky seemed aflame and many of us became violent feminists'.[23] This sense of possibility flows into the fiction that follows *African Farm*, especially in the 1890s. The romance plot of *An Australian Girl* does not end with lovers appropriately matched in temperament and intellect; it is notable for Martin's 'transcendence of an ostensibly conventional plot'.[24] There is no trajectory for Stella like that of George Eliot's Dorothea in *Middlemarch*, who, after marrying the dreadful Casaubon, finds a truer match and fuller life with Ladislaw. Stella marries badly to the rich but problem-drinking Ted when she is deceived into thinking her appropriate match Anselm is already married, but this is not resolved by her eventually finding romantic fulfilment with Anselm. Rather, she determines to live with, and in a sense tries to save, Ted by believing in him, armed with her new religious certainty.

While choosing marriage is inconceivable in *African Farm*, self-sacrifice is not. In the allegorical interlude that appears in the middle of *African Farm*, the eponymous 'hunter' dies on his quest for truth. Later stories by Schreiner, such as 'The Buddhist Priest's Wife' (1892) and others in the collection *Dreams* (1895), suggest that forms of martyrdom are a higher good than almost anything else. Sacrifice is transformed into a pleasure in these texts; similarly, Martin resolves her novel with a heroine who makes a sacrificial choice. In words that echo those from 'The Hunter', Stella tells Anselm, in their last tragic intimate conversation, 'In seeking after the best that we can reach, each cup of suffering, every pang of sorrow, may breathe into our lives that finer spirit of all knowledge'.[25] The dominant Victorian discourse of women's dutiful self-sacrifice is not overturned by either of these feminist writers, but it is transformed into an active choice on the part of their heroines.

While a superficial reading sees *An Australian Girl* as a domestic romance, the literary atmosphere – there are constant allusions to English, German, French and classical texts, and consideration of issues such as philosophy and socialism – demands that the novel be read as a thoughtful examination of many matters beyond the marriage plot. The book features unlikely elements such as complete speeches, including one by a socialist leader, covering many pages. Just as Schreiner's reviewer from the *Church Quarterly Review* complained with obvious exasperation: 'Whole chapters are devoted to soliloquy and dissertation, during which the tale does not advance one inch',[26] so Martin devotes whole chapters to readings of Kant.

While *An Australian Girl* does not contain Waldo's agonies before a Calvinistic God, Martin's novel reaches similar depths as Stella grapples with religious doubt and a conscience that must be satisfied, despite its conflict with her romantic desires. Stella is tempted by Waldo's conclusion – 'There is no God!'[27] – but ultimately experiences conversion: 'All the unsatisfied yearning for belief, which had so long been stilled and left a waste place in her heart, rose into new life' from which comes 'a faint dawn of hope'.[28] The recognition that self-sacrifice might itself be a fulfilling course confirms this hope. Before she enters the church in London where these developments unfold, Stella's mind keeps returning to the 'Mallee Scrub',[29] a landscape that she has responded to deeply throughout the text. The Mallee is often dismissed by those unfamiliar with it as bleak and repetitive, yet Martin depicts it as a place of depth and timeless solace, with hints of the infinite. Stella's relationship to the Mallee is reminiscent of Schreiner's affinity to the Karoo, especially the connection both feel with the truth-inducing capacity of country so removed from that of Britain: 'Those things which signified meaning in Europe – quest, vocation, romance – have been shown to be empty in the world of the Karroo [Schreiner's spelling], even irrelevant'.[30] Martin's romance and vocation plots are not so extreme nor despairing as Schreiner's, but they indicate nevertheless that the certainties of the European *Bildungsroman* are not possible for the new heroine in Australia.

Henry Havelock Ellis, Miles Franklin, Henry Handel Richardson

Schreiner's closest personal connection to Australia was through her friend Henry Havelock Ellis (1859–1939), who arrived in Sydney in 1875 and returned to London in 1879. Out of those 'gap years' came his short novel, *Kanga Creek: An Australian Idyll*, belatedly published in 1922. Ellis spent his last year in Australia as the only teacher at bush schools in New South Wales, one at Sparkes Creek, where he lived in a simple hut that doubled as the classroom; here, isolated and close to nature, he got to know himself – in his fevered imagination at least. As Geoffrey Dutton puts it in *Kanga Creek: Havelock Ellis in Australia*: 'an English boy [. . .] nineteen, with a small beard, a long thin body, virginal loins and a soul released by a strange, ancient, very new country [. . .] became a man'.[31] In *My Life* (1940), Ellis would refer to that time in Australia as the most eventful year of my life [...] in which I had discovered the universe, and discovered myself and my art and my science [...] and the sacred spot beneath the Southern Cross [...] where all these things were revealed to me.[32]

Ellis read *African Farm* on his return to England and wrote to Schreiner.

> What delighted me [...] was, in part, the touch of genius [...]; in part, my own personal sympathy with the mental evolution described, all the more since it had taken place, as largely had my own, in the solitude of a remote southern land.[33]

When they met, he shared his private Australian diaries with her and, inspired by her example, began his autobiographical short fiction. 'Sweet brother soul,' she responded to the first chapter,

> I have never before felt so tender to you. [...] I have been thinking just now with such longing of my little bedroom at Ganna Hoek with its hole in the roof and the stars shining through, and of your little hut in Australia where you too used to lie and look up at the stars through the roof.[34]

Kanga Creek imagines an ideal woman to share the young schoolmaster's emotional, spiritual and physical longings: a Schreiner in the Australian bush. It played out painfully, however, when 'Olive and Harry' spent intimate time together in England, hoping but failing to share their bodies as they bared their souls. 'We were not what can be technically, or even ordinarily, called lovers', Ellis later wrote.[35]

In *My Life*, Ellis reflected on the 'seminal work' that Sparkes Creek had done for him, recalling impulses ('truly related in *Kanga Creek*') that were 'fiercely urgent' while 'still remaining emotional rather than sensual'.[36] '*Kanga Creek* is a story of adolescence', writes John Heuzenroeder, introducing Nelson's 1970 reprint of the novel, and commending Ellis, among sojourning Englishmen, for his responsiveness to Australia on its own terms.[37] Ellis's idyll ends in anticipation of a future time when the young man will look back to these days and nights as:

> The sweetest thing that life could give, when he would thirst for the strange solitudes that the black man has left and the white man has not yet taken for his own, and where the mystery of the early world is still alive.[38]

Ellis published an essay on 'Fiction in the Australian Bush' in 1903 in which he argues against received ideas of 'weird melancholy' and stereotypes like 'the semi-imbecile swagman and the drunken swearing drover'.[39] He emphasises the 'innumerable traits of humanity and refinement one meets with throughout the bush', which he describes as 'full of exquisite beauty'.[40] He appreciates Henry Lawson but qualifies his praise of Miles Franklin: 'One feels that *My Brilliant Career* was inspired by the same impulse as another youthful book written from the recesses of another continent, Olive Schreiner's *Story of an African Farm*, but in intellectual force and artistic perception the two writers cannot be compared'.[41]

Written when Miles Franklin was nineteen, *My Brilliant Career* (1901) appeared nearly twenty years after *African Farm*. The Goulburn newspaperman who recognised the quality of *My Brilliant Career* in manuscript wrote to a London publisher about it in 1899, mentioning Schreiner – 'possibly the first occasion Miles Franklin heard of the famous South African writer', notes her biographer, Jill Roe.[42] Lawson called *My Brilliant Career* 'the Australian *African Farm*' when he endorsed the manuscript the following year, introducing Franklin to J. B. Pinker, his London agent. Blackwood in Edinburgh published Franklin's book in 1901 when she was twenty, the same year she actually read *African Farm*. She later called it 'one of the two most exalting novels I read in my girlhood'.[43] The 'brilliant careers' of these two remarkable women would continue to be linked in the minds of Australian readers and critics.

Franklin's next novel *Cockatoos* was set partly in South Africa during the Boer War, a conflict that her female protagonist back home in Australia opposed. Franklin wrote to Pinker that it was 'less outspoken than "the unsurpassable *Story of an African Farm*"'.[44] Later in Chicago, Franklin read Schreiner's *Woman and Labour* (1911), which she found no less powerful with its insights into the paradoxes of 'love and freedom'.[45] Franklin saw her idol in person at a public meeting in London in 1916 when Schreiner 'caused a scene [. . .] and had to be removed'.[46] And, after Schreiner's death, Franklin read Samuel Cronwright-Schreiner's biography of his wife and the letters he published, finding there a 'terrible warning' not to be diverted from the books she needed to write by all the other demands of a committed woman's writing life.[47]

When a new novel, *Old Blastus of Bandicoot*, eventually appeared under Miles Franklin's name in 1932, Nettie Palmer profiled her as 'The "Olive Schreiner" of Australian Literature'.[48] For Palmer, at once Australian nationalist and sophisticated cosmopolitan reader, Franklin had opened the way to Australian writers by following Schreiner's example in breaking through colonial attitudes and 'the cage' of her gender.[49] Moreover, she had done so in an Australian way. Yet Australia had not produced an author of comparable international standing, as was evident as far away as China in a frank assessment by Zhao Jingshen in 1929: 'Taking a closer look at Australia, the country with six million colonized people, however, we will find it even lags behind South Africa when it comes to literature. South Africa has Olive Schreiner, what about Australia?'[50] Zhao would publish Schreiner's *Dreams* in Chinese in Shanghai in 1931.

Henry Handel Richardson might have been mentioned, had Zhao been aware of her. She was a contender for the Nobel Prize in Literature with the international success of *The Fortunes of Richard Mahony*, published as a trilogy in 1930.[51] She was born Ethel Florence Lindesay Richardson in Melbourne in 1870, left Australia in 1888 and returned only once. She married and settled in England, where she died in 1946. *Maurice Guest* was published under her male pseudonym in London in 1908, only a few years after Franklin's *My Brilliant Career*. Richardson admired Schreiner, and *Woman and Labour* became a book she recommended to friends, as Franklin did too.[52] *Maurice Guest* struggled, despite the regard of discerning readers: 'it sits easily nowhere', suggests Carmen Callil in her introduction to the Text Classics edition in 2008, confessing her disappointment at its modest sales when she re-published it as a Virago Modern Classic in 1981.[53] Looking back in 1932, Nettie Palmer noted that it 'had some constant readers, but was hardly known as the work of an Australian'.[54]

Yet the woman at the centre of *Maurice Guest*, Louise Dufrayer, and the enigma at the core of Maurice Guest's tragic obsession, is Australian. Her origins are signalled in minimal but telling ways against the worldly musical background of *fin de siècle* Leipzig. What she is in flight from – its very absence – seems to explain something about the mystery she presents: a child's trauma by her father's grave, the dry, 'empty' land, isolation, singularity, a marked darkness.[55] There is a telling reference to the novels that a visiting American woman is reading: 'A circulating library, rich in English novels, had been discovered; Mrs Cayhill was content'.[56] When Maurice's friend Dove asks how she liked a book he has lent her, she replies:

> 'Let me see, it was ... no, that was yesterday: *Shadowed by Three*, a most delightful book. On Friday, *Richard Elsmere*, and—oh, yes, I know, it was about a farm, an Australian farm.'
> '*The Story of an African Farm*,' put in Dove mildly, returning to his seat.
> 'Australian or African, it doesn't matter which,' said Mrs Cayhill. 'Yes, a nice book, but a little coarse in parts, and very foolish at the end—the disguising, and the dying out of doors, and the looking-glass, and all that.'
> 'I must say I think it is a very powerful book,' said Dove solemnly. 'That part, you know, where the boy listens to the clock ticking in the night, and thinks to himself that with every tick, a soul goes home to God.'
> 'A very striking idea!'[57]

The passage depicts Mrs Cayhill as an up-to-date reader of contemporary fiction by women. The other novels mentioned are *Shadows by Three* (1879), a popular mystery by Lawrence L. Lynch, pseudonym of Emma Van Deventer, set and published in Chicago, and Mrs Humphrey Ward's *Richard Elsmere* (1888), about spiritual conflict. Mrs Cayhill's vagueness about the location of the farm is a memory lapse that makes Australia a version of Africa, while her criticism of Schreiner's novel allows the author of *Maurice Guest* an ironic foreshadowing of what is to come: 'the dying out of doors, and the looking-glass, and all that'.[58] Richardson signals a covert identification with Schreiner and a connection between her Louise and Schreiner's Lyndall. 'There are faint traces of Olive Schreiner's Lyndall in Louise', notes Dorothy Green.[59]

Soon after, as the relationship between Louise and Maurice develops, their mutual friend Madeleine states: 'Louise is a true Southerner', which Louise clarifies as 'I come from Australia':

> If she had said she was a visitant from another world, Maurice would not, at the moment, have felt much surprise; but on hearing the name of this distant land . . . a sense of desolation overcame him. . . .of her past life, her home, her country, he knew, and could know nothing.[60]

Louise is 'wild', 'savage'.[61] When Maurice determines 'to unearth the past', she rages 'I'm not your slave,' accusing him of wanting to 'remake [her] nature and correct it'.[62]

Her abjection is Australian settler-colonial, an acknowledgement, however veiled, of dispossession in the occupation of the land. In this context, Schreiner becomes an illuminating intertextual presence. The prospect of an emancipatory new world to which the novel frequently appeals is shadowed by the *actual* 'new world' from which Louise, restless and alone, is in flight. What remains is a gulf that ends in subjection and self-abasement:

> The real truth, the last-reaching truth about her, it would not be his to know. Soul would never be absorbed in soul; not the most passionate embraces could bridge the gulf; to their last kiss, they would remain separate beings, lonely and alone.[63]

White would find comparable words in *The Story of an African Farm* for the epigraphs to his novel treatment of another singular Australian woman at large in Europe: Theodora Goodman, the eponymous central figure of *The Aunt's Story*:

> *She thought of the narrowness of the limits within which a human soul may speak and be understood by its nearest of mental kin, of how soon it reaches*

that solitary land of the individual experience, in which no fellow footfall is ever heard. When your life is most real, to me you are mad.⁶⁴

2. Afterlife: Patrick White in Africa
The Story of an African Farm *and* The Aunt's Story

Patrick White transcribed the quotations from Schreiner in a wartime journal dated 1941 when he was an intelligence officer stationed with South African pilots in North Africa.⁶⁵ 'In the company of the South Africans, his habitual shyness turned into confidence', writes David Marr: '[t]hey read anything they could lay their hands on'.⁶⁶ White and Lieutenant 'Nick' Nicholas, the young South African officer sent to replace him, overlapped for a time in Eritrea and became friends. Nicholas, who was a reader and a writer too, went on to become Mr Justice Herbert Cecil Nicholas. In the citation for an honorary doctorate from the University of Witwatersrand in Johannesburg, his alma mater, his eloquence at the opening of the Oliver Schreiner Law Library at the university is remembered.⁶⁷ The library was named for the great judge – Olive Schreiner's nephew – who was passed over for the position of Chief Justice for political reasons in 1956 and 1959. Nicholas's speech places himself within the Schreiner family's orbit and indicates an allegiance with aunt and nephew. Did Nicholas introduce White to Schreiner's novel? Was there a copy of the 1939 orange Penguin paperback edition of *African Farm* lying around at Sidi Haneish, a proud example of South African literature that White read with a sense of elective affiliation as he considered his calling?⁶⁸

White later describes his anti-monarchical tendencies developing during his involvement in the allied war effort in North Africa and later Greece, but his politics bear little relation to Schreiner's feminism and socialism.⁶⁹ What, then, drew White to Schreiner's work, and how did he deploy her style and philosophy in his work? *The Aunt's Story* represents a shift in White's style; it is the first of his novels in which he successfully balances descriptions of a protagonist's interior life with descriptions of Australian and émigré social life, a style that characterises the rest of his work. These are also important questions for the study of Schreiner, particularly given recent debates on the place of Schreiner in the modernist canon and for the study of modernism in the colonial world generally.⁷⁰ It is, in short, White's modernist reading of Schreiner that enables his own modernism.

Rejected proposals and failed Bildung

The first part of *The Aunt's Story*, 'Meroë', comprises a condensed farm novella with all the topoi of the genre: rural isolation, thwarted *Bildung*, boarding schools, transformative meetings with strangers, and unfulfilling journeys to urban cultural centres; but the influence of *African Farm*, as opposed to any other farm novel, is most apparent in the protagonist, Theodora Goodman, who is a composite of Waldo and Lyndall. Waldo is the primary model for Theodora though. Both are marked as out-of-place in farm life because of their fixation on their interior worlds. Theodora is maligned and isolated for failing or refusing to ask 'the questions that have answers',[71] just as Waldo is scolded for asking questions about God and nature and beaten for reading J. S. Mill.[72] Theodora and Waldo are marginalised and persecuted, to paraphrase Schreiner's epigraph, for the madness others perceive in them, and their narratives concern their attempts to sustain themselves despite the dictates of farm society.

Lyndall and Theodora are linked by the gendered oppression they face, particularly the expectation of marriage. Both plots stage how marriage would destroy some part of them. Lyndall desires power to effect social change and articulates how marriage strips women of their agency, but ultimately lacks the power to change this social structure.[73] She flees to the Transvaal with her lover in an attempt to find a place where living in free union is possible, but dies after a traumatic childbirth. Theodora, similarly, fends off two suitors with a gun (not by shooting them, but by being a better shot than them) in the knowledge that she could not sustain her selfhood in such a bond.[74]

How these anti-marriage plots end is a crucial difference between *African Farm* and *The Aunt's Story*. Without the power to change the society that oppresses her, but with too much will to submit to it, Lyndall's plot ends unhappily. She dies, for her 'deliberate and principled transgression of the patriarchal code of feminine behaviour'.[75] Conversely, Theodora survives her (anti-)marriage plot and becomes 'that institution, an aunt'.[76] Theodora's modest aims are part of what facilitates this. Theodora never desires to change her world, merely to find a space within it where she can sustain her selfhood. White's primary question is not about marriage nor patriarchy. Instead, Schreiner's thwarted marriage plot offers White a way to reject a traditional marriage and *Bildungsroman* narratives and to open a space to ask: what happens to a character when she rejects her prescribed narrative and social roles?

The modesty of this aim, however, is insufficient to explain Theodora's survival; Waldo, whose preoccupations are similarly interior (intellectual and spiritual) also dies. The other difference between Theodora and Schreiner's protagonists (and between White and Schreiner herself) is access to wealth. Although none of these characters finds a space outside of or different to their oppressive societies, Theodora eventually gains independent means to live on – no longer as a daughter or prospective wife, but as a consumer. Lyndall, conversely, is a poor orphan who can only just afford to go to boarding school. The cyclically structured 'Meroë' begins and ends with Mrs Goodman's death, the moment when what remains of the Goodmans' wealth flows to Theodora. The characters who survive in *African Farm* are only those who inherit or marry into property: Em, Tant' Sannie, Gregory. Their relative security offers them a chance to participate in society and they take it, whereas Lyndall and Waldo are never offered this possibility of reconciliation, even if they would accept it. (We might add here that the source of wealth, in both novels, is stolen land in the settler-colonies). We can, however, hardly say Theodora uses her inheritance to participate in her society; rather, she sets about exhausting it. The individual's struggle with isolation and the need to protect individuality underlie Theodora's rejection of the marriage plot (rather than the emphasis on material and historical change found in Schreiner's *Woman and Labour*).

These themes, epitomised in the epigraphs from *African Farm* chosen by White, suggest their intense interest to the young homosexual man and ambitious creative writer. How was he to live? Like the artist Roy de Maistre and his other queer friends in London? But if not London, then where? Or entirely closeted? White's anti-marriage plot in *The Aunt's Story* can be read as a repressed closet narrative. This returns in *The Solid Mandala* (1966), in which the unmarried twins Arthur and Waldo live out their psychically split lives together, and 'comes out' in the tripartite *Twyborn Affair* (1979), in which Eddie/Eudoxia/Eadith is explicitly non-binary. In *The Aunt's Story*, years before White wrote about homosexuality directly, it was Schreiner's philosophical style and subversion of narrative tropes – applied to his class position and sexuality – that enabled him to write about and sublimate these themes.

Living with the epigraphs

In parts two and three of *The Aunt's Story*, 'Jardin Exotique' and 'Holstius', White leaves the farm novel behind, but Schreiner's ghost still looms over the language and philosophy of the text. 'Jardin' and 'Holstius' test where *African Farm* could have gone if it did not end, and take up a question implicit in the epigraphs: how can one sustain selfhood when the reality of that selfhood appears to others as madness?

How can one live among others when the limits in which a soul may speak and be understood are vanishingly narrow? Inhabiting these lines from Schreiner, White develops the style he will use to answer these questions and describe Australian life throughout his career.

In 'Jardin', Theodora uses her inheritance to stay in a cheap hotel in provincial France. There she imagines herself, and is imagined, into the lives of other guests – but her imaginary lives never take her beyond social roles she could, as an unmarried woman in the 1930s, be assigned. She becomes a nursemaid, a lady-in-waiting, and the sister of a White Russian General. Despite the proximity of these imaginary lives to her own, she never gains purchase in any of the other characters' minds; outside of her imaginings, the other guests at the hotel seldom address her by either her imagined or real names. Theodora's imaginary lives, and their unintelligibility to those around her, exemplify 'the narrowness of the limits within which a human soul may speak and be understood'.[77]

To ask questions about the narrow limits of selfhood, White appropriates the syntax in which Schreiner articulates them. Both novels' narrators break from narrative to offer aphoristic philosophical speculations. What we might call Schreiner's aphoristic syntax tends to employ general pronouns: the 'you' of 'to me you are mad'.[78] The sentences slip into the present tense. The epigraphs also tend to speak in abstractions ('narrowness of the limits') or metaphors ('solitary land'), and in the passive voice ('where no fellow footfall is ever heard').[79] None of these are necessary to generate Schreiner's aphoristic style, and none of them alone are sufficient; rather, a shifting array of them produces the style. These sentences are non-narrative; they transcend the temporality of their stories and cannot incontestably be attributed to any character's consciousness.

Schreiner did not, of course, invent the aphorism, and White's 1939–41 notebook, from before his reading of *African Farm*, contains a list of his own aphorisms.[80] What *African Farm* offers him however is a model for integrating aphorisms into narration, for narrativising questions of the limits of selfhood that fall beyond the limits of plot. For example, as Theodora walks along an esplanade with Sokolnikov, not yet talking and never managing to communicate when they do (and so not un-reminiscent of the passages in which Schreiner's epigraphs are originally uttered, where, for example, Lyndall has just attempted and failed to explain her political philosophy to Waldo),[81] White's narrator writes: 'The most one can expect from the led life is for it to be lit occasionally by a flash of wonder, which does not bear questioning, it is its own light'.[82] In both novels, the narrators turn to aphorism when characters fail to communicate. Both novels also use aphorism to speak of the unintelligibility of the self. Indeed, White seems to suggest that one's life also is unintelligible not only to others but also to oneself. The aphoristic style, detachable from any characters' consciousness, can thus articulate what they cannot. If we are to content ourselves with 'the led life' or the narrow limits, they will not bear questioning, and yet the style White appropriates from Schreiner allows readers to begin that questioning.

The last part of *The Aunt's Story* sees Theodora flee war torn Europe for another settler-colonial hinterland: New Mexico. Like Lyndall, she finds that even on the fringes of the colonies she cannot escape limiting social expectations. Theodora squats in an abandoned house on a mountain, where she communes with Holstius, the first of her imaginary figures who appears as a consciousness distinct from her own, and the first who is not an unmarried woman. We can read Holstius as the product of Theodora's imaginative agency; we can also read him as a symptom of her insanity. He is proof of Schreiner's lines: 'When your life is most real, to me you are mad', and this ambivalence concludes the novel.[83] Neighbours bring a doctor to institutionalise Theodora – to subject her to a psychiatric regime whose aim is to restructure her interiority. The reader, then, is left with the question of whether, given all we know about Theodora, her sense of self can subsist under this extreme limit case.

The narrative poses this question through Holstius, who speaks in the style of Schreiner's epigraphs: '[T]here is sometimes', he says, 'little to choose between the reality of illusion and the illusion of reality. Each of your several lives is evidence of this',[84] and warns her to keep these selves 'under our hats'.[85] Holstius's monologues can be read as extrapolations on the *African Farm* epigraphs, but to their exposition of the unintelligible self, they add this: Theodora must remain unintelligible to others, must keep the truth of herself under her hat if she is to survive institutionalisation. It is precisely the unintelligibility of the self that Schreiner's epigraphs deal with that may make it possible for Theodora to sustain her selfhood and for White to conclude his novel.

Confort moderne *in the colonies*

Marr traces the genealogy of White's modernism to D. H. Lawrence, Gertrude Stein and James Joyce.[86] White's indirect interior style, however, is first successfully realised in *The Aunt's Story* and emerges as much from his reading of Schreiner as from his antecedents in the Euro-American modernist canon. White described the stream-of-consciousness of *Happy Valley*, which bears the influence of Joyce and Stein more evidently than anywhere else in his work, as a 'cul de sac'.[87] This text imports an urban modernism – the polyphony of voices on the street in Paris and Dublin – to the Australian highlands, where one can still walk all day without hearing another human voice. In *African Farm*, White finds a model for voice and characterisation that can describe an alienated, modern and colonial subjectivity – an isolation that develops on the farm and that follows both Schreiner and White's protagonists wherever they go. Thus, the aspects of White's writing that we so often call modernist are influenced by his reading of Schreiner, down to the very sentence structure.

The influence of Schreiner also complicates another commonplace about White's style. White himself claims returning to Australia restored 'the colours' to his work and incepted the style that characterised the rest of his literary career.[88] This would mean that his mature style begins with *The Tree of Man*, the first novel he wrote after returning to Australia. His mature style, however – which balances descriptions of social life in the settler-colonies with isolated interior lives – develops in *The Aunt's Story* and, in part, because of his reading *African Farm* while serving with South Africans in the RAF in North Africa in 1941, seven years before his return to Australia. His imagery of Australia owes as much to Schreiner's Karoo as to his surroundings at Castle Hill. White's Australia abounds in African imagery; Theodora's childhood home in Australia 'Meroë', for example, is named for an ancient city on the Nile. This is not to underestimate the impact of the Australian landscape on his work, but rather to suggest the equal importance of his connection to literary and aesthetic life in other colonies, producing a provincial cosmopolitanism.

3. Conclusion: Into Solitary Lands

We might describe Schreiner and the Australian writers who drew influence from her work as 'nearest of mental kin [in] solitary lands'.[89] Separated by the Indian Ocean and by generations, each of these writers finds permission in Schreiner's work to narrate aspects of colonial life, and particularly of women's experience therein. Yet what Schreiner's fertilising work permits differs from writer to writer. For Martin, the style offers a way to inject philosophical and intellectual speculations into a narrative of colonial life while rejecting the romantic and vocational certainties of the European *Bildungsroman*; for Richardson, *African Farm* provides a model of the intellectual frustrations of colonials;

and for White, it becomes a way to narrate the unintelligibility and alienation of his characters. Beginning from *African Farm*, each of these writers soon reaches 'that solitary land of the individual experience, in which no fellow footfall is ever heard'.[90] The proximity recognised in Schreiner's world allowed Australian authors to find ways to narrate their own.

Acknowledgement

Our special thanks to Susan Sheridan for her inspiration, encouragement and guidance in this project, including many suggestions that we have gratefully taken on board. We also wish to thank Margaret Allen, Dorothy Driver and Susan Magarey, colleagues at the University of Adelaide in whose steps we follow, and all those in the University's Department of English, Creative Writing, and Film who have contributed to this research. Finally, we thank our editors Jade Munslow Ong and Andrew van der Vlies for conceiving this publication and inviting us in.

Works Cited

'Why Do Women Wilt!' *South Australian Register*, 11 December 1889.
Allen, Margaret. *Catherine Martin's Library*. Canberra: Mulini Press, 2002.
—. '"To put on record, as faithfully as possible": Catherine Martin (1847–1937)'. In *Uncommon Ground: White Women in Aboriginal History*, edited by Fiona Paisley, Anna Cole and Vicki Haskins, 241–56. Canberra: Aboriginal Studies Press, 2005.
Anon., 'Reviews.' *The Englishwoman's Review of Social and Industrial Questions* 124 (1883): 362–64.
—. 'Three Controversial Novels'. *Church Quarterly Review* 29 (1890). In *Olive Schreiner*, edited by Cherry Clayton, 74–75. Johannesburg: McGraw-Hill, 1983.
Ash, Bay. 'Olive Schreiner'. *The Australian Worker* (6 January 1921). Accessed 4 April 2022. http://nla.gov.au/nla.news-article145771861.
Barnard, E. L. 'Bookselling from 1880 to 1896 in Western Australia'. *The West Australian*, 13 May 1950, 22.
Boake, Capel. *Painted Clay*. London: Virago, 1986.
Bradstock, Margaret. 'Landscape and Environment in the Novels of Catherine Martin'. *Margin: Life and Letters in Early Australia* 36 (1995): 12–14.
Brantlinger, Patrick. *Dark Vanishings*. New York: Cornell University Press, 2013.
Cruse, Amy. *The Victorians and Their Books*. London: George Allen & Unwin, 1935.

Davidson, Jim. 'Also Under the Southern Cross: Federation Australia and South Africa – The Boer War and Other Interactions.' *Journal of Australian Colonial History* 14 (2012): 183–204.
Drooglever, R. W. F. (ed.). *From the Front: A. B. (Banjo) Paterson's Despatches from the Boer War*. Sydney: Macmillan, 2000.
Dutton, Geoffrey. *Kanga Creek: Havelock Ellis in Australia*. Sydney: Pan Books, 1989.
Franklin, Miles. *My Brilliant Career*. Sydney: Allen & Unwin, 2012.
Green, Dorothy. *Ulysses Bound: Henry Handel Richardson and Her Fiction*. Canberra: Australian National University Press, 1973.
Handel Richardson, Henry. *Maurice Guest*. Melbourne: Text Publishing, 2008.
—. *The Letters, Volume 2: 1874–1915*, edited by Clive Probyn and Bruce Steele. Melbourne: The Miegunyah Press, 2000.
Havelock Ellis, Henry. 'Fiction in the Australian Bush (1903)'. Reprint, *Kanga Creek: Havelock Ellis in Australia*, edited by Geoffrey Dutton. Sydney: Picador, 1989.
—. *Kanga Creek*. Melbourne: Nelson, 1970.
—. *My Life*. London: Neville Spearman, 1967.
Magarey, Susan. *Passions of the First-Wave Feminists*. Sydney: Pluto Press, 2001.
—. *Ever Yours C. H. Spence: Catherine Helen Spence's An Autobiography (1825–1910), Diary (1894) and Some Correspondence (1894–1910)*. Adelaide: Wakefield Press, 2005.
—. *Unbridling the Tongues of Women: A Biography of Catherine Helen Spence*. Adelaide: University of Adelaide Press, 2010.
Marr, David. *Patrick White: A Life*. Australia: Random House, 1991.
—. *Patrick White: Letters*. Australia: Random House, 1994.
Martin, Catherine. *An Australian Girl*, edited by Graham Tulloch. 2nd ed. Oxford: Oxford University Press, 1999.
—. *An Australian Girl*, edited by Rosemary Campbell. Queensland: University of Queensland Press, 2002.
Munslow Ong, Jade. *Olive Schreiner and African Modernism: Allegory, Empire and Postcolonial Writing*. London: Routledge, 2017.
Nicholas, Herbert Cecil. Honorary Graduate. University of Witwatersrand.
Roe, Jill. *Searching for the Spirit: Theosophy in Australia, 1879–1939*. Adelaide: Wakefield Press, 2020.
—. *Stella Miles Franklin*. Sydney: Fourth Estate, 2008.
Schreiner, Olive. *Dreams*. London: T. Fisher Unwin, 1895.
—. *The Story of an African Farm*. London: Penguin, 1971.
—. 'The Buddhist Priest's Wife'. In *Women Who Did: Stories by Men and Women, 1890–1914*, edited by Angelique Richardson, 9–20. London: Penguin, 2002.
—. *Woman and Labour*. London: T. Fisher Unwin, 1911.
Sheridan, Susan. *Along the Faultlines: Sex, Race and Nation in Australian Women's Writing, 1880s–1930s*. Sydney: Allen & Unwin, 1995.
—. 'Love and Ideology: Feminism and British Fiction, 1880–1950'. PhD diss., University of Adelaide, 1978.
—. Personal communication, email, 20 March 2022.
—. 'White Women Writing in the Contact Zone: Catherine Martin and Nancy Cato'. *Australian Feminist Studies* 27, no. 73 (2012): 249–57.

Smith, Vivian. *Nettie Palmer*. St Lucia: University of Queensland Press, 1988.
Treagus, Mandy. *Empire Girls*. Adelaide: Adelaide University Press, 2014.
White, Patrick. *Flaws in the Glass*. London: Penguin, 1981.
—. 'Notebook, including material for *Happy Valley* (1939), *The Living and the Dead* (1941), *The Aunt's Story* (1948) and *Voss* (1957), c. 1939–1941'. *The Papers of Patrick White*, National Library of Australia. Accessed 2 February 2022. https://nla.gov.au/nla.obj-224191956/findingaid?digitised=y#nla-obj-224192872.
—. *The Aunt's Story*. London: Penguin, 1963.
—. 'The Prodigal Son'. In *The Literature of Australia*, edited by Nicholas Jose, 557–60. New York: Norton. 2009.
—. 'War Journal, including material for *The Aunt's Story* (1948), c. 1941'. *The Papers of Patrick White*, National Library of Australia. Accessed 6 January 2021. https://nla.gov.au/nla.obj-224191956/findingaid?digitised=y#nla-obj-224192872.
White, Captain S. A. 'Olive Schreiner'. *The Adelaide Register*, 13 January 1921.
Wilde, William, Joy Hooton and Barry Andrews (eds). 'Martin, C. E. M. (Catherine Edith Macauley Martin)'. In *Oxford Companion to Australian Literature*. 2nd ed. Oxford: Oxford Reference, 1994. Accessed 1 February 2022.
Zhao, Jingshen. 'Modern Australian Literature'. *Short Story Press* 12, no. 1 (1921): 325–26. (Unpublished translation by Liu Shusen, personal communication, email).

Letters

Olive Schreiner to Havelock Ellis, 18 August 1885. *Olive Schreiner Letters Online*.

Notes

1. Green, *Ulysses Bound*, 177.
2. Drooglever, *From the Front*, 126; see also Davidson, 'Also Under the Southern Cross', 183–204.
3. Drooglever, *From the Front*, 127.
4. White, S. A., 'Olive Schreiner'.
5. Barnard, 'Bookselling', 22.
6. Sheridan, *Along the Faultlines*, 285.
7. Boake, *Painted Clay*, 284.
8. Ash, 'Obituary', 13. 'Bay Ash' is a pseudonym of Mary E. Lloyd; *The Australian Worker* was edited by the poet and journalist Mary Gilmore (1865–1962) (Susan Sheridan, personal communication, email, 20 March 2022).
9. In *Passions of the First Wave Feminists*, for example, Susan Magarey writes about the importance of Schreiner's allegories for Australian feminists: Maybanke Anderson quoted Schreiner in *The Woman's Voice*, the feminist newspaper she edited in Sydney, and cited 'Three Dreams' in a letter

to eminent feminist Rose Scott as a reminder of what 'their' first-wave feminism aspired to and achieved (67, 177, 179–84). Edna Ryan read Schreiner, Edward Carpenter and Havelock Ellis as a young Communist in Sydney in the 1920s, and named her daughter – now a distinguished historian – Lyndall (Ryan) (Sheridan, personal communication, email, 20 March 2022); Roe, *Searching for the Spirit*, 263.
10. Magarey, *Passions*, 42.
11. Spence, 'Why Do Women Wilt!' 6.
12. Spence, 'Why Do Women Wilt!' 6. See also Magarey, *Unbridling the Tongues of Women*, 145. In her diary for 3 March 1894 Spence writes: 'Read some stories by Olive Schreiner—very sad'. Magarey, *Ever Yours C. H.*, 248. Magarey notes that the 'stories' were probably 'Three Dreams in a Desert' (1887).
13. Spence, 'Why Do Women Wilt!' 6.
14. In tracing Martin's library, Margaret Allen found some 200 volumes, but speculates that Martin's itinerant lifestyle meant that her library was probably much larger and later divided across households. See Allen, *Catherine Martin's Library*, 5.
15. Campbell, 'Introduction', xlii.
16. L. Lawson, quoted in Sheridan, 'Wives and Mothers Like Ourselves', 77; Brantlinger, *Dark Vanishings*. Both note the widespread nineteenth-century understanding that the more 'primitive' races would inevitably die out in contact with Europeans.
17. Allen, 'To Put on Record', 254; Sheridan, 'White Women', 250.
18. See Treagus, *Empire Girls*, 37, 54–55.
19. Wilde, Hooton and Andrews, *Oxford Companion to Australian Literature*, 464.
20. See Schreiner, *Woman and Labour*.
21. Martin, *Australian Girl*, 188.
22. Martin, *Australian Girl*, 89.
23. Cruse, *The Victorians*, 363.
24. Wilde, Hooton and Andrews, *Oxford Companion to Australian Literature*, 464.
25. Martin, *Australian Girl*, 429.
26. Anon, 'Three Controversial Novels,' 75.
27. Schreiner, *African Farm*, 102; Martin, *Australian Girl*, 337.
28. Martin, *Australian Girl*, 615–16.
29. Martin, *Australian Girl*, 612.
30. Treagus, *Empire Girls*, 108.
31. Dutton, *Kanga Creek*, 15.
32. Ellis, *My Life*, 138–9.
33. Ellis, *My Life*, 182.
34. Schreiner to Havelock Ellis, 18 August 1885, *Olive Schreiner Letters Online*.
35. Dutton, *Kanga Creek*, 97.
36. Ellis, *My Life*, 182.
37. Ellis, *Kanga Creek*, xiii.
38. Dutton, *Kanga Creek*, 163–64.
39. Dutton, *Kanga Creek*, 231–34.
40. Dutton, *Kanga Creek*, 231–34.

41. Dutton, *Kanga Creek*, 231–34.
42. Roe, *Stella*, 57.
43. Roe, *Stella*, 36.
44. Roe, *Stella*, 83.
45. Roe, *Stella*, 150, 157.
46. Roe, *Stella*, 205.
47. Roe, *Stella*, 276.
48. Smith, *Nettie Palmer*, 419.
49. Smith, *Nettie Palmer*, 419, 421.
50. Zhao, 'Modern Australian Literature'.
51. Smith, *Nettie Palmer*, 405.
52. Richardson, *Letters*, 483; Roe, *Stella*, 465.
53. Richardson, *Maurice Guest*, vii.
54. Richardson, *Maurice Guest*, vii; Smith, *Nettie Palmer*, 416.
55. Richardson, *Maurice Guest*, 114, 387, 471–72.
56. Richardson, *Maurice Guest*, 83.
57. Richardson, *Maurice Guest*, 88.
58. Richardson, *Maurice* Guest, 88.
59. Green, *Ulysses Bound*, 177.
60. Richardson, *Maurice Guest*, 114.
61. Richardson, *Maurice Guest*, 512, 503.
62. Richardson, *Maurice Guest*, 479.
63. Richardson, *Maurice Guest*, 528.
64. White, *The Aunt's Story*, 9, 263; Dorothy Driver notes that White omits 'perhaps' from the start of the first quotation. For many Australian readers in recent decades, White's novel was a first introduction to Schreiner. (Personal testimony, Driver; personal testimony Sheridan, Jose and Sutcliffe.)
65. White, 'War Journal', 83.
66. Marr, *Patrick White: A Life*, 210.
67. Nicholas, Honorary Graduate, 11.
68. Nicholas kept a diary in which he writes about White. 'Diary in possession of the Hon. Mr Justice H. C. Nicholas', notes Marr, *Life*, 677. Its present whereabouts are unknown.
69. White, *Flaws in the Glass*, 106.
70. See Munslow Ong, *Olive Schreiner and African Modernism*.
71. White, *The Aunt's Story*, 42.
72. Schreiner, *African Farm*, 112, 125.
73. Schreiner, *African Farm*, 93, 190.
74. White, *The Aunt's Story*, 74, 124.
75. Sheridan, 'Love and Ideology,' 57.
76. White, *The Aunt's Story*, 12.
77. Schreiner, *African Farm*, 196.
78. Schreiner, *African Farm*, 102.
79. Schreiner, *African Farm*, 196.
80. White's 1939–41 aphorisms are not always as profound as Schreiner's; for example, he writes, 'Sex is one of the more fascinating subjects on earth, even to those who profess not to be interested'. See White, 'Notebook', 58.
81. Schreiner, *African Farm*, 196.

82. White, *The Aunt's Story*, 186.
83. Schreiner, *African Farm*, 102.
84. White, *The Aunt's Story*, 289.
85. White, *The Aunt's Story*, 295.
86. Marr, *Patrick White: A Life*, 151.
87. White, quoted in Marr, *Patrick White: A Life*, 151.
88. White, 'The Prodigal Son', 559.
89. Schreiner, *African Farm*, 196.
90. Schreiner, *African Farm*, 196.

Part V

South African Afterlives

Chapter 13

Passing It On: Olive Schreiner and Bessie Head
Dorothy Driver

On 3 January 1881, working as a governess on a Karoo farm, Schreiner made a brief diary entry about an occasion that would turn out to be momentous for her life and her writing, and also for what the editors of this collection of essays have called her afterlife:

> This afternoon I helped the poor coloured woman in the road when her baby was born. Mrs Fouché [her employer] wouldn't even give bread and sugar. I sent her my shawl [. . .] I hope I cut the string quite right.[1]

Seven years later she returned to the episode in a letter that accentuates the emergence of the new:

> There is always something so beautiful to me in the thought of a new little life coming into the world. [. . .] The first time I saw a birth it was a halfcaste prostitute at the Cape, who had lain down in her labour behind a hedge. None of the Boer women or black women would go near her, and I helped an old black *man*! It was so wonderful and beautiful to see that little new life coming out under a blue sky just like this, and a little older child of the woman's of two years old sat watching. I often wonder what has become of that little baby I brought into the world![2]

To respond to Schreiner's question about 'that little baby' turns out to be enormously productive both in relation to her own writing and to the manner in which it might be said to relate to Bessie Head's, generations later. The 'little ["halfcaste"] baby' reappears not only in Schreiner's novel, *From Man to Man* (1926) but also, arguably, in Head's novel *Maru* (1971). Its presence in Schreiner's novel helped develop the general theme of 'passing it on', as well as seeming both to signify a limit Schreiner could not overcome and to foreground her white character's sense of 'the coming dawn after the dark'.[3] In these regards Head's *Maru* seems to have been invoked by *From Man to Man* – or perhaps it is the later novel that re-invokes the earlier one through insisting on its re-reading.

Schreiner began *From Man to Man* in 1873 (under different titles and in a different form), and was still struggling to complete it twenty years later. The 'halfcaste' child was a late addition. In its earlier form, the novel had centred on 'the story of a prostitute & of a married woman who loves another man, & whose husband is sensual & unfaithful'.[4] Later, it came to include the white husband's infidelity with a Black domestic servant; this figure, named Clartje, appears in an 1886–87 manuscript fragment.[5] And now, in or by 1908, Schreiner introduced a new plot element derived in part from the 1881 diarised event. She did so at a time of increasing despair for her, largely on account of the treatment by colonial British and Boers of indigenous South Africans, treatment that would in due course come to its ominous conclusion with the Act of Union of 1910. Renaming the child as 'half-coloured' in a North American style that recalls her reading of W. E. B. Du Bois and its effect on her,[6] she explained the new narrative to her younger brother William (he had been Prime Minister of the Cape during the Anglo-Boer War and was still an influential MP):

> In my small way I am doing what I can. [. . .] [O]ne of the centre points of the story is that the wife has adopted & brings up as her own among the legitimate children a little half-coloured child who is her husbands [sic] by a coloured servant. [. . .] You will of course see how this opens up the whole question of our relation to the darker races, & the attitude which says "they are here for <u>our</u> interest [and] for our <u>pleasure</u>, & to hell with them when they aren't that!"[7]

In contrast to the husband's lack of concern and even distaste for his illegitimate offspring, the wife, Rebekah, assumes responsibility for the child, bringing her up alongside her four sons though under instructions to call her 'mistress'.[8] She educates the children through allegorical, often evolutionary, tales meant to usher them into a mode of thinking much like Schreiner's own: a thinking we can call – with a firm eye on the context of the time – feminist, anti-imperialist, anti-colonial, socialist, anti-racist. During one story-telling episode, Rebekah wears a black evening dress covered with star-shaped sequins that Sartje, the foster-child, occupies herself by counting, her eyes fuller of dreams than her white foster-mother's eyes.[9] The reference to dreams is central to the plot's unfolding and its embedded theme of passing it on, and will be central to the notion of Head as Schreiner's afterlife being developed in this essay.

So, too, in the case of Schreiner's theme of limitation. Responding to the refusal uttered by one of her sons to be seen with Sartje in public, Rebekah asks the boys to imagine *themselves* with 'tinted' skins, degraded, humiliated and overcome by a group of self-announced superior white invaders. She tells the boys the choice they have: passively waiting or fighting for change. When she pauses, one of her sons urges her to go on. Rebekah can only say: 'The dream ends there'.[10] And towards the end of the narrative, much in the manner of E. M. Forster's 'not yet',[11] this white foster-mother finds herself still stuck in a South African scene in which Sartje cannot freely walk the city streets, and certainly not with a white man.

Into this moment, half a century later, Head's writing intervenes. *Maru* portrays an outcast mother giving birth to a child on the outskirts of a Botswana village just before she dies. When, the following morning, no assistance is forthcoming from others (who shrink from touching the 'untouchable'), passers-by call on the missionaries, 'not' – Head adds acerbically – 'that the missionaries really liked to be involved with mankind'.[12] The white male missionary shows no interest, but his wife adopts and brings up the child, who, somewhat like Sartje in *From Man to Man*, will outstrip her foster-mother in imaginative power. Her eyes, moreover, are said to be 'as pretty as stars'.[13] This novel enters a realm Schreiner's did not, charting the transformation of the foster-child's dreams into art as well as their role in political reform.

Since several moments in Head's fiction, essays and correspondence rehearse 'allegories of self',[14] it is not difficult to imagine the birth and adoption scene in *Maru* as simply a version of Head's own birth and early childhood, offered in reaction to the narrative provided her from a racist South Africa. Certainly, the little she knew about the circumstances of her conception and birth had yelled 'outcast' to her (she was to be told that her father was 'a native', and her mother 'white' and 'insane'), as had her upbringing and education under apartheid.[15] Moreover, Head records in an autobiographical essay that her reading and drawing had been encouraged by a white teacher at the Anglican Mission orphanage, whose advice about sketching, Head noted, served as a metaphor for advice about writing as well: from 'harsh outlines' to 'soft, round curves'.[16] In *Maru*, Head uses the teacher's name – Margaret Cadmore – for the character, and has this figure pass on her own name to the foster-child, much as Head herself inherited her biological mother's name.

However, in the interests of 'afterlife' – which is to say, of a retrospective critical creation of an 'afterlife' – it is worth pursuing the former possibility: Head's identification as Schreiner's 'halfcaste' child, but with her own assertive exploration of a future freedom. Head had possibly seen or heard of Schreiner's diary entry, for it was quoted in the first of four brief essays on Schreiner published in 1955 in *New Age*,[17] a radical anti-apartheid broadsheet written, according to its imprint page, 'from the viewpoint of advanced democracy and Non-European liberation' and ardently read in Cape Town's District Six, where Head lived and worked in the late 1950s and early 60s. Moreover, Head's conceptualisation of her own writing and of her status as an author was bound up with Schreiner's, for when others spoke of her as Schreiner's 'reincarnation' she responded with pleasure.[18] And, as will be detailed in due course, she also referred in interviews to the relation between herself and Schreiner as if she were, indeed, her metaphorical 'reincarnation'.

One can only speculate how much these references stemmed from Head's own reading of Schreiner and how much they were shaped by the suggestions of others, critics and interviewers who were themselves readers of Schreiner and thus part of the earlier writer's afterlife. Nothing can be certain in this regard. But, still, the question of 'afterlife' leads us to ask how a literary 'tradition' is formed: how writing (and its meaning) is transmitted from one generation to the next. Furthermore, re-reading Head *after* Schreiner not only poses questions about how Head is to be positioned in a literary tradition already partially developed by Schreiner-Head critics; it also invites us to re-read Schreiner herself, and – crucially – to do so as if through Head's (imagined) eyes. The latter practice alerts us to the deepest of readerly contingencies, destabilising any notion of a final 'truth' in the act of reading. How, for instance – one might ask of the diary entry – would 'we' (the *we* produced as part of both Schreiner's and Head's afterlife) hear the young Schreiner's tone? As helpful and motherly, or as proprietorial, triumphalist? Might Head have heard the latter tone embedded in Rebekah's stance? And what might she have felt more generally when she came upon those of Schreiner's racial stereotypes reproduced in the writings she had access to? How would her pleasure at being called Schreiner's 'reincarnation' square with the intense hatred and rage she so vehemently expressed towards white South Africans? What purchase, in the end, is there in considering Head as Schreiner's 'afterlife'? And what benefits, and what risks, incur in using the term across so apparently gaping a cultural divide?

* * *

Betty McGinnis Fradkin, a US scholar who interviewed Head in 1975 (and was researching Schreiner's writing too), was not the first to speak to her about similarities between the two authors. Planning her Botswana visit, she wrote to Head:

> When people compare you to Olive it's certainly not in style of writing, it's a fierce, free way you both have. My theory is that it goes back to a rootless childhood in both cases, but you'll clear that up.[19]

In framing the published interview, Fradkin named the affinity in surprisingly close terms: Head as 'sister (or daughter?)' to Schreiner.[20] Beyond the shared childhood rootlessness, she gleaned a similarity in their adult experience of draining demands from others.[21] Fradkin also intimated a further literary likeness: both authors were concerned with 'the higher direction democracy and friendship and love would take in the future'.[22]

Head might have been influenced by such assessments, but in two later interviews she develops her own line. First, speaking to Jean Marquard in December 1976 about having 'much in common with Schreiner', and specifically of their shared 'pioneering role', she adds a crucial distinction.[23] Both she and Schreiner, Head notes, lived at a time of historical transition, thus both were concerned with questions about the future; but hers – she remarks – were to do with African independence, while Schreiner's remained particularly 'South African'.[24] A few years later, in 1983, Head extends this point to confirm her own discrete position. Prompted to amplify her comments to Marquard, she claims not 'quite remember[ing]' speaking of the similarity of their tasks, Schreiner's in South Africa, hers in Botswana, and notes, rather, that she had been categorised 'as the Olive Schreiner of South Africa'.[25] One of the interviewers corrects her: surely the 'Olive Schreiner of Botswana'? No, Head emphatically repeats: she has been called the 'Olive Schreiner of South Africa' instead.[26]

Offered an alternative position by these more recent interviewers, Head thus makes what I take to be an assertive choice of her own. Startling though it is to hear her imaginatively re-locate herself in the country she felt had never been home – denied a South African passport, issued only with an exit permit, she even rejected the label 'exile'[27] – we need to ask what positioning herself thus might have meant for her (and might mean for us). The one epithet suggests mere repetition: to be honoured simply as the first English novelist from Botswana, as was Schreiner in South Africa, for example. But the preferred one – the 'Schreiner of South Africa' – shows her taking Schreiner's place *as a South African*, and in the process redefining South Africa itself: as a country hospitable to a writer such as herself, and placed in so honoured a position as Schreiner had occupied before her. As this essay will suggest, then, Head redefines what it means to be 'South African' by including 'Africa' within it, letting the fact of African independence *and* a Black woman writer's autonomy reincarnate the country itself.

Before pursuing the aesthetic and political implications of Head's cross-ethnic and transnational re-positioning, it is worth noting how precarious critical views can be. Readers familiar with the views of the literary critics hitherto occupied with the Schreiner-Head relation, namely Cherry Clayton, Christopher Heywood, Robin Visel, and Jade Munslow Ong,[28] will have spotted key differences. Writing across changing times, and Writing across changing times, and coming from varying sociological and intellectual milieux, and perhaps even with different axes to grind, the specificity of each position calls attention to different ways of understanding how 'afterlife' crosses geographical and ethnic lines. So, too, with my own critical position: a white South African critic not only long removed from the country Schreiner and Head were born into, unfamiliar with the country Head resided in and mostly wrote of and also distanced – generationally or politically or both – from a milieu that is in some cases dismissive of Head as not quite 'African', whatever she herself claimed. I refer in the latter regard both to Lewis Nkosi's assertion that Head's 'vision of a "power-hungry" and "exclusive" Africa' was 'rooted in her insecurity as a mulatto',[29] and to L. J. Rafapa, A. Z. Nengoma and H. S. Tshamano's seemingly related comment about Head's 'superiority complex towards the Batswana black Africans' (she saw herself as 'more attractive').[30] Mompoloki Bagwasi, publishing in Botswana, has further argued that Head was ignorant of the 'culture of the people she [was] writing about'.[31] Such claims come in contrast not only to any argument about Head's precocious line in the politics of difference (an argument made by Desirée Lewis, a leading South African feminist and author of a pathbreaking book on Head). It also contrasts with Leloba Molema's forthright comment from Botswana: Head uncovered 'certain special, unspoken-of peculiarities of our seemingly placid society'; 'we disclaimed her contentions publicly to save face, but we cannot disclaim them privately to ourselves without being guilty of self-deceit and hypocrisy'.[32]

***

None of the four critics who have hitherto compared Schreiner and Head investigate the extent to which Head might have known Schreiner's writing. Much would have been uncertain: Head spoke in 1983 – in an interview published in 1986 – of owning only *African Farm* and Uys Krige's *Olive Schreiner: A Selection*.[33] She singled out simply Schreiner's political writings for comment (she announced them as 'very attractive').[34] Moreover, when in essays she named the writers and thinkers she most admired, she did not include Schreiner. She referred generously and often extensively to European writers – Bertolt Brecht, Doris Lessing, D. H. Lawrence, Boris Pasternak, Fyodor Dostoevsky and others – but when she listed 'the greats of southern African literature', she first quoted a colleague's selection – Sol T. Plaatje, S. M. Molema,

C. L. S. Nyembezi – and then settled on Plaatje, Robert Sobukwe and Steve Biko as her own. These were the figures who carried forward, for her, the 'theme of continuous growth' so important to her vision of humanity.[35]

Head would have accessed Schreiner's political essays through Krige's *Selection*, which included other material too, but she acquired this book, along with *African Farm*, only after publishing her first trilogy, *When Rain Clouds Gather* (1968), *Maru*, and *A Question of Power* (1974). Although she tells Fradkin she had had 'no contact with [Schreiner's] ideas' before Fradkin sent Krige, she speaks of having read 'a lot of by-the-way articles on her', including an essay Nadine Gordimer published 'in a magazine some time ago' (this would have been in 1959).[36] She may also have heard something of Schreiner in Durban in the mid-50s, perhaps via the influential teacher recalled in *Maru*, or, as suggested earlier, from reading *New Age* in District Six. Moreover, her wider social circle included the writer and literary scholar Richard Rive, who officially began research on Schreiner only in 1971 but would have been acquainted with her work during the 1950s and 60s.[37]

The year 1955 had brought widespread observances of the centenary of Schreiner's birth. The four short *New Age* pieces on Schreiner by the left-wing activist Michael Harmel, published in the independent weekly, *New Age*, were gathered into a centenary booklet, with its cover page announcing Schreiner in the following manner: 'South Africa's greatest creative writer was a fearless fighter for human rights, for the equality of all men and women'.[38] For Harmel, Schreiner was 'a revolutionary by nature and intellectual conviction'.[39] In overwhelmingly positive prose verging on the hagiographic, he praised her 'materialist and dialectical philosophy' and her 'ceaseless struggles [. . .] for the rights of workers and the non-European people'.[40] Such terms would have attracted Head, selling her own newsletter from the doorway of the Stakesby Lewis Hostel: this building was named for Schreiner's older sister, Henrietta (Ettie), married into the Stakesby Lewis family, and known throughout South Africa in the last decades of the nineteenth century as a public speaker and social worker. Over 10,000 people attended her funeral in Cape Town in 1912.[41]

Harmel summarised *From Man to Man*, his favourite among Schreiner's writings.[42] The passages he quoted are largely from Rebekah's allegories in which Schreiner's views are writ large. Head joined the Pan-Africanist Congress in 1959 and, had she perused the essays or booklet, would have felt her socialist, anti-colonial and anti-imperial politics matched by what Harmel drew from Schreiner. In one instance, he drew Schreiner on 'the wave of exploitation and destructiveness vomited forth by the nations of Europe, led by England in her drunken orgy of imperialism based on capitalism which swept across the earth, disrupting and destroying its peoples and their individuality'.[43] With her own burgeoning interest in the similarities between African and Eastern religious and philosophical thought,[44] Head's attention would also likely have been drawn to Rebekah's definition of European civilisation, as quoted in Harmel: 'From the ancient civilisations of Asia and Africa, ancient and complete when we were merely savage, have we not got all the foundation and much of the superstructure of what we possess?'[45] And, given Head's attraction to Hinduism and Gandhi's teachings,[46] her interest would also have been piqued by Rebekah's portrayal, again as quoted by Harmel, of a 'broad road of opposition to law and authority' where the 'heroes, the prophets, the thinkers, the leaders, [. . .] white-robed sons of the gods' hear the call of 'infinitely higher goals' than those offered by 'laws and conventions', and become 'the new pathfinders of the race'.[47]

Head's statement to Fradkin in 1975, 'More than anything I want to be noble',[48] echoes a key word in Harmel's praise of Schreiner: her 'noble endeavour on behalf of the oppressed and the exploited'; her 'noble soul'; Rebekah's 'noble spirit'.[49] It also echoes the concept of nobility Schreiner herself used, in a passage from *From Man to Man* reprinted in Krige's *Selection*, where Rebekah speaks of the contribution that each individual can make to the accumulated layers of 'things good and beautiful' that constitute humanity: 'just one tiny grain', just 'one layer, perhaps one thin layer', which can be 'so well and truly laid' that 'all coming after shall say – "It was nobly done!"'.[50] Writing to Fradkin in 1977 about how much she appreciated having access, through Krige, to Schreiner's 'huge and generous view of life',[51] Head also singles out one of the letters Krige reprinted, using it to praise Schreiner's vision: an 'ideal world [in which] each person has something, a little something, he is prepared to give up' for the good of that world.[52] Schreiner and Head spoke of their literary mission in similar terms. For Schreiner: 'It is to lessen the suffering of others that I have to live [. . .] for this that I have led the life that I have'.[53] And for Head: 'I'm not the kind of person that's just born for being born sake. It's very significant that I've been born in Southern Africa. All these years I've been trying to find the purpose in it'.[54] The 'nobility' of their shared literary project, then, informed by the shared 'huge and generous view of life' as well as by the social, allegorical use both authors made of their individual selves (displaced, often, into a key fictional character), is the major connection between Schreiner and Head. However, it is also shot through with a key difference: Schreiner's analogical or allegorical writing increasingly concerned with the limitations of whiteness, Head's increasingly expanding on how to be 'black' in the world.

A crucial aspect of their shared but also unshared literary vision relates to their concern with, the capacity to see and act in accord with, a common humanity, a capacity that Schreiner yearned to retrieve and that Head felt she was indeed able to portray in her Botswana community. Through several of the extracts in Krige, Head would have seen references to the 'social instinct', which Schreiner saw as a 'primitive' characteristic that was being lost among 'civilised' people, and as only a might-have-been among 'primitive' Boers since they were particularly incapable of letting their social sympathies cross the 'limits of race'.[55] For Schreiner, it was evident in the 'primitive' African: 'We find him in the land of his growth with all the instincts of the free man intact', provided (she sharply points out) that he has not been 'indoctrinated' with the 'vices [. . .] of our civilization'.[56] 'Man is not meant to live striving against his fellows, but living in an organised union with them', Schreiner wrote to her husband in 1908, deploring the condition of Africans who had been alienated from their 'tribe', and were 'organically united to nothing'.[57]

Schreiner did not, at least in the extracts Head would have seen in Krige, associate the social instinct with the 'Bushman'. However, she spoke of it as a crucial aspect of the human imagination, issuing in certain 'exceptional individuals gifted with those rare powers of sympathetic insight [. . .] to see clearly those far more important elements of a common humanity which underlie and unite them'.[58] In addition, as Head would have seen, Schreiner's definition of the social instinct as 'instinctive and unconscious' segued into a metonymic association with what she thought of as dreaminess.[59] In a piece of writing clearly intended to be strategic, Schreiner claimed that this 'element' was to be found in South Africans born to the land, figures imbued with a propensity to be 'more easily guided through our affections and sympathies' than other nations are.[60] She also associated that 'dreamy' capacity with 'a certain gentle passivity'.[61] This association recalls Head's complex representation of passivity as a feature of key characters in *The Cardinals*, *Maru* and *A Question of Power*, figures characterised by a strong creative force, as she took pains to explain to her set of South African interviewers in 1983.[62]

Reading Krige, then, Head would have developed an admiration for Schreiner that was in many ways attuned to her own self-image and interests as a writer. We may also imagine Head to have welcomed the adjustments evident in his *Selection* as it moves from *Thoughts on South Africa* (1896) to *Closer Union* (1908–9), adjustments relating, for instance, to Schreiner's use of the word 'race'. Throughout the former book it signifies the human race while in *Closer Union* Schreiner uses the term to insist that 'distinctions of race and colour' should go.[63] In addition, Head may have noticed Schreiner's shift in racial terminology, which in *Closer Union* she revises to 'the South African Bantu' (adds Schreiner: 'a race probably with a large admixture of Arab blood!') from whom white South Africans might learn, in order for 'our nation [to] be shaped'.[64]

Yet even here we need to ponder how Head might have heard Schreiner's tones:

> We find him in the land of his growth with all the instincts of the free man intact; with all the instincts of loyalty to his race and its chiefs still warm in his heart; with his social instincts almost abnormally developed and fully active; we have only with wisdom and patient justice slowly to transfer them to our own larger society [...] the proudest of us may envy many of the social virtues which the Bantu displays. We have a great material here, wisely handled.[65]

Surely, elsewhere in Krige, Head would have heard Schreiner's progressive thinking overarched by a discourse of superiority — 'we are here to teach them all we know if they will learn'[66] — and peppered with periodic expectations of [their] 'gratitude'.[67] She would also have seen Schreiner's sharp division between 'the Kaffir working in our kitchen' and 'the little human ape Bushman', even when (through the latter) referring to the 'line of growth' extending between peoples,[68] and as in *African Farm*, being associated with the 'dreamy element' of creativity.[69] What, then, would she have made here of Schreiner's 'we'? What would she have thought on hearing Schreiner traducing human exchange as the 'transfer' of 'material'?

However much their shared interests, then, and however similarly phrased or felt was their sense of mission as writers, no suggestion of 'afterlife' should mask the differences between the two writers. Krige's *Selection* does show Schreiner's interest in 'the most careful intellectual self-examination',[70] and *From Man to Man*, as already been suggested, certainly portrays a degree of self-examination in nascent form, albeit coming to settle into a moment of stasis that this essay has already identified as the novel's self-conscious limitation. However, Head's creative work shows no interest in the stasis of such limits, nor indeed in the capacities or incapacities of white culture and what it might 'transfer' from the Black; her own focus was on Black communities, and if whites were incorporated, it was on the basis of their assimilation into those communities, as shown in her novel *When Rain Clouds Gather* and her collection of interviews, *Serowe: Village of the Rain Wind* (1981).

And the discourse of white or Western culture was radically interrogated in *A Question of Power* and *A Bewitched Crossroad* (1984).

While Head, thanking Fradkin for the *Selection*, acknowledges Schreiner for the extraordinary writer she was – 'Olive was truly a startling woman for her times' – she also notes to Fradkin that she had 'paused over her portraits of the Boer'.[71] The 'beautiful world' Schreiner had outlined 'never came into being', for 'something very evil grew there'.[72] Thinking of this brings to mind, Head adds, Schreiner's hostility to Cecil John Rhodes (Krige's extracts from letters show the growth of this hostility), but she barely conceals her surprise at Schreiner's failure to recognise evil in any other form: however 'beautiful' Schreiner's Boer world may have 'looked [. . . .] It was never [really] so'.[73] She immediately recalls 'a line [she herself] had written' in *A Question of Power*: 'You don't realise the point at which you become evil'.[74] Her own novel, she knew, boldly investigates the damage done by oppressive discourses and their effects on the unconscious. So, to quote from the novel itself, if a 'first group brought about dark times [. . .] [w]e had to dream a nobler dream'.[75]

Despite Head's forgiving phrasing about Schreiner ('for her times'), we may easily imagine her becoming infuriated reading Krige's *Selection*, especially since she did not hold back when friends and other correspondents failed to meet her standards.[76] Yet when Schreiner draws a moral equivalence between South Africa's 'sons, black [and] white' in the struggle over the land and – rather than acknowledge and lament European dispossession of African land – argues that 'South Africa has no reason to be ashamed of the way in which either of [them] fought in those old, terrible days',[77] Head responds politely but pointedly (she is writing to Fradkin), 'She was not near the Transvaal when the battle for the land was fought where the Boer displayed his land greed'.[78]

***

In her youth Schreiner had met a 'person of genius', a 'Betuanna' [Bechuana/Botswana] woman from whom she received instruction about the part played by gender and labour relations in the 'social instinct'.[79] Head would not have read of this, for the relevant texts were not reprinted in Krige. Nor would she have seen the portrayal in *From Man to Man* of a 'Bushman' woman who lived and died in service to her community, and was thus, in Schreiner's thinking, more important to the human race than any Bismarck.[80] She would not have seen, either, the novel's so-called 'Bushman girl', Griet, who has about her the kind of magical quality Head might well have appreciated, and who also – arguably – functions as a figure of authorial 'subversion'.[81] If, as already suggested through the figure of Sartje, *From Man to Man* develops an uncanny vocative relation to Head, so too do these various figures bring forth another kind of evocation, which is then underlined by the novel's expanding gaze: from a white-dominated, colonial South Africa to a more northerly region called 'Central Africa'. This includes the territory around Lake Ngami (in present-day Botswana) and what we may take as a figure of 'Bushman' resistance ('three Bushman arrows').[82] Schreiner thus imagines a land not yet colonised by the British, and points forward in this regard to the land of Head's imagination: the place where Head could escape the stultifying effects of apartheid South Africa on her writing. Schreiner's own gaze had, in real life, made a similar turn. Exhausted by the society of English-speaking South Africans she now lived among, a society that lacked both an aristocracy and a working class, and having felt connected only to 'the Boers and the Kaffirs', she had longed to 'go up to the centre of Africa'.[83]

How might Head have responded to such an imagined evocation? In many ways her writing produces, at least in this reader, the uncanny impression of an author writing back, *avant-la-lettre*, to a novel by Schreiner she had not yet read. And this impression could not be stronger than when it comes to imagining her reaction to Schreiner's disturbing use of 'Bushmen' skulls.

In 1901, while Schreiner was producing the transformative *Closer Union* and was returning once again to *From Man to Man*, she wrote to her sister Ettie about how the Prelude to the novel had flashed upon her. This exemplified for Schreiner the manner in which 'the ideal which we strive after must first shape itself within us'.[84] *From Man to Man* further dramatises this shaping process through a series of related icons that track their way through Rebekah's consciousness – notably, the statue of Hercules holding a child, the fossil remains of a winged reptile, and the dicynodont's head 'come out to see the sunshine it once loved'.[85] All these throb with a life force, a power that has been temporarily buried, a latent energy whose time will once again come.

Schreiner spoke of this moment in an earlier letter – it occurred while she was 'writing an article on the Bushmen and giving a description of their skulls'[86] – and uses it in *From Man to Man* to ground the crucial moment of creative inspiration upon 'African' soil, at least as she imagined it. Perhaps in such a space – the uncolonised Africans' 'land of growth'[87] – the ideal of 'a common humanity' would develop.[88] She gives over the flash of inspiration not to Rebekah but to Rebekah's soul-mate Drummond, a decision motivated partly by the fact that he, as a traveller and explorer, is the plausible medium for the evocation of Africa that the theme of 'passing it on' requires. She uses much the same terms as she used for her own real-life experience, but for Drummond adds a detail about 'the exact measurement of some skulls'.[89] It is remarkable that neither the novel nor the two letters offer comment on this: the pseudo-scientific practice of craniometry, the calibration of skulls designed to produce evidence of racial hierarchies descending into the sub-human and the degenerate. Instead, in describing both her own and Drummond's experience of inspiration, her focus is the romantic image of communication between dead skull and living writer.[90]

The image of a skull does not appear in Schreiner's text in quite the same manner as the fossilised dicynodont's head, that is, as an object lovingly collected and preserved (which might have led us back into yet another burning question about Schreiner's tendency to conflate animals and 'Bushmen'). But its entry into Schreiner's writing recalls various other highly insensitive and historically blind and irresponsible moments, such as in relation to the young Rebekah's distress at hearing an account of the Ninth Frontier War, where affective focus is placed rather more on a white child than on the Gcaleka warriors 'blown away' by cannon fire.[91] In other ways too, her allegorical tales may well read as primarily serving a sympathetic imagination rather than opening out into possibilities of material change.

Schreiner means differently, of course, and – had she read *From Man to Man* – Head might truly have been moved by the thought that in this unfinished, often inchoate novel, sporadically composed and over a time during which its author was undergoing political change, Schreiner's inspirational shaping of the future was trying to root itself in the multi-layered soil of a racially interwoven society. For Schreiner, the skull may well signify a latent potential, thus functioning similarly to the other icons in the novel, but it remains less developed in this way than the other icons are. However, there is a further point to be pursued before addressing how the idea of the skull reaches into Head's writing.

Schreiner's displacement of the real-life flash of inspiration onto Drummond rather than Rebekah possibly implies a degree of ironic distance, but it has a disturbing effect. It absolves Rebekah of the responsibility (a responsibility that is actually Schreiner's) for utilising the 'Bushmen' skulls in so historically myopic a manner. Perhaps unconsciously, the absolution of responsibility embeds itself into the novel's theme of 'passing it on': *passing* on responsibility, with all the ambiguity of that word 'passing', an ambiguity already inscribed into Rebekah's passing the fossil of the winged reptile to Drummond to send off to the Vienna museum: '"It's better so," she said. "Someone might make use of it. I never will"'.[92] Schreiner has built into the novel its own ambiguous afterlife, inviting us to see an 'Africa' beyond the colonial but nonetheless represented in terms of the colonial; calling up the 'halfcaste' child as dreamer and writer without recognising the problematic nature of 'Bushmen' skulls; cushioning her female character from culpability.

***

The 'Bushman' skull, that dead experimental object lurking so troublingly in Schreiner's own thinking as well as in her fiction, springs up alive in Head's writing, in a performance that insists on a vitality, autonomy and agency of far greater power than exists in the 'Bushman' art referred to in *African Farm*. The performance of re-vitalisation is dramatised very differently in *Maru* and *A Question of Power*, but in both novels Head transforms her own name into a fictional signifier, *head*, and its metonym, *skull*, and in the process expands on the word's potential as the source of a creative imagination. Such a transformation underlines Head's desire to make social, even political, use of her personal situation, involving as it did a profound reconstruction of 'self' as she moved from South Africa to Botswana. To allegorise 'self' meant, for Head, to allegorise a self reincarnated into a broader geographical and social experience than had been available to Schreiner: to be made politically aware through, variously, being 'black' in South Africa, not 'black' enough in Botswana, and of 'mixed-race' in both countries, with race all the while being intersected by gender and class. Her writing developed a specific, and ironic, angle of vision on both 'blackness' and 'whiteness' and their associated attributes. Most certainly Head's writing shows how 'the oppressed can access the restorative, anticipatory and transformative potential of creativity and imagination', as Munslow Ong has so usefully put it, but it dramatises far more than any mere 'strength to endure'.[93] Head's writing articulates a world in which a powerful creative inspiration derives from being 'comfortably' Black in the world in such a way that it becomes a power 'in which all mankind can share'.[94] Blackness, for her, was a protean position, developed from what she called the 'horizon', the definition of which depended on a 'huge view of life' and a 'long-term view'.[95] Dismissive of those who liked to 'hog the black skin' as an exclusive identification of self or nation, she proclaimed to her correspondent Randolph Vigne: 'You know, my friend, a combination such as I of two nations finally establishes the human race'.[96]

While still in South Africa, in a 1963 review of James Baldwin's *The Fire Next Time*, Head claimed that those labelled 'black' were capable of achieving a humanity beyond the reach of racist whites. Neither she nor

Baldwin understood Blackness according to the standard binarism of white racism. To be Black in their terms in effect transcended what Frantz Fanon had diagnosed as an envious and self-destructive desire among the colonised to take 'the settler's place'.[97] Indeed, as Baldwin wrote and Head approvingly quotes, whites' estimation of their own worth could 'scarcely be corroborated', and 'a vast amount of the energy that goes into what we call the Negro problem is produced by the White man's profound desire not to be judged by those who are not White'.[98] Baldwin used the term 'Negro', but his wording shows that he saw Blackness not as essentialist but as a positive cultural construct. This, too, was the direction taken by Head: 'identity [. . .] as strategy rather than essence', as the critic and fiction writer Zoë Wicomb has put it.[99]

In *Maru*, the missionary woman's implicit injunction to her ward to help 'your people' not only foregrounds the tones of white superiority.[100] It also ignores the fact that the 'help' that is needed (as Baldwin brilliantly sees it) is for whites to retrieve the humanity they lost in their assumption of power. Head's *Maru* uses both the archetypal and social positions of the 'Bushman' to refer to a vital imaginative position from which to envisage a perspective that may be said to be pre-Babel: that is, not at all dependent on the symbolic processes of self and other from which racism may be said to develop.[101] Head deploys the term 'Bushman' to refer to both 'Masarwa' and 'coloured' (that is, to the racisms practised and experienced in both Botswana and South Africa). It was, as she noted, 'not that hard to put myself in the shoes of a Masarwa' for, as regards 'the language used to exploit Basarwa people, [and] the methods used to exploit them, the juxtaposition between white and Black in South Africa and Black and Basarwa in Botswana is so exact'.[102] The novel thus adopts a perspective developed across both countries, reaching forward to the universality of oppressive power structures addressed in *A Question of Power*.

Crucial, too, are Head's critical references in *Maru* to the science of the time, which recall not only Schreiner's pseudoscientific use of 'Bushmen' skulls but also her interest in the role of the environment in creating or allowing for change. When the child, now a young woman, claims her identity as 'Masarwa', she retains the ethnic term, radically adapting her foster-mother's mantra about 'environment everything; heredity nothing'.[103] Taking what she needs from her European education (that is, what has been provided for her by the changed environment of her life), she retains but redefines her identity as 'Masarwa' by becoming 'something new and universal, a type of personality that would be unable to fit into a definition of something as narrow as tribe or race or nation'.[104] Head's own position in this regard is also made quite clear in her essays and letters: where she acknowledges the need to transcend racial categories and at the same time to claim one's racial or ethnic belonging.

Another reference to the science of the time occurs with the concept of 'experiment' used thrice in the novel.[105] It describes, first, the way the 'Masarwa' child is used by the missionary woman; and, secondly, the way the Tswana leader takes the 'Masarwa' figure as a wife in order to signal to the wider community the establishment of social equality between the Batswana and the Basarwa. He marries her *as a 'Masarwa'* just as the missionary woman has rescued her *as a 'Masarwa'*. Margaret's dreams manifest as paintings that spur the Tswana leader to social reform, but, despite the 'voices of the gods in his heart',[106] his reform remains limited, as does his aesthetic interpretation, receiving the kind of ironic treatment – with its distancing metadiscursive regard – that, in retrospect, makes Schreiner's Rebekah look somewhat too earnest. The process the Tswana leader engages in involves a sharp separation between Margaret's body and head ('the threads went snap, snap, snap behind her neck').[107] Although there is a 'slow inpouring of life' once again, such that Margaret survives, she survives as a wife, not – the novel strongly implies – as a practising artist.[108] However, the novel's remarkable prolepsis keeps the notion of the artist and artistry fully alive by portraying a complex unconscious at work in a world of dreams where Margaret is *other* than wife, *other* than any experiment.

In *A Question of Power*, the idea of the skull functions differently, for it draws in the protagonist's responsibility as well. In obvious ways, the skull is the echo chamber for a cacophony of hostile voices, among which the protagonist keeps hearing a recurring, monotonous song 'right inside her head: "Dog, filth, the Africans will eat you to death. Dog, filth, the Africans will eat you to death"'.[109] As Jacqueline Rose tells us, '[p]aranoia – voices in the head – is of course the perfect metaphor for colonisation'.[110] Much more than British colonisation is involved here: a plethora of invasive voices (not just from South Africa and Botswana) degrade the central character, Elizabeth, racially and sexually, politically and spiritually, as when the novel's central figure of evil power 'opened her skull', 'bent his mouth towards the cavity and talked right into the exposed area'.[111] These oppressive voices have a history, a contingency of sources, emanating from a set of discourses that gradually reveal themselves through the novel; they speak not the voice of truth but of power. The maternal voice that once called for a different world to be created now also calls for interrogation of the very discourses through which a white woman such as she was defined as 'mad'.[112] At another moment in the novel, too, the protagonist fears that the creative function moving 'the dreamer of new dreams' may itself have been taken over by destructive discourses: hence the nightmarish thrust of the dreams.[113] If Head's voice throughout *Maru* is a cautionary one that reminds us to look closely at how we read, how we look, how we interpret, in *A Question of Power* it calls us to examine the discourses that create us, and that we ourselves may participate in creating. To see these discourses as historical constructions is to find a different position for the self, a different environment for the self to inhabit and to be defined by, a different way of defining heredity, all in a continuous and exemplary process of awareness and detachment. Here the theme of what Head thought of as creative passivity is writ large: the creative self as 'passive, inactive, impersonal', detached from regulation: 'the essential ingredient in creativity is to create and let the dreams fly away with a soft hand and heart'.[114]

***

While the focus of this essay has been on the uncanny relation between *From Man to Man* and *Maru* and, to a lesser extent, *A Question of Power*, let it be said that Head published *Serowe*, *The Collector of Treasures*, and *A Bewitched Crossroad* after she had read and commented on Krige's *Selection*. As already suggested, Schreiner had turned first to the Boers for her proto-modernist appreciation of 'primitive' life – their organic connection to the land, the concomitant distancing from materialist values (their 'primitive conditions of life'), and their refusal to submit to ideological forces that they did not respect – and then to what she called the 'tribal African', finding there the social instinct she felt to be so crucial to human progress.[115] Head's second trilogy similarly portrayed a world where such an instinct was in play, a world made up of the 'ordinary' people of Botswana, who – she felt – had remained undamaged by colonisation and could run their own affairs without the abstractions of dogma or overbearing leadership, working through for themselves the muddles of everyday life. In creating this kind of African country for her primary setting, Head did not leave South Africa behind, but in many ways bypassed its damaging impact. The connection and disconnection between the two writers become particularly clear at this point.

When Head announced – as mentioned earlier in this essay – the 'theme of continuous growth' as the keynote of the authors she most highly respected (with no mention of Schreiner), she implicitly bound her interests with Schreiner's, for both writers addressed the possibilities of social harmony through allegorical or analogical relations between the individual and the group. However, Head includes and inhabits the position of the 'Bushman' in a way Schreiner did not herself attempt, and was indeed incapable of doing. Moreover, Head quite remarkably lets that position expand beyond any definition current in her day. It is in this expansive gesture, above all, that we can see Head as the reincarnated 'Olive Schreiner of South Africa', acknowledging but also rejecting the racialised labels Schreiner struggled to transcend. We can also see the Southern African land she created as a reincarnation of the South Africa that had given birth to Schreiner and to herself as well. Line of growth, land of growth: their basis in Schreiner's and Head's creative imagination lies, to different degrees and in different ways, in African soil, but also in the soul, again in the two authors' respective configurations, for Head's writing explicitly conceptualised the evolution of the soul. The two authors certainly shared an interest in social progress: in Schreiner this was a gradual process, taking place particle by particle or layer by layer, to use her sedimentary metaphors; but in Head's cyclic imagination, her reincarnative consciousness, the term 'revolutionary' seems more appropriate.

While Head's deepest literary drives seem similar to Schreiner's at several points, in their sensitivities the writers often appear far apart. Much more remains to be explored between them: among those topics already touched on – the shared desire for social change, their avowed interest in shaping the future through acts of writing, a common interest in the soul – and much not yet referred to: a unity felt to exist among all living things, a shared interest in the relations between human and animal, and human and plant-life as well, where the poetics of plants speaks out of an African soil. This essay has focused on the analogical relations between the individual and collective, suggesting that in this very similarity between the two writers is revealed that stark difference, here tentatively called Schreiner's progressive, and Head's revolutionary, politics. Head heard, through Krige, how limited an investigation of the evils of the South African past Schreiner was able to provide. Yet she seems also to have felt in Schreiner's vision of the future the limits imposed by her historical present and the fact that Schreiner turned to listen was, perhaps, part of what Head thought of as 'huge and generous'. Still, rereading Schreiner as if through Head's imagined eyes has inevitably been a speculative process. It has not necessarily retrieved the Schreiner Head herself found, nor the Schreiner other readers may find. While it remains tempting to imagine Schreiner welcoming Head's portrayal of what the younger author identified as an 'African' perspective, 'a vast feeling that encompasses everyone, not a narrow, horrific, exclusive world',[116] it must be recognised that Head moved much further in this regard, so much further indeed that one can only fantasise what impact it might have had on Schreiner to have encountered a Bessie Head.

But let me give the younger writer the last word. Writing to Fradkin about the claim (Fradkin's and Heywood's) that 'Bessie Head is of the tradition stemming from Olive Schreiner', Head herself retorted:

> People might have meeting points only in so far as they feel driven by a passion to shed some light on human affairs. It is hardly 'belonging to a tradition' but the sheer force of ones [sic] living experience.[117]

Works Cited

Adler, Michelle, Susan Gardner, Tobeka Mda and Patricia Sandler. 'Bessie Head Interviewed.' In *Between the Lines: Interviews with Bessie Head, Sheila Roberts, Ellen Kuzwayo, Miriam Tlali*, edited by Craig MacKenzie and Cherry Clayton, 5–30. Grahamstown: National English Literary Museum, 1989.

Bagwasi, Mompoloki. 'Identity and Race in Bessie Head's *Maru*.' In *Writing Bessie Head in Botswana: An Anthology of Remembrance and Criticism*, edited by Mary S. Lederer and Seatholo M. Tumedi, 87–96. Gaborone: Pentagon Publishers, 2008.

Beard, Linda Susan. 'Bessie Head in Gaborone, Botswana: An Interview.' *Sage* 3, no. 2 (1986): 44–47.

Bolaane, Maitseo. 'Bessie Head and the Dynamics of Social Relations in Serowe.' In *Writing Bessie Head in Botswana: An Anthology of Remembrance and Criticism*, edited by Mary S. Lederer and Seatholo M. Tumedi, 61–73. Gaborone: Pentagon Publishers, 2007.

Clayton, Cherry. 'The Face of Africa.' *English in Africa* 10, no. 1 (1983): 1–13.

Cronwright-Schreiner, S. C. *The Life of Olive Schreiner*. London: T. Fisher Unwin, 1924.

Driver, Dorothy. 'Olive Schreiner's *From Man to Man* and the "Copy Within"'. In *Changing the Victorian Subject*, edited by Maggie Tonkin, Mandy Treagus, Madeleine Seys and Sharon Crozier-De Rosa, 123–50. Adelaide: University of Adelaide Press, 2014.

Eilersen, Gillian Stead. *Bessie Head: Thunder Behind Her Ears*. [1995] Second edition. Johannesburg: Wits University Press, 2001.

Fanon, Frantz. *The Wretched of the Earth*, translated by Constance Farrington. New York: Grove Weidenfeld, 1963.

Forster, E. M. *A Passage to India*. [1924] Edited by Oliver Stallybrass. Harmondsworth: Penguin, 1983.

Fradkin, Betty McGinnis. 'Conversations with Bessie.' *World Literature Written in English* 17, no. 2 (1978): 427–34.

Harmel, Michael. *Olive Schreiner, 1855–1955*. Cape Town: Real Printing & Publishing, 1955.

—. 'Olive Schreiner, South Africa's Greatest Creative Writer.' *New Age* 1, no. 18 (24 February 1955): 7.

Head, Bessie. *A Question of Power*. London: Heinemann, 1974.
—. '"African Religions".' [1969] Review of *African Religions and Philosophy*, by John S. Mbiti.' In *A Woman Alone: Autobiographical Writings*, edited by Craig MacKenzie, 50–53. London: Heinemann, 1990.
—. 'Bessie Head Reviews *The Fire Next Time*.' *Contact* 6, no. 15 (26 July 1963): 8.
—. 'Claiming a Great Heritage.' *English in Africa* 28, no. 1 (2001): 42–47.
—. *Maru*. [1971] London: Heinemann, 1987.
—. 'Some Notes on Novel Writing.' [1978] In *A Woman Alone: Autobiographical Writings*, edited by Craig MacKenzie, 61–64. London: Heinemann, 1990.
—. 'Writing out of Southern Africa.' [1985] In *A Woman Alone: Autobiographical Writings*, edited by Craig MacKenzie, 93–100. London: Heinemann, 1990.
Heywood, Christopher. 'Traditional Values in the Novels of Bessie Head.' In *Individual and Community in Commonwealth Literature*, edited by Daniel Massa, 12–19. Malta: University Press, 1979.
Krige, Uys. *Olive Schreiner: A Selection*. Cape Town: Oxford University Press, 1968.
Lederer, Mary S., and Leloba S. Molema. '"That troublemaker": Bessie Head in Botswana.' In *Emerging Perspectives on Bessie Head*, edited by Huma Ibrahim, 109–20. Trenton: Africa World Press, 2004.
Lewis, Desirée. *Living on a Horizon: Bessie Head and the Politics of Imagining*. Trenton: Africa World Press, 2007.
Marquard, Jean. 'Bessie Head: Exile and Community in Southern Africa.' *London Magazine* (1978/1979): 52–53.
Molema, Leloba. '"The End is Where We Start From": A Tribute to Bessie Head.' In *Writing Bessie Head in Botswana: an Anthology of Remembrance and Criticism*, edited by Mary S. Lederer and Seatholo M. Tumedi, 2–3. Gaborone: Pentagon Publishers, 2007.
Munslow Ong, Jade. *Olive Schreiner and African Modernism: Allegory, Empire and Postcolonial Writing*. London: Routledge, 2018.
Ngcobo, Lauretta. 'A Black South African Woman Writing Long After Schreiner.' In *The Flawed Diamond: Essays on Olive Schreiner*, edited by Itala Vivan, 189–99. Sydney: Dangaroo Press, 1991.
Nkosi, Lewis. *Tasks and Masks: Themes and Styles of African Literature*. London: Longman, 1981.
Rafapa, L. J., A. Z. Nengoma, and H. S. Tshamano, 'Instances of Head's Distinctive Feminism, Womanism and Africanness in her Novels.' *Tydskrif vir Letterkunde* 48, no. 2 (2011): 112–21.
Rose, Jacqueline. 'On the 'Universality' of Madness: Bessie Head's *A Question of Power*.' *Critical Inquiry* 20, no. 3 (1994): 401–08.
Samuelson, Meg. 'Writing Women.' *Cambridge History of South African Literature*, edited by David Attwell and Derek Attridge, 757–78. Cambridge: Cambridge University Press, 2012.
Schoeman, Karel. *Olive Schreiner: A Woman in South Africa 1855–1881*, translated by Henri Snijders. Johannesburg: Jonathan Ball, 1991.
Schreiner, Olive. 'Chapter 6: The Diary of a Prig.' Olive Schreiner Collection. Humanities Research Center, Austin, Texas.
—. 'Closer Union.' [1908] In *Words in Season: The Public Writings with Her Own Remembrances Collected for the First Time*, edited by Stephen Gray, 160–89. Johannesburg: Penguin, 2005.

—. *From Man to Man or Perhaps Only*. [1926] Edited by Dorothy Driver. Cape Town: University of Cape Town Press, 2015.
—. 'Introduction to the Life of Mary Wollstonecraft and the Rights of Woman.' Transcribed by Carolyn Burdett. *History Workshop Journal* 37 (Spring 1994): 188–93.
—. *The Story of an African Farm*. [1883] London: Benn's Essex Library, 1929.
—. *Thoughts on South Africa*. [1923] Parklands: Ad Donker, 1992.
—. *Woman and Labour*. [1911] London: Virago, 1978.
Viljoen, Shaun. *Richard Rive: A Partial Biography*. Johannesburg: Wits University Press, 2001.
Visel, Robin. '"We Bear the World and We Make It": Bessie Head and Olive Schreiner.' *Research in African Literatures* 21, no. 3 (1990): 115–24.
Wicomb, Zoë. 'Identity, Writing, and Autobiography: The Case of Bessie Head's *The Cardinals* (1994).' In *Race, Nation, Translation: South African Essays, 1990–2013*, edited by Andrew van der Vlies, 217–28. New Haven: Yale University Press, 2018.

Letters

Betty Fradkin to Bessie Head, 2 February 1975, Bessie Head Papers, Khama III Memorial Museum. Serowe, Botswana.
Bessie Head to Betty Fradkin, 22–23 February 1975, Bessie Head Papers, Khama III Memorial Museum, Serowe, Botswana.
Betty Fradkin to Bessie Head, 23 March 1975, Bessie Head Papers, Khama III Memorial Museum. Serowe, Botswana.
Betty Fradkin to Bessie Head, 1 September 1975, Bessie Head Papers, Khama III Memorial Museum. Serowe, Botswana.
Betty Fradkin to Bessie Head, 4 December 1975, Bessie Head Papers, Khama III Memorial Museum. Serowe, Botswana.
Bessie Head to Betty Fradkin, 23 June 1977, Bessie Head Papers, Khama III Memorial Museum. Serowe, Botswana.
Olive Schreiner Letters Online.
Rive, Richard. *Olive Schreiner Letters 1871–1899*, vol. 1. Oxford: Oxford University Press, 1987.
Vigne, Randolph. *A Gesture of Belonging: Letters from Bessie Head, 1965–1979*. Johannesburg: Wits University Press, 1991.

Notes

1. Schreiner, Lelie Kloof Journal, quoted in Cronwright-Schreiner, *The Life of Olive Schreiner*, 142; reprinted in Schreiner, *From Man to Man*, 433.
2. Schreiner to Edward Carpenter, 8 January 1888, in Rive, *Olive Schreiner Letters 1871–1899*, 133; see also *Olive Schreiner Letters Online* (OSLO).
3. Schreiner, *From Man to Man*, 383.
4. Schreiner to Havelock Ellis, 31 October 1884, quoted in Schreiner, *From Man to Man*, 436; see also *OSLO*.

5. Schreiner, 'Chapter 6: The Diary of a Prig', 1886–87 mss. MS-3734, Humanities Research Center, University of Texas; for a transcription, see UCT Libraries Digital Collections.
6. See Schreiner to John X. Merriman, 31 October 1905, quoted in Schreiner, *From Man to Man*, 457; see also *OSLO*.
7. Schreiner to W. P. Schreiner, 4 June 1908, quoted in Schreiner, *From Man to Man*, 462–63; see also *OSLO*.
8. Schreiner, *From Man to Man*, 353.
9. Schreiner, *From Man to Man*, 379.
10. Schreiner, *From Man to Man*, 365.
11. Forster, *A Passage to India*, 289.
12. Head, *Maru*, 13, 12.
13. Head, *Maru*, 19.
14. For this term and some relevant discussion, see Lewis, *Living on a Horizon*, 93–126 and Wicomb, 'Identity, Writing, and Autobiography,' 217–228.
15. Head, quoted in Eilersen, *Thunder Behind Her Ears*, 24–25.
16. Head, quoted in Eilersen, *Thunder Behind Her Ears*, 31.
17. See Harmel, 'Olive Schreiner, South Africa's Greatest Creative Writer,' 7.
18. Adler et al., 'Bessie Head Interviewed,' 17. Here Head, who believed in reincarnation, used the term figuratively. See Head to Fradkin, 22–23 February 1975, KMM 015 BHP 4: 'I have some other idea of my previous reincarnations, but I'm very flattered all the same.'
19. Fradkin to Head, 23 March 1975, KMM 015 BHP 5.
20. Fradkin, 'Conversations with Bessie,' 427–434.
21. Fradkin to Head, 4 December 1975, KMM 015 BHP 18.
22. Fradkin to Head, 1 September 1975, KMM 015 BHP 13.
23. Head, quoted in Marquard, 'Bessie Head: Exile and Community in Southern Africa,' 52–53.
24. Head, quoted in Marquard, 'Bessie Head: Exile and Community in Southern Africa,' 52–53.
25. Adler et al., 'Bessie Head Interviewed,' 16–17.
26. Adler et al., 'Bessie Head Interviewed,' 17.
27. Head, 'Some Notes on Novel Writing', 62. See also Beard, 'Bessie Head in Gaborone,' 44, where Head speaks of apartheid South Africa as 'such a choking, throttling, death-like kind of world'.
28. Clayton, 'The Face of Africa,' 1–13; Heywood, 'Traditional Values in the Novels of Bessie Head,' 12–19; Visel, 'We Bear the World and We Make It,' 115–24; Munslow Ong, *Olive Schreiner and African Modernism*, 158–60.
29. Nkosi, *Tasks and Masks*, 101. The chapter that this quote was taken from was first published as 'Southern Africa: Protest and Commitment' (1966).
30. Rafapa, Nengoma and Tshamano, 'Instances of Head's Distinctive Feminism,' 115.
31. Bagwasi, 'Identity and Race in Bessie Head's *Maru*,' 89. See also Bolaane, 'Bessie Head and the Dynamics of Social Relations,' 61–73.
32. Molema, 'The End is Where We Start From,' 2. This essay was first published (under her then last name Young) as an obituary in *Mmegi wa*

Dikgang (26 April 1986). See also Mary S. Lederer and Molema, '"That troublemaker": Bessie Head in Botswana'.
33. Adler et al., 'Bessie Head Interviewed,' 17.
34. Adler et al., 'Bessie Head Interviewed,' 17.
35. Head, 'Claiming a Great Heritage,' 43. Eilersen dates the essay as 1982.
36. See Head to Fradkin, 2 February 1975, KMM 015 BHP 2. Fradkin sent Head a copy of *Thoughts on South Africa* in 1976 and of *African Farm* in 1977.
37. Head met Rive in 1958 and, although they did not make friends, he socialised with many of those in Head's circle, such as James Matthews and Barney Desai (the latter edited *Golden City Post* from 1955 where Head worked as a journalist from 1958 or 1959); see Viljoen, *Richard Rive*, 38 *et passim*. Head would later write to Fradkin about Rive's comments about Schreiner in an essay he published in 1977.
38. The essays, which made up a 12-page centenary booklet, Harmel's *Olive Schreiner, 1855–1955*, were originally published as follows: 'Olive Schreiner, South Africa's Greatest Creative Writer', *New Age* 1, 18 (24 February 1955), 7; 'Olive Schreiner – Fearless Fighter Against Injustice', *New Age* 1, 20 (10 March 1995), 7; 'Olive Schreiner's deeply sensitive and sympathetic nature . . .', *New Age* 1, 21 (17 March 1955), 6; and 'Olive Schreiner's Writings are Part of the Inheritance of S outh Africa', *New Age* 1, 22 (24 March 1955), 7. Subsequent quotations are from this booklet.
39. Harmel, *Olive Schreiner, 1855–1955*, 7.
40. Harmel, *Olive Schreiner, 1855–1955*, 11, 4.
41. Schoeman, *Olive Schreiner: A Woman in South Africa*, 467.
42. Harmel, *Olive Schreiner, 1855–1955*, 11. For Harmel, *From Man to Man* was Schreiner's 'finest work and the greatest achievement of South African literature'. See *Olive Schreiner, 1855–1955*, 3.
43. Harmel, *Olive Schreiner, 1855–1955*, 7, quoting from Schreiner, *Thoughts on South Africa*, 344.
44. See Head, 'African Religions' [1969] [Review of *African Religions and Philosophy* by John S. Mbiti]. See also: 'If [the existing practice of humility] was also transported to the realm of the spirit there might be no more caste and class wars in the name of God' (52).
45. Harmel, *Olive Schreiner, 1855–1955*, 10, quoting from Schreiner, *From Man to Man*, 164 but dropping a comma.
46. See Eilersen, *Thunder Behind Her Ears*, 35–38; Lewis, *Living on a Horizon*, 83–89.
47. Harmel, *Olive Schreiner, 1855–1955*, 10; quoting from *From Man to Man*, 161–62.
48. Head, quoted in Fradkin, 'Conversations with Bessie,' 433.
49. Harmel, *Olive Schreiner, 1855–1955*, 2, 3, 9.
50. Krige, *Olive Schreiner: A Selection*, 111. See also Schreiner, *From Man to Man*, 375.
51. Adler et al., 'Bessie Head Interviewed,' 17.
52. Head to Fradkin, 23 June 1977, KMM 015 BHP 53.
53. Schreiner to Havelock Ellis, 12 July 1884, in Krige, *Selection*, 196. See also *OSLO*.

54. Head, letter to Vigne, 14 May 1966, in *A Gesture of Belonging*, 31.
55. Krige, 'The Colour Question,' in *Selection*, 157, from 'The Psychology of the Boer' (1892); see also Schreiner, *Thoughts on South Africa*, 255.
56. Krige, 'The Native Question,' in *Selection*, 187, 188, from *Closer Union* (1909). The title of the extract is Schreiner's original title, 'The Native Question', as used in the *Transvaal Leader* in 1908.
57. Schreiner to S. C. Cronwright-Schreiner, 25 March 1908, reprinted in Krige, *Selection*, 212; from Cronwright-Schreiner's *The Letters of Olive Schreiner* (1926). See also *OSLO*.
58. Krige, 'The Colour Question,' in *Selection*, 158, from 'The Psychology of the Boer' (1892); see also Schreiner, *Thoughts on South Africa*, 256.
59. Krige, 'The Colour Question,' in *Selection*, 158–159, from 'The Psychology of the Boer' (1892); see also Schreiner, *Thoughts on South Africa*, 256.
60. Krige, 'A Strange Gentleness,' in *Selection*, 159, 161, from 'The Psychology of the Boer' (1892); see also Schreiner, *Thoughts on South Africa*, 258, 259.
61. Krige, 'A Strange Gentleness,' in *Selection*, 160, from 'The Psychology of the Boer' (1892); see also Schreiner, *Thoughts on South Africa*, 259.
62. Adler et al., 'Bessie Head Interviewed,' 21–22.
63. Krige, 'Fatal Distinctions,' in *Selection*, 183, from *Closer Union* (1909). See also Schreiner, 'Closer Union', 166.
64. Krige, 'The Native Question,' in *Selection*, 187, from *Closer Union* (1909); see also Schreiner, 'Closer Union,' 181.
65. Krige, 'The Native Question,' in *Selection*, 187–188, from *Closer Union* (1909); see also Schreiner, 'Closer Union', 182.
66. Krige, 'England's Stroke of Genius,' in *Selection*, 172, from 'The Englishman' (1892); see also Schreiner, *Thoughts on South Africa*, 311.
67. Krige, 'The Native Question,' in *Selection*, 188, from *Closer Union* (1908); see also Schreiner, 'Closer Union', 182.
68. Krige, 'England's Stroke of Genius,' in *Selection*, 173, from 'The Englishman' (1892); see also Schreiner, *Thoughts on South Africa*, 312.
69. See Munslow Ong's astute analysis of the novel's creativity; she links Waldo's 'spiritual affinity to the San people' with his 'dreamy look' (67, 83).
70. Krige, 'The Colour Question,' in *Selection*, 158, from 'The Psychology of the Boer' (1892); see also Schreiner, *Thoughts on South Africa*, 256.
71. Head to Fradkin, 23 June 1977, KMM 015 BHP 53.
72. Head to Fradkin, 23 June 1977, KMM 015 BHP 53.
73. Head to Fradkin, 23 June 1977, KMM 015 BHP 53. Krige includes several of Schreiner's letters about Rhodes, starting in 1890 before he and Schreiner met, and ending in 1896 (*Selection* 208–209).
74. Head to Fradkin, 23 June 1977, KMM 015 BHP 53. See also Head, *A Question of Power*, 96.
75. Head, *A Question of Power*, 34.
76. See Lewis, *Living on a Horizon*, 43–91.
77. Krige, 'A Possible Foundation,' in *Selection*, 141, from 'The Boer and His Republics' (1892); see also Schreiner, *Thoughts on South Africa*, 209. Krige's extract may give the impression Schreiner is generalising, but she refers specifically to the war between the Boers and Zulus in 1836.
78. Head to Fradkin, 23 June 1977, KMM 015 BHP 53.

79. Schreiner, *Woman and Labour*, 13; Schreiner, 'Introduction to the Life of Mary Wollstonecraft and the Rights of Woman,' 193. I am indebted for this reference to Meg Samuelson, 'Writing Women,' 759 n2.
80. Schreiner, *From Man to Man*, 160.
81. Schreiner, *From Man to Man*, 69; see also Meg Samuelson, 'Writing Women,' 759.
82. Schreiner, *From Man to Man*, 395.
83. Schreiner to Havelock Ellis, 15 April 1890, in Krige, *Selection*, 208; see also *OSLO*.
84. Schreiner to Ettie Schreiner, 25 December 1901, in Schreiner, *From Man to Man*, 455; see also *OSLO*.
85. Schreiner, *From Man to Man*, 400. See also Driver, 'Olive Schreiner's *From Man to Man* and the "Copy Within"', 123–150.
86. Schreiner to Adela Villiers-Smith, October 1909, in Schreiner, *From Man to Man*, 464; see also *OSLO*.
87. Krige, 'The Native Question', in *Selection*, 187–88, from *Closer Union* (1909); see also Schreiner, 'Closer Union,' 182.
88. Krige, 'The Colour Question', in *Selection*, 158, from 'The Psychology of the Boer' (1892); see also Schreiner, *Thoughts on South Africa*, 256.
89. Schreiner, *From Man to Man*, 406.
90. For Schreiner: 'My mind must have been working at it *unconsciously*, though I knew nothing of it—otherwise how did it come?' Schreiner to Adela Villiers Smith, October 1909, quoted in Schreiner, *From Man to Man*, 464.
91. Schreiner, *From Man to Man*, 376.
92. Schreiner, *From Man to Man*, 402.
93. Munslow Ong, *Olive Schreiner and African Modernism*, 160.
94. See Head, 'Writing out of Southern Africa,' *A Woman Alone*, 97, where Head credited Robert Sobukwe for giving her a 'comfortable black skin in which to live and work'; Head, *A Question of Power*, 135.
95. Adler et al., 'Bessie Head Interviewed,' 13.
96. Vigne, *A Gesture of Belonging*, 64.
97. Fanon, *The Wretched of the Earth*, 39.
98. Head, 'Bessie Head Reviews *The Fire Next Time*,' 8.
99. Wicomb, 'Identity, Writing, and Autobiography: The Case of Bessie Head's *The Cardinals* (1994),' 224.
100. Head, *Maru*, 20.
101. See Head, *Maru*, 11–12.
102. Head, quoted in Beard, 'Bessie Head in Gaborone,' 46; Adler et al., 'Bessie Head Interviewed,' 11.
103. Head, *Maru*, 24, 40, 15.
104. Head, *Maru*, 16.
105. Head, *Maru*, 19, 62, 70.
106. Head, *Maru*, 8.
107. Head, *Maru*, 120.
108. Head, *Maru*, 123.
109. Head, *A Question of Power*, 46.
110. Rose, 'On the "Universality" of Madness,' 405.
111. Head, *A Question of Power*, 45.

112. Head, *A Question of Power*, 17. Of her never-known white mother as a woman who (Head surmised) had fallen in love with a Black man at a time when such sexual liaisons were illegal, Head wrote: 'there is no world as yet for what she has done. She left me to figure it out.' Head to Vigne, 31 October 1968, in Vigne, *A Gesture of Belonging*, 68.
113. Head, *A Question of Power*, 42.
114. Head, *A Question of Power*, 38.
115. Krige, 'The Boer's Simplicity,' in *Selection*, 134, 135, from 'The Wanderings of the Boer' (1891); see also Schreiner, *Thoughts on South Africa*, 140, 141.
116. Head, quoted in Marquard, 'Bessie Head: Exile and Community in Southern Africa,' 51.
117. Head to Fradkin, 23 June 1977, Bessie Head Papers, KMM 015 BHP 53. Head's text is reproduced verbatim.

Chapter 14

Coetzee's Schreiner, Schreiner's Coetzee: Provincialising Allegory
Andrew van der Vlies

Speaking to the poet Stephen Watson in 1978, J. M. Coetzee, then the author of two short books and a handful of essays of criticism, shared with his University of Cape Town colleague a conviction that the writing of South Africa was 'not a great literature'; 'there are no really gigantic figures in it', Coetzee charged, and he had little interest, he continued, in writers 'who are *classed* as gigantic, say Schreiner and Campbell'.[1] Precisely two decades later, in an interview published only in Korean, Coetzee offered a slightly different assessment. Of all South African writers, he suggested on this occasion, '[o]nly Olive Schreiner has meant a great deal to me'.[2] The qualification 'of all South African writers' is worth noting, as is the fact that Coetzee has often disavowed – or sought to downplay – the influence of writing from the country of his birth. In a lecture given at Berkeley in 1991, published under the title 'Homage' in the *Threepenny Review* in 1993, Coetzee suggested for example that when he had first looked in South Africa for a model for the kind of writer he imagined becoming, there simply was none.[3] To be more precise, his claim was that

> in 1960 there was no South African writer, novelist or poet, to whom I as a young man could turn for a significant and vital lead in how to respond to, how to feel about, and therefore how to write about, my homeland. Certain times and places throw up writers who measure up to the challenge they provide, others do not. Australia threw up Patrick White, a writer who could go into the heart of the country and return with a version of that country powerful enough for his readers to believe in and take a lead from [. . .]. South Africa threw up nothing comparable [. . .].[4]

One could, as others have done, follow a trail that leads from Patrick White back to Schreiner.[5] One might also, in Coetzee's formulation of what White is claimed to have done (journeyed 'into the heart of the country'), hear an echo of the title of his own second book, *In the Heart of the Country* (1977), which several critics have noted is in conversation not only with Schreiner's *The Story of an African Farm* (1883), but also her posthumously published *From Man to Man* (1926) and *Undine* (1928).[6] I wish instead to note an interesting moment earlier in 'Homage' when Coetzee wonders whether he ought, in addressing the question of influence, to be talking (or writing) not about literary 'paternity', but 'maternity'.[7] The point is not pursued, and he continues without pause 'to tell at least some of the paternal truth, as it seems to me now', offering a now-familiar genealogy (at least to Coetzee scholars), and an exclusively male one, including Samuel Beckett, Ford Madox Ford, T. S. Eliot and Ezra Pound, as well as early and mid-twentieth-century Middle- and Eastern-European writers like Robert Musil and Hans Magnus Enzensberger, Joseph Brodsky and Zbigniew Herbert.[8] As David Attwell remarks, the 'profound influences' on Coetzee's style, as well as his interests in 'language, aesthetics, and philosophy [. . .] do not come from his native country' but from such European writers, as well as from others like 'Kafka, Barthes, Derrida, and further back, Dostoevsky, Defoe, and Cervantes'.[9]

'Homage', however, encourages the reader to approach any such lists with a degree of scepticism. 'In a deep sense, like the child in Freud's family romance', Coetzee notes in this lecture, 'we may want to disown our real parents and claim for ourself a much finer-sounding lineage'; any 'reader versed in the vicissitudes of autobiography', he warns (and we might imagine Coetzee delivering these lines with a wry smile), should 'receive' his words 'with due caution'.[10] What then *can* we say about literary maternity? And how might Schreiner feature in such a telling of 'some of the [maternal] truth' about other forms of inheritance or influence? Who or what is Coetzee's Schreiner – or indeed *Schreiner*'s *Coetzee* – the work gathered under the sign 'J. M. Coetzee' for which Schreiner might be said to stand in some attitude of maternal relation?

***

In 1988, midway between Coetzee's interview with Watson (in which he implied Schreiner had been cast improperly as 'gigantic' in South African literary circles by the later 1970s) and the conversation with the Korean journalist (in which he claimed Schreiner nonetheless 'meant a great deal' to him), Coetzee published *White Writing*, a collection of essays on the culture of letters descended from European models in Southern Africa, writing – in the book's gloss on the category its title names – 'no longer European, not yet African'.[11] *White Writing*'s third chapter, 'Farm Novel and *Plaasroman*' (the genre's twentieth-century,

Afrikaans-language embodiment), turns to Schreiner's contribution to this genre, more specifically to her subversion of the expectations of the pastoral in *The Story of an African Farm* (hereafter *African Farm*), the region's first great anti-pastoral novel. 'What kind of place is the African farm of which Schreiner's novel is the story?' Coetzee asks, before answering that it is 'one of the key "topoi" of South African literature' and its key constituent, 'the veld' (the bush), the 'site of wholesale absence', specifically – in Schreiner's case – 'of a personal God'.[12]

Schreiner's use of scale – 'between the infinitesimal and the infinite, the farm tries to assert its own measure of time and space by which to carry on its self-absorbed existence' – and her counterposing of farm to town (and farmstead to the expanse of the Karoo) make of this topos something allegorical, too, Coetzee suggests.[13] The farm is 'Schreiner's microcosm of colonial South Africa', a

> tiny community set down in the midst of the vastness of nature, living a closed-minded and self-satisfied existence, driving out those of its number who seek the great white bird Truth by venturing out into the unexplored veld or by reading outside the One (closed) Book. The farm is pettiness in the midst of vastness.[14]

Coetzee's allusion here is to one of the central allegories in *African Farm*, a novel replete with allegorists and allegorical interludes. We might also note that his endorsement of those who 'read outside the One (closed) Book' is offered in strikingly similar terms to those Coetzee used in his defence of the invitation issued to Salman Rushdie to attend a literary festival in Cape Town in 1988; the invitation was withdrawn, to Coetzee's alarm, in the wake of hostile responses to *The Satanic Verses*, an action Coetzee decried as pandering to those who sought to police heterodox reading.[15] What is worth emphasising here is Coetzee's appreciative endorsement of Schreiner's essentially allegorical endeavour. 'Rather than taking Schreiner's farm as a realistic representation of an African stock farm', he writes, 'we should read it as a figure in the service of her critique of colonial culture'.[16]

This chapter of *White Writing* ends, however, with a rhetorically powerful warning that readers ought not to overdo any tendency (or desire) to read for allegory, or rather to see in what is absent an allegory of presence:

> True, the silences in the South African farm novel, particularly its silence about the place of the black man in the pastoral idyll [. . .], speak more loudly now than they did fifty years ago. Our ears today are finely attuned to modes of silence. We have been brought up on the music of Webern: substantial silence structured by tracings of sound.[17]

The consequence, Coetzee muses, is that critique, a mode of reading that Eve Sedgwick would later label paranoid (rather than reparative), is focused less on what is present than what is hidden: 'Only part of the truth, such a reading asserts, resides in what writing says of the hitherto unsaid; for the rest, its truth lies in what it dare not say for the sake of its own safety, or in what it does not know about itself: in its silences'.[18] Here again it serves to read these observations alongside Coetzee's reflections – in his 1987 *Weekly Mail* Book Fair address, published as 'The Novel Today' in the same year as *White Writing* – on the ways in which politics threatened to overwhelm the literary in late-apartheid South Africa.[19] Such a 'mode of reading' – against the grain and for an obscured idea that relies on external validation indexed to an extra-literary hierarchy of value – nonetheless runs the risk, 'like all triumphant subversion, of becoming the dominant in turn', Coetzee warns.[20] 'Our craft', he concludes (the craft of criticism, we might infer, but not without hearing the implied irony), 'is all in reading *the other*: gaps, inverses, undersides; the veiled; the dark, the buried, the feminine; alterities'.[21]

It is difficult not to hear in this a warning to those in search of a hidden maternity, a 'buried, [. . .] feminine' genealogy. Jade Munslow Ong reads this rhetorical conclusion at face value: 'the "truth"' of the farm novel lies '"in its silences"; therefore "[o]ur craft is all in reading"' to uncover these.[22] For Munslow Ong, taking Coetzee's lead requires uncovering the hidden genealogy that places Schreiner's example at the centre of all Anglophone South African writing, at least that which participates in one way or another (through its engagement with the consequences of capitalist uneven development) in modernist experiment. 'Anglophone South African literature emerges as modernism in the work of Olive Schreiner, and persists as modernism even to the present day', she argues.[23] In this reading, the crucial difference between Schreiner's anti-pastoralism and that of writers like Gordimer (in *The Conservationist* [1974]) and Coetzee (*In the Heart of the Country*) is that the later writers 'repurpose the form to emphasise loss and lack rather than future hope'.[24] Schreiner's writing remains open-ended and hopeful.

Whether or not we agree that the repurposing of Gordimer and Coetzee shares a modus operandi, we should ask what else we might infer from Coetzee's response to Schreiner. In 1993, five years after *White Writing* appeared, Coetzee taught a Masters-level course on South African literature at the University of Cape Town. Amongst his course preparation papers, held at the Amazwi archives in Makhanda, is a page of notes on Schreiner.[25] Attwell suggests about these that it appears less to have been Schreiner's work than her career – not least her propensity to be drawn into public debate and her frustration at never repeating the success of her first novel – that provided a cautionary model for Coetzee; the notes do not 'seek to understand Schreiner's work per se', instead providing a 'mirror', a prompt to reflect 'on his own career', Attwell suggests.[26] '[T]here is little anxiety of influence in Harold Bloom's sense', he continues, and while *African Farm* is undoubtedly an intertext for *In the Heart of the Country*, 'it is there as a fairly neutral precedent, one that lends itself to re-inscription, rather than a work whose intellectual weight leaves a deep impression'.[27] For Coetzee, according to these reflections, Schreiner lost touch with the source of her inspiration, with 'the Karoo landscape' in which 'a certain confluence of environment and ideas and the intellectual excitement of growth' spurred her early work.[28] The problem with the later writing, specifically the posthumously published *From Man to Man*, is that Schreiner 'ultimately failed [. . .] to absorb herself deeply enough into the project to transform it and allow it to transform her so that in the end she and it should discover where/what they were'.[29] The suggestion here is that what matters is how an artist fuses content and form to produce something more than the sum of parts. Furthermore, that for an artist whose inspiration is intimately connected to place, removal from that place (which might also be a time, which is to say a moment in a place in which 'confluence of environment and ideas' interact) diminishes creative power. If *African Farm* was 'a bank account' that underwrote Schreiner's public career, in Coetzee's analysis, without such power being augmented and further transformed by 'more poesis' (Coetzee's words), 'the result' – in Attwell's paraphrase – would inevitably be 'attenuation, anxiety, bad faith'.[30]

Attwell does not quote an aside that Coetzee offers in the notes after his assessment of Schreiner's failure to rise above the success of her first book, or the interaction of ideas and place that gave rise to it:

> Of course I am talking about myself. Whenever we talk about something else we are talking about ourselves. In this case, because the subject is so near to home, the relevance is unusually obvious. But I choose not to reflect on it, turn myself back to look upon it (like Orpheus). Life is too short. (The meaning of the Orpheus story: you kill your inspiration by turning back to look at it).[31]

This is an unusually frank and affecting acknowledgement of an influence less disavowed than deliberately uninterrogated, cast again (we might notice) in implicitly feminine terms. Coetzee's 'subject' here is compared to Eurydice, who ought – in the terms of the conclusion to chapter 3 of *White Writing* – to remain hidden ('veiled'): 'dark, [. . .] buried, [. . .] *feminine* [. . .]'.[32] 'Ideas are certainly important – who would deny that?', Coetzee remarks in 'Homage', but one of the lessons he claims to have learned from Herbert is that style might in fact be more important than content, 'style that is also an approach to the world and to experience, political experience included'.[33] Indeed, Coetzee continues:

> the ideas that operate in novels and poem, once they are unpicked from their context and laid out on the laboratory table, usually turn out to be uncomplicated, even banal. Whereas a style, an attitude to the world, as it soaks in, becomes part of the personality, part of the self, ultimately indistinguishable from the self.[34]

What is at stake here is an anxiety on Coetzee's part about the relationship between form and content, ideas and place, early achievement and what might follow. He is also asking whether style is enough, especially if one feels drawn away from the early sources of inspiration or entanglement, or even towards modes of direct engagement with politics at the expense of poesis. In his own case, if style is indistinguishable from the (male writerly) self, what hope is there of establishing the nature of a relationship to what is veiled, or 'feminine'? Is there some other complex Oedipal relationship to the feminine operating in these musings, in which Schreiner and the maternal are aligned?[35]

***

Perhaps the only way to approach (some of) these issues with anything other than speculation is by posing a different set of questions entirely. To do so, we must pivot from discussing Coetzee's own discussions of Schreiner, as well as other critics' discussions of these discussions, to ask instead what another approach might yield. What if we looked beyond the claim that Coetzee's *In the Heart of the Country* – or indeed *Disgrace* (1999) – is in conversation with Schreiner's *African Farm*? What if we instead placed two different texts, one by each author, side by side, and considered not what the comparison suggests about direct influence, but instead what their respective engagements with the dichotomy Coetzee sketches between 'the ideas that operate in novels' and 'style' (as 'an attitude to the world') suggests about each author's response to a broadly similar set of dilemmas, however differently contextualised by their historical moments?[36] Concomitantly, and in a not unrelated vein, how does each think with or against allegory – understood as a text that 'fulfills its rhetorical purpose (whatever that purpose might be) by means of the transformation of some phenomenon into a figural narrative'?[37] As we will see, a strong case for influence might be evident, though impossible to confirm, as I have found in more than one other such comparison.[38] A more interesting question is what such parallel readings suggest about the usefulness of questions of inheritance, influence or indebtedness in the first place.

The texts I have in mind are *Trooper Peter Halket of Mashonaland* (1897, hereafter *Trooper Peter*), the last sustained work of allegorical fiction Schreiner would publish in her lifetime, and Coetzee's first published book, *Dusklands* (1974). *Trooper Peter* offers a pointed attack on Cecil Rhodes and the British South Africa Company's genocidal campaign in Mashonaland in 1896, which followed the conclusion of the Second Matabele War, known to Zimbabweans as the First Chimurenga (war of independence). *Dusklands* contains two parts that also engage with imperial or neo-imperialist violence. 'The Vietnam Project' is a portrait of the mental breakdown of Eugene Dawn, an expert in psychological warfare tasked with providing a report on future directions for US propaganda during the conflict in Southeast Asia. The second part, 'The Narrative of Jacobus Coetzee', offers a disturbing account of another genocidal campaign, this time in southern Africa during the mid-eighteenth century. Each part features versions of characters named 'Coetzee'. In the first part, the protagonist's demanding line-manager is Coetzee; in the second's paratexts, the translator and author of a preface ('J. M.') as well as the translator's father ('S. J.'), ostensibly editor of his ancestor's 'Narrative' and author of an afterword, share the protagonist's surname. These repetitions offer a characteristically playful instantiation of the author's reflections on style's transformation into something 'ultimately indistinguishable from the self'.[39] 'There remains the matter of getting past Coetzee', Dawn remarks at one point, later reporting his manager's quip about Dawn's work-in-progress that he 'never imagined this department would one day be producing work of an *avant garde* nature'.[40] There is (in other words) a great deal to be said about the author's staging of the problem of authority through an invitation to question the authority of personae bearing his name.

Like *Dusklands*, Schreiner's *Trooper Peter* is also a work in two parts, though they are not separate narratives; its structure revisits the contrast between night and day that so memorably opens *African Farm*, the first part set on 'a dark night', the second 'a hot day'.[41] In the first, Halket, an English migrant, not yet twenty-one, who has abandoned prospecting and enlisted as a volunteer in the British South Africa Company's campaign, is separated from his party while delivering maize to a nearby camp.[42] Disoriented (and likely delirious), he waits up through the night on a hillock, pensive, though we read that

'Peter Halket had never been given to much thinking'.[43] His musings reveal the degree to which Halket has bought into the narrative of imperial expansion and, more importantly, capitalist exploitation of southern Africa. 'All men made money when they came to South Africa —Barney Barnato, Rhodes—they all made money out of the country', he thinks.[44] His fantasies of setting up one company 'and another', forming a 'syndicate', selling shares in London in something like a pyramid scheme (cashing out just at the right time), give way to memories of the extreme violence in which he has participated, 'working a maxim gun' that 'seemed to him [...] more like the reaping machine he used to work in England', destroying villages and burning granaries for miles around.[45] British forces also routinely dynamited caves in which the fleeing Mashona took shelter.

Into this scene of disturbed and disturbing revery comes a stranger the reader is invited to understand as Christ.[46] Declaring himself '[a] friend', and with uncanny knowledge not only of Halket's life but of the goings on for miles around (including in those caves and other hiding places), the stranger proceeds to encourage the young man to apprehend his complicity in unjustifiable acts of violence.[47] The Stranger asks Halket to think himself into the position of the Mashona, drawing a comparison with the then very topical Armenian rising against Ottoman rule being reported in the illustrated papers. Are the Armenians also rebels, as the Company had cast the Matabele and Mashona, he asks? 'Oh, the Armenians aren't rebels, [...] they are on our side!', Halket responds.[48] Crucially, they are (also) Christian, and yet to be Christian is to offer hospitality and aid irrespective of race or creed, the Stranger argues, presenting a series of case studies and allegories to win Halket over.[49] Soldiers are merely pawns in a larger game in which 'the speculator and the monopolist' are the villains, he explains.[50] In one example of principled resistance to these structures of exploitation, a minister in Cape Town brandishes from the pulpit the Cape Parliament's report into the Jameson Raid, a recent, failed, Company-backed insurgency in the Transvaal Republic over New Year 1895–96 intended to extend British control over Johannesburg's gold reserves.[51] The minister admonishes his congregation to stop supporting war mongering and exploitation, much to the chagrin of his status-conscious wife.

Halket is sent to proclaim his new conviction that the Company's war is unjust, and in part II, set a day or two later, we are in the encampment after Halket has taken issue with his Captain's treatment of a captive Shona man. We overhear other soldiers, some of them Cape colonials rather than English volunteers, who have a clearer sense of the forces manipulating events but who nonetheless toe the line.[52]

They are horrified when, rather than being made to execute the captive himself as punishment for advocating on his behalf, Halket releases the prisoner and appears to stab himself. They find his body at the base of the tree to which the Shona man had been bound, Halket's corpse here a replacement – in a gruesome inversion – of the Matabele man in a photograph of a lynching that Halket described to the Christ-Stranger in Part I: 'I saw a photograph of the [. . .] hanging, our fellows standing around smoking [. . .]'.[53] A similar image appeared as the frontispiece to Schreiner's text in its early editions.

This gruesome exhibit has its counterpart in those photographs that Eugene Dawn, the narrator of 'The Vietnam Project', carries 'around in [his] briefcase' to provide himself with 'the slight electric impulse' he requires to 'free' his 'imagination' for his work.[54] Amongst these are images of a rape, of soldiers with three severed heads, and stills from a propaganda film of imprisoned Communist rebels. There is much to connect these instances of brutality in Indochina to imperial misadventures in southern Africa – down to the particularities of decapitation and the widespread use of sexual violence (implicit in many of Halket's accounts of Black women used as sex slaves; 'I got her cheap', he tells Christ at one point).[55] If Marilyn Dawn shares with the Capetonian minister's wife (in *Trooper Peter*) an anxiety about losing a position of comfort and respect on account of her husband's deviation from orthodoxy ('Marilyn's great fear is that I will drag her out of the suburbs into the wilderness'), her concern that Dawn has 'become addicted to violent and perverse fantasies' also makes her a voice of conscience not unlike Halket's remembered mother.[56] Indeed, an approach that seeks to read against the grain of *Trooper Peter* as allegory might view Halket's intuition of his mother's likely displeasure at his actions in Mashonaland manifesting in the apparition (during a delirium) of the Stranger as a kind of superego.[57] Peter has already recalled a poster of Christ on his childhood schoolroom wall, and we know he is prone to suggestion. He is also exhausted.[58]

Eugene Dawn likewise has a dark night of the soul, one that leads to dreams of 'total air-war', paranoia and violence.[59] He kidnaps his son and holes up in a motel room with the child. Tracked down by his wife and federal agents, he stabs the boy with a fruit knife (the child survives) and is subsequently institutionalised. On Dawn's bedside table are copies of Patrick White's *Voss* (1957) and Saul Bellow's *Herzog* (1964), about which he reflects: 'I spend many analytic hours puzzling out the tricks which their authors perform to give their monologues [. . .] the air of a real world through the looking-glass'.[60] Dawn does not see the hubristic failure of his own grand designs (no less than a blueprint for 'a new mythology') foreshadowed in those novels of imperial overreach and wounded male pride.[61] 'I have an exploring temperament', he declares at one point: 'Had I lived two hundred years ago I would have had a continent to explore, to map, to open to colonization'.[62] This is precisely what we see in the second part of *Dusklands*, the 'Narrative' of an explorer-freebooter two centuries earlier, licensed by a different but no less exploitative Company than that in *Trooper Peter* one century later – and no less restrained than Halket admits Rhodes and his agents to be in present-day Zimbabwe.[63]

In 'The Narrative of Jacobus Coetzee', framed by paratexts that present the fiction as an historical document (mediated by a translator and explicated in an afterword), the eighteenth-century narrator offers his own version of the 1760 hunting and trading expedition to the interior described in a deposition (also translated in an appendix), and augments this account too with a description of a subsequent outing the following year. This expedition features extreme violence visited on the Namaqua people, who had nursed Coetzee to health after serious illness during his first journey. He had been expelled from the settlement after injuring a child during a delirium (mirroring of the events of Part 1) and, in late 1761, returns to the settlement 'as a storm-cloud': 'Fill in the morning smoke rising straight into the air, the first flies making for the corpse, and you have the tableau'.[64] Jacobus Coetzee's attempt to separate his own people (Calvinist Dutch, French Huguenot, German) from the country's indigenous inhabitants recalls Halket's defence of the Armenians against the Turks. 'We are Christian, a folk with a destiny', Coetzee claims.[65] By contrast, the /Xam ('Bushmen') are to be hunted like animals, and Black and other autochthonous men, Namaqua, Griqua, 'Hottentot', pressed into service, and the women (in his words, 'completely disposable') into sex slavery.[66]

If Dawn sees his role as counterposing a new mythography in support of neo-imperialist US hegemony in Vietnam, the eighteenth-century Coetzee sees his own role in similar terms. Both view as inevitable the process of colonization through redescription. 'I am a hunter, a domesticator of the wilderness, a hero of enumeration', the genocidal explorer declares, 'a tool in the hands of history'.[67] His Coetzee descendant, 'S. J.', the editor ostensibly responsible for the afterword, echoes this assessment in a statement. *Dusklands* invites us, via the information in the preface that the afterword is based on lectures delivered between 1934 and 1948 at the University of Stellenbosch (the institution most associated with the intellectual support for Afrikaner nationalism, 'National Christian' pedagogy and conservative Calvinist theology in the period of the rise of the National Party), to read as an article of apartheid faith: 'The Company's men were only playing the role of the angel with the flaming sword in this drama of God's creation'.[68] Halket might well have agreed before his encounter with his Stranger. Those who objected in the older Coetzee's period (and just after), like John Barrow, are dismissed (by S. J. Coetzee) as 'victim[s] of many of the enthusiasms and prejudices of Enlightenment Europe'.[69] So, too, are liberals dismissed by the Company in *Trooper Peter*. If Schreiner's political critique relies on readers to applaud Halket's Damascene turn and understand his death as a Christ-like sacrifice, the political message of *Dusklands* appears to rely more heavily on irony than on straightforward allegory, and the key to reading against the grain of the first-person records that constitute each part is recognising the lack of congruence between the attitude to the world of Coetzee's book's megalomaniacal narrators and that of the author, which is to say that style (as 'attitude to the world') is central to understanding the 'ideas that operate' in this book (whether or not a novel).[70]

***

Whether *Dusklands* is itself allegorical depends on how we understand the term. For Gary Johnson, allegory 'emerges from a complex interaction among authorial intention, the nature of the narrative text in question, the rhetorical situation that gave rise to that text, and the reader's response to it'; in other words, it is 'a kind of gestalt'.[71] Perhaps there is common ground here with Derek Attridge's suggestion that we not regard allegory as a mode that requires the reader constantly to look outside the text, but rather – and at least in Coetzee's hands – one that requires readers to think differently about aspects of the text that might appear allegorical; 'we need to ask how allegory is thematized in the fiction, and whether this staging of allegory as an *issue* provides any guidance in talking about Coetzee's *use* of allegory (and about allegory more generally)', Attridge argues.[72] Michael Titlestad reminds us that, for Paul de Man, allegory was inherently temporal because indexed to historical reality,[73] and in *Dusklands* we see allegory itself presented as at the heart of the colonial condition. It is Titlestad's view that:

> In a compelling, if disturbing, sense, Jacobus Coetzee is an allegorical figure committed to maintaining an allegorical order of being; allegory, in an act of imperial will, becomes ontology. Without the border between savagery and civilization, his presence asserts, where would the settler be? Without the assurances of allegory, how would we tell settlers from savages? [. . . .] It is allegory, the settler facing the savage, which permits the demarcation of the colony and the protection of its territory: allegory, in other words, rather than only theorizing and abstracting from the real, is potentially its very basis.[74]

It is this that we intuit Eugene Dawn realises about his new mythography of the USA's presence in Vietnam, and the epiphany drives him mad. This realisation is not vouchsafed to Peter Halket, though Schreiner's allegory teeters on the edge of realising that style might not need to be sacrificed to idea. It would perhaps have taken only a frame narrator (or the device of a letter from Peter to his mother) to reveal the antecedental proximity of Schreiner's anti-colonial allegory to Conrad's *Heart of Darkness*, serialised in *Blackwoods* magazine in early 1899, less than two years later (Conrad's Kurtz is an antecedent, too, for *Dusklands*'s monomaniacal anti-heroes, and *In the Heart of the Country*'s title is surely allusive). Peter is not Marlow, though he is a proto-Marlovian figure whose doubts about the authority of his own inherited vocabularies do become clear, and lead – in one reading of Schreiner's novella's ending – to suicide.[75]

Irene Gorak's illuminating discussion of Schreiner's use of allegory, chiefly in *African Farm*, observes that

> [a]t the back of Schreiner's novels lurks a half-examined link between allegory and colonial occupation: the first, a trope based on parallels between different orders of experience; the second, a kind of nightmare comparison, proceeding by physical as well as verbal expropriation, between two cultures, a 'higher,' colonizing power, and a 'lower,' less developed culture, to be attacked, absorbed, emptied, and cast aside.[76]

Here Gorak has in mind Abdul JanMohamed's elaboration of the centrality of Manichean allegory to colonial power relations. 'Nonhegemonic colonial texts, observes JanMohamed' – Gorak writes, quoting – '"tend to be less preoccupied with maintaining the stability and coherence of the individual and the community", and, conversely, "more tolerant of heterogeneous definitions of self and society"'.[77] *African Farm*, she argues, is however one such text only imperfectly, deploying a variety of allegories and allegorists and serving as a 'test case for the recuperability of allegory in progressive social narrative'.[78] Those of Schreiner's characters who are the most suggestive as allegorists, Gorak argues, are those whose experience returns them to 'the body'; these seem most able to negotiate the dangers of allegory's association with external authority.[79] By the time we find Schreiner despairing at the mendacity of the repressive and extractive infrastructure she identifies most closely with Rhodes in *Trooper Peter*, however, allegory is put to more direct and less subtle purpose, though the prescription for the ills identified seems clearer than in *African Farm*. According to Gorak, what *Trooper Peter* seems to call for is 'to substitute an openhearted, Whitmanesque spirit for the structures of exploitation set in place by capitalists and entrepreneurs'.[80]

There is a structural irony here in that allegory itself, in tying representation to referent, replicates a pattern of domination that privileges the qualifying point of reference. Gorak attempts to cast allegory recuperatively as effecting an unsettling of a 'promised pattern of stable exchange' that replicates that which the colony hopes for from 'metropolitan parent' (in a relationship that mirrors that of allegory to referent).[81] And yet, as Gorak acknowledges, '[c]olonies remedy trading deficiencies and surpluses in the parent economy, but with little value added for themselves', with a resulting 'play between two orders of settlement that dissolves into a mirage, an erosion of cultural identity rather than a fructifying birth'.[82]

I want to suggest that Coetzee learns a formal or structural lesson from this conundrum, one that, in his reading of Schreiner's derogation of style (at least in the later works) in place of ideas, might be seen in his scrupulous attention, at least in his early (apartheid-era) career, to undermining narrative authority by presenting occasions of narration that are rigorously contextualised, undermined, compromised or impossible. This draws attention to the hand that writes – in *Dusklands* literally Eugene Dawn's and Jacobus Coetzee's, as well as the latter's transcriber, translator, and (later) editor. The result is a text – or series of texts – that requires of the reader an awareness of irony closer to that invited by the first part of *African Farm* (where for example we see through Blenkins before Otto, or indeed Tant Sannie, does). *Dusklands* is nothing if not a 'formally peculiar work' – in Attwell's judgment – precisely because it offers an unsettling of assumptions about the connection between realism and the novel as form with which the mainstream Anglo-American – and certainly South African – literary establishment had operated for a century.[83]

Dusklands presents texts that are ostensibly realist and non-allegorical, but the context of their production, the author-persona standing behind them, along with the context of their first publication, mean that readers in that moment, and certainly readers ever after, have to see their function as complex allegory, and not only for Apartheid. Dawn's narrative presents America's imperial atrocities as allegory for Apartheid's and European colonialism and presents Jacobus Coetzee as allegory for America's war in Vietnam as well as for the ongoing emergency in South Africa. The mirror state of the two texts produces the first degree of allegory while the context of production and authorship produces the second, and all of this is managed without recourse to the supernatural or the magical (*Peter Halket*), or the timeless/indeterminate setting of Coetzee's 1980 novel *Waiting for the Barbarians*. For these reasons, perhaps, it is possible to see why

Coetzee in a certain moment would have been dismissive of Schreiner even as the model of *Peter Halket* might have been generative. Disavow what looks aesthetically/formally bankrupt (the Christian supernaturalism) even as the political commentary and use of a more obvious form of allegory provide prompts for Coetzee's more sophisticated formal inventions and innovations.

Russell Samolsky's study of violence, allegory and futurity in work by Conrad, Kafka and Coetzee (chiefly *Waiting for the Barbarians*) invokes Walter Benjamin's 'figuration of history as ruin' as riposte to Hegel's view that history's progression was toward apotheosis 'as absolute spirit'; for Benjamin, by contrast (in particular the secular Baroque drama that inherited its form from the medieval mystery plays), allegory served 'in the realm of thoughts, what ruins are in the realm of things'.[84] Allegories encode reflections on time's ruin and invite us to learn to see past how promise might have unfolded differently. Insofar as Schreiner's *Trooper Peter* and Coetzee's *Dusklands* are invitations to imagine different outcomes to acts of colonial and imperial excess, they partake of allegory's utopian energies; the difference in their approach is perhaps ultimately one of degree, favouring one side or the other of a style-idea dichotomy that is finally less a dualism than itself an allegory for any writer's response to the exigencies of their socio-political moment.

Works Cited

Attridge, Derek. *J. M. Coetzee and the Ethics of Reading: Literature in the Event*. Chicago: University of Chicago Press, 2004.

Attwell, David. 'Mother – Age of Iron'. In *J. M. Coetzee and the Life of Writing: Face to Face with Time*, 161–76. Oxford: Oxford University Press, 2015.

—. 'J. M. Coetzee's South African Intellectual Landscapes.' In *The Intellectual Landscape in the Works of J. M. Coetzee*, edited by Tim Mehigan and Christian Moser, 274–93. New York: Camden House, 2018.

Benjamin, Walter. *On the Origin of German Tragic Drama*, translated by John Osborne. New York: Verso, 1977.

Chrisman, Laura. *Rereading the Imperial Romance: British Imperialism and South African Resistance in Haggard, Schreiner, and Plaatje*. Oxford: Clarendon Press, 2000.

Coetzee, J. M. *Dusklands*. [1974] London: Vintage, 1998.

—. 'Homage.' *The Threepenny Review* 53 (Spring 1993): 5–7.

—. Interview with Chull Wang, 1998, Coetzee Papers. Harry Ransom Research Center, Austin.

—. Lecture and Seminar Notes for the Comparative African Literature Module,

MA Literary Studies, 1991, Coetzee Collection. University of Cape Town, Cape Town.
—. 'The Novel Today.' *Upstream* 6, no. 1 (Summer 1988): 2–5.
—. *White Writing: On the Culture of Letters in South Africa*. New Haven: Yale University Press, 1988.
de Man, Paul. 'The Rhetoric of Temporality'. In *Blindness and Insight: Essays in the Rhetoric of Contemporary Criticism*, 188–89. Oxon: Routledge, 1983.
Gorak, Irene E. 'Olive Schreiner's Colonial Allegory: *The Story of an African Farm*'. *Ariel: A Review of International English Literature* 23, no. 4 (October 1992): 53–72.
JanMohamed, Abdul R. *Manichean Aesthetics: The Politics of Literature in Colonial Africa*. Amherst: University of Massachusetts Press, 1983.
Johnson, Gary. *The Vitality of Allegory*. Athens: Ohio State University Press, 2012.
Kannemeyer, J. C. *J. M. Coetzee: A Life in Writing*, translated by Michiel Heyns. Jeppestown: Jonathan Ball, 2012.
Kosofsky Sedgwick, Eve. 'Paranoid Reading and Reparative Reading, or, You're So Paranoid, You Probably Think this Essay is About You'. In *Touching Feeling: Affect, Pedagogy, Performativity*, 123–51. Durham: Duke University Press, 2003.
Lewis, Simon. 'The Transnational Circulation of Dissent: Olive Schreiner and the Colonial Counter-flows of Unitarian Freethinking'. *Safundi: The Journal of South African and American Studies* 14, no. 1 (February 2013): 1–15.
Munslow Ong, Jade. *Olive Schreiner and African Modernism: Allegory, Empire and Postcolonial Writing*. London: Routledge, 2018.
Rorty, Richard. *Contingency, Irony, and Solidarity*. Cambridge: Cambridge University Press, 1989.
Samolsky, Russell. *Apocalyptic Futures: Marked Bodies and the Violence of the Text in Kafka, Conrad, and Coetzee*. New York: Fordham University Press, 2011.
Schreiner, Olive. *Trooper Peter Halket of Mashonaland*. London: T. Fisher Unwin, 1905.
Titlestad, Michael. 'Unsettled Whiteness: The Limits of Allegory in Three South African Novels'. In *Authority Matters: Rethinking the Theory and Practice of Authorship*, edited by Stephen Donovan, Danuta Fjellestad, and Rolf Lundén, 223–56. Amsterdam: Brill, 2008.
Van der Vlies, Andrew. *Present Imperfect: Contemporary South African Writing*. Oxford: Oxford University Press, 2017.
—. *South African Textual Cultures*. Manchester: Manchester University Press, 2007.
—. 'World Literature, the Opaque Archive, and the Untranslatable: J. M. Coetzee and Some Others'. *Journal of Commonwealth Literature* 58, no. 2 (2023): 480–97.
—. 'Writing, Politics, Position: Coetzee and Gordimer in the Archive'. In *J. M. Coetzee and the Archive: Fiction, Theory, and Autobiography*, edited by Marc Farrant, Kai Easton, and Hermann Wittenberg, 59–75; 63–65. London: Bloomsbury Academic, 2021.

Watson, Stephen. 'Speaking: J. M. Coetzee'. *Speak* 1, no. 3 (June 1978): 21–24.
Wittenberg, Hermann. 'Towards an Archaeology of *Dusklands*'. *English in Africa* 38, no. 3 (October 2011): 71–89.

Notes

1. Watson, 'Speaking: J. M. Coetzee', 22, emphasis added.
2. Coetzee, Interview with Chull Wang, 8 April 1998, unpublished in English translation, Coetzee Papers, Harry Ransom Research Center, MS-0842, box 83.4.
3. Coetzee, 'Homage', 7. Coetzee is here revisiting an assessment of the infertile local grounds for production of something that could ever be regarded as a 'Great South African Novel' that he offered in *Leadership* magazine in 1983.
4. Coetzee, 'Homage', 7. The sentence ends, after a semi-colon, with the qualification 'or rather, South Africa produced three or four versions of the land which today I regard as, and even thirty years ago suspected to be, false and corrupt'.
5. See for example the chapter in this collection by Nicholas Jose, Mandy Treagus and Alex Sutcliffe.
6. Munslow Ong, *Olive Schreiner and African Modernism*, 164. See also my own discussion of Coetzee's book as a 'deconstruction of, and in part an homage to, the anti-pastoralism of Schreiner's *The Story of an African Farm*' in Van der Vlies, *South African Textual Cultures*, 134. Many others have made similar connections.
7. Coetzee, 'Homage', 5.
8. Coetzee, 'Homage', 5. Several of these writers are also addressed as models for Coetzee's partially fictionalised younger self in *Youth*.
9. Attwell, 'J. M. Coetzee's South African Intellectual Landscapes', 276.
10. Coetzee, 'Homage', 5.
11. Coetzee, *White Writing*, 11.
12. Coetzee, *White Writing*, 64. The chapter appeared first as an essay with the same title in *English in Africa*, 1–19. My references are to the text in *White Writing*.
13. Coetzee, *White Writing*, 64.
14. Coetzee, *White Writing*, 65.
15. See Van der Vlies, 'Writing, Politics, Position: Coetzee and Gordimer in the Archive', 63–65. For the full text of Coetzee's remarks on this occasion, see Kannemeyer, *J. M. Coetzee: A Life in Writing*, 658–61 (n91).
16. Coetzee, *White Writing*, 66.
17. Coetzee, *White Writing*, 81.
18. Coetzee, *White Writing*, 81. See also Sedgwick, 'Paranoid Reading and Reparative Reading'.
19. Coetzee, 'The Novel Today'.
20. Coetzee, *White Writing*, 81.
21. Coetzee, *White Writing*, 81, Coetzee's italics.
22. Munslow Ong, *Olive Schreiner and African Modernism*, 162 (quoting Coetzee, *White Writing*, 81).

23. Munslow Ong, *Olive Schreiner and African Modernism*, 143.
24. Munslow Ong, *Olive Schreiner and African Modernism*, 147.
25. Coetzee, 'Lecture and Seminar Notes for the Comparative African Literature Module'.
26. Attwell, 'J. M. Coetzee's South African Intellectual Landscapes', 274 (quoting Coetzee, 'Lecture and Seminar Notes').
27. Attwell, 'J. M. Coetzee's South African Intellectual Landscapes', 276.
28. Coetzee, 'Lecture and Seminar Notes', quoted in Munslow Ong, *Olive Schreiner and African Modernism*, 162.
29. Coetzee, 'Lecture and Seminar Notes', quoted in Munslow Ong, *Olive Schreiner and African Modernism*, 162.
30. Attwell, 'J. M. Coetzee's South African Intellectual Landscapes', 275.
31. Coetzee, 'Lecture and Seminar Notes', quoted in Munslow Ong, *Olive Schreiner and African Modernism*, 162.
32. Coetzee, *White Writing*, 81, Coetzee's italics.
33. Coetzee, 'Homage', 7.
34. Coetzee, 'Homage', 7. The passage continues: 'To put it another way: in the process of responding to the writers one intuitively chooses to respond to, one makes oneself into the person whom in the most intractable but also perhaps the most deeply ethical sense one wants to be.'
35. For Attwell's reflections on Coetzee's long engagement with his own mother's example in his writing, see for example the chapter 'Mother – *Age of Iron*'.
36. Coetzee, 'Homage', 7.
37. Johnson, *The Vitality of Allegory*, 7–8.
38. I have considered a broadly similar set of questions about the usefulness of arguing for direct influence or indebtedness in two other engagements with Coetzee's work and its possible intertexts; in chapter 2 of *Present Imperfect: Contemporary South African Writing* in relation to the similar challenges to conventional autobiography staged in Coetzee's *Scenes from Provincial Life* trilogy and Gregor von Rezzori's *Memoirs of an Anti-Semite* (1981), and in an essay on the similarities between Ingrid Winterbach's Afrikaans-language novel *Erf* (1987) and Coetzee's *Age of Iron* (1990), which raises questions about the visibility of minor-language literatures in constructions of 'World Literature' as discipline in the Euro-American academy. See Van der Vlies, 'World Literature, the Opaque Archive'.
39. Coetzee, 'Homage', 7.
40. Coetzee, *Dusklands*, 15, 2.
41. Schreiner, *Trooper Peter Halket of Mashonaland*, 13, 193.
42. Schreiner, *Trooper Peter Halket of Mashonaland*, 63, where we are also told Halket volunteered because of the promise of 'lots of loot to be got, and land to be given out, and that sort of thing [. . .]'.
43. Schreiner, *Trooper Peter Halket of Mashonaland*, 23. Compare 'The Vietnam Project', in which Dawn declares himself 'a thinker' while his manager, Coetzee, tells him that the military, by contrast, 'are, as a class—to put it frankly—slow thinking [. . .]', Coetzee, *Dusklands*, 4.
44. Schreiner, *Trooper Peter Halket of Mashonaland*, 28.
45. Schreiner, *Trooper Peter Halket of Mashonaland*, 31, 30, 40, 16.

46. Halket first supposes him '[o]ne of the Soudanese Rhodes brought with him from the north [...]'. Schreiner, *Trooper Peter Halket of Mashonaland*, 48.
47. Schreiner, *Trooper Peter Halket of Mashonaland*, 44.
48. Schreiner, *Trooper Peter Halket of Mashonaland*, 94.
49. As Laura Chrisman suggests, Christ's speeches 'target intellectuals, women, and workers as potential opponents of Rhodesian expansionism', though she also notes that Peter voices her own critique of the British class system in doubting that he will be afforded a hearing because of his class status: 'Schreiner upholds the possibility of an oppositional anti-imperial metropolis but at the same time exposes it for what it is, a fiction that cannot be realized until the British class structure, with its impoverishment, degradation, and snobbish exclusivity of its own subjects, is destroyed'. Chrisman, *Rereading the Imperial Romance*, 9.
50. Schreiner, *Trooper Peter Halket of Mashonaland*, 130.
51. The minister was based on David Faure, founder of the Free Protestant Church in Cape Town in 1867, and a friend of Schreiner's in the 1890s. See Lewis, 'The Transnational Circulation of Dissent', 11–12.
52. 'It's a damned convenient thing to have a war like this to turn on and off'. Schreiner, *Trooper Peter Halket of Mashonaland*, 208–9.
53. Schreiner, *Trooper Peter Halket of Mashonaland*, 78.
54. Coetzee, *Dusklands*, 13. Hermann Wittenberg's archival work on the publication of *Dusklands* showed how Coetzee had thought about 'a gravure plate titled "Hottentotten Mädchen" from Leonard Schultze's treatise *Aus Namaland und Kalahari* (1907)' as basis for the book's cover; Wittenberg speculates the image was to function 'ironically, in keeping with the anti-colonial critique of the Jacobus Coetzee narrative'. In the event, a watercolour by early nineteenth-century British painter Thomas Baines was used, '[p]resumably [...] to strengthen the fictive historical framing', Wittenberg suggests. See Wittenberg, 'Towards an Archaeology of *Dusklands*', 81. One might say also to index both the operation of the European gaze and emphasize its banality.
55. Schreiner, *Trooper Peter Halket of Mashonaland*, 57.
56. Coetzee, *Dusklands*, 9.
57. Peter recalls his mother admonishing him not to use violence on those weaker than himself. Schreiner, *Trooper Peter Halket of Mashonaland*, 80.
58. Schreiner, *Trooper Peter Halket of Mashonaland*, 25.
59. Coetzee, *Dusklands*, 28.
60. Coetzee, *Dusklands*, 37.
61. Dawn writes that 'The highest propaganda is the propaganda of a new mythology'. Coetzee, *Dusklands*, 25.
62. Coetzee, *Dusklands*, 31–2.
63. Schreiner, *Trooper Peter Halket of Mashonaland*, 82.
64. Coetzee, *Dusklands*, 100.
65. Coetzee, *Dusklands*, 58.
66. Coetzee, *Dusklands*, 65, 61.
67. Coetzee, *Dusklands*, 80, 106.
68. Coetzee, *Dusklands*, 110.
69. Coetzee, *Dusklands*, 111.

70. Coetzee, 'Homage', 7.
71. Johnson, *Vitality*, 17.
72. Attridge, *J. M. Coetzee and the Ethics of Reading*, 34.
73. Titlestad, 'Unsettled Whiteness', 226. The reference to De Man is to 'The Rhetoric of Temporality', 188–89.
74. Titlestad, 'Unsettled Whiteness', 252, 253.
75. I am here invoking Richard Rorty's definition of the ironist as the person who 'has Socratic doubts about the final vocabulary he inherited', about 'his own moral identity, and perhaps his own sanity' and who 'desperately needs to *talk* to other people [. . .] because only conversation enables him [. . .] to keep his web of beliefs and desires coherent enough to enable him to act'. Rorty, *Contingency, Irony and Solidarity*, 187. I acknowledge Peter D. McDonald for having convinced me twenty years ago that this is amongst the most useful ways to understand Marlow's compulsion to narrate his own moral confusion in *Heart of Darkness*, *Lord Jim*, and other Conrad texts in which he appears.
76. Gorak, 'Olive Schreiner's Colonial Allegory', 57.
77. Gorak, 'Olive Schreiner's Colonial Allegory', 56 (quoting Abdul R. JanMohamed, *Manichean Aesthetics*, 267).
78. Gorak, 'Olive Schreiner's Colonial Allegory', 57.
79. Gorak, 'Olive Schreiner's Colonial Allegory', 67.
80. Gorak, 'Olive Schreiner's Colonial Allegory', 60.
81. Gorak, 'Olive Schreiner's Colonial Allegory', 65–66.
82. Gorak, 'Olive Schreiner's Colonial Allegory', 66.
83. Attwell, *J. M. Coetzee and the Life of Writing*, 63, see also 62, and on the composition of 'The Vietnam Project' from 1972, see also 59–60.
84. Samolsky, *Apocalyptic Futures*, 155 (quoting Benjamin, *On the Origin of German Tragic Drama*, 177–78).

Chapter 15

Olive Schreiner In/Beyond the Museum

Paul Walters and Jeremy Fogg

If the function of a museum is, as Karin de Jager claims, the collection and preservation of 'artefacts which are representative or symbolic of the past', then Samuel Cron Cronwright-Schreiner's reburial of Olive Schreiner – in a specially constructed tomb of local ironstone, on a mountaintop south of the small Eastern Cape town of Cradock, South Africa, on 13 August 1921 – can be seen as a deliberate museological act, albeit a seemingly private and somewhat macabre one.[1] On the surface, and as presented by Cronwright (in the unpublished but detailed typescript 'The Reinterment on Buffelskop'), he was honouring a wish expressed by Schreiner only two months after their marriage.[2] In April 1894, when the 'briefly transfigured pair' stood together on Buffelskop, Schreiner had expressed the wish that they be buried there.[3] Given Cronwright's proprietorial attitude to Schreiner's life *and* letters (indeed all her writings, as the copyright holder after her death), however, it is at least arguable that the reinterment was his final attempt to link his life with that of his much more famous wife.

In this chapter, we have taken a predominantly historical approach to the origins and development of the Schreiner House Museum in Cradock. One reason is that we were, in our different capacities, participants and eye-witnesses in that process. More importantly, we hope that our description may suggest the roles that a research-based 'parent' institution may play in the creation and evolution of an 'author museum' located at some distance from the parent.[4] The National English Literary Museum (NELM, now Amazwi South African Museum of Literature) was itself initially a project of the Institute for the Study of English in Africa. Our discussion will touch on these developments before turning to the details of the House itself.

As Cronwright was carrying out his elaborate plans for the reinterment of the mortal remains of Schreiner, their baby daughter, and a favourite dog on the top of Buffelskop, it is unlikely that he was aware that a Cradock child, then about three-and-a-half years old, would grow up to become a professor of English and establish a national literary museum that would contribute signally to the preservation and promotion of Schreiner's legacy. Yet Cronwright relied on that child's aunt, Miss Mary Butler,[5] for the draft eye-witness account of Schreiner's reinterment; he 'corrected' it before giving it to her father, James Butler, to publish.[6] James was founder and editor of Cradock's English language newspaper, *The Midland News*, and he set up his daughter's account, after which Cronwright proofread it and approved it for publication. Mary, by her nephew Professor Guy Butler's later account,[7] would see to it that her nephews and nieces grew up aware of South African literature, 'introducing [them] to Olive Schreiner and to books by F. C. Slater and Pauline Smith as they appeared'.[8]

This was not Cronwright's first contact with James Butler. While managing John E. Wood's farm 'Krantz Plaats' (of which Buffelskop forms the highest point) for more than nine years from December 1884 onwards, he had been a 'frequent contributor to the paper, both through the letter columns and as the pseudonymous author of a "Karoo Farmers" Column'.[9] It was Cronwright's attack in his column on Rhodes's proposed 'Strop Bill' that first brought Cronwright to Schreiner's notice, and led to her asking her friend and former employer, Erilda Cawood, to try to find out the identity of the writer. Schreiner, too, had had past dealings with James Butler, most notably over his refusal to publish her highly emotional 'Letter to the Women of Somerset East' (1900) in his columns.[10] Thus both Schreiner and Cronwright, the Butler family, and Cradock share several links that ought not to be overlooked in considering the attention that NELM was to give the Schreiner House in Cradock, even though Schreiner herself spent a mere three years of her early teens there. (One has, however, only to read the first page of *The Story of an African Farm* to see how powerfully the landscape of the Karoo region had inscribed itself on the consciousness of this impressionable young woman).

After the reinterment in 1921, Cronwright was to visit the tomb on at least two further occasions:[11] 29 November 1922, with Anna Purcell (who had wished to be part of the original burial party) and W. W. Lidbetter, the outstanding photographer who lived in Cradock; and 28 March 1925, 'when introducing his new English-born wife to his favourite landscapes'.[12] Butler believes the 1922 expedition was to gather photographic material for a projected separate publication on the 'Reinterment'.[13] Cronwright's second climb was undertaken alone.[14]

Fast forward 28 years to 1964: the victory of the Afrikaner Nationalist Party over Jan Smuts's United Party in the General Election of 1948, and successively larger majorities for the party in each subsequent election, has entrenched and intensified the fragmentation of South Africa along racial and linguistic lines. Despite an official policy of equal rights for English and Afrikaans, the nationalist regime is promoting Afrikaner dominance in every sphere of public life. There are four – almost exclusively white – universities at which the medium of instruction is English: Cape Town, the Witwatersrand (Wits), Natal (two campuses) and the numerically tiny Rhodes in Grahamstown (Makhanda) in the Eastern Cape. These institutions somewhat vainly attempt to cling to a more inclusive, liberal notion of academic freedom, and seek to reserve the right to determine for themselves matters of curricula and the racial composition of their staff and student bodies – an allegiance that is structurally jeopardised by their almost total financial reliance on the Nationalist Government for their very existence (in some instances for 80 percent or more of their funding). Nevertheless, these universities seek to promote a degree of divergence from Afrikaner Nationalist ideologies and policies (its 'grand narrative'), and, in particular, to uphold values that are seen as 'inclusive', 'democratic', sceptical of uncritical allegiance to an alien and alienating dogma, and with an emphasis on human rights.[15]

Guy Butler, grandson of James and nephew of Mary, has occupied the Chair of English at Rhodes University, Grahamstown (the nearest university to Cradock, his home town), since 1952. After matriculating from the Cradock High School for Boys, Butler entered Rhodes University in Grahamstown – then several hours away on unpaved roads – where he finished a Master's Degree in English Literature before volunteering to serve in South Africa's National Defence Force in the British Empire's fight against the Axis powers in World War II. The latter part of that service would expose him for the first time to European 'high culture' in the form of what was visible amidst the ruins of war-torn Italy as the Allies fought their way northwards from the 'toe'. After the War, an ex-serviceman's grant enabled him to read English at Brasenose College, Oxford.

Butler returned to South Africa to teach briefly at a private boys' school in Johannesburg before accepting a junior post in the Department of English at the University of the Witwatersrand, whence, in late 1951, with a prize-winning play to his credit, Butler was appointed to the Chair of English at his alma mater. In the course of a long and distinguished career in this post, Butler enabled the founding at Rhodes University of the departments of Linguistics and English Language, of Speech and Drama, and of Journalism. He was one of the founders of the National Festival of the Arts, held in Grahamstown every July from 1974 (until 2020), and of Rhodes University's Institute for the Study of

English in Africa (ISEA), founded in 1964. Butler wryly commented in 1991 (in the third volume of his autobiography) that '[this] Institute has shown a talent for giving birth to other institutes'.[16] Apart from anchoring *New Coin Poetry* and *English in Africa* for many decades, ISEA was to become the home of the *Oxford Dictionary of South African English on Historical Principles*, and the Molteno Institute for Language and Literacy, which had a major impact on the acquisition of mother-tongue literacy and accelerated learning of English as an additional language in segregated primary schools for Black children from the late 1970s to the early 1990s.

Most relevant to this chapter, however, is the formation under the umbrella of the ISEA of what was to become the National English Literary Museum (NELM). The story of its founding has been told several times: initially and briefly by Butler himself in the third volume of his autobiography, quoted in the paragraph above. Then in 2005 by Malcolm Hacksley – NELM's director at the time – in the twenty-fifth Anniversary Edition of *NELM News*.[17] More recently, it was dealt with briefly by Paul Walters (2016) and in much greater detail by de Jager (2016) in the same publication.[18] In contrast to its financial dependence on government funding, NELM's relative independence in outlook and policy of Pretoria and its Afrikaner Nationalist hegemony was assured by its being recognised in 1981 as an 'Associated Research Institute' of Rhodes University.

One of the principal aims in the founding of NELM was to provide a home for the preservation and study of manuscripts, published works and other memorabilia of all South African writers in English, and the writings of Schreiner clearly fall within this purview. As a published poet and dramatist, Butler had long been concerned about the fate of the manuscripts of all South African writers in English, especially when lucrative offers were being made by comparatively wealthy British and American research institutes and libraries. In 1970, the Human Sciences Research Council (HSRC), based in Pretoria and funded by the Afrikaner Nationalist Government, established a 'National Documentation Centre'. Butler's response was to appeal in 1972 to the HSRC – part of whose function was to support larger research projects – to fund a documentation centre for English based at Rhodes University and under the auspices of the ISEA. He donated his own considerable private collection of manuscripts and first editions to launch this centre, known initially as the 'Thomas Pringle Collection' in honour of South Africa's earliest poet writing in English.

After considerable anxiety lest the Afrikaner Nationalist Government under the aegis of the HSRC might simply appropriate this project – and some astute negotiating – this venture of Butler's in 1980 achieved the status of a 'National Declared Cultural Institution', to be known as NELM and based in Grahamstown. This new status was proclaimed in the *Government Gazette* in April 1980, and in that month the new national Museum moved to the rented premises it was to occupy for the next thirty-six years: the 'Priest's House' in Beaufort Street, owned by the local Albany Museum.

Despite considerable constraints on available physical space, NELM and its collections thrived, and demand for its services grew steadily. The increasing presence of Southern African texts in school syllabi meant a growing demand from schools for assistance with teaching and contextualising these texts. There was simply no space at all for such educational work or for outreach within the Museum's premises, so NELM made a virtue of a necessity, and took the education work out of the physically limited and limiting Museum and into the bush.

This step gave rise to a series of literary and environmental camps where learners – usually in the ten to fourteen years age-range – would spend one or two nights under canvas at a site of literary significance. Here they would be introduced to literary texts and authors relevant to that site; would sometimes participate in activities designed to recreate the conditions under which some texts were written; and would be encouraged to reflect on the stimulus experiences provided and to respond by producing their own creative work.

The award-winning programme of innovative and highly successful camps was largely the brain-child of NELM's Basil Mills. Perhaps the most taxing, but undoubtedly the most popular (open to all age groups from ten upwards), was the climb up Buffelskop to the Schreiner sarcophagus (dealt with below), which often included nights under canvas in the Buffelshoek valley. The spectacular 360-degree view from the Kop has changed little – if at all – since 1921, and the sarcophagus itself only in the repointing of the stone joints in the early 2000s. Compared to other commemorative sites today, it takes very little imagination to picture oneself there with Schreiner and Cronwright in April 1894, or as a member of the burial party in August 1921. If museums at their best have the capacity to stimulate an informed re-imagination of what it must have been like to have lived at the time of the incident or period depicted, then the unchanged landscape in its sheer three-dimensional vastness and power transcends the work of display artists working within the confines of a museum building.[19]

Three years after NELM's founding in 1983, a small house 'in near derelict state' at 9 Cross Street, Cradock, was discovered to be the house in which Schreiner had lived briefly with her siblings, Theophilus (Theo) and Henrietta (Het or Ettie), while Theo was principal of the Boys' School there. With the help of a national insurance company, NELM was able to acquire this cottage and the large piece of ground on which it stands.[20] After considerable research, excavation and reconstruction, the Schreiner House Museum came into existence as a 'satellite' of NELM, with a curator jointly funded by NELM and the Cradock Municipality. This acquisition by NELM of the Schreiner cottage provided the fledgling National English Literary Museum with an unprecedented occasion for a museum to commemorate, in a highly author-specific way, the first internationally recognised South African novelist in English. Today the restored and amplified Schreiner House bears comparison with such sites as Wordsworth's Dove Cottage in Cumbria, or Hardy's home in Dorchester, and offers similar opportunities for education, outreach and the exercise of the historical imagination.

The superb fifth chapter, 'Cradock', in Karel Schoeman's 1991 biography of Schreiner should ideally be read in full to provide an adequate context for what the move in 1868 from Balfour to Cradock was to mean to Schreiner. It began, as Schoeman notes:

> her association with the town and district in which she was to spend eight or nine years of her life, write the major portions of her three novels, and finally be buried; a town that has become [. . .] inextricably associated with her fame and memory.[21]

In Chapter IX, 'Cart Tracks in the Sand', of Schreiner's posthumously published novel, *From Man To Man*, Schreiner sketches 'her' Cradock:

> Up-country, in the red karroo, was the town where Aunt Mary-Anna lived, red karroo to the right of it, red karroo to left. A river bed ran below the town, in winter full of dried mud banks and reaches of gravel and bare stone, but in the summer rains, coming down red and full, the dark sand-laden water lying level with the banks and bearing on its waves trees and stumps, the carcasses of drowned animals, and even sometimes at long intervals a human corpse.
> All round the plain were flat-topped mountains, some broken into jagged points, but still bearing the marks, in their flat structure, of what had been the shores of seas and lakes, the remains of whose mammoth amphibious beasts lay still within the stratified shale, turned in the course of ages to stone themselves.[22]

Schoeman points out that the 'Karoo' (modern spelling) covers about one third of the area of the present Republic of South Africa, and Cradock, at 870 metres above sea level, lies on part of 'the high plateau of the South African interior'. He also notes:

> In the neglected part of the modern Cradock, behind the Schreiners' former house in Cross Street, something remains of that rural community with its modest houses, large plots, vegetable gardens, huge pear trees, quince hedges, stone walls and paved furrow, the white walls and green gardens in vivid contrast to the great, barren circle of mountains around the town .... On [Schreiner's] walks up and down the street outside the Schreiner home – the pensive pacing noted by a contemporary – that panorama of mountains would have been before her eyes.[23]

On the eve of the South African War (17 July 1899), writing to Betty Molteno from Johannesburg (which she loathed), Schreiner explored some of the significances of these mountains for herself:

> I like to think you and Miss Greene look at my mountains and love them. I have loved them so all my life since I was a child. It is on the top of that highest point that you see from Cradock that I have bought my two acres of ground and where Cron and I and my baby are to be buried.
> [...]
> it's such an unchanging joy and *rest* to me to think of that mountain top. Oh, the peace, the beauty of it up there. You can see far away [...] Often since I have been in Johannesburg there has seemed nothing else on earth beautiful to me personally but that mountain top.[24]

Schoeman, at the beginning of his chapter on Cradock, provides a factual description of the Karoo as a region, into which the opening paragraphs of *African Farm* plunge the reader.[25]

The heritage site now known as the Schreiner House Museum consists of two major elements: the first is the Schreiner House itself (behind which is a small garden) and the Ikhamanga Hall (which includes a bookshop and toilets); the second a much larger site (erf 2701) surrounding these buildings, still to be fully developed.[26] Both these erven are now owned by Amazwi.[27]

For three years, in the late 1860s, the four youngest surviving children of Gottlob and Rebecca Schreiner lived together at 9 Cross Street. Olive Schreiner (born in 1855) was the ninth child. Another sibling, and certainly, after Olive, the most notable today, was William Philip (born in 1857), the tenth child, who became premier of the Cape Colony and a major force in South African politics at the time of the South African War of 1899–1902. Two others, also forceful characters with strong convictions, made their mark on their era as well. They were Theo, born in 1844, and Ettie born in 1850. In Schoeman's words: '[t]he Schreiner children were ... the products of heredity as well as the atmosphere in which they had grown up; all of them were difficult, intense, self-willed and emotional people who might, in some respects, be described as abnormal'.[28]

Schreiner's years at 9 Cross Street marked a period of precocious intellectual growth and personal unhappiness. Persecuted for her religious doubts by her devout sister Ettie and conservative brother Theo, she turned increasingly for company to the world of books. Her wide reading as a teenager was in large part enabled by the resources of the Cradock Public Library, then newly established by a local medical practitioner, Dr George Grey. Schreiner's own collection of books, as they are preserved today at the Schreiner House and Amazwi, include the works of Ralph Waldo Emerson, Herbert Spencer, Henry David Thoreau, Edward Gibbon, Charles Darwin, John Stuart Mill, Thomas Huxley, John Ruskin and Johann Wolfgang von Goethe. Many of these texts are intensively annotated, as Schreiner, denied the debate of a classroom, furiously 'wrote back' to the authors she was reading. This was a habit that lasted until her death. When her body was discovered on the morning of 11 December 1920, her right hand still held one of her 'little mapping pens', and the book she had been reading 'lay open in her left hand on her chest'.[29]

The reconstruction was undertaken by the Cradock Town Engineer's Department along lines determined by a professor of architecture, Professor J. C. Radford, of Wits. His aim was to restore the house in form and content as closely as possible to the state in which Schreiner would have known it. This involved a considerable amount of detective work, for the house had been substantially altered over the intervening years: no original wooden windows or doors remained, floors were of concrete, and the Victorian fireplaces had been removed. Only the shell of the house remained to give some clue as to the original appearance, while several additions to the original core of the house were discerned only by carefully examining the various roof coverings.

It seems from the title deeds that the original core of the house was built sometime between 1847 and 1852. Radford's analytical process suggested strongly that the earliest structure had only three rooms: the front two including the passage, and the kitchen. This core is of mud brick 400mm thick, with yellowwood beams and plank ceilings.

Structural and archaeological evidence made it possible to ascertain the probable form of the house in the late 1860s. This consisted of five rooms: the original three (probably a bedroom, lounge and kitchen) on to which a dining-room and *stoepkamer* (a small room opening off the veranda) had been added. The careful research that went into this project has contributed substantially to the understanding of the layout of the typical nineteenth-century home in Cradock and has helped to inform other restoration projects in Cradock, most notably the restoration of an entire street of simple townhouses, now known as the 'Tuishuise'.

The degree of care with which the restoration was carried out includes the maintaining of an authentic colour scheme and other details. For instance, although turquoise may strike a present-day visitor as an unusual choice for the walls of the kitchen, it was widely used at the time in the belief that the high lead content of this paint would serve as a deterrent to flies. In the kitchen, reflecting the custom of the time, the old *misvloer* [dung floor] was relaid.[30] In the oldest part of the house, a panel has been left to show to visitors the composition and method of construction of the walls during the mid-nineteenth century. At that time, cement was imported and expensive, and therefore usually used only for plastering externally. An examination of the panel area shows that soft sun-dried brick set in mud mortar was used. Unlike the more sophisticated but less flexible building methods of the present era, this form of construction has the advantage of allowing the building to move with the effects of seasonal changes without cracking. Radford states that whilst it might not be immediately apparent, the Schreiner House is of some cultural significance as it represents in 'its plan and spaces' a very typical late nineteenth-century middle-class home in Cradock: 'This particular aspect became very important during the restoration process, especially as there is virtually no surviving documentation which would give us any specific idea of what the house looked like or how it was used during the Schreiners' residence'.[31]

In addition, the House is of some architectural value, especially in its restored state. 'Little building fabric remains from the early days of Cradock, particularly in an unaltered state, so that the house as it now is gives us a fairly good picture of the domestic architecture of the times'.[32] Many other of the early buildings have been swept away in the periodic floods of the Great Fish River. Another architect and enthusiast of Karoo architecture, Gabriel Fagan, wrote in 2008 of these:

> simple buildings, so modest and similar, yet each with its own identity, economically planned and built with basic materials – mud, stone, wood and sometimes whitewashed with lime. Each is planned with care and aptly detailed with good proportions and symmetrical facades to contribute to the serenity of the street as a whole.[33]

Radford adopted 'restoration by anastylosis as the only viable method that could be employed' to achieve the policy's aim [of restoring the house as it would most probably have looked during the 1860's].[34] This meant reconstructing the original appearance of the house by closely examining a wide range of existing old houses in Cradock and by studying all relevant visual material, such as sketches and photographs of the period: 'From this a pattern was abstracted, and onto the shell of the existing building a series of "typical" solutions were imposed to give it a definite form'.[35] After this substantial restoration, the house was officially opened on 7 November 1986.

Nearly twenty years later, in a democratic South Africa, Schreiner received belated national recognition: President Thabo Mbeki awarded her the Order of Ikhamanga in Gold (posthumous) on 2 December 2003.[36] The accompanying citation proclaimed that the Award was made 'for her exceptional contribution to literature and her commitment to the struggle for human rights and democracy'.[37] It was accepted on behalf of the Schreiner family by sitting ANC Member of Parliament Jenny Schreiner, a published poet in her own right, and a great-granddaughter of Schreiner's beloved younger brother, William Philip.[38]

In 2004, NELM was given a one-off grant to improve its exhibitions. As the Schreiner House was the only property NELM owned, the Council decided to apply these funds to improve facilities there, and to mark the 150th anniversary of Schreiner's birth in March 2005 with the construction of a building behind the extant building. The existing bookshop was incorporated into the plan, and in March 2005 it was officially opened by Judge Chris Nicolson. It was named the Ikhamanga Hall in honour of the Award made to Schreiner two years earlier and, in addition to an attractive bookshop and improved visitor facilities, provides approximately sixty-five square metres of space for meetings, book launches and lectures, as well as substantial wall space for the display of exhibition material. As an interpretation centre, it relieves visitor pressure on the somewhat fragile structure of the restored House.

This rigorously professional and historically sensitive approach to the restoration of a significant building was later extended to other sites associated with Schreiner's Cradock years: with the support of the Cawood family of Ganna Hoek, Mills was able to conduct an investigation of the remains of Klein Ganna Hoek Farmhouse (strongly associated with early drafts of *African Farm*),[39] and, later, to explore the slender remains of the Krantz Plaats farmhouse to which Cronwright brought his bride in 1894 (now on the farm 'Riverview').[40] The latter site formed the focus of a visit by the Grahamstown Historical Association in October 2006; four years later, delegates to the first 'Spirit of Schreiner' Festival in 2010 were able to visit both sites on a field trip led by Mills.[41]

Exploration and 'mapping' were extended from buildings to the terrain itself: in 1991, members of the Education and Outreach Department of NELM used the evidence provided by Cronwright's diaries and his meticulous notes under numerous photographs to identify the probable routes up the mountain of the various parties involved in Schreiner's reinterment. This exploration subsequently provided three different possible hiking trails up Buffelskop. These trails, varying in length and difficulty, have been used to good effect during the countless expeditions to the Schreiner sarcophagus organised subsequently by the Outreach Department of NELM/Amazwi. From 1996 for nearly twenty years, NELM staff also led an annual expedition for members of the English Honours class at Rhodes University.[42]

As we were drafting this chapter, an important article on the Schreiner House Museum was published by Dana Lande in *Narrative Culture*.[43] We are grateful to Jade Munslow Ong for bringing it to our attention, and would recommend it as an essential complement to this chapter, especially for readers not able to visit Cradock for themselves. Lande's text, at its simplest level, provides precise and detailed descriptions of the exhibitions currently on display in both the Schreiner House and the adjacent Ikhamanga Hall. Lande goes much further, though: by employing the discourse of critical narrative analysis, Lande contextualises the House within many of the present and past social, historical and political narratives within South Africa, which she perceives as 'intersecting' in this particular site. Her analysis is perceptive and illuminating.[44]

The significance of Cradock (and its mountains in particular) in the life of Schreiner is further underscored by an important incident in her early married life. Shortly after Schreiner and Cronwright were married in February 1894, they climbed up to the summit of Buffelskop on the farm Krantz Plaats, which Cronwright had been managing for nearly ten years. Despite what must have been a particularly strenuous walk for her, once at the summit, Schreiner was thrilled by the beauty of the panorama. Cronwright describes the incident:

> Before we went down she said: 'We must be buried here, you and I, Cron. I shall buy one morgen of this top and we must be buried up here'. It jumped with my own desire, and so it came to be decided.[45]

After her reinterment, the spectacular site they chose rapidly became a focus of pilgrimage for Schreiner enthusiasts: perhaps the first was Schreiner's staunch friend and fellow campaigner for women's rights, the aforementioned Purcell, conducted by Cronwright himself.[46] Mary Butler (a member of the burial party) certainly saw to it that the Butler family made the climb. From the 1980s onwards, the climb to the sarcophagus – although the most physically demanding of the NELM literary excursions – has proven by far the most popular. It is open to all age groups from age ten upwards, and never fails to grip the imagination of all who have undertaken it. With school or university groups, a deliberate attempt is usually made to encourage participants to spend some time alone and in silence to allow the site to do its work. Reading and personal writing always formed an important part of the literary camps for schools.

One such response is captured in an extract from an essay written by Stefania, a ten-year-old pupil at Victoria Primary School in Grahamstown (Makhanda). It may be taken as indicative of NELM's success in communicating something of Schreiner's legacy to a rising generation. She writes about nearing the summit of Buffelskop:

> Then, out of the blue, two black eagles were circling above us, it was exquisite! I had only seen them in captivity before and felt proud to have been one to have experienced that glorious moment. Then the top . . . we could see the top! We only had a few hundred metres to go and then we would be there.
>
> As I stepped onto the flat piece of ground at the summit I could hear my friends' voices, but as I looked around me they seemed to disappear, for I was surrounded by, by, the most spectacular view and a place with much history. And for one moment, just that one moment, I felt king of the world. I had made it, I had really truly conquered Mount Buffelskop. I had done it![47]

Many changes – almost all for the better – have taken place since the youthful Stefania penned those lines: NELM/Amazwi has achieved a home of its own in a splendid purpose-built building in Grahamstown, which itself has been renamed 'Makhanda'; Amazwi's remit has been broadened to include all the languages and literatures of South Africa; and it is now possible to drive nearly to the summit of Buffelskop in a vehicle with 4 × 4 traction. Most exciting for Cradock and the Schreiner House Museum, though, is the issuing in January 2022 of invitations from Amazwi to tender for the development of the full Erf 2701. There is every possibility that this ongoing project will result in Schreiner and her works being even more widely appreciated in Cradock and the communities that the Schreiner House Museum serves.

Works Cited

'Archive of Compositions from Victoria Primary School'. NELM, Grahamstown.
Beeton, Ridley. *Facets of Olive Schreiner: A Manuscript Source Book*. Johannesburg: Ad Donker, 1987.
Butler, Guy. *A Local Habitation: An Autobiography 1945–90*. Cape Town: David Philip, 1991.
—. *Karoo Morning: An Autobiography 1918–1935*. Cape Town: David Philip, 1977.
—. *Tales from the Old Karoo*. Johannesburg: Ad Donker, 1989.
Cronwright-Schreiner, Samuel. *Her South African Ancestors* London: Philip Allan & Co, 1930.
—. *The Life of Olive Schreiner*. London: T. Fisher Unwin, 1924.

—. ed., *The Letters of Olive Schreiner 1876–1920*. London: T. Fisher Unwin, 1924.
de Jager, Karin. 'The Story of NELM: from Filing Cabinet to International Museum'. In *ISEA 1964–2014*, edited by Monica Hendricks, 85–99. Grahamstown: NISC, 2016.
De Villiers, Andre. 'Memories of NELM'. In *NELM News Anniversary Edition (25 Years)*, edited by Malcolm Hacksley, 14–15. Grahamstown: NELM, 2005.
Driver, Dorothy. 'Memories of NELM'. In *NELM News Anniversary Edition (25 Years)*, edited by Malcolm Hacksley, 13–14. Grahamstown: NELM, 2005.
Eve, Jeanette, and Basil Mills. *A Literary Guide to the Eastern Cape*. Cape Town: Double Storey Books, 2003.
Fagan, Gabriel. *Brakdak*. Cape Town: Breestraat Publikasies, 2008.
Fogg, Jeremy. *The Schreiner House, Cradock*. Grahamstown: NELM, 1993.
Government of South Africa. 'Recipients of the National Order Awards, 2003'. https://www.gov.za/sites/default/files/schreiner.pdf.
Hacksley, Malcolm. 'Memories of NELM'. In *NELM News Anniversary Edition (25 Years)*, edited by Malcolm Hacksley, 1–3. Grahamstown: NELM, 2005.
Horrabin, Winifred. Unpublished Papers, 1935–1937. Hull University Archives, Hull.
Lande, Dana. 'Narrative Intersections in an Author Museum: The Olive Schreiner House'. *Narrative Culture* 7, no. 1 (Spring 2020): 60–78.
Mills, Basil. 'Klein Gannahoek: An Archaeo-Architectural Investigation of an African Farmhouse'. *Southern African Field Archaeology* 1 (1992): 42–53.
Palmer, Eve. *The Plains of Camdeboo*. London: Collins, 1966.
Radford, J. C. 'The Architectural Background to the Restoration of the Schreiner House, Cradock'. *Restorica* 22 (October 1987): 8–12.
Rive, Richard, ed., *Olive Schreiner: Letters 1871–99*. Cape Town: David Philip, 1987.
Schoeman, Karel. *Olive Schreiner: A Woman in South Africa 1855–1881*. Johannesburg: Jonathan Ball Publishers, 1991.
Schreiner, Olive. *The Story of an African Farm*, edited by Stephen Gray. Johannesburg: Penguin Books, 2008.
—. *From Man to Man or Perhaps Only*, edited by Dorothy Driver. Cape Town: UCT Press, 2015.
Walters, Paul. '"The Child is Father to the Man . . ." Origin and Early History of the ISEA'. In *ISEA 1964–2014*, edited by Monica Hendricks, 8–33. Grahamstown: NISC, 2016.
Walters, Paul, and Jeremy Fogg (eds). *Olive Schreiner: Her Reinterment on Buffelskop*. Grahamstown: National English Literary Museum, 2005.
—. '"This morning a year ago . . .": Annotated Extracts from Samuel Cronwright's *Diaries* (Sept. 1921–Nov. 1923)'. *English in Africa* 42, no. 1 (2015): 103–129.
—. '"When in Doubt Leave Out": The Country Editor Who Declined to Publish a Long Letter From Olive Schreiner'. *English in Africa* 47, no. 2 (2020): 41–58.

Letters

Henry Havelock Ellis to Winnifred Horrabin, 19 February 1935. Henry Havelock Ellis: Letters to Winnifred Horrabin 1935–1937. Brenthurst Archive. Brenthurst Library, Johannesburg.

—. 'Letter to the Women of Somerset East'.In *The Letters of Olive Schreiner 1876–1920*, edited by S. C. Cronwright-Schreiner, 378–85. London: T. Fisher Unwin, 1900.

Lynn Cronwright to Henry Havelock Ellis, 22 October 1936. Correspondence between Henry Havelock Ellis and Samuel Cron Cronwright-Schreiner. Harry Ransom Research Center, Austin.

Samuel Cron Cronwright-Schreiner to Gerald Orpen, 23 January 1926. W. P. Schreiner Papers. University of Cape Town, Cape Town.

Notes

1. de Jager, 'The Story of NELM', 87.
2. Walters and Fogg, *Olive Schreiner*, 12.
3. As early as 1886, according to a letter at Harry Ransom Research Center from Erilda Cawood to Rebecca Schreiner, Schreiner had expressed the wish to be buried among [Cawood's] mountains (Beeton, 1987, n57). Buffelskop forms part of the same massif. This, together with the date of their climb, casts serious doubt on the theory that Schreiner was influenced by Cecil John Rhodes's choice of the Matopos in her choice of burial site.
4. See also Lande, 'Narrative Intersections in an Author Museum'.
5. For more on Mary Butler, see Note 84 in Walters and Fogg, *Olive Schreiner*, 154 and our recent article '"When in Doubt Leave Out . . ."'.
6. See Walters and Fogg, *Olive Schreiner*, 122–23 and 'Diary II' entries for 14 and 15 August 1921 respectively.
7. Butler, *Karoo Morning*, 22.
8. John L. Hodgson (with whose family at Leighton Buzzard, Bedfordshire Cronwright had spent the Christmas of 1920 after Schreiner's death) in writing to a later would-be biographer of Schreiner, Winifred Horrabin, called Cronwright 'something of a tuft-hunter' – a now outmoded word for people who attempt to associate with persons more famous or socially more eminent than themselves. If Hodgson was justified in this perception, then the reinterment can also be seen as an act of self-promotion and what might be unkindly termed a publicity stunt on Cronwright's part. See Unpublished Papers, [1935–1937], Hull University Archives, U/DWH/2/3.
9. Rive, *Olive Schreiner: Letters 1871–99*, 281, n4. In the same letter to her sister Ettie, Schreiner mentions that, in 1892, she had seen Cronwright's leader on the 'Strop Bill', and had written to Mrs Erilda Cawood to find out the author's identity. Cronwright and Schreiner met some nine months later in Mrs Cawood's front room at Ganna Hoek.
10. See Walters and Fogg, '"When in Doubt Leave Out . . ."'.

11. We say 'at least' because, in Butler (1989), there is an implied visit in 1930. Although this is a work of fiction, most of the detail is factually accurate. It is also our authority for the date of Cronwright's interment.
12. Walters and Fogg, *Olive Schreiner*, 30. Also see his *Her South African Ancestors* (1930). This was part of an extended tour to the Eastern Cape, during which Cronwright was doing field research for this book on his family and his daughter's British Settler forebears.
13. Walters and Fogg, *Olive Schreiner*, 30.
14. There is a rather sad epilogue to Cronwright's elaborately planned commemoration of his famous wife: his own interment in the sarcophagus on 12 September 1936. His brother, Morthland, travelled from Johannesburg to oversee the procedure, as Cronwright's second wife, Lynn, presumably refused any part in it. On 22 October 1936, she writes a rather thin, formal note to Henry Havelock Ellis, confirming Cronwright's death, and enclosing the *Cape Times* account. See Cronwright to Havelock Ellis, 27.
15. It can be counter-argued that, if this ethos existed at all, it was singularly ineffective in achieving any significant change in the racially skewed status quo. Yet some staff and a significant number of students and student leaders at these universities dared to speak out, and were rewarded for their pains with imprisonment without trial, violent interrogation, banning orders, exile and even, in certain instances, death. Within the faith communities, Anglican clerics from Trevor Huddleston and Ambrose Reeves to Desmond Tutu maintained a stream of critical public commentary; dominies of the Dutch Reformed Church such as Albert Geyser, Beyers Naude and Allen Boesak also suffered a variety of sanctions from the very people they had been appointed to lead.
16. Butler, *A Local Habitation*, 235.
17. Hacksley, *NELM News Anniversary Edition (25 Years)*, 1–3; see also contributions by Driver (13–14) and De Villiers (14–15) in the same volume.
18. Hendricks, *ISEA 1964–2014*, 85–99; see also her extensive bibliography.
19. If we might be permitted for a moment our own 'flight of fancy': could Schreiner's admiration for Emily Brontë's *Wuthering Heights* (1847) have had something to do with her wish for a mountain-top burial? In his *Life of Olive Schreiner*, Cronwright writes: 'Olive once remarked to me that in her opinion Emily Brontë . . . was the greatest woman of genius the English-speaking peoples had produced' (181). He takes up this point again in *Her South African Ancestors* (1930), where he writes of sending his mother a copy of Brontë's novel, 'telling her she was to read it, because Olive said I was "Heathcliff with a good mother"' (188–89). Readers of Brontë's novel will recall Lockwood (one of the least reliable of the novel's multiple narrators) visiting the trio of adjacent graves of Edgar Linton, Cathy and Heathcliff in the graveyard of the ruined hillside 'kirk'. His reported thoughts end the book. Only paragraphs before, Nelly Dean has reported local legends of the ghosts of Heathcliff and Cathy being seen walking together on the moors. Lockwood's failure to understand the emotional intensity of the principal characters in the book has been repeatedly made plain, yet Brontë gives him the final sentence: 'I lingered round them, under that benign sky; watched the moths fluttering among the heath and harebells, listened to the soft wind breathing through the grass, and wondered

how anyone could ever imagine unquiet slumbers for the sleepers in that quiet earth'. Well aware of her own (un-Victorian) passionate nature at the time of her marriage (had she not written to Havelock Ellis for several years as 'My Other Self' in a phrase reminiscent of Cathy Linton's famous 'I am Heathcliff!'?), perhaps Schreiner hoped to share something of the peace of that quiet coda to that most passionate of novels. Judging by her letter to Betty Molteno from Johannesburg on the eve of the South African War, Schreiner emphasises the sense of peace and the silence she remembers. Writing about his mother's response to 'that wonderful book', Cronwright recalls that 'Olive said to me "[it] is one gasp of passion from the first page to the last"' (*Her South African Ancestors*, 189). Cronwright seems to have shared something of Brontë's love of the wild weather of the Heights when he extolled the virtues of Buffelskop as a burial site for Schreiner: 'How the thunderstorms roar and crash over the Kop! How the lightning strikes on it! [It is capped by a sheet of ironstone] .... How her "Karoo stars" shine over it!'. See Walters and Fogg, *Olive Schreiner*, 54.

20. The restoration of the house was funded by AA Mutual Life, which had become interested in it through Lucille Gillwald, who in 1983 directed Stephen Gray's *Schreiner: A One Woman Play*. The production won one of the quarterly VITA Awards sponsored and administered by the company. At the celebratory luncheon, Gillwald drew attention to the existence and uncertain future of Schreiner's former home, which she had visited during the course of her research. AA Mutual Life took the initiative and, with active support from NELM and the Cradock Town Council, acquired the house and began the work of restoration.
21. Schoeman, *Olive Schreiner*, 148.
22. Schreiner, *From Man to Man*, 266–67.
23. Schoeman, *Olive Schreiner*, 149–150; 159.
24. Rive, *Olive Schreiner: Letters 1871–99*, 369. Schoeman quotes one sentence from this letter (195). We are indebted to him for this link.
25. Perhaps for those unfamiliar with this evocative semi-desert, a paragraph from the first volume of Guy Butler's autobiography is worthy of comparison with Schreiner's: 'The Karoo, once you have been given the hint, is the eroded ruins of a world, the great lake and its giant reptiles gone but for a few bones and ripple marks, gone ... in earthquake and fire, epochs of reptilian life abolished, stone scorched and purged, and then sculpted clean and bare into noble shapes, the tactics of the elemental artist spelt out in the fine sand of the watercourses, his signature clear in the cirrus clouds. You can see all this because the air is dry, distances clear, and scarcely a shrub grows higher than your knees. In that vast semi-desert it is difficult to forget your smallness, and the colour and size of the shrubs is shy; growth slow and stubborn .... The extremities of the seasons, from snow to blinding sun, drive the lesson home: no luxury here; every year frost and fire will search you and find you out'. See Butler, *A Local Habitation*, 173.
26. An erf is a deeds-registered piece of land in South Africa.
27. On 7 June 1984, the Minister of National Education, then responsible for the funding of NELM, approved that the property known as 'Schreiner House' be accepted by the Council of NELM as donated by the AA Mutual Life Assurance Association, and on 13 September 1989, the same

Government department approved that the Council of NELM accept the donation of Erf 2701 from the Cradock Municipality. The consent of the Minister of Finance to the acceptance of this donation by NELM was received on 15 October 1990.
28. Schoeman, *Olive Schreiner*, 65.
29. Cronwright-Schreiner, *Life*, 382.
30. See Schreiner, *African Farm*, Chapter 19: 195–208.
31. Radford, 'The Architectural Background to the Restoration of the Schreiner House, Cradock', 8–12.
32. Radford, 'The Architectural Background to the Restoration of the Schreiner House, Cradock', 8.
33. Radford, 'The Architectural Background to the Restoration of the Schreiner House, Cradock', 8.
34. Radford, 'The Architectural Background to the Restoration of the Schreiner House, Cradock', 8.
35. Radford, 'The Architectural Background to the Restoration of the Schreiner House, Cradock', 8.
36. Ikhamanga is the indigenous name for the strelitzia, or 'bird of paradise' plant.
37. See Government of South Africa, 'Recipients of the National Order Awards, 2003'.
38. NELM News, 41 July 2004, 1.
39. Mills, 'Klein Gannahoek', 46–53.
40. The original farm Krantz Plaats was subdivided some time after Cronwright and Schreiner left. It is bisected by the district road to Mortimer, as well as the main railway line from Port Elizabeth to Johannesburg. The portion of the farm lying to the east of these transport arteries and on which the original homestead stood was renamed 'Riverview'; the portion above the railway line became 'Buffelshoek'.
41. This became the precursor of the annual 'Schreiner Karoo Writers Festival' – a deliberate widening of scope. The Ikhamanga Hall has played a central role in these activities. In recent years, sponsorship for a schools-focused poetry festival that runs in conjunction with the Schreiner Festival has sought to draw in learners from all the Cradock schools. In addition, NELM/AMAZWI staff have in the past contributed modules on Schreiner to learners studying 'Tourism and Hospitality' in Cradock schools. A previous curator of the Schreiner House, distinguished South African museologist Brian Wilmot, developed a number of popular Walking Tours of Cradock's heritage, and pioneered links with commemorations of the 'Cradock Four'– activists killed by apartheid security forces in 1984.
42. This field trip soon became extended to include Helen Martins's 'Owl House' in Nieu-Bethesda, the Valley of Desolation outside Graaff-Reinet, and Reinet House Museum (whose gabled grandeur contrasts so strongly with the typical Karoo domestic dwelling). As opportunity allowed, visits were sometimes made to 'Eildon' and the site of Thomas Pringle's grave (another reinterment), and to Cranemere, the home of Eve Palmer, author of a non-fictional introduction to the Karoo, *The Plains of Camdeboo* (1966). For almost all of these visits, NELM/AMAZWI is dependent on the

goodwill of the present owners of the farms concerned, and great thanks are due to their ready hospitality.
43. Lande, 'Narrative Intersections in an Author Museum'.
44. As researchers who have been exploring the bundle of contradictions (not to say competing narratives) surrounding Cronwright for more than a decade, we would like to suggest that the transition from Cronwright's distorted narratives to Stanley's is not as simple as Lande suggests. Many scholars from the 1980s onwards have contributed to the much richer (and less biased) Schreiner narrative, which undoubtedly reached a high point in Stanley's work. Moreover, the 'Cronwright narrative' is not as straightforward as Lande suggests: he is, and has been, too readily demonized. It is interesting that Havelock Ellis, who knew both Olive and Cronwright well, cautioned another would-be biographer of Schreiner against being too 'prejudiced against him': 'Of course I am far from admiring his deficiencies in literary skill and tact, & his own character ... comes out only too conspicuously in his writing. But his character makes his unfailing worship and devotion all the more remarkable. His task was really very difficult (I should have found it so myself had I accepted it [he had been Schreiner's first choice]) & in his loyalty to Olive he said nothing at all of some features of her character'. Unpublished letter to Winnifred Horrabin, 15 November 1935, Brenthurst Library, MS 143/5f.
45. Cronwright-Schreiner, *Life*, 382.
46. Before leaving De Aar for England in November 1913, Schreiner had entrusted a great deal of her MSS to Anna Purcell for safe-keeping at Purcell's estate 'Bergvliet' then outside Cape Town. See Walters and Fogg, *Olive Schreiner*, 21–23. From 13 February 1922, Cronwright spent days at Bergvliet sorting the Schreiner MSS there. See also Walters and Fogg, '"This morning a year ago..."'.
47. 'Archive of Compositions from Victoria Primary School'. NELM, Grahamstown.

Index

References to notes are indicated by n.

Abdurahman, Abdullah, 125
Act of Union, 270
African National Congress (ANC), 93, 117, 126, 129; *see also* South African Native Convention; South African Native National Congress
Afrikaner (Boer), 94, 115, 118, 120–1, 122, 143, 145, 146, 183–5, 187, 188, 192, 198n90, 202, 206–8, 269, 270, 277, 279, 280, 285, 304, 316; *see also* South African War (1899–1902)
Afrikaner Nationalist Government, 304, 315, 316, 317
allegory, 9, 25, 27, 32, 39, 41, 47–51, 54, 118, 138, 146–7, 150, 163–5, 171, 189, 200, 227–31, 233, 276–7, 295, 297, 300, 303, 305–8
Allen, Margaret, 247, 260, 263n14
anarchism, 11, 157–73
Andrews, C. F., 8, 85–95
androgyny, 70; *see also* gender
angel of the bush, 227
Anglo-Boer War *see* South African War (1899–1902)
animism, 69, 74
anti-apartheid, 14, 271, 330n41; *see also* apartheid
anti-colonial, anti-colonialism, 8, 14, 85, 91, 95, 117, 188, 270, 275, 306; *see also* colonialism
anti-imperial, anti-imperialism, 1, 2, 40, 206, 245, 270, 275, 312n49
anti-racism, anti-racist, 1, 6, 8, 85, 88, 94, 95, 115–16, 126, 139–40, 213, 270; *see also* racism
apartheid, 14, 15, 271, 280, 298, 304, 307; *see also* anti-apartheid
Ardis, Ann, 1
Armenia, Armenians, 302, 304
art, 24, 25, 35n2, 39, 46, 62, 66, 67, 119, 203–4, 233, 236, 245, 250, 271, 282, 284; *see also* illustration

Art Nouveau, 204
Ash, Bay, 245, 262n8
Attridge, Derek, 305
Attwell, David, 296, 298–9, 307
Australia, 5, 9, 12, 162, 223, 225, 229, 232, 233, 235, 244–60, 295
author-function, 178

Bagchi, Barnita, 5, 7, 8
Bagwasi, Mompoloki, 274
Baker, Louisa Alice, (Alien) 9, 224–5, 227–32, 237
Baldwin, James, 282–3
Ballinger, Margaret, 213
Balzac, Honoré de, 43, 47, 58nn9,20
Bambatha Rebellion, 106, 109, 113n26
Bantu, 89, 93, 99, 185, 278
Baraitser, Marion, 14
Bardsley, Jan, 11
Barends, Heidi, 6, 8, 228
Barnes, Emma, 5, 9, 12
Barrow, John, 305
Batavian myth, 187, 197n60
Beckett, Samuel, 296
Bellow, Saul, 303
  Herzog, 303
beloved community, 139, 148–50
Berkman, Joyce Avrech, 62, 70
Biko, Steve, 275
Bildungsroman, 4, 246, 249, 255, 259; *see also The Story of an African Farm*
birds, 68, 69, 71, 73, 74, 75, 117, 119, 130, 141, 297; *see also* Chapungu bird
Black, Barbara, 14
Black, Clementina, 41–2
Black, Constance, 41–2
Black South Africa, Black South Africans, 7, 8, 12, 50, 86, 88, 89, 90, 92, 93, 103, 105, 107, 109, 111, 115–131, 143, 144–5, 146, 185, 188, 269, 270, 273, 277, 278, 279, 282–3
Bloomsbury (London), 5, 39–42, 55, 58n7, 61

Index   333

Boake, Capel, 245
  Painted Clay, 245
Boehmer, Elleke, 5
Boer, Boers *see* Afrikaner
Botswana, 5, 271, 272–3, 274, 277, 279, 280, 282, 283, 284, 285
Bourke-Marston, Philip, 41
Brecht, Bertolt, 274
Bremer, Fredrika, 211
British South Africa Company, 117, 301; *see also* Rhodes, Cecil John; Rhodesia
Brittain, Vera, 2
Brodsky, Joseph, 296
Brown, Eliza, 100–1, 104–5, 108–9
Brown, Mary, 9
Buffelshoek, 318
Buffelskop, 13, 72, 314–15, 318, 324–5
Burdett, Carolyn, 4, 14, 25–7, 75, 159
Butler, Guy, 315–18, 329n25
Butler, James, 315, 316
Butler, Mary, 315, 316, 324

C. & E. Gernandts (publisher), 203
Caird, Mona, 1, 41, 245–6
Callil, Carmen, 252
Campbell, Roy, 14, 295
Carpenter, Edward, 2, 40, 65, 103, 104, 106, 107, 145, 157–8, 199, 223
Cederschiold, Maria, 211
Chapungu bird, 117, 119, 130; *see also* Zimbabwe
Chrisman, Laura, 3, 51, 228, 229
Christianity, Christian spirituality, 45, 46, 49, 50–1, 68, 85, 91–4, 104, 148, 179, 180, 189–90, 192, 206, 225, 246, 302, 304, 308
church, 41, 91, 92, 139, 179, 212, 249, 312n51, 328n15
Civil Rights, 8, 138–40, 150
Clayton, Cherry, 274
Coetzee, J. M., 12, 13, 295–308
  Disgrace, 300
  Dusklands, 13, 301, 304–6, 307–8
  'Homage', 295–6, 300
  In the Heart of the Country, 298, 299, 300, 306
  'The Narrative of Jacobus Coetzee', 301, 304, 305, 307
  'The Novel Today' 298; *see also* Weekly Mail Book Fair, 298
  'The Vietnam Project', 301, 303
  Waiting for the Barbarians, 307–8
  White Writing, 296–8, 299
colonialism, 86, 88, 91, 93, 95, 117, 120, 135n4, 211, 223, 307; *see also* anti-colonialism
  settler colonialism, 86, 93, 95, 237
'coloured' South Africans, 7, 13, 19n26, 92, 102, 103, 105, 106, 124, 269, 270, 283
Comyn, Sarah, 5, 9, 223, 225–6, 232

Conrad, Joseph, 306, 308
  Heart of Darkness, 306
Contagious Diseases Acts, 9
copyright, 159, 169–71, 314
Cradock, 13, 15, 314–16, 318–25
  Boys' School, 316, 319
  Public Library, 321
Crane, Walter, 204
craniometry, 281
Cronwright-Schreiner, Samuel Cron, 61, 106, 113n21, 119, 153n25, 183, 188, 208, 251, 314–15, 318, 320, 323, 324

D'Eaubonne, Françoise, 63
Danielsson, Elma, 212
Darwin, Charles, 62, 67, 70, 71, 74–5, 321
  Social Darwinism, 25, 26, 32, 185
Davidson, Apollon, 11
Davison, Emily, 8
de Man, Paul, 305
Dickens, Charles, 45, 242n65
Disraeli, Benjamin, 45
District Six, 272, 275
dogs, 23, 53, 71–2, 284, 314
Dostoevsky, Fyodor, 274, 296
Dovey, Lindiwe, 14
dream, 10, 25, 50, 54, 65, 72, 85, 87, 95, 139, 141, 147, 150, 158, 164–5, 228, 230–2, 270–1, 277, 278, 279, 282, 284–5, 303;
Driver, Dorothy, 5, 7, 12, 13, 14, 62, 143, 228, 260
Drwal, Małgorzata, 6, 11
Du Bois, W. E. B., 100, 101, 106–8, 109, 110, 118, 127, 145–6, 147, 149, 270
  The Souls of Black Folk, 101, 106–7, 109, 145
Dube, John Langalibalele, 93, 117
Dutton, Geoffrey, 249

ecology, ecological, 5, 71, 73, 229, 233
Egerton, George, 1
Eilersen, Gillian Stead, 290nn15,16, 291nn35,46
Eliot, George, 242n65, 248
  Middlemarch, 248
Eliot, T. S., 296
Emerson, Ralph Waldo, 24, 36n14, 160, 321
Engels, Friedrich, 30, 42–3, 54
Enzensberger, Hans Magnus, 296
epiphany, 99, 100, 101, 109, 110, 306
Esty, Jed, 4, 39, 44, 51
eugenics, 7, 25, 27, 168
Eurydice, 299
evolution, theory of, 26, 45, 62, 67, 74–5, 87, 134–5n1, 197n42, 270; *see also* Darwin, Charles
exchange system (in the press), 160, 163–4, 199, 201, 205
excursions, literary/historical, 324
exoticism, 202, 207
Eyre, Anghalad, 49, 50

Fabian, Bernhard, 200
Fabianism, Fabian Society, 157, 163
factory, 31, 33, 180
Fallen Woman, 233–5
Fanon, Frantz, 283
farm novel, 255, 256, 296, 297, 298; *see also* *The Story of an African Farm*
farms, farming, 23–4, 27, 35–6n11, 102, 103, 108, 202, 252, 253, 255, 259, 269, 297, 315, 323, 324, 330n40, 330–1n42; *see also* Ganna Hoek, Gannahoek; Krantz Plaats; Phoenix Farm
Fellowship of the New Life, 40, 157, 163
feminism, feminist, 1, 5, 6, 8–9, 11, 12, 25, 40, 41, 62, 63, 64, 69, 70, 71, 74, 126, 127, 130, 138, 140, 158, 164, 166, 172, 178, 180–1, 190–3, 202, 211–12, 213, 214, 223–37, 245, 247, 248, 254, 262–3n9, 270, 274
  anarchist-, 161, 163, 165, 166, 167
  bourgeois, 192, 193
  eco-, 3, 5, 6, 61–76
  proto-, 1–2, 61–3
  transnational, 193, 210–12, 213
  see also gender; women's suffrage
Fermanis, Porscha, 5, 9, 223, 225–6, 232
Filatova, Irina, 11
fin de siècle, 2, 33, 40, 47, 224, 233, 252
Flygare, Hanni, 210
Flynn, Leontia, 14
Fogg, Jeremy, 13, 19n43
Ford, Ford Madox, 296
Forster, E. M., 271
Foucault, Michel, 178
Fradkin, Betty McGinnis, 272, 273, 275, 276, 279, 287
Franklin, Miles, 12, 249, 251–2
  Cockatoos, 251
  My Brilliant Career, 251, 252
  Old Blastus of Bandicoot, 251
free love, 167, 168, 169, 172
freethinking, 1, 148, 154n54, 159, 172
Frontier Wars, 281

Gaard, Greta, 63–4
Gandhi, Leela, 2
Gandhi, Mohandas K., 6, 7–8, 85, 86, 88, 90–5, 124, 129, 139, 144, 147, 276
Ganna Hoek, Gannahoek, 69, 250, 323, 327n9
Gaskell, Elizabeth, 45, 242n65
Gcaleka, 281
Gebers Förlag, Hugo, 201
gender, 2, 5, 9, 10, 15, 49, 50, 54, 63, 64, 70–1, 76, 94, 95, 115, 117, 126, 130, 139, 140, 141, 149, 150, 179, 181, 191, 193, 223, 225–7, 229, 247, 251, 255, 279, 282; *see also* androgyny
Gibbon, Perceval, 210
Gill, Clare, 6, 11, 14

Gilman, Charlotte Perkins (Charlotte Perkins Stetson), 2, 146, 190
Gissing, George, 33
Global South, 6, 95
Gorak, Irene, 306–7
Gordimer, Nadine, 275, 298
Grand, Sarah, 1, 190, 224
Gray, Stephen, 14, 329n20
Green, Dorothy, 244, 253
Grey, George, 321
Griqua, 105, 304
Grossman, Edith Searle, 224, 225

Haggard, Henry Rider, 41
Haraway, Donna, 67, 74
Harkness, Margaret, 5, 39–56, 157, 158
  Out of Work, 39, 41, 43–9, 51, 52–4, 55
  'The Gospel of Getting On', 41, 49, 50
Harmel, Michael, 275–6
Havelock Ellis, Henry, 2, 40, 41, 47–8, 102, 157, 249–50, 331n44
  'Fiction in the Australian Bush', 250
  Kanga Creek, 249, 250
  My Life, 249–50
Head, Bessie, 12, 13, 269–87
  Bewitched Crossroad, A, 279, 285
  Maru, 13, 269, 271, 275, 277, 282, 283–4, 285
  Question of Power, A, 275, 277, 279, 282, 283, 284–5
  reading of Olive Schreiner, 272
  Serowe: Village of the Rain Wind, 278, 285
  The Cardinals, 277
  The Collector of Treasures, 285
  When Rain Clouds Gather, 275, 278
Hearn, Lafcadio, 210
Helgesson, Stefan, 213
Herbert, Zbiegniew, 296, 300
Heuzenroeder, John, 250
Heywood, Christopher, 274, 287
Hinduism, Hindus, 90, 276
Hobhouse, Emily, 223
Hofmeyr, Isabel, 5, 85, 199, 205
Holmes, Sarah. E., 159, 165–7, 172
Horrabin, Winnifred, 327n8
Humphrey Ward, Mrs, 253
  Richard Elsmere, 252, 253

illustrations, 203–5, 218n34n; *see also* art
imprisonment, 58n16, 188, 208–9, 303, 328n15
indentured labour, 85, 91, 92, 94, 95, 226
India, 2, 5, 6, 7–8, 85, 88–95, 139, 210
Indigenous peoples, indigeneity, 7, 61, 225–26, 227, 228–9, 246–7, 270, 304, 330n36; *see also* Black South Africa, Black South Africans; Bantu; Gcaleka; Mashona (Shona); Matabele (Ndebele); San, Khoisan, Bushman, Bushmen; Xhosa; Zulu
Iron, Ralph (Olive Schreiner), 24, 58n9, 201

Jabavu, John Tengo, 118, 121, 124, 125
Jacobs, Aletta, 6, 190–2, 193
Jameson, Fredric, 4
Jameson Raid, the, 118–19, 120, 121, 302
JanMohamed, Abdul R., 306
Jarlbrink, Johan, 200, 201, 206, 208
Johnson, Gary, 305
Jose, Nicholas, 5, 9, 12, 310n5

Karoo, karroo, 7, 13, 61, 62, 100, 102, 249, 259, 269, 297, 299, 315, 318–20, 322, 329n25, 330n42; *see also* landscape
Khoikhoi, Khoi, 7, 103, 113(8n), 185; *see also* San, Khoisan, Bushman, Bushmen
King, Martin Luther, Jr., 8, 138–40, 146, 148–50; *see also* beloved community
Kipling, Rudyard, 13, 103, 210
Kleen, Ingeborg, 203–4
Kleen, Tyra, 203–5
Klinger, Max, 204
Knechtel, Ruth, 69
Krantz Plaats, 315, 323, 324, 330n40
Krige, Uys, 274–79, 285, 286
    ed., *Olive Schreiner: A Selection*, 274, 275, 276, 277, 278, 279, 285
Kruger, Paul (Oom Paul), 208, 219n57

labour, 5, 7, 23–33, 36–7n19, 37n38, 70, 85, 89–90, 91, 115, 118, 120, 123, 130, 144, 146, 159, 160, 161, 163, 164, 165, 167, 170, 191, 211, 225–6, 237, 279
    as reproductive, 27–8, 33
    see also indentured labour; work
Lande, Dana, 324
landscape, 62–3, 64, 100–4, 108, 111, 113n10, 202, 229, 235, 249, 259, 299, 315, 318
language
    Afrikaans, 7, 184, 198n90, 208, 212, 297, 316
    Cape Dutch (proto-Afrikaans), 7
    Dutch, 177–93
    French, 7, 48
    Italian, 7
    isiXhosa, 7
    Swedish, 199–214
Lawrence, D. H., 258, 274
Lee, Vernon (Violet Paget), 41
Lessing, Doris, 14, 274
Levy, Amy, 41, 42
    'Women and Club Life', 42
Lewis, Desirée, 274, 290n14
Lewis, Simon, 2–3, 143
Lister, David, 14
literary model, 210
Livesey, Ruth, 53, 163
Lukács, Georg, 39, 43–4, 47, 48–9, 51–2, 55
Lynch, Lawrence L. (Emma Van Deventer), 253
    Shadows by Three, 253
Lytton, Constance, 2

machine, 5, 23–34, 36n14, 37n21, 37n38, 38n52, 171, 302; *see also* mechanisation
Mackie, Vera, 11
Magarey, Susan, 245, 260, 262–3n9
Mander, Jane, 9, 224, 225, 227, 232–7
Mansfield, Katherine, 13, 224
Marquard, Jean, 273
Marr, David, 254, 258
marriage, 9, 32, 41, 51, 70, 86, 90, 104, 158, 159, 167–69, 171, 192, 211, 225, 228, 230, 231–2, 235, 236, 245, 246–8, 255–6, 270, 284, 314, 324
Martin, Catherine, 9, 12, 245–49, 259
    Australian Girl, An, 246–49
    The Incredible Journey, 247
Marx, Eleanor, 2, 30, 41, 157
Marx, Karl, 30
Marx, Leo, 24
Marxism, 3; *see also* Karl Marx
Mashona (Shona), 302
Mashonaland, 119, 183, 301, 303; *see also* Rhodesia, Zimbabwe
Matabele (Ndebele), 302, 303
Matabeleland, 117, 119; *see also* Rhodesia, Zimbabwe
Matjiesfontein, 7, 13, 55, 100, 102, 103, 104, 108
Matthews, James, 291n37
mechanisation, 23–34
Men and Women's Club, 25, 40, 157
Merriman, John X., 88, 97n26, 105, 107, 108–9, 120, 121, 129
migration, 224–6, 232–6
Millin, Sarah Gertrude, 224
Milner, Sir Alfred, 120, 208, 219n57
modernism, modernist, 1, 3, 4–6, 12, 13, 15, 39, 40, 42–9, 51, 53, 55, 62, 224, 236, 244, 254, 258–59, 285, 298
modernity, 3, 4–5, 64, 116, 225
Molema, Leloba, 274
Molteno, Betty, 85, 88, 92–3, 95, 320, 329n19
Moore, George, 41
Msezane, Sethembile, 117, 119, 130
Multatuli (Eduard Douwes Dekker), 182, 183, 192, 196n29
Munslow Ong, Jade, 4, 5, 7, 34, 62, 116, 132–3n1, 228, 260, 274, 282, 298, 324
museum, 3, 41, 281, 314–25, 330n42
    Amazwi South African, of Literature, 15, 298, 314, 320, 321, 324–5
    Apartheid, 15
    British, 41
    National English Literary (NELM, forerunner of Amazwi), 314–15, 317–19, 323–5
    Olive Schreiner House, 13, 15, 314, 315, 319, 320–3, 324, 325
    see also restoration of buildings
Musil, Robert, 296

narrator, 23, 39, 45–7, 49–54, 65, 257, 259–60, 303–7, 328n19

Nations, Carly, 14, 50
Natives Land Act, 129, 130, 144, 145
Naturalism, 39–41, 43–5, 47–9, 51, 55
Nengoma, A. Z., 274
Netherlands, the, 5, 11, 177, 181, 183–4, 190, 192, 193
  press in, 177–93;
  confessional, 11, 179, 185, 188–9, 192
  pedagogical, 189–90
  pillarised, 11–12, 177, 179–81, 184, 189, 192
  socialist, 177, 179–80, 182–3, 184, 189, 191–2, 193
New Age, 271, 275
New Man, 70, 211
New Woman, 1, 9, 11, 12, 37n21, 41, 70, 190, 223–37, 245
New World, 224, 253
New Zealand (Aotearoa), 5, 9, 12, 223–7, 229, 232–5, 237
newspapers
  Australian Worker, 245
  Imvo Zabantsundu, 121, 124
  Indian Opinion, 124, 129
  Izwi Labantu, 121–2, 124
  Lagos Standard, 127
  Lagos Weekly Record, 127
  Liberty, 159–73
  Lucifer, the Light Bearer, 166–7
  Otago Witness, 224, 227
  Rand Daily Mail, 124
  Sierra Leone Weekly News, 124
  Tsala ea Becoana, 127, 128
  see also periodicals
Nicholas, Herbert Cecil, 254
Nivesjö, Sanja, 6, 12, 228
Nkosi, Lewis, 274
Nord, Deborah Epstein, 4, 42
Norway, 199, 216n2
Nya Idun (women's organisation), 203
Nyembezi, C. L. S., 275

obituary, 150, 210, 212, 245, 291n32
office work, 32–3, 36n14, 42, 200
Ouida (Maria Louise Ramé), 187, 188

pacifism, pacifist, 94, 106, 126, 138, 186, 191, 208
Palmer, Nettie, 251, 252
Pan-African Conference (1900), 118
Pan-Africanist Congress (1959), 275
parasitism
  class, 33
  sex, 25–6, 28–9, 30–1, 32, 33, 211, 247
Pasternak, Boris, 274
pastoral, 23–4, 297, 298; see also farm novel; farms, farming
Paterson, A. B. (Banjo), 244
Pearson, Karl, 2, 7, 25, 27, 33, 40, 68, 71, 163
Pearson, W. W. (Willie), 85, 88, 92, 94, 95

periodicals
  Church Quarterly Review, 248
  Fortnightly Review, 163, 166, 184
  The Englishwoman's Review, 247
  see also newspapers; the Netherlands: press in; Sweden: press in
Peterson, Derek R., 199, 205
Pethick-Lawrence, Frederick, 106
Phoenix Farm, 86, 93, 94, 97n22
pillarisation, 11–12, 177, 179–81, 184, 189, 192; see also the Netherlands: press in
Plaatje, Sol T., 7, 8, 93, 122, 127–30, 274–5
  Native Life in South Africa, 129–30
Plumage Bill, 73
post-colonial, postcolonial, postcolonialism, 3, 6, 14, 15, 52, 63
Potter, Beatrice (Beatrice Webb), 41, 47
Pound, Ezra, 296
prostitute, prostitution, 9, 10, 25, 29, 30, 31, 32, 33, 54, 192, 247, 269, 270; see also Contagious Diseases Act
protest, 14, 49, 91, 116–17, 126, 129, 139, 144, 187, 188–9, 192, 206, 230
Protestant, 177, 179, 180, 185, 188–9, 192
public persona, 177, 178, 188, 189
Pukekaroro, 232, 234–5

race, 2, 3, 7, 8, 13, 15, 19n26, 28–9, 49, 50, 62, 64, 72, 85–95, 99–111, 113n8, 113n26, 113–14n29, 114n32, 115–31, 134–5n1, 136n46, 138–50, 159, 184, 185, 188, 197n42, 207, 208, 247, 263n16, 270–2, 276–87, 302, 303, 316, 328n15
  mixed-, 13, 19n26, 99, 101, 102, 104–6, 109, 185, 197n42, 270, 282
  see also Black South Africa, Black South Africans; 'coloured' South Africans; Indigenous peoples, indigeneity; white South Africa, white South Africans
racism, racist, 7, 14, 35n5, 85, 86, 88, 91, 92–4, 99, 113n16, 117, 126–7, 138, 143–4, 145, 207, 247, 271, 282–5, 302–3, 328n15
  'black peril', 99, 126–7, 144, 207
  white superiority, white supremacy, 117, 126, 283
  see also anti-racism
Radford, Dollie, 41
Rafapa, L. J., 274
Rainbow Nation, 15
realism, realist 43, 44, 48–9, 53, 202, 297, 307
Remmington, Janet, 7, 8, 12, 14
restoration of buildings, 321–3, 329n20
Rhodes, Cecil John, 6, 8, 13, 14, 103, 116–22, 124, 130, 143, 206, 279, 301, 302, 304, 306, 315, 327n3
Rhodes University, 316–17, 324
  Institute for the Study of English in Africa (ISEA), 314, 316–17
Rhodesia, 104, 117, 118, 126, 185, 312n49; see also Zimbabwe

#RhodesMustFall, 14–15, 115–17, 119–20
Richardson, Henry Handel, 12, 244, 249, 252, 253, 259
  Fortunes of Richard Mahony, The, 252
  Maurice Guest, 252–3
Rive, Richard, 275, 291n37
Roe, Jill, 251
Roos, Anna Maria, 211, 212
rose, 86, 225, 228–32
Rose, Jacqueline, 284
Rubusana, Mpilo Walter Benson, 121, 124, 125
rumours, 109, 126, 184, 188, 208–9
Rushdie, Salman, 297
Rydberg, Victor, 203

Samolsky, Russell, 308
Samuelson, Meg, 293n79
San, Khoisan, Bushman, Bushmen, 7, 100, 103, 104, 105, 113n8, 185, 277, 278, 279, 280, 281–3, 286, 304
Sanders, Mark, 4, 5
Sauer, J. W., 120, 121, 129
Schoeman, Karel, 61, 319, 320
Schreiner, Frances ('Fan'), 55
Schreiner, Henrietta ('Ettie', Ettie Stakesby-Lewis), 88, 104, 118, 275, 280, 319, 320–1
Schreiner, Olive
  diary, 13, 62, 269, 270, 271
  portrait of, 208
  reception of, 10, 11, 12, 95, 146, 177–93, 199–214
  Translations of works:
    Drömmar (Dreams), 203–5
    Kvinnan och arbetet (Woman and Labour), 210
    Soldaten Peter Halket: en berättelse från Sydafrika (Trooper Peter Halket of Mashonaland), 206
    Under Afrikas himmel (The Story of an African Farm), 201
  Writings:
    'A Message to the English People', 206–7
    'An English-South African's View of the Situation', 6, 178, 184, 206
    Closer Union, 85, 89–90, 110, 113–14n29, 120, 123–4, 128, 277–8, 280
    'Dream Life and Real Life: A Little African Story', 225, 228, 232–3
    Dreams, 1, 8, 10, 12, 14, 39, 88, 146, 158, 163, 181–2, 183, 184, 189, 192, 193, 200, 202–4, 208, 212, 229, 248, 252
    From Man to Man, or Perhaps Only, 9, 13, 14, 68, 69, 73, 75–6, 85, 86–7, 90, 102, 108, 112n6, 141, 199, 228, 233, 269–71, 275, 276–7, 278, 279–82, 285, 296, 299, 319
    'I Thought I Stood...', 202, 205
    'In a Far-Off World', 202–3
    'In a Ruined Chapel', 189, 202
    'Life's Gifts', 202
    'Message to the Universal Races Congress', 127–8
    'Speech on the Boer War', 207
    'The Gardens of Pleasure', 202, 204, 229–31
    'The Lost Joy', 182, 202
    'The Political Situation', 118, 122, 206
    The Story of an African Farm, 1, 4, 9, 10, 11, 12, 14, 15, 23–5, 31, 33–4, 61, 62–3, 64–65, 72, 102, 103, 149, 150, 162, 168–72, 177, 181, 184, 199, 201–3, 208, 212, 213, 224–5, 227–8, 232, 233, 244–60, 274, 275, 278, 282, 296, 297, 299, 300, 301, 306, 307, 315, 320, 323
    'The Sunlight Lay Across My Bed', 39, 48–52, 54, 55, 189
    'The Woman's Rose', 202–3, 228, 232
    Thoughts on South Africa, 101, 102, 115, 277–8
    'Three Dreams in a Desert', 9, 25, 27, 32, 146–7, 150, 162–7, 171, 173, 182, 192, 200, 225, 232, 234, 236, 263n12
    Trooper Peter Halket of Mashonaland, 6, 10, 13, 107, 118, 143, 145, 148, 182–3, 185, 188, 189, 193, 206, 207, 233, 301–8
    Undine, 65, 102, 228, 296
    Woman and Labour, 1, 5, 12, 25, 26–9, 31–4, 37n30, 190–2, 193, 200, 210–13, 230, 247, 251, 252, 256
Schreiner, Theophilus ('Theo'), 318–19, 320, 321
Schreiner, William Philip ('Will'), 6, 40, 41, 55, 110, 120, 121, 125, 126, 127, 130, 157, 187, 199, 208, 270, 320, 323
Schreiner Karoo Writers Festival, 13, 323, 330n41
Scott, Bonnie Kime, 42, 63, 76
Sedgwick, Eve Kosofsky, 298
sermon, 46, 92, 140, 189, 212
sex, 7, 26, 28–30, 32, 42, 70–1, 76, 115, 120, 129, 144, 157, 159, 167–9, 172, 173, 176n38, 211, 224, 226, 245; *see also* gender; parasitism (sex)
sexual, sexuality, 9, 26, 29, 32, 33, 64, 71, 102, 126, 140, 167–9, 172, 224, 232–6, 256, 284, 303, 304
Shaw, Anna, 191, 212
Shaw, George Bernard, 41, 165
Sheridan, Susan, 245, 247, 260
Showalter, Elaine, 62
Sixth Conference of the International Woman Suffrage Alliance, 212; *see also* feminism
slave, slavery, 26, 28, 29, 31, 35n5, 91, 105, 106, 184–5, 225, 230, 233, 253, 303; *see also* indentured labour
Smuts, Jan Christiaan, 115–16, 145, 315
Snaith, Anna, 40
Snickars, Pelle, 201
Sobukwe, Robert, 275, 293n94

socialism, socialist, 1, 2, 5, 25, 39–43, 47–52, 55, 63, 103, 126, 138, 145, 146, 157–9, 161, 163, 164, 168, 172, 177, 179, 180, 182–3, 184, 189, 191, 192, 193, 199, 223, 248, 254, 270, 275
Somerset East Women's Meeting, 186, 207
South Africa, 1, 2, 4, 5–8, 11, 12, 13–15, 24, 25, 40, 55, 61, 85, 86, 87, 88–94, 100, 103, 104–6, 107, 109, 113–14n29, 115–31, 139, 140, 142–5, 149, 178, 183–8, 192, 206–10, 212, 213, 223–5, 229, 244, 251, 252, 254, 270, 271, 273, 275, 277, 279, 280, 282–3, 284, 285–6, 295–8, 301, 302, 307, 314, 316–17, 319, 320, 323–5
  Union of, 126
  see also Afrikaner (Boer); Afrikaner Nationalist government; race; South African War (1899–1902)
South African National Native Congress, 121, 145
South African Native Convention, 124; see also African National Congress (ANC)
South African War (1899–1902), 27, 106, 115, 118, 183, 185–6, 191, 200, 205–9, 210, 212, 213, 251, 270, 320
Spence, Catherine Helen, 9, 12, 245–6
Spencer, Herbert, 68, 69–70, 75, 321
Spydell, Anna, 14
Stakesby Lewis Hostel, 275
Stanley, Liz, 7, 8, 10, 11, 14, 115, 134–5n1, 138, 143, 144–5, 149, 331n44
Stead, W. T., 55, 118, 169, 186, 188
Stellenbosch University, 304
Stevenson, Robert Louis, 210
Stobie, Caitlin, 14
Stowe, Harriet Beecher, 101, 107, 145, 182, 192
  Uncle Tom's Cabin, 107, 108, 145, 182, 183
stream of consciousness, 47, 258
Strindberg, August, 211
suffrage, women's, 1, 2, 106, 113n24, 144, 146, 180, 190–1, 212, 223
Suffragette (film), 8, 14
Sutcliffe, Alex, 5, 9, 12, 311n5
Sweden, 5, 199, 200, 202–3, 204, 206, 208, 211, 212, 213–14, 216n2
  press in, 199–214
symbol, symbolic, Symbolism, 12, 23, 24, 40, 70, 117, 164, 203, 225, 228, 229, 283, 314
Symons, Arthur, 41

Tagore, Rabindranath, 85, 86, 88, 90, 91, 92, 97n22
terra nullius, 247
Thurman, Howard, 8, 138–50
  Jesus and the Disinherited, 139, 140, 141

ed., *A Track to the Water's Edge: An Olive Schreiner Reader*, 139, 141, 145, 146
Titlestad, Michael, 305
Tomida, Hiroko, 11
Treagus, Mandy, 5, 9, 12, 227, 310n5
Tshamano, H. S., 274
Tucker, Benjamin R., 159–72

Universal Races Congress, 106, 108, 110, 127, 128, 137n66
Unwin, T. Fisher, 10, 187
utopia, 6, 8, 51–2, 85–6, 87, 91, 93, 95, 308

Valman, Nadia, 52
Van der Vlies, Andrew, 5, 11, 12, 13, 14, 260
Van Heerden, Etienne, 14
Vietnam, 304, 306, 307
Vigne, Randolph, 282
Visel, Robin, 274
Vivan, Itala, 11

Wägner, Elin (Devinez), 211
Wairoa river, 233–6
Walters, Paul, 13, 19n43, 317
Watson, Stephen, 295, 296
West, Rebecca, 2
White, Patrick, 12, 244, 253, 254–60, 295, 303
  The Aunt's Story, 244, 253–6, 258, 259
  The Solid Mandala, 256
  The Tree of Man, 259
  The Twyborn Affair, 256
  Voss, 303
'War Journal', 254
white South Africa, white South Africans, 14, 61, 86, 92, 93, 95, 99, 103, 105, 109, 111, 120, 121, 122–4, 126–7, 129, 142, 185, 207, 208, 223, 272, 274, 277, 278–9, 280, 282–3, 316
Wibaut, Mathilde, 192
Wicomb, Zoë, 283
Wilde, Oscar, 41
Williams, Michelle, 5
Wollstonecraft, Mary, 26, 29, 48, 62, 70
Woman Question, the, 26, 62, 140, 157, 159, 167, 211, 224, 247
Woolf, Virginia, 5, 13, 61–76
Wylie, Dan, 4, 5, 34

Xhosa, 7, 100, 103, 121

Zhao, Jingshen, 251–2
Zimbabwe, Zimbabwean, 117, 119, 130, 301, 304; see also Chapungu bird; Rhodesia
Zola, Émile, 40, 43, 47–8
Zulu 93, 94, 185

EU representative:
Easy Access System Europe
Mustamäe tee 50, 10621 Tallinn, Estonia
Gpsr.requests@easproject.com